INTRODUCTION TO

DIGITAL IMAGE PROCESSING
WITH MATLAB

ALASDAIR
MCANDREW

School of Computer Science and Mathematics
Victoria University
Melbourne, Victoria, Australia

Australia • Canada • Mexico • Singapore • Spain
United Kingdom • United States

Introduction to Digital Image Processing with MATLAB®

by Alasdair McAndrew

Executive Editor: Mac Mendelsohn
Product Manager: Alyssa Pratt
Associate Product Manager: Mirella Misiaszek
Editorial Assistant: Amanda Piantedosi
Production Editor: Philippa Lehar
Cover Designer: Joel Sadagorsky

Compositor: Shepherd, Inc.
Senior Manufacturing Coordinator: Trevor Kallop
Production Service: Shepherd, Inc.
Copy Editor: Jane Loftus
Interior Design: Lisa Henry
Coverprinting and Binding: Quebecor World

To my dear wife Felicity,
for all her love, support and understanding
while this book was written.

CONTENTS

uman beings are predominantly visual creatures, and our computing environments reflect this. We have the World Wide Web, filled with images of every possible type and provenance, and our own computers are crammed with images from the operating system, downloaded from elsewhere, or taken with our digital cameras. Then there are the vast applications that use digital images: remote sensing and satellite imaging, astronomy, medical imaging, microscopy, industrial inspection . . . .

This book is an introduction to **digital image processing,** from a strictly elementary perspective. We have selected only those topics that can be introduced with simple mathematics; however, these topics provide a very broad introduction to the discipline.

This book is based on some very successful image-processing subjects that have been taught for the past few years at Victoria University in Melbourne, Australia. The topics chosen, and their method of presentation, are the result of many hours of talking to and learning from the hundreds of students who have taken these subjects.

There are a great many books on the subject of image processing, and this book differs from all of them in several important respects:

Not too much mathematics. Some mathematics is necessary for the explanation and discussion of image-processing algorithms. But this book attempts to keep the mathematics at a level commensurate with elementary undergraduate computer science.

The level of mathematics required is about one year's study at a tertiary level, including calculus and linear algebra.

A discrete approach. Since digital images are discrete entities, we have adopted an approach using mainly discrete mathematics. Although calculus is required for the development of some image-processing topics, we attempt to connect the calculus-based (continuous) theory with its discrete implementation.

A strong connection between theory and practice. Since we have used a mainly discrete approach to explain the material, it becomes much easier to extend the theory into practice. This becomes particularly significant when we develop our own MATLAB functions for implementing specific image-processing algorithms.

Software based. There are image-processing books that are based on programming languages, generally C or Java. The problem is that to use such software, a specialized image-processing library must be used, and, at least for C, there is no standard for this. A problem with the Java image-processing libraries is that they are not really suitable for beginning students.

This book is based entirely on MATLAB and its Image Processing Toolbox. This provides a complete environment for image processing that is easy to use, easy to explain, and easy to extend.

Plenty of examples. *All* the example images in this text are accompanied by MATLAB commands. Thus, if you work carefully through the book, you can create the images as given in the text.

Exercises. Chapters finish with a selection of exercises that enable the student to consolidate and extend the material. Some of the exercises are pencil-and-paper, designed for better understanding of the material, and others are MATLAB based to explore the algorithms and methods of that chapter.

What Is In the Book

The first three chapters set the scene for much of the rest of the book, exploring the nature and use of digital images and how they can be obtained, stored, and displayed. Chapter 1 provides a brief introduction to the field of image processing and attempts to give some idea as to its scope and areas of practice. We also define some common terms. Chapter 2 shows how MATLAB handles images as matrices and how the manipulation of these matrices forms the background of all of subsequent work. Chapter 3 investigates aspects of image display and looks at resolution and quantization, and discusses how they affect the appearance of the image.

Chapter 4 looks at some of the simplest, yet most powerful and widely used, of all image-processing algorithms. These are the point operations, where the value of a pixel (a single dot in a digital image) is changed according to a single function of its value.

Chapter 5 introduces spatial filtering. Spatial filtering can be used for a vast range of image-processing operations, from removing unnecessary detail to sharpening edges and removing noise.

Chapter 6 looks at the geometry of an image—its size and orientation. Resizing an image may be necessary for inclusion in a Web page or printed text; we may need to reduce it to fit, or enlarge it.

Chapter 7 introduces the Fourier transform. This is possibly the single most important transform for image processing. To get a feeling for how the

Fourier transform works and what information it provides, we need to spend some time exploring its mathematical foundations. This chapter contains the most mathematics in this book and requires some knowledge of complex numbers. In keeping with our philosophy, we use discrete mathematics only. We then show how images can be processed with great efficiency using the Fourier transform and how various operations can be performed using only the Fourier transform.

Chapter 8 discusses the restoration of an image from different forms of degradation. Among these is the problem of noise, or errors in an image. Such errors are a natural consequence of electronic transmission of image signals, and although error correction of the signal can go a long way to ensure that the image arrives "clean," we may still receive images with noise. We also look at the removal of blur.

Chapter 9 addresses the problems of thresholding and of finding edges in an image. Edges are a vital aspect of object recognition: we can classify the size, shape, and type of object by an analysis of its edges. As well, edges form a vital aspect of human visual interpretation, and thus the sharpening of edges is often an important part of image enhancement.

Chapter 10 introduces morphology or mathematical morphology, which is an area of image processing very much wedded to set theory. Historically, morphology developed from the need for granulometry, or the measurement of grains in ore samples. It is now a very powerful method for investigating shapes and sizes of objects. Morphology is generally defined in terms of binary images (which is what we do here) and then can be extended to grayscale images. With the latter, we can also perform edge detection and some noise reduction.

Chapter 11 investigates the topology of digital images. This is concerned with the neighborhoods of pixels and how the exploration of different neighborhoods leads to an understanding of the structure of image objects.

We continue the investigation of shapes in Chapter 12, but from a more spatial viewpoint; we look at traversing the edges of an object and how the traversal can be turned into descriptors of the size and shape of the object.

Chapter 13 looks at color. Color is one of most important aspects of human interpretation. We look at the definition of color from physical and digital perspectives and examine how a color image can be processed using the techniques we have developed so far.

Chapter 14 discusses some basic aspects of image compression. Image files tend to be large, and their compression can be a matter of some concern, especially if there are many of them. We distinguish two types of compression: lossless, where there is no loss of information, and lossy, where higher compression rates can be obtained at the cost of losing some information.

Chapter 15 introduces wavelets, which have become a very hot topic in image processing. In some places they are replacing the use of the Fourier transform. Our treatment is introductory only. We show how wavelets and waves differ, how wavelets can be defined, how they can be applied to images, and the effects that can be obtained. In particular, we look at image compression and show how wavelets can be used to obtain very high rates of lossy compression with no apparent loss of image quality.

Chapter 16 is intended to be a bit more lighthearted than the others. Here we look at some special effects used on images. These are often provided with image-editing programs—if you have a digital camera, chances are the accompanying software will allow this. Our treatment attempts to provide an understanding of the nature of these algorithms.

Appendix A provides a brief introduction to MATLAB and MATLAB programming, and Appendix B introduces the fast Fourier transform.

What This Book Is Not

This book is *not* an introduction to either MATLAB or its Image Processing Toolbox. We have used only a small fraction of the many commands and functions available; we used only those useful for an elementary text such as this. There are an enormous number of books on MATLAB available; a fine general introduction is the text by Hanselman and Littlefield [10]. To really come to grips with the Image Processing Toolbox, you can either use its excellent manual or browse through the comprehensive online documentation.

How To Use This Book

This book can be used for two separate streams of image processing: one very elementary, another a little more advanced. A first course consists of the following:

- Chapter 1
- Chapter 2, except for Section 2.5
- Chapter 3, except for Section 3.6
- Chapter 4
- Chapter 5
- Chapter 7
- Chapter 8
- Chapter 9, except for Sections 9.4, 9.5, and 9.9
- Chapter 10, except for Sections 10.8 and 10.9
- Chapter 13
- Chapter 14, Sections 14.2 and 14.3 only

A second course fills in the gaps:

- Section 2.5
- Section 3.6
- Section 6
- Sections 9.4, 9.5 and 9.9
- Sections 10.8 and 10.9
- Chapter 11
- Chapter 12
- Section 14.4
- Chapter 15

As taught at Victoria University of Technology, for the first course we concentrate on introducing students to the principles and practices of image processing, and we don't worry about the implementation of the algorithms. In the second course, we spend time discussing programming issues and encourage the students to write their own programs and edit programs already written. Both courses have been very popular since their inception.

Acknowledgments

This book began as set of notes written to accompany an undergraduate introductory course to image processing; these notes were then extended for another course. Thanks must go to the many students who have taken these courses and who have discussed the subject material and its presentation with me.

I would like to thank my colleagues at Victoria University for many stimluating conversations about teaching and learning. I would also like to thank David Booth and Grenville Armitage of Swinburne University of Technology for providing me with a very pleasant environment for seven months, during which much of the first draft of this book was written.

Kallie Swanson, of Brooks/Cole Publishing Company, has been an editor whose help over the production of this book has been invaluable. Her ready and detailed answers to my many foolish questions and her presence as a helping hand have made the writing of this book not only painless, but enjoyable.

I would also like to thank Courtney Esposito, of the Book Program at The Mathworks (creators of MATLAB) for her very helpful discussion on the use of MATLAB and for her help obtaining permission to use some of their images.

I would like also to thank the reviewers for their close and careful reading of the original draft, and for their thoughtful, detailed and constructive comments.

Finally, heartfelt thanks to my long-suffering wife Felicity, and my children Angus, Edward, Fenella, William, and Finlay, who have for far too long, put up with absentmindedness, grunts instead of conversation, and blank stares at meal times.

A Note on the Images

Some of the images used in this book are the author's and may be used freely and without restriction. They are:

```
arch.tif
blocks.tif
buffalo.tif
cat.tif
emu.tif
engineer.tif
iguana.tif
newborn.tif
nicework.tif
pelicans.tif
twins.tif
wombats.tif
```

CRC Press has kindly allowed the use of the following images from *The Image Processing Handbook* by John Russ [31]:

```
bacteria.tif
circles.tif, circlesm.tif
flowers.tif
ic.tif
lily.tif
rice.tif
text.tif
tire.tif
```

The Mathworks has allowed the use of the images:

```
board.tif
cameraman.tif
circbw.tif
coins.tif
nodules1.tif
paper.tif
```

```
pout.tif
spine.tif
```

The image

```
caribou.tif
```

has been cropped from the NOAA image `anim0614.jpg`, a photograph of a caribou (*Rangifer tarandus*) by Capt. Budd Christman of the NOAA Corps.

CHAPTER ONE

INTRODUCTION

1.1 Images and Pictures

As we mentioned in the preface, human beings are predominantly visual creatures: we rely heavily on our vision to make sense of the world around us. We not only look at things to identify and classify them, but we can scan for differences and obtain an overall rough feeling for a scene with a quick glance.

Humans have evolved very precise visual skills: we can identify a face in an instant, we can differentiate colors, and we can process a large amount of visual information very quickly.

However, the world is in constant motion. Stare at something for long enough and it will change in some way. Even a large solid *object*, like a building or a mountain, will change its appearance depending on the time of day (day or night), amount of sunlight (clear or cloudy), or various shadows falling upon it.

We are concerned with single images, snapshots, if you like, of a visual scene. Although image processing can deal with changing scenes, we will not discuss it in any detail in this text.

For our purposes, an **image** is a single picture that represents something. It may be a picture of a person, or animals, or an outdoor scene, or a microphotograph of an electronic component, or the result of medical imaging. Even if the picture is not immediately recognizable, it will not be just a random blur.

1.2 What Is Image Processing?

Image processing involves changing the nature of an image in order to either

1. improve its pictorial information for human interpretation, or
2. render it more suitable for autonomous machine perception.

(a)   (b)

FIGURE 1.1 *Image sharpening. (a) The original image. (b) Result after sharpening.*

We shall be concerned with **digital image processing,** which involves using a computer to change the nature of a **digital image** (see above). It is necessary to understand that these two aspects represent two separate but equally important aspects of image processing. A procedure that satisfies condition 1—a procedure that makes an image look better—may be the very worst procedure for satisfying condition 2. Humans like their images to be sharp, clear, and detailed; machines prefer their images to be simple and uncluttered.

Examples of condition 1 may include

- enhancing the edges of an image to make it appear sharper. An example is shown in Figure 1.1. Note how the second image appears cleaner; it is a more pleasant image. Sharpening edges is a vital component of printing. For an image to appear at its best on the printed page, some sharpening is usually performed.

- removing noise from an image, noise being random errors in the image. An example is given in Figure 1.2. Noise is a very common problem in data transmission: all sorts of electronic components may affect data passing through them, and the results may be undesirable. As we shall see in Chapter 8, noise may take many different forms, each type of noise requiring a different method of removal.

- removing motion blur from an image. An example is given in Figure 1.3. Note that in the deblurred image Figure 1.3(b) it is easier to read the

(a)   (b)

FIGURE 1.2 *Removing noise from an image. (a) The original image. (b) After removing noise.*

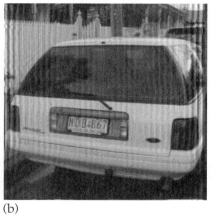

(a)   (b)

FIGURE 1.3 *Image deblurring. (a) The original image. (b) After removing the blur.*

number plate and to see the spikes on the fence behind the car, as well as other details not at all clear in the original image Figure 1.3(a). Motion blur may occur when the shutter speed of the camera is too long for the speed of the object. In photographs of fast-moving objects, athletes or vehicles, for example, the problem of blur may be considerable.

Examples of condition 2 may include

- obtaining the edges of an image. This may be necessary for the measurement of objects in an image. An example is shown in Figure 1.4 (a and b). Once we have the edges we can measure their spread and the area contained within them. We can also use edge-detection algorithms

(a) (b)

FIGURE 1.4 *Finding edges in an image. (a) The original image. (b) Its edge image.*

(a) (b)

FIGURE 1.5 *Blurring an image. (a) The original image. (b) Blurring to remove detail.*

as a first step in edge enhancement, as we saw above. From the edge result, we see that it may be necessary to enhance the original image slightly, to make the edges clearer.

- removing detail from an image. For measurement or counting purposes, we may not be interested in all the detail in an image. For example, when a machine inspects items on an assembly line, the only matters of interest may be shape, size, or color. For such cases, we might want to simplify the image. Figure 1.5 shows an example: in image Figure 1.5(a) there is a picture of an African buffalo, whereas image Figure 1.5(b) shows a blurred version in which extraneous detail (such as the logs of wood in the background) have been removed. Notice that in image

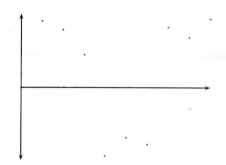

FIGURE 1.6 *Sampling a function—undersampling.*

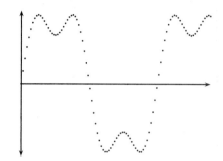

FIGURE 1.7 *Sampling a function with more points.*

Figure 1.5(b) all the fine detail is gone; what remains is the coarse structure of the image. We could, for example, measure the size and shape of the animal without being distracted by unnecessary detail.

1.3 Image Acquisition and Sampling

Sampling refers to the process of digitizing a continuous function. For example, suppose we take the function

$$y = \sin(x) + \frac{1}{3}\sin(3x)$$

and sample it at 10 evenly spaced values of x only. The resulting sample points are shown in Figure 1.6. This shows an example of **undersampling,** where the number of points is not sufficient to reconstruct the function. Suppose we sample the function at 100 points, as shown in Figure 1.7. We now can clearly reconstruct the function; all its properties can be determined from this sampling. To ensure that we have enough sample points, we require that the sampling period is not greater than one-half the finest

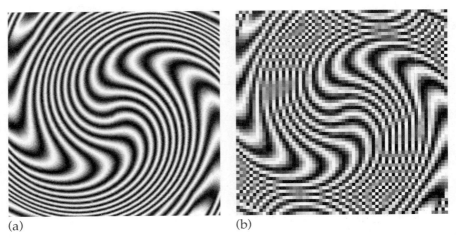

(a)   (b)

FIGURE 1.8 *Effects of sampling. (a) Correct sampling; no aliasing. (b) An undersampled version with aliasing.*

detail in our function. This is known as the **Nyquist criterion** and can be formulated more precisely in terms of frequencies, which are discussed in Chapter 7. The Nyquist criterion can be stated as the **sampling theorem,** which says, in effect, that a continuous function can be reconstructed from its samples provided that the sampling frequency is at least twice the maximum frequency in the function. A formal account of this theorem is provided by Castleman [4].

Sampling an image again requires that we consider the Nyquist criterion, when we consider an image as a continuous function of two variables and we wish to sample it to produce a digital image.

An example is shown in Figure 1.8 where an image is shown, and then with an undersampled version. The jagged edges in the undersampled image are examples of **aliasing.** The sampling rate will, of course, affect the final resolution of the image; we discuss this in Chapter 3. To obtain a sampled (digital) image, we may start with a continuous representation of a scene. To view the scene, we record the energy reflected from it; we may use visible light, or some other energy source.

1.3.1 Using Light

Light is the predominant energy source for images, simply because it is the energy source that human beings can observe directly. We are all familiar with photographs, which are a pictorial record of a visual scene.

Many digital images are captured using visible light as the energy source; this has the advantage of being safe, cheap, easily detected, and readily processed with suitable hardware. Two very popular methods of producing a digital image are with a digital camera or a flat-bed scanner.

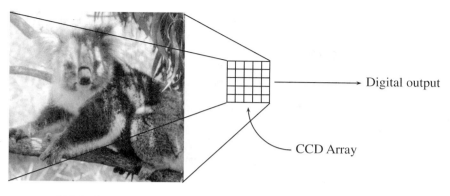

Original scene

FIGURE 1.9 *Capturing an image with a CCD array.*

CCD CAMERA   CCD stands for "charge-coupled device." This is an array of light sensitive cells called "photosites" each of which produces a voltage proportional to the intensity of light falling on them. Colors are obtained by the use of red, green, and blue filters. CCDs are used in most digital cameras as they produce very good results, can be made with high resolution, and are robust against noise. A good account of CCD technology is given by Castleman [4].

A complementary technology is the use of CMOS (complementary metal oxide semi-conductor) chips. These have the advantage of being cheaper to produce and require less power to run than a CCD chip; however they are more susceptible to noise. Thus they are only used in low-end cameras, such as in some webcams.

For a camera attached to a computer, information from the photosites is then output to a suitable storage medium. Generally, this is done on hardware, which is much faster and more efficient than software, using a **frame-grabbing card.** This allows a large number of images to be captured in a very short time—in the order of 1/10,000 of a second each. The images can then be copied onto a permanent storage device at some later time.

This is shown schematically in Figure 1.9.

The output will be an array of values, each representing a sampled point from the original scene. The elements of this array are called **picture elements,** or more simply **pixels.**

Digital still cameras use a range of devices, from floppy disks and CD's to various specialized cards and memory sticks. The information can then be downloaded from these devices to a computer hard disk.

FLAT-BED SCANNER   This works on a principle similar to the CCD camera. Instead of the entire image being captured at once on a large array, a single row of photosites is moved across the image, capturing it row by row as it moves. This is shown schematically in Figure 1.10.

Original scene

FIGURE 1.10 *Capturing an image with a CCD scanner.*

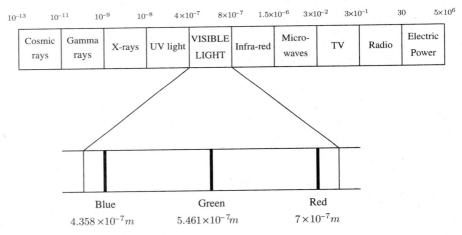

Blue
$4.358 \times 10^{-7} m$

Green
$5.461 \times 10^{-7} m$

Red
$7 \times 10^{-7} m$

FIGURE 1.11 *The electromagnetic spectrum.*

Since this is a much slower process than taking a picture with a camera, it is quite reasonable to allow all capture and storage to be processed by suitable software.

1.3.2 Other Energy Sources

Although light is popular and easy to use, other energy sources may be used to create a digital image. Visible light is part of the **electromagnetic spectrum**, radiation in which the energy takes the form of waves of varying wavelength. These range from cosmic rays of very short wavelength to electric power, which has very long wavelength. Figure 1.11 illustrates this.

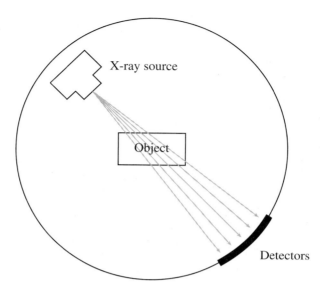

FIGURE 1.12 *X-ray tomography.*

For microscopy, we may use x-rays, or electron beams. As we can see from Figure 1.11, x-rays have a shorter wavelength than visible light and thus can be used to resolve smaller objects than are possible with visible light. See Clark [5] for a good introduction to this. X-rays are, of course, also useful in determining the structure of objects usually hidden from view, such as bones.

An additional method of obtaining images is by the use of **x-ray tomography,** where an object is encircled by an x-ray beam. As the beam is fired through the object, it is detected on the other side of the object, as shown in Figure 1.12. As the beam moves around the object, an image of the object can be constructed; such an image is called a **tomogram.** In a CAT (computed axial tomography) scan, the patient lies within a tube around which x-ray beams are fired. This enables a large number of tomographic slices to be formed, which can then be joined to produce a three-dimensional image. A good account of such systems (and others) is given by Siedband [31].

1.4 Images and Digital Images

Suppose we take an image, a photo, say. For the moment, let's make things easy and suppose the photo is monochromatic (that is, shades of gray only), so no color. We may consider this image as being a two-dimensional function, where the function values give the brightness of the image at any given

$f(x, y) = 0.8$

FIGURE 1.13 *An image as a function.*

point, as shown in Figure 1.13. We may assume that in such an image brightness values can be any real numbers in the range 0.0 (black) to 1.0 (white). The ranges of x and y will clearly depend on the image, but they can take all real values between their minima and maxima.

Such a function can, of course, be plotted, as shown in Figure 1.14. However, such a plot is of limited use to us in terms of image analysis. The concept of an image as a function, however, will be vital for the development and implementation of image-processing techniques.

A **digital image** differs from a photo in that the x, y, and $f(x,y)$ values are all discrete. Often the $f(x,y)$ values take only integer values, so the image shown in Figure 1.13 will have x and y ranging from 1 to 256 each and the brightness values ranging from 0 (black) to 255 (white). A digital image, as we have seen above, can be considered as a large array of sampled points from the continuous image, each point with a particular quantized brightness; these points are the **pixels,** which constitute the digital image. The pixels surrounding a given pixel constitute its **neighborhood.** A neighborhood can be characterized by its shape in the same way as a matrix: we can speak, for example, of a 3 × 3 neighborhood or of a 5 × 7 neighborhood. Except in very special circumstances, neighborhoods have odd numbers of rows and columns; this ensures that the current pixel is in the center of the neighborhood. An example of a neighborhood is given in Figure 1.15. If a neighborhood has an even number of rows or columns (or both), it may be necessary to specify which pixel in the neighborhood is the current pixel.

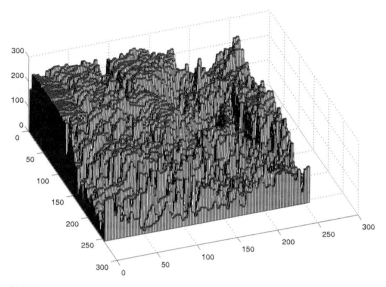

FIGURE 1.14 *The image of Figure 1.13 plotted as a function of two variables.*

48	219	168	145	244	188	120	58
49	218	87	94	133	35	17	148
174	151	74	179	224	3	252	194
77	127	87	139	44	228	149	135
138	229	136	113	250	51	108	163
38	210	185	177	69	76	131	53
178	164	79	158	64	169	85	97
96	209	214	203	223	73	110	200

Current pixel

3×5 neighborhood

FIGURE 1.15 *Pixels with a neighborhood.*

1.5 Some Applications

Image processing has an enormous range of applications; almost every area of science and technology can make use of image-processing methods. Here is a short list to give some indication of the range of image-processing applications.

1. Medicine

   - Inspection and interpretation of images obtained from x-rays, MRI or CAT scans
   - Analysis of cell images and chromosome karyotypes

2. Agriculture

- Satellite/aerial views of land, for example, to determine how much land is being used for different purposes or to investigate the suitability of different regions for different crops
- Inspection of fruit and vegetables—distinguishing good and fresh produce from old

3. Industry

- Automatic inspection of items on a production line
- Inspection of paper samples

4. Law enforcement

- Fingerprint analysis
- Sharpening or deblurring of speed-camera images

A good introduction to the many applications of digital image processing is provided by Baxes [1].

1.6 Aspects of Image Processing

It is convenient to subdivide different image-processing algorithms into broad subclasses. There are different algorithms for different tasks and problems, and often we would like to distinguish the nature of the task at hand.

IMAGE ENHANCEMENT   Processing an image so that the result is more suitable for a particular application is called image enhancement. Examples include

- sharpening or deblurring an out-of-focus image,
- highlighting edges,
- improving image contrast or brightening an image, and
- removing noise.

IMAGE RESTORATION   An image may be restored by the damage done to it by a known cause, for example,

- removing of blur caused by linear motion,
- removal of optical distortions, and
- removing periodic interference.

IMAGE SEGMENTATION   Segmentation involves subdividing an image into constituent parts or isolating certain aspects of an image, including

- finding lines, circles, or particular shapes in an image, and
- identifying cars, trees, buildings, or roads in an aerial photograph.

These classes are not disjoint; a given algorithm may be used for both image enhancement or for image restoration. However, we should be able to decide what it is that we are trying to do with our image: simply make it look better (enhancement) or remove damage (restoration).

1.7 An Image-Processing Task

We will look in some detail at a particular real-world task and see how the above classes may be used to describe the various stages in performing this task. The job is to obtain, by an automatic process, the postal codes from envelopes. Here is how this may be accomplished:

1. **Acquiring the image.** First we need to produce a digital image from a paper envelope. This can be done using either a CCD camera or a scanner.

2. **Preprocessing.** This is the step taken before the major image-processing task. The problem here is to perform some basic tasks in order to render the resulting image more suitable for the job to follow. In this case it may involve enhancing the contrast, removing noise, or identifying regions likely to contain the postal code.

3. **Segmentation.** Here is where we actually get the postal code; in other words we extract from the image that part of it that contains only the postal code.

4. **Representation and description.** These terms refer to extracting the particular features that allow us to differentiate between objects. Here we will be looking for curves, holes, and corners that allow us to distinguish the different digits that constitute a postal code.

5. **Recognition and interpretation.** This means assigning labels to objects based on their descriptors (from the previous step) and assigning meanings to those labels. We identify particular digits, and we interpret a string of digits at the end of the address as the postal code.

1.8 Types of Digital Images

We shall consider four basic types of images.

1. **Binary.** Each pixel is just black or white. Since there are only two possible values for each pixel, we need only 1 bit per pixel. Such images can therefore be very efficient in terms of storage. Images for which a binary representation may be suitable include text (printed or handwriting), fingerprints, or architectural plans.

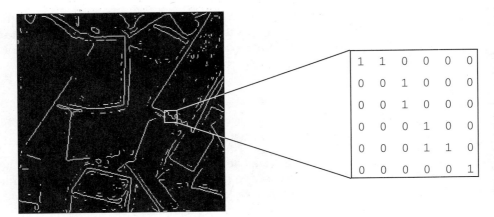

1	1	0	0	0	0
0	0	1	0	0	0
0	0	1	0	0	0
0	0	0	1	0	0
0	0	0	1	1	0
0	0	0	0	0	1

FIGURE 1.16 *A binary image.*

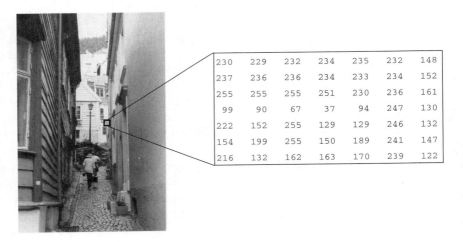

230	229	232	234	235	232	148
237	236	236	234	233	234	152
255	255	255	251	230	236	161
99	90	67	37	94	247	130
222	152	255	129	129	246	132
154	199	255	150	189	241	147
216	132	162	163	170	239	122

FIGURE 1.17 *A grayscale image.*

An example was the image shown in Figure 1.4(b). In this image, we have only the two colors: white for the edges and black for the background. See Figure 1.16.

2. **Grayscale.** Each pixel is a shade of gray, normally from 0 (black) to 255 (white). This range means that each pixel can be represented by 8 bits, or exactly 1 byte. This is a very natural range for image file handling. Other grayscale ranges are used, but generally they are a power of 2. Such images arise in medicine (x-rays), and images of printed works; indeed, 256 different gray levels are sufficient for the recognition of most natural objects.

An example is the street scene shown in Figure 1.1 and in Figure 1.17.

3. **True color or red-green-blue.** Here each pixel has a particular color, that color being described by the amount of red, green, and blue in it. If each

49	55	56	57	52	53
58	60	60	58	55	57
58	58	54	53	55	56
83	78	72	69	68	69
88	91	91	84	83	82
69	76	83	78	76	75
61	69	73	78	76	76

Red

64	76	82	79	78	78
93	93	91	91	86	86
88	82	88	90	88	89
125	119	113	108	111	110
137	136	132	128	126	120
105	108	114	114	118	113
96	103	112	108	111	107

Green

66	80	77	80	87	77
81	93	96	99	86	85
83	83	91	94	92	88
135	128	126	112	107	106
141	129	129	117	115	101
95	99	109	108	112	109
84	93	107	101	105	102

Blue

FIGURE 1.18 *A true color image.*

of these components has a range 0–255, this gives a total of $255^3 = 16,777,216$ different possible colors in the image. This is enough colors for any image. Since the total number of bits required for each pixel is 24, such images are also called **24-bit color images.**

Such an image may be considered as consisting of a stack of three matrices; representing the red, green, and blue values for each pixel. This means that for every pixel there correspond three values.

An example is shown in Figure 1.18.

4. **Indexed.** Most color images have only a small subset of the more than 16 million possible colors. For convenience of storage and file handling, the image has an associated **color map,** or **color palette,** which is simply a list of all the colors used in that image. Each pixel has a value that does not give its color (as for a red-green-blue [RGB] image), but an **index** to the color in the map.

It is convenient if an image has 256 colors or fewer, for then the index values will require only 1 byte each to store. Some image file formats (for example, Compuserve GIF), allow only 256 colors or fewer in each image for precisely this reason.

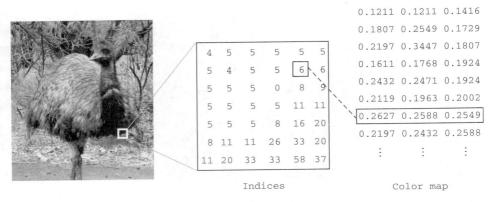

FIGURE 1.19 *An indexed color image.*

Figure 1.19 shows an example. In this image the indices, rather than being the gray values of the pixels, are simply indices into the color map. Without the color map, the image would be very dark and colorless. In the figure, for example, pixels labeled 5 correspond to 0.2627 0.2588 0.2549, which is a dark grayish color.

1.9 Image File Sizes

Image files tend to be large. We shall investigate the amount of information used in different image types of varying sizes. For example, suppose we consider a 512×512 binary image. The number of bits used in this image (assuming no compression and neglecting, for the sake of discussion, any header information) is

$$512 \times 512 \times 1 = 262{,}144$$
$$= 32768 \, \text{bytes}$$
$$= 32.768 \, \text{Kb}$$
$$\approx 0.033 \, \text{Mb}.$$

(Here we use the convention that a kilobyte is 1,000 bytes, and a megabyte is 1 million bytes.)

A grayscale image of the same size requires

$$512 \times 512 \times 1 = 262{,}144 \, \text{bytes}$$
$$= 262.14 \, \text{Kb}$$
$$\approx 0.262 \, \text{Mb}.$$

 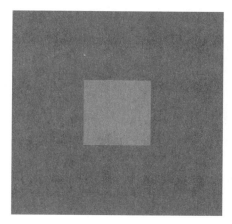

FIGURE 1.20 *A gray square on different backgrounds.*

If we now turn our attention to color images, each pixel is associated with 3 bytes of color information. A 512×512 image thus requires

$$512 \times 512 \times 3 = 786{,}432 \text{ bytes}$$
$$= 786.43 \text{ Kb}$$
$$\approx 0.786 \text{ Mb}.$$

Many images are, of course, much larger than this; satellite images may be of the order of several thousand pixels in each direction.

1.10 Image Perception

Much of image processing is concerned with making an image appear better to human beings. We should therefore be aware of the limitations of the human visual system. Image perception consists of

1. capturing the image with the eye, and
2. recognizing and interpreting the image with the **visual cortex** in the brain.

The combination and immense variability of these steps influences the ways in which we perceive the world around us.

There are a number of things to bear in mind:

1. **Observed intensities** vary as to the background. A single block of gray will appear darker if placed on a white background than if it were placed on a black background. That is, we don't perceive gray scales as they are, but rather as they differ from their surroundings. In Figure 1.20 a gray

FIGURE 1.21 *Continuously varying intensities.*

square is shown on two different backgrounds. Notice how much darker the square appears when it is surrounded by a light gray. However, the two central squares have exactly the same intensity.

2. We may observe nonexistent intensities as bars in continuously varying gray levels. See, for example, Figure 1.21. This image varies continuously from light to dark as we travel from left to right. However, it is impossible for our eyes not to see a few horizontal edges in this image.

3. Our visual system tends to undershoot or overshoot around the boundary of regions of different intensities. For example, suppose we had a light gray blob on a dark gray background. As our eye travels from the dark background to the light region, the boundary of the region appears lighter than the rest of it. Conversely, going in the other direction, the boundary of the background appears darker than the rest of it.

EXERCISES

1. Watch the TV news, and see if you can observe any examples of image processing.

2. If your TV set allows it, turn down the color as far as you can to produce a monochromatic display. How does this affect your viewing? Is there anything that is hard to recognize without color?

3. Look through a collection of old photographs. How can they be enhanced or restored?

4. For each of the following, list five ways in which image processing could be used:

- Medicine
- Astronomy
- Sports
- Music
- Agriculture
- Travel

5. Image-processing techniques have become a vital part of the modern movie production process. Next time you watch a film, take note of all the image processing involved.

6. If you have access to a scanner, scan in a photograph and experiment with all the possible scanner settings.
   a. What is the smallest file you can create that shows all the detail of your photograph?
   b. What is the smallest file you can create in which the major parts of your image are still recognizable?
   c. How do the color settings affect the output?

7. If you have access to a digital camera, photograph a fixed scene, using all possible camera settings.
   a. What is the smallest file you can create?
   b. How do the light settings affect the output?

8. Suppose you were to scan in a monochromatic photograph and then print out the result. Then suppose you scanned in the printout and printed out the result of that, and repeated this process a few times. Would you expect any degradation of the image during this process? What aspects of the scanner and printer would minimize degradation?

9. Look up *ultrasonography*. How does it differ from the image-acquisition methods discussed in this chapter? What is it used for? If you can, compare an ultrasound image with an x-ray image. How do they differ? In what ways are they similar?

10. If you have access to an image-viewing program (other than MATLAB) on your computer, make a list of the image-processing capabilities it offers. Can you find imaging tasks it is unable to do?

CHAPTER TWO

IMAGES AND MATLAB

MATLAB is a data analysis software package with powerful support for matrices and matrix operations. For a brief introduction, see Appendix 1. Digital images may be considered as matrices whose elements are the pixel values of the image. In this chapter we shall investigate how the matrix capabilities of MATLAB allow us to investigate images and their properties. From now on, we shall use the term "image" to mean "digital image."

2.1 Grayscale Images

Suppose you are sitting at your computer and have started MATLAB. You will have a MATLAB **command window** open and in it the MATLAB prompt

```
>>
```

ready to receive commands. Type in the command

```
>> w=imread('wombats.tif');
```

This command takes the gray values of all the pixels in the grayscale image wombats.tif and puts them all into a matrix w. This matrix w is now a MATLAB variable, and thus we can perform various matrix operations on it. In general the imread function reads the pixel values from an image file and returns a matrix of all the pixel values.

There are two things to note about this command:

1. It ends in a semicolon, which has the effect of not displaying the results of the command to the screen. The result of this particular command is a matrix of size 256×256, or 65,536 elements, thus we don't really want all its values displayed.

2. The name wombats.tif is given in single quotation marks. Without them, MATLAB would assume that wombats.tif was the name of a variable rather than the name of a file.

Now we can display this matrix as a grayscale image:

```
>> figure, imshow(w), pixval on
```

This is really three commands on one line. MATLAB allows many commands to be entered on the same line, using commas to separate the different commands. The three commands we use here are:

figure, which creates a figure on the screen. A figure is a window in which a graphics object can be placed. Objects may include images or various types of graphs.

imshow(g), which displays the matrix g as an image.

pixval on, which turns on the pixel values in our figure. This is a display of the gray values of the pixels in the image. They appear at the bottom of the figure in the form

$$c \times r = p$$

where c is the column value of the given pixel; r its row value, and p its gray value. Because wombats.tif is an 8-bit grayscale image, the pixel values appear as integers in the range 0–255.

This is shown in Figure 2.1.

If there are no figures open, then an imshow command, or any other command that generates a graphics object, will open a new figure for displaying the object. However, it is good practice to use the figure command whenever you wish to create a new figure.

We could display this image directly, without saving its gray values to a matrix, with the following command:

```
imshow('wombats.tif')
```

However, it is better to use a matrix, because these are handled very efficiently in MATLAB.

2.2 RGB Images

As we will discuss in Chapter 13, we need to define colors in some standard way, usually as a subset of a three-dimensional coordinate system; such a subset is called a **color model.** There are, in fact, a number of different methods for describing color, but for image display and storage a standard

FIGURE 2.1 *The wombats image with* `pixval on`.

model is RGB, for which we may imagine all the colors sitting inside a color cube of side 1 as shown in Figure 2.2. The colors along the black-white diagonal, shown in the diagram as a dotted line, are the points of the space where all the R, G, B values are equal. They are the different intensities of gray. We may also think of the axes of the color cube as being discretized to integers in the range 0–255.

RGB is the standard for the display of colors on computer monitors and TV sets. But it is not a very good way of describing colors. How, for example, would you define light brown using RGB? As we will see in Chapter 13, there are some colors that are not possible with the RGB model in that they would require negative values of one or two of the RGB components. MATLAB handles 24-bit RGB images in much the same way it does grayscale. We can save the color values to a matrix and view the result:

```
>> a=imread('autumn.tif');
>> figure,imshow(a),pixval on
```

Note that the pixel values now consist of a list of three values, giving the red, green, and blue components of the color of the given pixel.

An important difference between this type of image and a grayscale image can be seen by the command

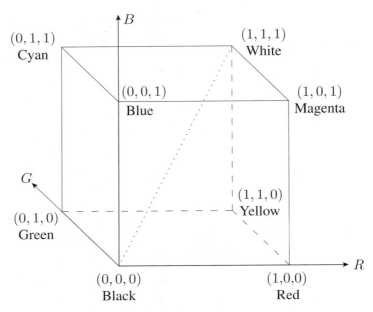

FIGURE 2.2 *The color cube for the RGB color model.*

```
>> size(a)
```

which returns *three* values: the number of rows, columns, and "pages" of a, which is a three-dimensional matrix, also called a **multidimensional array**. MATLAB can handle arrays of any dimension, and a is an example. We can think of a as being a stack of three matrices, each of the same size.

To obtain any of the RGB values at a given location, we use similar indexing methods as above. For example,

```
>> a(100,200,2)
```

returns the second color value (green) at the pixel in row 100 and column 200. If we want all the color values at that point, we can use

```
>> a(100,200,1:3)
```

However, MATLAB allows a convenient shortcut for listing all values along a particular dimension just by using a colon on its own:

```
>> a(100,200,:)
```

A useful function for obtaining RGB values is `impixel`; the command

```
>> impixel(a,200,100)
```

returns the RGB values of the pixel at column 200, row 100. Notice that the order of indexing is the same as that which is provided by the `pixval on` command. This is opposite the row/column order for matrix indexing. This command also applies to grayscale images:

```
>> impixel(g,100,200)
```

will return three values, but because g is a single two-dimensional matrix, all three values will be the same.

2.3 Indexed Color Images

The command

```
>> figure,imshow('emu.tif'),pixval on
```

produces a nice color image of an emu. However, the pixel values, rather than being three integers as they were for the RGB image, are three fractions between 0 and 1. What is going on here?

If we try saving to a matrix first and then displaying the result,

```
>> em=imread('emu.tif');
>> figure,imshow(em),pixval on
```

we obtain a dark, barely distinguishable image with single-integer gray values, indicating that em is being interpreted as a single grayscale image.

In fact, the image emu.tif is an example of an **indexed image,** consisting of two matrices: a **color map,** and an **index** to the color map. Assigning the image to a single matrix picks up only the index; we need to obtain the color map as well:

```
>> [em,emap]=imread('emu.tif');
>> figure,imshow(em,emap),pixval on
```

MATLAB stores the RGB values of an indexed image as values of type double, with values between 0 and 1.

2.3.1 Information about Your Image

A great deal of information can be obtained with the imfinfo function. For example, suppose we take our indexed image emu.tif from above.

```
>> imfinfo('emu.tif')
ans =
                       Filename: 'emu.tif'
                    FileModDate: '26-Nov-2002 14:23:01'
                       FileSize: 119804
                         Format: 'tif'
                  FormatVersion: []
                          Width: 331
                         Height: 384
                       BitDepth: 8
                      ColorType: 'indexed'
                FormatSignature: [73 73 42 0]
                      ByteOrder: 'little-endian'
                 NewSubfileType: 0
                  BitsPerSample: 8
                    Compression: 'PackBits'
       PhotometricInterpretation: 'RGB Palette'
                    StripOffsets: [16x1 double]
                SamplesPerPixel: 1
                   RowsPerStrip: 24
                 StripByteCounts: [16x1 double]
                    XResolution: 72
                    YResolution: 72
                 ResolutionUnit: 'Inch'
                       Colormap: [256x3 double]
             PlanarConfiguration: 'Chunky'
                      TileWidth: []
                     TileLength: []
```

(continued)

```
       TileOffsets: []
    TileByteCounts: []
       Orientation: 1
         FillOrder: 1
  GrayResponseUnit: 0.0100
    MaxSampleValue: 255
    MinSampleValue: 0
      Thresholding: 1
```

Much of this information is not useful to us, but we can see the size of the image in pixels, the size of the file (in bytes), the number of bits per pixel (given by BitDepth), and the color type (in this case indexed).

For comparison, let's look at the output of a truecolor file (showing only the first few lines of the output):

```
>> imfinfo('flowers.tif')

ans =

           Filename: [1x57 char]
        FileModDate: '26-Oct-1996 02:11:09'
           FileSize: 543962
             Format: 'tif'
      FormatVersion: []
              Width: 500
             Height: 362
           BitDepth: 24
          ColorType: 'truecolor'
```

Now we shall test this function on a binary image:

```
>> imfinfo('text.tif')

ans =

           Filename: [1x54 char]
        FileModDate: '26-Oct-1996 02:12:23'
           FileSize: 3474
             Format: 'tif'
      FormatVersion: []
              Width: 256
             Height: 256
           BitDepth: 1
          ColorType: 'grayscale'
```

What is going on here? We have a binary image, and yet the color type is given as "grayscale." The fact is that MATLAB does not distinguish between grayscale and binary images: a binary image is just a special case of a grayscale image that has only two intensities. However, we can see that text.tif is a binary image because the number of bits per pixel is only one.

2.4 Data Types and Conversions

Elements in MATLAB matrices may have a number of different numeric data types. The most common are listed in Table 2.1. There are others, but those listed will be sufficient for all our work with images. These data types are also functions that can be used to convert from one type to another. For example:

```
>>  a=23;
>> b=uint8(a);
>> b

b =

    23

>> whos a b
  Name        Size            Bytes  Class

    a          1x1                8   double array
    b          1x1                1   uint8 array
```

Even though the variables a and b have the same numeric value, they are of different data types. An important consideration is that arithmetic operations are not permitted with the data types int8, int16, uint8, and uint16.

TABLE 2.1   *Data types in MATLAB*

Data Type	Description	Range
int8	8-bit integer	−128–127
uint8	8-bit unsigned integer	0–255
int16	16-bit integer	−32768–32767
uint16	16-bit unsigned integer	0–65535
double	Double precision real number	Machine specific

TABLE 2.2   *Converting images in* MATLAB

Function	Use	Format
ind2gray	Indexed to grayscale	y=ind2gray(x,map);
gray2ind	Grayscale to indexed	[y,map]=gray2ind(x);
rgb2gray	RGB to grayscale	y=rgb2gray(x);
gray2rgb	Grayscale to RGB	y=gray2rgb(x);
rgb2ind	RGB to indexed	[y,map]=rgb2ind;
ind2rgb	Indexed to RGB	y=ind2rgb(x,map);

A grayscale image may consist of pixels whose values are of data type uint8. These images are thus reasonably efficient in terms of storage space, since each pixel requires only 1 byte. However, arithmetic operations are not permitted on this data type; a uint8 image must be converted to double before any arithmetic is attempted.

We can convert images from one image type to another. Table 2.2 lists all of MATLAB's functions for converting between different image types. Note that the gray2rgb function does not create a color image, but an image all of whose pixel colors were the same as before. This is done by simply replicating the gray values of each pixel: grays in an RGB image are obtained by equality of the RGB values.

2.5 Image Files and Formats

We have seen in Section 1.8 that images may be classified into four distinct types: binary, grayscale, colored, and indexed. In this section we consider some of the different image file formats, their advantages and disadvantages. You can use MATLAB for image processing very happily without ever really knowing the difference between GIF, TIFF, PNG, and all the other formats. However, some knowledge of the different graphics formats can be extremely useful in order to make a reasoned decision as to which file type to use and when.

There are a great many different formats for storing image data. Some have been designed to fulfill a particular need (for example, to transmit image data over a network); others have been designed around a particular operations system or environment.

As well as the gray values or color values of the pixels, an image file will contain some **header information.** This will, at the very least, include the size of the image in pixels (height and width). It may also include the color map, compression used, and a description of the image. MATLAB recognizes many standard formats and can read image data from them and write image data to them. The examples above are all images with extension .tif, indicating that they are TIFF (tagged image file format) images. This is a particularly general format, because it allows binary, grayscale, RGB, and indexed color images, as well as different amounts of compression. TIFF is thus a good format for transmitting images between different operating systems and environments. TIFF also allows more than one image per file; the particular image can be read into MATLAB by using an optional numeric argument to the imread function.

The imread and imwrite functions of MATLAB currently support the following formats:

JPEG These images are created using the Joint Photographics Experts Group compression method. We will discuss this more in Chapter 14.

TIFF Tagged Image File Format is a very general format that supports different compression methods, multiple images per file, and binary, grayscale, truecolor, and indexed images.

GIF Graphics Interchange Format is a venerable format designed for data transfer. It is still popular and well supported, but is somewhat restricted in the image types it can handle.

BMP Microsoft Bitmap format has become very popular and is used by Microsoft operating systems.

PNG Portable Network Graphics is designed to overcome some of the disadvantages of and become a replacement for GIF.

HDF Hierarchical Data Format is an extensible, versatile format designed principally for use with scientific images.

PCX This format was originally designed for use with the MS-DOS-based software PC Paintbrush. It is also used by some Microsoft products.

XWD X Window Dump is used to store images created by screen dumps from the X Window system. This is the standard windowing system used by Unix operating systems.

ICO This format is used to display icons in Microsoft Windows operating systems. It allows multiple images per file.

CUR This format is used to display the mouse cursor in Microsoft Windows operating systems.

We will discuss some of these formats briefly below.

A HEXADECIMAL DUMP FUNCTION   To explore binary files, we need a simple function that will enable us to list the contents of the file as hexadecimal values. If we try to list the contents of a binary file directly, for example with the type function (which prints the file contents to the screen), we will see masses of garbage. The trouble is that the contents are being interpreted as ASCII characters, which means that most characters will be either unprintable or nonsensical as values.

```
function dumphex(filename, n)
%
% DUMPHEX(FILENAME,N) prints the first 16*n bytes of the file FILENAME
% in hex and ASCII.  For example:
%
%    dumphex('picture.bmp',4)
%
fid = fopen(filename, 'r');
if fid==-1
  error('File does not exist or is not in your Matlab path');
end;
a=fread(fid,16*n,'uchar');
idx=find(a>=32 & a<=126);
ah=dec2hex(a);
b=repmat([' '],16*n,3);
b2=repmat('.',16,n);
b2(idx)=char(a(idx));
b(:,1:2)=ah;
[reshape(b',48,n)' repmat(' ',n,2) reshape(b2,16,n)']
```

FIGURE 2.3 *A function for producing hexadecimal dumps.*

A simple hexadecimal dump function is shown in Figure 2.3. The first three lines read in the required amount of information from the file and format it as hexadecimal values. The next three lines put those values into a matrix for display. For example:

```
>> dumphex('dataread.mexglx',4)

ans =

7F 45 4C 46 01 01 01 00 00 00 00 00 00 00 00 00    .ELF............
03 00 03 00 01 00 00 00 10 11 00 00 34 00 00 00    ............4...
E4 66 00 00 00 00 00 00 34 00 20 00 03 00 28 00    .f......4. ...(.
1B 00 18 00 01 00 00 00 00 00 00 00 00 00 00 00    ................
```

2.5.1 Vector versus Raster Images

We may store image information in two different ways: as a collection of lines or vectors or as a collection of dots. We refer to the former as **vector** images and to the latter as **raster** images. The great advantage of vector images is that they can be magnified to any desired size without losing any sharpness. The disadvantage is that are not very good for the representation of natural scenes in which lines may be scarce. The standard vector format is Adobe PostScript, which is an international standard for page layout. PostScript is the format of choice for images consisting mostly of lines and mathematically described curves, such as architectural and industrial plans, font information, and mathematical figures. Its reference manual [16] provides all necessary information about PostScript.

```
P2
# CREATOR: The GIMP's PNM Filter Version 1.0
256 256
255
  41  53  53  53  53  49  49  53  53  56  56  49  41  46  53  53  53
  53  41  46  56  56  56  53  53  46  53  41  41  53  56  49  39  46
```

FIGURE 2.4 *The start of a PGM file.*

The great bulk of image file formats store images as raster information, that is, as a list of the gray or color intensities of each pixel. Images captured by digital means, digital cameras or scanners, will be stored in raster format.

2.5.2 A Simple Raster Format

As well as containing all pixel information, an image file must contain some **header information;** this must include the size of the image, but may also include some documentation, a color map, and the compression used. To show the workings of a raster image file, we shall describe briefly the ASCII PGM format. This format was designed to be a generic format used for conversion between other formats. Thus, to create conversion routines between, say, 40 different formats, rather than have $40 \times 39 = 1560$ different conversion routines, all we need is the $40 \times 2 = 80$ conversion routines between the formats and PGM.

Figure 2.4 shows the beginning of a PGM file. The file begins with P2; this indicates that the file is an ASCII PGM file. The next line gives some information about the file. Any line beginning with a hash symbol is treated as a comment line. The next line gives the number of columns and rows and the following line the number of grayscales. Finally, we have all the pixel information, starting at the top left of the image and working across and down. Spaces and carriage returns are delimiters, so the pixel information could be written in one very long line or one very long column.

Note that this format has the advantage of being very easy to write to and to read from; it has the disadvantage of producing very large files. Some space can be saved by using raw PGM. The only difference is that the header number is P3 and the pixel values are stored one per byte. There are corresponding formats for binary and colored images (PBM and PPM, respectively); colored images are stored as three matrices, one for each red, green and blue, either as ASCII or raw. The format does not support color maps.

Binary, grayscale, or color images using these formats are collectively called PNM images. MATLAB does not support PNM images directly; however, functions for reading and writing them can be found at the Mathworks Central File Exchange.[1]

---

[1] http://www.mathworks.com/matlabcentral/fileexchange, in the External Interface →
Image and Movie Formats subdirectory.

2.5.3 Microsoft BMP

The Microsoft Windows BMP image format is a fairly simple example of a binary image format. Like the PGM format discussed previously, it consists of a header followed by the image information. The header is divided into two parts: the first 14 bytes (bytes 0–13) are the File Header, and the following 40 bytes (bytes 14–53) are the Information Header. The header is arranged as follows:

Bytes	Information	Description
0–1	Signature	BM in ASCII = 42 4D in hexadecimal.
2–5	FileSize	The size of the file in bytes.
6–9	Reserved	All zeros.
10–13	DataOffset	File offset to the raster data.
14–17	Size	Size of the information header = 40 bytes.
18–21	Width	Width of the image in pixels.
22–25	Height	Height of the image in pixels.
26–27	Planes	Number of image planes (= 1).

28–29	BitCount	Number of bits per pixel:
		    1: Binary images; two colors,
		    4: $2^4 = 16$ colors (indexed),
		    8: $2^8 = 256$ colors (indexed),
		    16: 16-bit RGB; $2^{16} = 65,536$ colors,
		    24: 24-bit RGB; $2^{24} = 17,222,216$ colors.

30–33	Compression	Type of compression used:
		    0: No compression (most common),
		    1: 8-bit RLE encoding (rarely used),
		    2: 4-bit RLE encoding (rarely used).

34–37	ImageSize	Size of the image. If compression is 0, then this value may be 0.
38–41	HorizontalRes	The horizontal resolution in pixels per meter.
42–45	VerticalRes	The vertical resolution in pixels per meter.
46–49	ColorsUsed	The number of colors used in the image. If this value is zero, then the number of colors is the maximum obtainable with the bits per pixel, that is, $2^{BitCount}$.
50–53	ImportantColors	The number of important colors in the image. If all the colors are important, then this value is set to zero.

After the header comes the Color Table, which is only used if BitCount is less than or equal to 8. The total number of bytes used here is $4 \times$ ColorsUsed. This format uses the Intel "least-endian" convention for byte ordering, where in each word of 4 bytes the least valued byte comes first. To see an example of this, consider a simple example:

```
>> dumphex('blocksets.bmp',4)

ans =

42 4D 6E 18 00 00 00 00 00 00 36 00 00 00 28 00   BMn.......6...(.
00 00 42 00 00 00 1F 00 00 00 01 00 18 00 00 00   ..B.............
00 00 38 18 00 00 C4 0E 00 00 C4 0E 00 00 00 00   ..8.............
00 00 00 00 00 00 00 00 00 00 00 00 00 00 00 00   ................
```

The image width is given by bytes 18–21; they are in the second row

```
00 00 42 00
```

To find the actual width, we reorder these bytes back-to-front:

```
00 00 00 42
```

Now we can convert to decimal

$$(4 \times 16^1) + (2 \times 16^0) = 66$$

which is the image width in pixels. We can do the same thing with the image height: bits 22–25

```
00 00 1F 00
```

Reordering and converting to hexadecimal results in

$$(1 \times 16^1) + (F \times 16^0) = 16 + 15 = 31.$$

2.5.4 GIF and PNG

Compuserve GIF (pronounced *jif*) is an image format that was first proposed in the late 1980s as a means for distributing images over networks. Like PGM, it is a raster format, but it has the following properties:

1. Colors are stored using a color map. The GIF specification allows a maximum of 256 colors per image.
2. GIF doesn't allow binary or grayscale images, except as can be produced with RGB values.
3. The pixel data is compressed using LZW (Lempel-Ziv-Welch) compression. This works by constructing a "codebook" of the data. The first time a pattern is found, it is placed in the codebook. Subsequently, the encoder will output the code for that pattern. LZW

compression can be used on any data; however, it is a patented algorithm, and legal use requires a license from Unisys.

4. The GIF format allows multiple images per file. This aspect can be used to create animated GIFs.

A GIF file will contain a header including the image size (in pixels), the color map, the color **resolution** (number of bits per pixel), a flag indicating whether or not the color map is ordered, and the color map size.

The GIF format is commonly used; it has become one of the standard formats supported by the World Wide Web and by the Java programming language. Full descriptions of the GIF format can be found in reference books [2], [20].

The PNG (pronounced *ping*) format has been more recently designed to replace GIF and to overcome some of GIF's disadvantages. Specifically, PNG does not rely on any patented algorithms, and it supports more image types than GIF. PNG supports grayscale, truecolor, and indexed images. Moreover, its compression utility, zlib, *always* results in genuine compression. This is not the case with LZW compression, which can result in a compression larger than the original data. PNG also includes support for **alpha channels,** which are ways of associating variable transparencies with an image, and **gamma correction,** which associates different numbers with different computer display systems to ensure that a given image will appear the same independently of the system.

PNG is described in detail [28]. PNG is certainly to be preferred to GIF, but being newer, it is not yet as well supported.

2.5.5 JPEG

The compression methods used by GIF and PNG are lossless: the original information can be recovered completely. The JPEG algorithm uses lossy compression, in which not all the original data can be recovered. Such methods result in much higher compression rates, and JPEG images are in general much smaller than GIF or PNG images. Compression of JPEG images works by breaking the image into 8×8 blocks, applying the discrete cosine transform (DCT) to each block, and removing small values. JPEG images are best used for the representation of natural scenes, in which case they are preferred.

For data with any legal significance or scientific data, JPEG is less suitable for the very reason that not all information is preserved. However, the mechanics of the JPEG transform ensures that a JPEG image, when restored from its compression routine, will generally look the same as the original image. The differences are, in general, too small to be visible to the human eye. JPEG images are thus excellent for display.

We shall investigate the JPEG algorithm in Section 14.4. More detailed accounts are available [7], [27].

A JPEG image then contains the compression data with a small header providing the image size and file identification. We can see a header by using our dumphex function:

```
>> dumphex('ngc6543a.jpg',4)

ans =

FF D8 FF E0 00 10 4A 46 49 46 00 01 01 00 00 01    ......JFIF......
00 01 00 00 FF FE 00 47 43 52 45 41 54 4F 52 3A    .......GCREATOR:
20 58 56 20 56 65 72 73 69 6F 6E 20 33 2E 30 30     XV Version 3.00
62 20 20 52 65 76 3A 20 36 2F 31 35 2F 39 34 20    b  Rev: 6/15/94
```

An image file containing JPEG-compressed data is usually just called a JPEG image. But this is not quite correct; such an image should be called a JFIF image, where JFIF stands for JPEG File Interchange Format. The JFIF definition allows the file to contain a **thumbnail** version of the image; this is reflected in the header information:

Bytes	Information	Description
0–1	Start of image marker	Always FF D8.
2–3	Application marker	Always FF E0.
4–5	Length of segment	
5–10	JFIF\ 0	ASCII JFIF.
11–12	JFIF version	In our example above 01 01 or version 1.1.
13	Units	Values are: 0 arbitrary units; 1 pixel/inch; 2 pixels/centimeter.
14–15	Horizontal pixel density	
16–17	Vertical pixel density	
18	Thumbnail width	If this is 0, there is no thumbnail.
19	Thumbnail height	If this is 0, there is no thumbnail.

The thumbnail information (stored as 24-bit RGB values) and further information required for decompressing the image data would follow. For further information available see [2], [20].

2.5.6 TIFF

The **Tagged Image File Format,** or TIFF, is one of the most comprehensive image formats. It can store multiple images per file. It allows different compression routines (none at all, LZW, JPEG, Huffman, run-length encoding) and different byte orderings (little-endian ordering, as used in BMP, or big-endian ordering, in which the bytes retain their order within words). It allows binary, grayscale, truecolor or indexed images, and allows opacity or transparency.

For that reason it requires skillful programming to write image-reading software that will read all possible TIFF images. But TIFF is an excellent format for data exchange.

The TIFF header is, in fact, very simple; it consists of just 8 bytes:

Bytes	Information	Description
0–1	Byte order	Either 4D 4D: ASCII MM for big endian, or 49 49: ASCII II for little endian.
2–3	TIFF version	Always 00 2A or 2A 00 (depending on the byte order) = 42.
4–8	Image offset	Pointer to the position in the file of the data for the first image.

We can see this with

```
>> dumphex('newborn.tif',4)

ans =

49 49 2A 00 E0 01 01 00 32 7C 5B 2D 23 19 0E 15    II*.....2|[-#...
10 0E 0D 0F 10 0F 0E 10 11 11 0E 12 13 12 10 17    ................
10 1D 70 8E 99 A0 AE B5 BB BA C2 C6 C6 CB D3 D0    ..p.............
D2 D1 CA DB DE DE E1 E5 E6 DF E4 E9 FE EB 0B ED    ................
```

This particular image uses the little-endian byte ordering. The first image in this file (which is in fact the only image), begins at byte

```
E0 01 01 00
```

Because this is a little-endian file, we reverse the order of the bytes: 00 01 01 E0. This works out to 66016.

As well as the previously cited references, Baxes [1] provides a good introduction to TIFF.

2.5.7 DICOM

The DICOM (Digital Imaging and Communications in Medicine) 3.0 standard defines an image format that, like GIF, may hold multiple image files. However, the files may be considered as slices or frames of a three-dimensional object. Thus a DICOM file, in contrast to the image formats described above, may describe a three-dimensional image. DICOM has become a standard for medical digital-imaging modalities. More recently, it has been used as much in pathology as in diagnosis.

A DICOM file contains a header, which contains image information (size, number of slices), as well as the modality used (CAT, magnetic resonance imaging, positron-emission tomography, etc.), patient information, and compression used. Image data in a DICOM file may be compressed with either lossy or lossless methods: the former uses the DCT as does the JPEG format, and the latter either a lossless version of the DCT or **run-length encoding,** where a string of repeated characters is stored simply as the character plus the number of times it occurs.

The DICOM specification is huge and complex. Drafts have been published on the World Wide Web, or information can be obtained from the National Electrical Manufacturers Association, one of the creators of this format.

2.5.8 Files in MATLAB

An image matrix may be written to an image file with the `imwrite` function. Its general form is

```
imwrite(X,map,'filename','fmt')
```

which writes the image stored in matrix X with color map `map` (if appropriate) to file `filename` with format `fmt`. Without the `map` argument, the image data is supposed to be grayscale or RGB. For example, suppose we have read an image as follows:

```
a=imread('autumn.tif');
```

We can write this RGB matrix a to an PNG file with

```
imwrite(a,'autumn.png','png');
```

EXERCISES

1. Type in the command

    ```
    >> help imdemos
    ```

    This will give you a list of, among other things, all the sample TIFF images that come with the Image Processing Toolbox. Make a list of these sample images, and for each image:

    a. Determine its type (binary, grayscale, true color or indexed color).
    b. Determine its size (in pixels).
    c. Give a brief description of the picture (what it looks like; what it seems to be a picture of).

2. Pick a grayscale image, say `cameraman.tif` or `wombats.tif`. Using the `imwrite` function, write it to files of type JPEG, PNG, and BMP. What are the sizes of those files?

3. Repeat question 2 with:

    a. A binary image.

    b. An indexed color image.

    c. A true-color image.

4. The following shows the hexadecimal dump of a BMP file:

```
42 4D 7E 05 02 00 00 00 00 00 36 04 00 00 28 00
00 00 23 01 00 00 C2 01 00 00 01 00 08 00 00 00
00 00 48 01 02 00 00 00 00 00 00 00 00 00 00 01
00 00 00 00 00 00 00 00 00 00 01 01 01 00 02 02
```

Determine the height and width of this image (in pixels) and whether it is a grayscale or color image.

5. Repeat Question 4 with

```
42 4D 36 00 09 00 00 00 00 00 36 00 00 00 28 00
00 00 00 02 00 00 80 01 00 00 01 00 18 00 00 00
00 00 00 00 09 00 00 00 00 00 00 00 00 00 00 00
00 00 00 00 00 00 00 00 7D 02 01 7F 05 04 84 07
```

CHAPTER THREE

IMAGE DISPLAY

3.1 Introduction

We have touched briefly on image display in Chapter 2. In this chapter, we investigate this matter in more detail. We take a closer look at the use of the imshow function and show how spatial resolution and quantization can affect the display and appearance of an image. In particular, we look at image quality and how that may be affected by various image attributes. Quality is, of course, a highly subjective matter: no two people will agree precisely as to the quality of different images. However, for human vision in general, the preference is for images to be sharp and detailed. This is a consequence of two properties of an image: its spatial resolution and its quantization.

3.2 Basics of Image Display

An image may be represented as a matrix of the gray values of its pixels. The problem here is to display that matrix on the computer screen. There are many factors that will affect the display. They include

1. ambient lighting,
2. the monitor type and settings,
3. the graphics card, and
4. monitor resolution.

The same image may be very different when viewed on a dull CRT monitor compared with a bright LCD monitor. The resolution can also affect the display of an image. A higher resolution may result in the image taking up less physical area on the screen, but this may be counteracted by a loss in the color depth: the monitor may be only to display 24-bit color at low resolutions. If the monitor is bathed in bright light (sunlight, for example), the display of the image may be compromised. Furthermore, the individual's own visual system will affect the appearance of an image. The same image, viewed by two people, may appear to have different characteristics to each person. For our purpose, we shall assume that the computer set up is optimal and that the monitor is able to accurately reproduce the necessary gray values or colors in any image.

A very basic MATLAB function for image display is image. This function simply displays a matrix as an image. However, it may not necessarily give very good results. For example:

```
>> c=imread('cameraman.tif');
>> image(c)
```

will certainly display the cameraman, but possibly in an odd mixture of colors and with some stretching. The strange colors come from the fact that the image command uses the current color map to assign colors to the matrix elements. The default color map is called jet and consists of 64 very bright colors, which is inappropriate for the display of a grayscale image.

To display the image properly, we need to add several extra commands to the image line.

1. truesize, which displays one matrix element (in this case an image pixel) for each screen pixel. More formally, we may use truesize([256 256]), where the vector components give the number of screen pixels vertically and horizontally to use in the display. If the vector is not specified, it defaults to the image size.

2. axis off, which turns off the axis labeling,

3. colormap(gray(247)), which adjusts the image color map to use shades of gray only. We can find the number of gray levels used by the cameraman image with

```
>> size(unique(c))

ans =

   247      1
```

Since the cameraman image thus uses 247 different gray levels, we need only that number of grays in the color map.

Thus, a complete command for viewing this image will be

```
>> image(c),truesize,axis off, colormap(gray(247))
```

We may to adjust the color map to use fewer or more colors; however, this can have a dramatic effect on the result. The command

```
>> image(c),truesize,axis off, colormap(gray(512))
```

will produce a dark image. This happens because only the first 247 elements of the color map will be used by the image for display, and these will all be in the first half of the color map, thus all dark grays. On the other hand,

```
>> image(c),truesize,axis off, colormap(gray(128))
```

will produce a very light image, because any pixel with gray level higher than 128 will simply pick that highest gray value (which is white) from the color map.

The image command works well for an indexed color image, as long as we remember to use imread to pick up the color map as well:

```
>> [x,map]=imread('cat.tif');
>> image(x),truesize,axis off,colormap(map)
```

For true color images, the image data will be read (by imread) as a three-dimensional array. In such a case, image will ignore the current color map and assign colors to the display based on the values in the array. So

```
>> t=imread('twins.tif');
>> image(t),truesize,axis off
```

will produce the correct twins image.

In general the image function can be used to display any image or matrix. However, there is a command that is more convenient and does most of the work of color mapping for us; we discuss this in the next section.

3.3 The imshow Function

GRAYSCALE IMAGES   We have seen that if x is a matrix of type uint8, then the command

```
imshow(x)
```

will display x as an image. This is reasonable, since the data type uint8 restricts values to be integers between 0 and 255. However, not all image

Capt. Budd Christman/NOAA Corps.

(a)   (b)

FIGURE 3.1 *An attempt at data type conversion. (a) The original image. (b) After conversion to type* double.

matrices come so nicely bundled up into this data type, and lots of MATLAB image-processing commands produce output matrices that are of type double. We have two choices with a matrix of this type:

1. Convert to type uint8 and then display.
2. Display the matrix directly.

The second option is possible because imshow will display a matrix of type double as a grayscale image as long as the matrix elements are between 0 and 1. Suppose we take an image and convert it to type double:

```
>> c=imread('caribou.tif');
>> cd=double(c);
>> imshow(c),figure,imshow(cd)
```

The results are shown in Figure 3.1.

However, as you can see, Figure 3.1(b) doesn't look much like the original picture at all! This is because for a matrix of type double, the imshow function expects the values to be between 0 and 1, where 0 is displayed as black and 1 is displayed as white. A value v with $0 < v < 1$ is displayed as gray scale $\lfloor 255v \rfloor$. Conversely, values greater than 1 will be displayed as 1 (white) and values less than 0 will be displayed as 0 (black). In the caribou image, every pixel has value greater than or equal to 1 (in fact the minimum value is 21), so that every pixel will be displayed

Capt. Budd Christman/NOAA Corps.

(a)   (b)

FIGURE 3.2 *Scaling by dividing an image matrix by a scalar. (a) The matrix* cd *divided by 512. (b) The matrix* cd *divided by 128.*

as white. To display the matrix cd, we need to scale it to the range 0–1. This is easily done simply by dividing all values by 255:

```
>> imshow(cd/255)
```

and the result will be the caribou image as shown in Figure 3.1(a).

We can vary the display by changing the scaling of the matrix. Results of the commands

```
>> imshow(cd/512)
>> imshow(cd/128)
```

are shown in Figure 3.2.

Dividing by 512 darkens the image, because all matrix values are now between 0 and 0.5, so that the brightest pixel in the image is a midgray. Dividing by 128 means that the range is 0–2 and all pixels in the range 1–2 will be displayed as white. Thus the image has an overexposed, washed-out appearance.

The display of the result of a command whose output is a matrix of type double can be greatly affected by a judicious choice of a scaling factor.

We can convert the original image to double more properly using the function im2double. This applies correct scaling so that the output values are between 0 and 1. So the commands

```
>> cd=im2double(c);
>> imshow(cd)
```

will produce a correct image. It is important to make the distinction between the two functions double and im2double. The function double changes the data type but does not change the numeric values; im2double changes both the numeric data type and the values. The exception, of course, is if the original image is of type double, in which case im2double does nothing. Although the command double is not of much use for direct image display, it can be very useful for image arithmetic. We have seen examples of this above with scaling.

Corresponding to the functions double and im2double are the functions uint8 and im2uint8. If we take our image cd of type double, properly scaled so that all elements are between 0 and 1, we can convert it back to an image of type uint8 in two ways:

```
>> c2=uint8(255*cd);
>> c3=im2uint8(cd);
```

Use of im2uint8 is preferred. It takes other data types as input and always returns a correct result.

BINARY IMAGES   Recall that a binary image will have only two values: 0 and 1. MATLAB does not have a binary data type as such, but it does have a logical flag, where uint8 values 0 and 1 can be interpreted as logical data. The logical flag will be set by the use of relational operations such as ==, < or >, or any other operations that provide a yes/no answer. For example, suppose we take the caribou matrix and create a new matrix with

```
>> cl=c>120;
```

(we will see more of this type of operation in Chapter 9.) If we now check all of our variables with whos, the output will include the line

```
cl      256x256      65536 uint8 array (logical)
```

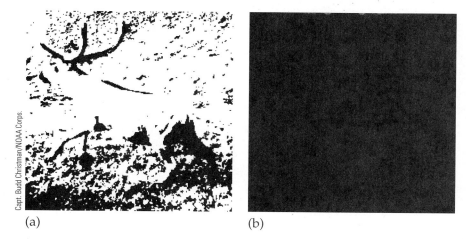

Capt. Budd Christman/NOAA Corps.

(a)   (b)

FIGURE 3.3 *Making the image binary. (a) The caribou image turned binary. (b) After conversion to type* uint8.

This means that the command

```
>> imshow(cl)
```

will display the matrix as a binary image. The result is shown in Figure 3.3.
    Suppose we remove the logical flag from cl. This can be done by a simple command:

```
>> cl = +cl;
```

Now the output of whos will include the line

```
cl      256x256      65536 uint8 array
```

If we now try to display this matrix with imshow, we obtain the result shown in Figure 3.3(b). A very disappointing image! But this is to be expected; in a matrix of type uint8, white is 255, 0 is black, and 1 is a very dark gray, indistinguishable from black.
    To get back to a viewable image, we can either turn the logical flag back on and view the result:

```
>> imshow(logical(cl))
```

or simply convert to type `double`:

```
>> imshow(double(c1))
```

Both these commands will produce the image seen in Figure 3.3(a).

3.4 Bit Planes

Grayscale images can be transformed into a sequence of binary images by breaking them up into their **bit-planes.** If we consider the gray value of each pixel of an 8-bit image as an 8-bit binary word, then the zeroth bit plane consists of the last bit of each gray value. Since this bit has the least effect in terms of the magnitude of the value, it is called the **least significant bit,** and the plane consisting of those bits the **least significant bit plane.** Similarly the eighth bit plane consists of the first bit in each value. This bit has the greatest effect in terms of the magnitude of the value, so it is called the **most significant bit,** and the plane consisting of those bits the **most significant bit plane.**

If we take a grayscale image, we start by making it a matrix of type `double`; this means we can perform arithmetic on the values.

```
>> c=imread('cameraman.tif');
>> cd=double(c);
```

We now isolate the bit planes by simply dividing the matrix `cd` by successive powers of 2, throwing away the remainder, and seeing if the final bit is 0 or 1. We can do this with the `mod` function.

```
>> c0=mod(cd,2);
>> c1=mod(floor(cd/2),2);
>> c2=mod(floor(cd/4),2);
>> c3=mod(floor(cd/8),2);
>> c4=mod(floor(cd/16),2);
>> c5=mod(floor(cd/32),2);
>> c6=mod(floor(cd/64),2);
>> c7=mod(floor(cd/128),2);
```

These are all shown in Figure 3.4. Note that the least significant bit plane, `c0`, is to all intents and purposes a random array and that as the index value

FIGURE 3.4 *The bit planes of an 8-bit grayscale image.*

of the bit plane increases, more of the image appears. The most significant bit plane, $c7$, is actually a threshold of the image at level 127:

```
>> ct=c>127;
>> all(c7(:)==ct(:))
ans =
      1
```

We will discuss thresholding in Chapter 9.

We can recover and display the original image with:

```
>> cc=2*(2*(2*(2*(2*(2*(2*c7+c6)+c5)+c4)+c3)+c2)+c1)+c0;
>> imshow(uint8(cc))
```

3.5 Spatial Resolution

Spatial resolution is the density of pixels over the image: the greater the spatial resolution, the more pixels are used to display the image. We can experiment with spatial resolution with MATLAB's imresize function. Suppose we have an 256×256 8-bit grayscale image saved to the matrix x. Then the command

```
imresize(x,1/2);
```

will halve the size of the image. It does this by taking out every other row and every other column, thus leaving only those matrix elements whose row and column indices are even:

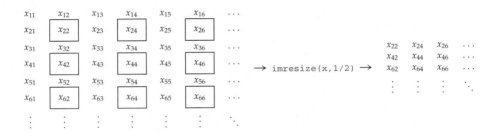

If we apply imresize to the result with the parameter 2 rather than 1/2, all the pixels are repeated to produce an image with the same size as the original, but with half the resolution in each direction:

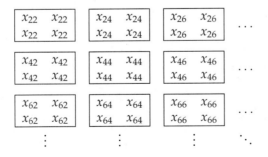

The effective resolution of this new image is only 128×128. We can do all this in one line:

```
x2=imresize(imresize(x,1/2),2);
```

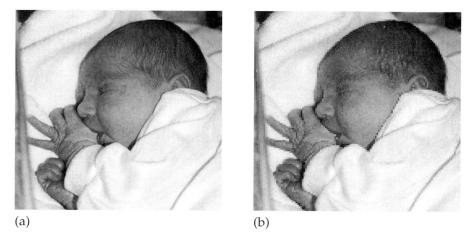

(a) (b)

FIGURE 3.5 *Reducing resolution of an image. (a) The original image. (b) Image at 128 × 128 resolution.*

By changing the parameters of imresize, we can change the effective resolution of the image to smaller amounts:

Command	Effective resolution
imresize(imresize(x,1/4),4);	64 × 64
imresize(imresize(x,1/8),8);	32 × 32
imresize(imresize(x,1/16),16);	16 × 16
imresize(imresize(x,1/32),32);	8 × 8

To see the effects of these commands, suppose we apply them to the image newborn.tif:

```
x=imread('newborn.tif');
```

The effects of increasing blockiness or **pixelization** become more pronounced as the resolution decreases. At only 128 × 128 resolution, such as in Figure 3.5(b), some fine detail, such as the edges of the baby's fingers, are less clear, and at 64 × 64 resolution, as shown in Figure 3.6(a), all edges are now quite blocky. At 32 × 32 resolution, as shown in Figure 3.6(b) the image is all but unrecognizable, and at resolutions 16×16 and 8×8, as shown in Figure 3.7(a and b) respectively, the image is reduced to unrecognizable blocks of gray.

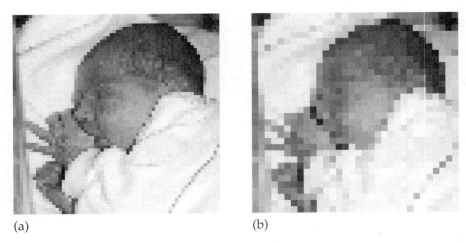

(a)   (b)

FIGURE 3.6 *Further reducing the resolution of an image. (a) Image at* 64 × 64 *resolution.*
(b) Image at 32 × 32 *resolution.*

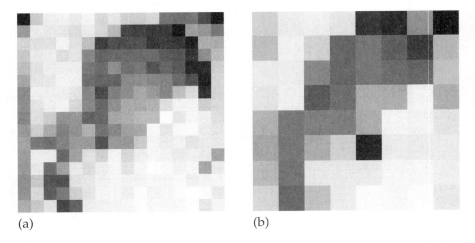

(a)   (b)

FIGURE 3.7 *Even more reducing the resolution of an image. (a) Image at* 16 × 16 *resolution.*
(b) Image at 8 × 8 *resolution.*

3.6 Quantization and Dithering

Quantization refers to the number of grayscales used to represent the image.
As we have seen, most images will have 256 grayscales, which is more than
enough for the needs of human vision. However, there are circumstances in
which it may be more practical to represent the image with fewer grayscales.
One simple way to do this is by **uniform quantization**: to represent an
image with only n grayscales, we divide the range of grayscales into n equal

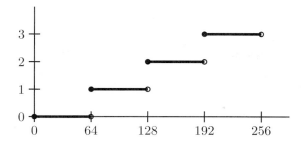

FIGURE 3.8 *A mapping for uniform quantization.*

(or nearly equal) ranges and map the ranges to the values 0 to $n - 1$. For example, if $n = 4$, we map grayscales to output values as follows:

Original values	Output value
0–63	0
64–127	1
128–191	2
192–255	3

The values 0, 1, 2, 3 may need to be scaled for display. This mapping can be shown graphically, as in Figure 3.8.

To perform such a mapping in MATLAB, we can perform the following operations, supposing x to be a matrix of type uint8:

```
f=floor(double(x)/64);

q=uint8(f*64);
```

Since the grayscales are in the range 0–255, the first command simply applies the function shown in Figure 3.8. The second command scales the values to more appropriate values for display. These commands can be done as one, with different values used to change the number of output grayscales:

Command	Number of grayscales
uint8(floor(double(x)/2)*2)	128
uint8(floor(double(x)/4)*4)	64
uint8(floor(double(x)/8)*8)	32
uint8(floor(double(x)/16)*16)	16
uint8(floor(double(x)/32)*32)	8
uint8(floor(double(x)/64)*64)	4
uint8(floor(double(x)/128)*128)	2

There is, however, a more elegant method of reducing the grayscales in an image, and it involves using the grayslice function. Given an image

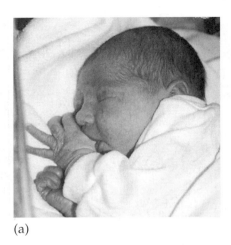
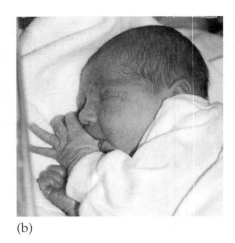

(a)   (b)

FIGURE 3.9 *Quantization (1). (a) The image quantized to 128 grayscales. (b) The image quantized to 64 grayscales.*

matrix x and an integer n, the command grayslice(x,n) produces a matrix whose values have been reduced to the values $0, 1, \ldots, n-1$. So, for example,

```
>> grayslice(x,4)
```

will produce a uint8 version of our image with values 0, 1, 2, and 3. We can't view this directly, because it will appear completely black: the four values are too close to zero to be distinguishable. We need to treat this matrix as the indices to a color map, and the color map we will use is gray(4), which produces a color map of four evenly spaced gray values between 0 (black) and 1.0 (white). Thus, for display, we can implement the above commands as the following:

Command	Number of grayscales
imshow(grayslice(x,128),gray(128))	128
imshow(grayslice(x,64),gray(64))	64
imshow(grayslice(x,32),gray(32))	32
imshow(grayslice(x,16),gray(16))	16
imshow(grayslice(x,8),gray(8))	8
imshow(grayslice(x,4),gray(4))	4
imshow(grayslice(x,2),gray(2))	2

If we apply these commands to our baby image, we obtain the results shown in Figures 3.9– 3.12. One immediate consequence of uniform quantization is that of false contours, most noticeable with fewer grayscales. For example, in

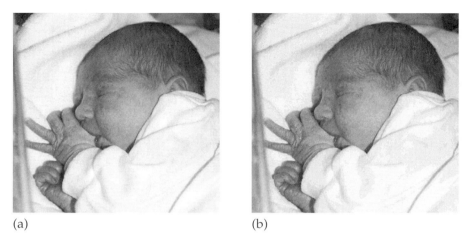

(a)   (b)

FIGURE 3.10 *Quantization (2). (a) The image quantized to 32 grayscales. (b) The image quantized to 16 grayscales.*

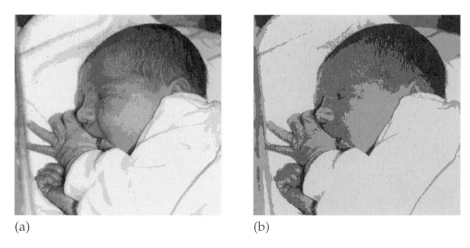

(a)   (b)

FIGURE 3.11 *Quantization (3). (a) The image quantized to eight grayscales. (b) The image quantized to four grayscales.*

Figure 3.10(b), we can see on the sleeves and on the baby's face that the gray texture is no longer smooth; there are observable discontinuities between different gray values. This effect is even more obvious in Figure 3.11(a and b). We expect that if fewer grayscales are used, and the jumps between consecutive grayscales become larger, such false contours will occur.

DITHERING   Dithering, in general terms, refers to the process of reducing the number of colors in an image. For the moment, we are concerned only with grayscale dithering. Dithering is necessary sometimes for display, if the image must be displayed on equipment with a limited number of colors or

FIGURE 3.12 *The image quantized to two grayscales.*

for printing. Newsprint, in particular, has only two scales of gray: black and white. Representing an image with only two tones is also known as **halftoning.**

One method of dealing with such false contours involves adding random values to the image before quantization. Equivalently, for quantization to two grayscales we may compare the image to a random matrix r. The trick is to devise a suitable matrix so that grayscales are represented evenly in the result. For example, an area containing midgray level (around 127) would have a checkerboard pattern. A darker area will have a pattern containing more black than white, and a light area will have a pattern containing more white than black. Figure 3.13 illustrates this. One standard matrix is

$$D = \begin{bmatrix} 0 & 128 \\ 192 & 64 \end{bmatrix}$$

which is repeated until it is as big as the image matrix, when the two are compared. Suppose $d(i,j)$ is the matrix obtain by replicating D. Thus an output pixel $p(i,j)$ is defined by

$$p(i,j) = \begin{cases} 1 & \text{if } x(i,j) > d(i,j) \\ 0 & \text{if } x(i,j) \le d(i,j) \end{cases}$$

This approach to quantization is called **dithering,** and the matrix D is an example of a **dither matrix.** Another dither matrix is given by

$$D_2 = \begin{bmatrix} 0 & 128 & 32 & 160 \\ 192 & 64 & 224 & 96 \\ 48 & 176 & 16 & 144 \\ 240 & 112 & 208 & 80 \end{bmatrix}$$

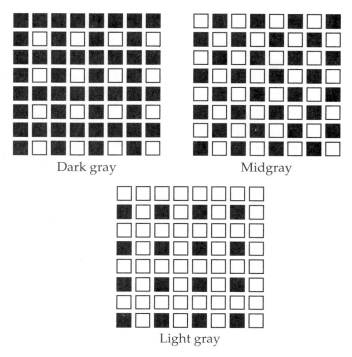

Dark gray   Midgray

Light gray

FIGURE 3.13 *Patterns for dithering output.*

We can apply the matrices to our newborn image matrix x by using the following commands:

```
>> D=[0 128;192 64]
>> r=repmat(D,128,128);
>> x2=x>r;imshow(x2)
>> D2=[0 128 32 160;192 64 224 96;48 176 16 144;240 112 208 80];
>> r2=repmat(D2,64,64);
>> x4=x>r2;imshow(x4)
```

The results are shown in Figure 3.14. The dithered images are an improvement on the uniformly quantized image shown in Figure 3.12. General dither matrices are provided by Hawley [12].

Dithering can be extended easily to more than two output gray values. Suppose, for example, we wish to quantize to four output levels 0, 1, 2, and 3. Since $255/3 = 85$, we first quantize by dividing the gray value $x(i, j)$ by 85:

$$q(i, j) = [x(i, j)/85].$$

This will produce only the values 0, 1, and 2, except for when $x(i, j) = 255$. Suppose now that our replicated dither matrix $d(i, j)$ is scaled so

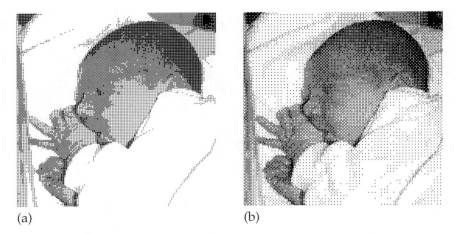

(a)   (b)

FIGURE 3.14 *Examples of dithering. (a) The newborn baby image dithered using D. (b) The newborn baby image dithered using D_2.*

that its values are in the range 0 . . . 85. The final value $p(i,j)$ is then defined by

$$p(i,j) = q(i,j) + \begin{cases} 1 & \text{if } x(i,j) - 85q(i,j) > d(i,j) \\ 0 & \text{if } x(i,j) - 85q(i,j) \leq d(i,j) \end{cases}$$

This can be easily implemented in a few commands, modifying D slightly from above:

```
>> D=[0 56;84 28]
>> r=repmat(D,128,128);
>> x=double(x);
>> q=floor(x/85);
>> x4=q+(x-85*q>r);
>> imshow(uint8(85*x4))
```

and the result is shown in Figure 3.15(a). We can dither to eight gray levels by using $255/7 = 37$ (we round the result up to ensure that our output values stay within range) instead of 85 above; our starting dither matrix will be

$$D = \begin{bmatrix} 0 & 24 \\ 36 & 12 \end{bmatrix}$$

and the result is shown in Figure 3.15(b). Note how much better these images look than the corresponding uniformly quantized images in Figure 3.11(a and b). The eight-level result, in particular, is almost indistinguishable from the original, despite the quantization.

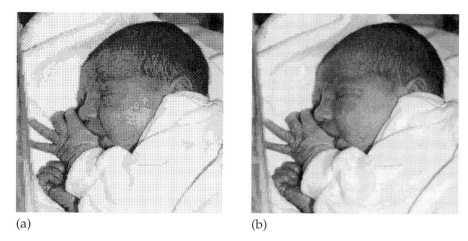

(a)   (b)

FIGURE 3.15 *Dithering to more than two grayscales. (a) Dithering to four output grayscales. (b) Dithering to eight output grayscales.*

ERROR DIFFUSION A different approach to quantization from dithering is that of **error diffusion.** The image is quantized at two levels, but for each pixel we take into account the error between its gray value and its quantized value. Since we are quantizing to gray values 0 and 255, pixels close to these values will have little error. However, pixels close to the center of the range, 128, will have a large error. The idea is to spread this error over neighboring pixels. A popular method, developed by Floyd and Steinberg, works by moving through the image pixel by pixel, starting at the top left and working across each row in turn. For each pixel $p(i, j)$ in the image we perform the following sequence of steps:

1. Perform the quantization.
2. Calculate the quantization error. This is defined as

$$E = \begin{cases} p(i,j) & \text{if } p(i,j) < 128 \\ p(i,j) - 255 & \text{if } p(i,j) >= 128 \end{cases}.$$

3. Spread this error E over pixels to the right and below according to this table:

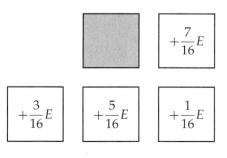

```
function y = fl_stein(x)
%
% FL_STEIN applies Floyd-Steinberg error diffusion to an image x, which is
% assumed to be of type uint8.
%
height=size(x,1);
width=size(x,2);
y=uint8(zeros(height,width));
z=zeros(height+2,width+2);
z(2:height+1,2:width+1)=x;
for i=2:height+1,
   for j=2:width+1,
     if z(i,j) < 128
        y(i-1,j-1) = 0;
        e = z(i,j);
     else
        y(i-1,j-1) = 255;
        e = z(i,j)-255;
     end
     z(i,j+1)=z(i,j+1)+7*e/16;
     z(i+1,j-1)=z(i+1,j-1)+3*e/16;
     z(i+1,j)=z(i+1,j)+5*e/16;
     z(i+1,j+1)=z(i+1,j+1)+e/16;
   end
end
```

FIGURE 3.16 *A* MATLAB *function for applying Floyd-Steinberg error diffusion to a grayscale image.*

There are several points to note about this algorithm:

- The error is spread to pixels *before* quantization is performed on them. Thus, the error diffusion will affect the quantization level of those pixels.
- Once a pixel has been quantized, its value will never be affected because the error diffusion affects pixels only to the right and below, and we are working from the left and above.
- To implement this algorithm, we need to embed the image in a larger array of zeros so that the indices do not go outside the bounds of our array.

The dither function, when applied to a grayscale image, actually implements Floyd-Steinberg error diffusion. However, it is instructive to write a simple MATLAB function to implement the error ourselves. One possibility is shown in Figure 3.16.

The result of applying this function to our newborn image is shown in Figure 3.17. Note that the result is very pleasing, so much so that it's hard to believe that every pixel in the image is either black or white so that we have a binary image.

Other error-diffusion schemes are possible; two such methods, Jarvis-Judice-Ninke and Stucki, have these error diffusion schemes:

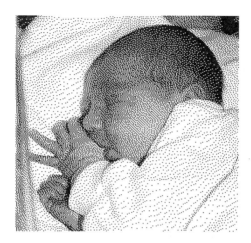

FIGURE 3.17 *The newborn baby image after Floyd-Steinberg error diffusion.*

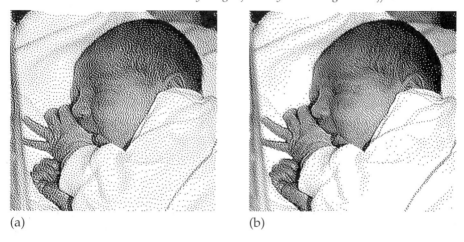

(a)   (b)

FIGURE 3.18 *Using other error-diffusion schemes. (a) Result of Jarvis-Judice-Ninke error diffusion. (b) Result of Stucki error diffusion.*

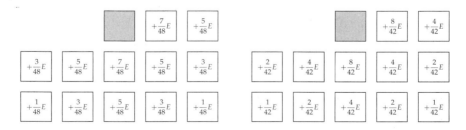

They can be applied by modifying the Floyd-Steinberg function shown in Figure 3.16. The results of applying these two error diffusion methods are shown in Figure 3.18.

A good introduction to error diffusion (and dithering) is given by Schumacher [32].

EXERCISES

1. Open the grayscale image `cameraman.tif` and view it. What data type is it?
2. Enter the following commands:

```
>> em,map]=imread('emu.tif');
>> e=ind2gray(em,map);
```

These will produce a grayscale image of type `double`. View this image.
3. Enter the command

```
>> e2=im2uint8(e);
```

and view the output.
What does the function `im2uint8` do? What effect does it have on the following?
   a. The appearance of the image.
   b. The elements of the image matrix.
4. What happens if you apply `im2uint8` to the cameraman image?
5. Experiment with reducing spatial resolution of the following images. In each case note the point at which the image becomes unrecognizable.
   a. `cameraman.tif`
   b. The grayscale emu image
   c. `blocks.tif`
   d. `buffalo.tif`
6. Experiment with reducing the quantization levels of the images in Question 5. Note the point at which the image becomes seriously degraded. Is this the same for all images, or can some images stand lower levels of quantization than others? Check your hypothesis with some other grayscale images.
7. With a magnifying glass look at a grayscale photograph in a newspaper. Describe the colors you see.

8. Show that the 2×2 dither matrix D provides appropriate results on areas of unchanging gray. Find the results of $D > G$ when G is 1 2×2 matrix of values
   a. 50
   b. 100
   c. 150
   d. 200

9. What are the necessary properties of D to obtain the appropriate patterns for the different input gray levels?

10. How do quantization levels affect the result of dithering? Use gray2ind to display a grayscale image with fewer grayscales and apply dithering to the result.

11. Apply each of Floyd-Steinberg, Jarvis-Judice-Ninke, and Stucki error diffusions to the images in Question 5. Which of the images looks best? Which error-diffusion method seems to produce the best results? Can you isolate what aspects of an image will render it most suitable for error diffusion?

CHAPTER FOUR

POINT PROCESSING

4.1 Introduction

Any image-processing operation transforms the gray values of the pixels. However, image-processing operations may be divided into three classes based on the information required to perform the transformation. From the most complex to the simplest, they are as follows:

1. **Transforms.** A transform represents the pixel values in some other, but equivalent form. Transforms allow for some very efficient and powerful algorithms, as we shall see later on. We may consider that in using a transform, the entire image is processed as a single large block. This may be illustrated by the diagram shown in Figure 4.1.

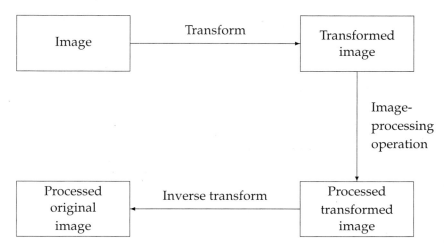

FIGURE 4.1 *Schema for transform processing.*

2. **Neighborhood processing.** To change the gray level of a given pixel we need only know the value of the gray levels in a small neighborhood of pixels around the given pixel.

3. **Point operations.** A pixel's gray value is changed without any knowledge of its surroundings.

Although point operations are the simplest, they contain some of the most powerful and widely used of all image-processing operations. They are especially useful in image preprocessing, where an image is required to be modified before the main job is attempted.

4.2 Arithmetic Operations

These operations act by applying a simple function

$$y = f(x)$$

to each gray value in the image. Thus $f(x)$ is a function that maps the range 0 . . . 255 onto itself. Simple functions include adding or subtracting a constant value to each pixel:

$$y = x \pm C$$

or multiplying each pixel by a constant:

$$y = Cx.$$

In each case we may have to adjust the output slightly in order to ensure that the results are integers in the 0 . . . 255 range. We can do this by first rounding the result (if necessary) to obtain an integer and then "clipping" the values by setting

$$y \leftarrow \begin{cases} 255 & \text{if } y > 255, \\ 0 & \text{if } y < 0. \end{cases}$$

We can obtain an understanding of how these operations affect an image by plotting $y = f(x)$. Figure 4.2 shows the result of adding or subtracting 128 from each pixel in the image. Notice that when we add 128, all gray values of 127 or greater will be mapped to 255. When we subtract 128, all gray values of 128 or less will be mapped to 0. By looking at these graphs, we observe that, in general, adding a constant will lighten an image and subtracting a constant will darken it.

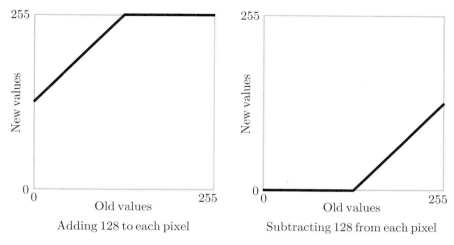

Adding 128 to each pixel   Subtracting 128 from each pixel

FIGURE 4.2 *Adding and subtracting a constant.*

We can test this on the blocks image `blocks.tif`, which we have seen in Figure 1.4. We start by reading the image in

```
>> b=imread('blocks.tif');
>> whos b
  Name      Size    Bytes  Class
   b       256x256  65536  uint8 array
```

The point of the second command was to find the numeric data type of b; it is `uint8`. The `unit8` data type is used for data storage only; we can't perform arithmetic operations. If we try, we just get an error message:

```
>> b1=b+128
??? Error using ==> +
Function '+' not defined for variables of class 'uint8'.
```

We can get round this in two ways. We can first turn b into a matrix of type `double`, add the 128, and then turn back to `uint8` for display:

```
>> b1=uint8(double(b)+128);
```

A second, and more elegant, way is to use the MATLAB function `imadd`, which is designed precisely to do this:

```
>> b1=imadd(b,128);
```

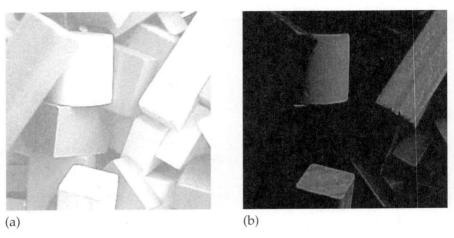

(a)   (b)

FIGURE 4.3 *Arithmetic operations on an image: adding or subtracting a constant. (a)* b1*: Adding 128; (b)* b2*: Subtracting 128.*

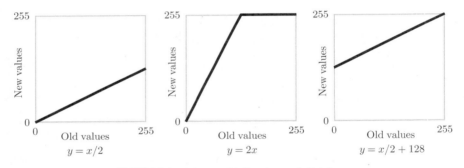

FIGURE 4.4 *Using multiplication and division.*

Subtraction is similar. We can transform out matrix in and out of `double` or use the `imsubtract` function:

```
>> b2=imsubtract(b,128);
```

And now we can view them,

```
>> imshow(b1),figure,imshow(b2)
```

and the results are seen in Figure 4.3.

We can also perform lightening or darkening of an image by multiplication. Figure 4.4 shows some examples of functions that will have these effects. To implement these functions we use the `immultiply` function.

TABLE 4.1   *Implementing pixel multiplication by MATLAB commands.*

$y = x/2$	b3=immultiply(b,0.5); or b3=imdivide(b,2)
$y = 2x$	b4=immultiply(b,2);
$y = x/2 + 128$	b5=imadd(immultiply(b,0.5),128);
	or b5=imadd(imdivide(b,2),128);

b3 : $y = x/2$ b4 : $y = 2x$ b5 : $y = x/2 + 128$

FIGURE 4.5 *Arithmetic operations on an image: multiplication and division.*

Table 4.1 shows the particular commands required to implement the functions of Figure 4.4. All these images can be viewed with imshow; they are shown in Figure 4.5.

Compare the results of darkening b2 and b3. Note that b3, although darker than the original, is still quite clear, whereas a lot of information has been lost by the subtraction process, as can be seen in image b2. This is because in image b2 all pixels with gray values 128 or less have become zero.

A similar loss of information has occurred in the images b1 and b4. Note in particular the edges of the light-colored block in the bottom center; in both b1 and b4 the right-hand edge has disappeared. However, the edge is quite visible in image b5.

COMPLEMENTS   The **complement** of a grayscale image is its photographic negative. If an image matrix m is of type double and thus its gray values are in the range 0.0 to 1.0, we can obtain its negative with the command

```
>> 1-m
```

If the image is binary, we can use

```
>> ~m
```

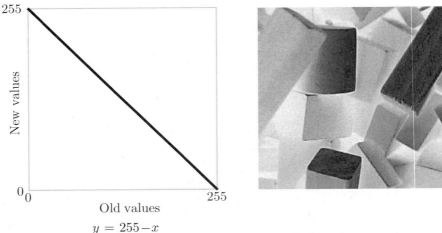

$$y = 255 - x$$

FIGURE 4.6 *Image complementation.*

If the image is of type `uint8`, the best approach is the `imcomplement` function. Figure 4.6 shows the complement function $y = 255 - x$, and the result of the commands

```
>> bc=imcomplement(b);
>> imshow(bc)
```

Interesting special effects can be obtained by complementing only part of the image, for example, by taking the complement of pixels of gray value 128 or less and leaving other pixels untouched. Or, we could take the complement of pixels that are 128 or greater and leave other pixels untouched. Figure 4.7 shows these functions. The effect of these functions is called **solarization** and will be discussed further in Chapter 16.

4.3 Histograms

Given a grayscale image, its **histogram** consists of its gray levels; that is, it is a graph indicating the number of times each gray level occurs in the image. We can deduce a great deal about the appearance of an image from its histogram, as the following examples indicate:

- In a dark image, the gray levels (and hence the histogram) would be clustered at the lower end.
- In a uniformly bright image, the gray levels would be clustered at the upper end.

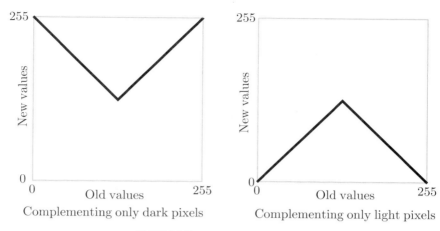

Complementing only dark pixels   Complementing only light pixels

FIGURE 4.7 *Part complementation.*

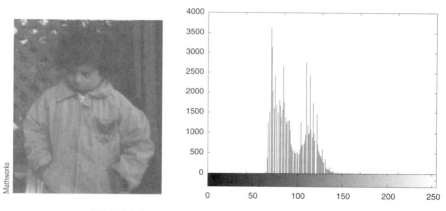

FIGURE 4.8 *The image* pout.tif *and its histogram.*

- In a well-contrasted image, the gray levels would be well spread out over much of the range.

We can view the histogram of an image in MATLAB by using the imhist function,

```
>> p=imread('pout.tif');
>> imshow(p),figure,imhist(p),axis tight
```

(the axis tight command ensures the axes are scaled so that all the histogram bars fit entirely within the Figure). The result is shown in Figure 4.8. Because the gray values are all clustered together in the center of the histogram, we would expect the image to be poorly contrasted, as indeed it is.

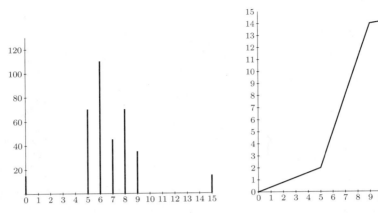

FIGURE 4.9 *A histogram of a poorly contrasted image and a stretching function.*

Given a poorly contrasted image, we would like to enhance its contrast by spreading out its histogram. There are two ways of doing this.

4.3.1 Histogram Stretching (Contrast Stretching)

Suppose we have an image with the histogram shown in Figure 4.9, which is associated with a table of the numbers n_i of gray values,

Gray level i	0	1	2	3	4	5	6	7	8	9	10	11	12	13	14	15
n_i	15	0	0	0	0	70	110	45	70	35	0	0	0	0	0	15

(with $n = 360$, as before). We can stretch out the gray levels in the center of the range by applying the piecewise linear function shown at the right in Figure 4.9. This function has the effect of stretching the gray levels 5–9 to gray levels 2–14, according to the equation

$$j = \frac{14 - 2}{9 - 5}(i - 5) + 2,$$

where i is the original gray level and j is its result after the transformation. Gray levels outside this range are either left alone (as in this case) or transformed according to the linear functions at the ends of the graph above. This yields

i	5	6	7	8	9
j	2	5	8	11	14

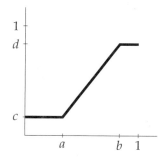

FIGURE 4.10 *The stretching function given by* `imadjust`.

and the corresponding histogram,

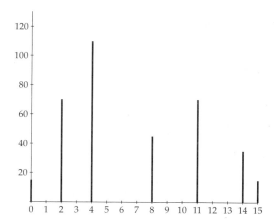

which indicates an image with greater contrast than the original.

USE OF Imadjust To perform histogram stretching in MATLAB, the `imadjust` function may be used. In its simplest incarnation, the command

```
imadjust(im,[a,b],[c,d])
```

stretches the image according to the function shown in Figure 4.10. Because `imadjust` is designed to work equally well on images of type `double`, `uint8`, or `uint16`, the values of a, b, c, and d must be between 0 and 1; the function automatically converts the image (if needed) to be of type `double`.

Note that `imadjust` does not work quite in the same way as shown in Figure 4.9. Pixel values less than a are all converted to c, and pixel values greater than b are all converted to d. If either `[a,b]` or `[c,d]` are

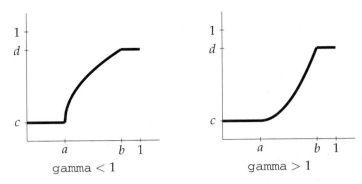

FIGURE 4.11 *The imadjust function with gamma not equal to 1.*

chosen to be [0,1], the abbreviation [] may be used. Thus, for example, the command

```
>> imadjust(im,[],[])
```

does nothing, and the command

```
>> imadjust(im,[],[1,0])
```

inverts the gray values of the image to produce a result similar to a photographic negative.

The imadjust function has one other optional parameter: the gamma value, which describes the shape of the function between the coordinates (a, c) and (b, d). If gamma is equal to 1, which is the default, then a linear mapping is used, as shown in Figure 4.10. However, values less than 1 produce a function that is concave downward, as shown on the left in Figure 4.11, and values greater than 1 produce a figure that is concave upward, as shown on the right in Figure 4.11.

The function used is a slight variation on the standard line between two points:

$$y = \left(\frac{x - a}{b - a}\right)^{\gamma} (d - c) + c$$

Use of the gamma value alone can be enough to substantially change the appearance of the image. For example,

```
>> t=imread('tire.tif');
>> th=imadjust(t,[],[],0.5);
>> imshow(t),figure,imshow(th)
```

produces the result shown in Figure 4.12.

FIGURE 4.12 *The tire image and after adjustment with the gamma value.*

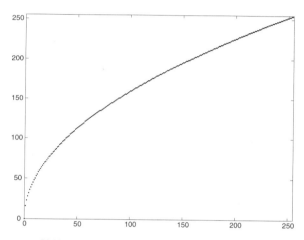

FIGURE 4.13 *The function used in Figure 4.12.*

We may view the `imadjust` stretching function with the `plot` function. For example,

```
>> plot(t,th,'.'),axis tight
```

produces the plot shown in Figure 4.13. Since p and ph are matrices that contain the original values and the values after the `imadjust` function; the `plot` function simply plots them, using dots to do it.

A PIECEWISE LINEAR-STRETCHING FUNCTION   We can easily write our own function to perform piecewise linear stretching as shown in Figure 4.14. To do this, we make use of the `find` function to find the pixel values in the image between

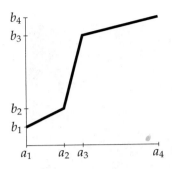

FIGURE 4.14 *A piecewise linear-stretching function.*

a_i and a_{i+1}. Because the line between the coordinates (a_i, b_i) and (a_{i+1}, b_{i+1}) has the equation

$$y = \frac{b_{i+1} - b_i}{a_{i+1} - a_i}(x - a_i) + b_i,$$

the heart of our function will be the lines

```
pix=find(im >= a(i) & im < a(i+1));
out(pix)=(im(pix)-a(i))*(b(i+1)-b(i))/(a(i+1)-a(i))+b(i);
```

where im is the input image and out is the output image. A simple procedure that takes as inputs images of type uint8 or double is shown in Figure 4.15. As an example of the use of this function,

```
>> th=histpwl(t,[0 .25 .5 .75 1],[0 .75 .25 .5 1]);
>> imshow(th)
>> figure,plot(t,th,'.'),axis tight
```

produces the figures shown in Figure 4.16.

4.3.2 Histogram Equalization

The trouble with any of the above methods of histogram stretching is that they require user input. Sometimes a better approach is provided by histogram **equalization**, which is an entirely automatic procedure. The idea is to change the histogram to one that is uniform; that is, every bar on the histogram is of the same height. In other words, each gray level in the image occurs with the same frequency. In practice this is generally not possible, although, as we will see, the result of histogram equalization provides very good results.

Suppose our image has L different gray levels, $0, 1, 2, \ldots, L - 1$, and gray level i occurs n_i times in the image. Suppose also that the total number

```
function out = histpwl(im,a,b)
%
% HISTPWL(IM,A,B) applies a piecewise linear transformation to the pixel values
% of image IM, where A and B are vectors containing the x and y coordinates
% of the ends of the line segments.  IM can be of type UINT8 or DOUBLE,
% and the values in A and B must be between 0 and 1.
%
% For example:
%
%    histpwl(x,[0,1],[1,0])
%
% simply inverts the pixel values.
%
classChanged = 0;
if ~isa(im, 'double'),
    classChanged = 1;
    im = im2double(im);
end

if length(a) ~= length (b)
   error('Vectors A and B must be of equal size');
end

N=length(a);
out=zeros(size(im));

for i=1:N-1
  pix=find(im>=a(i) & im<a(i+1));
  out(pix)=(im(pix)-a(i))*(b(i+1)-b(i))/(a(i+1)-a(i))+b(i);
end

pix=find(im==a(N));
out(pix)=b(N);

if classChanged==1
  out = uint8(255*out);
end
```

FIGURE 4.15 *A* MATLAB *function for applying a piecewise linear-stretching function.*

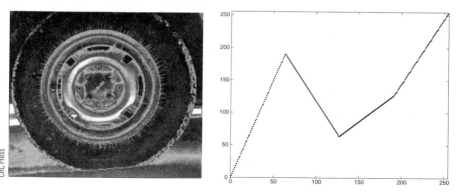

FIGURE 4.16 *The tire image and after adjustment with the gamma value.*

of pixels in the image is n (so that $n_0 + n_1 + n_2 + \cdots + n_{L-1} = n$). To transform the gray levels to obtain a better contrasted image, we change gray level i to

$$\left(\frac{n_0 + n_1 + \cdots + n_i}{n} \right) (L - 1),$$

and this number is rounded to the nearest integer.

EXAMPLE Suppose a 4-bit grayscale image has the histogram shown in Figure 4.17, associated with a table of the numbers n_i of gray values

Gray level i	0	1	2	3	4	5	6	7	8	9	10	11	12	13	14	15
n_i	15	0	0	0	0	0	0	0	0	70	110	45	80	40	0	0

(with $n = 360$). We would expect this image to be uniformly bright, with a few dark dots on it. To equalize this histogram, we form running totals of the n_i and multiply each by $15/360 = 1/24$:

Gray level i	n_i	Σn_i	$(1/24)\Sigma n_i$	Rounded value
0	15	15	0.63	1
1	0	15	0.63	1
2	0	15	0.63	1
3	0	15	0.63	1
4	0	15	0.63	1
5	0	15	0.63	1
6	0	15	0.63	1
7	0	15	0.63	1
8	0	15	0.63	1
9	70	85	3.65	4
10	110	195	8.13	8
11	45	240	10	10
12	80	320	13.33	13
13	40	360	15	15
14	0	360	15	15
15	0	360	15	15

We now have the following transformation of gray values obtained by reading off the first and last columns in the table above,

Original gray level i	0	1	2	3	4	5	6	7	8	9	10	11	12	13	14	15
Final gray level j	1	1	1	1	1	1	1	1	1	4	8	10	13	15	15	15

and the histogram of the j values is shown in Figure 4.18. This is far more spread out than the original histogram, and thus the resulting image should exhibit greater contrast.

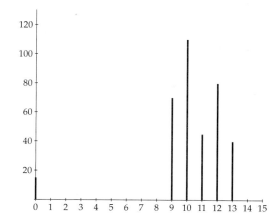

FIGURE 4.17 *Another histogram indicating poor contrast.*

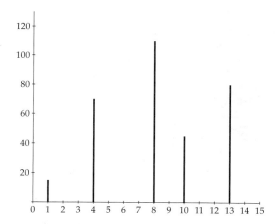

FIGURE 4.18 *The histogram of Figure 4.17 after equalization.*

To apply histogram equalization in MATLAB, use the `histeq` function; for example,

```
>> p=imread('pout.tif');
>> ph=histeq(p);
>> imshow(ph),figure,imhist(ph),axis tight
```

applies histogram equalization to the `pout` image and produces the resulting histogram. These results are shown in Figure 4.19. Notice the far greater spread of the histogram. This corresponds to the greater increase of contrast in the image.

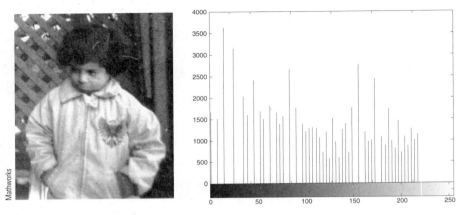

FIGURE 4.19 *The histogram of Figure 4.8 after equalization.*

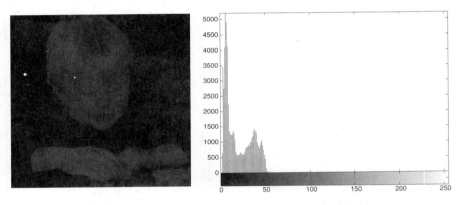

FIGURE 4.20 *The darkened version of* `engineer.tif` *and its histogram.*

We give one more example, that of a very dark image. We can obtain a dark image by taking an image and using `imdivide`.

```
>> en=imread('engineer.tif');
>> e=imdivide(en,4);
```

Because the matrix e contains only low values, it will appear very dark when displayed. We can display this matrix and its histogram with the usual commands:

```
>> imshow(e),figure,imhist(e),axis tight
```

The results are shown in Figure 4.20.

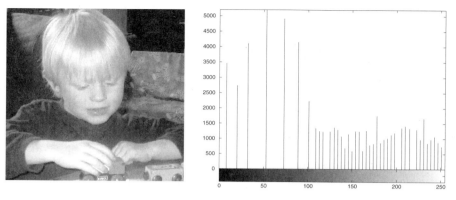

FIGURE 4.21 *The image from Figure 4.20 equalized and its histogram.*

As you see, the very dark image has a corresponding histogram heavily clustered at the lower end of the scale.

But we can apply histogram equalization to this image and display the results,

```
>> eh=histeq(e);
>> imshow(eh),figure,imhist(eh),axis tight
```

which are shown in Figure 4.21.

WHY IT WORKS   Consider the histogram in Figure 4.17. To apply histogram stretching, we would need to stretch out the values between gray levels 9 and 13. Thus, we would need to apply a piecewise function similar to that shown in Figure 4.9.

Let's consider the cumulative histogram, which is shown in Figure 4.22. The dashed line is simply joining the top of the histogram bars. However, it can be interpreted as an appropriate histogram stretching function. To do this, we need to scale the y values so that they are between 0 and 15 rather than 0 and 360. But this is precisely the method described in Section 4.3.2.

As we have seen, after equalization none of the example histograms are uniform. This is a result of the discrete nature of the image. If we were to treat the image as a continuous function $f(x, y)$ and the histogram as the area between different contours (see for example Castleman [4]), then we can treat the histogram as a probability density function. But the corresponding cumulative density function will always have a uniform histogram; see, for example, Hogg and Craig [14].

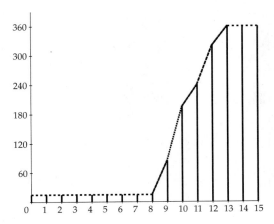

FIGURE 4.22 *The cumulative histogram.*

4.4 Lookup Tables

Point operations can be performed very effectively by using a **lookup table**, known more simply as an **LUT**. For operating on images of type uint8, such a table consists of a single array of 256 values, each value of which is an integer in the range 0 . . . 255. Our operation can then be implemented by replacing each pixel value p by the corresponding value t_p in the table.

For example, the LUT corresponding to division by 2 looks like

Index:	0	1	2	3	4	5	. . .	250	251	252	253	254	255
LUT:	0	0	1	1	2	2	. . .	125	125	126	126	127	127

This means, for example, that a pixel with value 4 will be replaced with 2; a pixel with value 253 will be replaced with value 126.

If T is a lookup table in MATLAB and im is our image, the lookup table can be applied by the simple command

```
T(im)
```

For example, suppose we wish to apply the above lookup table to the blocks image. We can create the table with

```
>> T=uint8(floor(0:255)/2);
```

and apply it to the blocks image b with

```
>> b2=T(b);
```

The image b2 is of type uint8, so can be viewed directly with imshow.

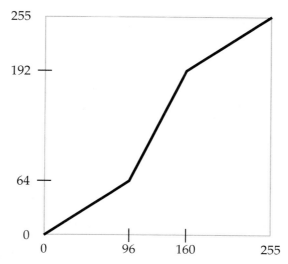

FIGURE 4.23 *A piecewise linear contrast-stretching function.*

As another example, suppose we wish to apply an LUT to implement the contrast-stretching function shown in Figure 4.23. Given the equation used in Section 4.3.1, the equations of the three lines used are

$$y = \frac{64}{96}x,$$

$$y = \frac{192 - 64}{160 - 96}(x - 96) + 64,$$

$$y = \frac{255 - 192}{255 - 160}(x - 160) + 192,$$

and these equations can be written more simply as

$$y = 0.6667x,$$

$$y = 2x - 128,$$

$$y = 0.6632x + 85.8947.$$

We can then construct the LUT with the commands

```
>> t1=0.6667*[0:64];
>> t2=2*[65:160]-128;
>> t3=0.6632*[161:255]+85.8947;
>> T=uint8(floor([t1 t2 t3]));
```

Note that the commands for t1, t2, and t3 are direct translations of the line equations into MATLAB, except that in each case we are applying the equation only to its domain.

EXERCISES

Image Arithmetic

1. Describe LUT for the following:
   a. Multiplication by 2.
   b. Image complements.

2. Enter the following command on the blocks image b.

```
>> b2=imdivide(b,64);
>> bb2=immultiply(b2,64);
>> imshow(bb2)
```

   Comment on the result. Why is the result not equivalent to the original image?

3. Replace the value 64 in Question 2 with 32 and 16.

Histograms

4. Write informal code to calculate a histogram $h[f]$ of the gray values of an image $f[row][col]$.

5. The following table gives the number of pixels at each of the gray levels 0–7 in an image with those gray values only.

0	1	2	3	4	5	6	7
3244	3899	4559	2573	1428	530	101	50

   Draw the histogram corresponding to these gray levels and then perform a histogram equalization and draw the resulting histogram.

6. The following tables give the number of pixels at each of the gray levels 0–15 in an image with those gray values only. In each case draw the histogram corresponding to these gray levels and then perform a histogram equalization and draw the resulting histogram.
   a.

0	1	2	3	4	5	6	7	8	9	10	11	12	13	14	15
20	40	60	75	80	75	65	55	50	45	40	35	30	25	20	30

	0	1	2	3	4	5	6	7	8	9	10	11	12	13	14	15
b.	0	0	40	80	45	110	70	0	0	0	0	0	0	0	0	15

7. The following small image has gray values in the range 0–19. Compute the gray level histogram and the mapping that will equalize this histogram. Produce an 8×8 grid containing the gray values for the new histogram-equalized image.

```
12    6    5   13   14   14   16   15
11   10    8    5    8   11   14   14
 9    8    3    4    7   12   18   19
10    7    4    2   10   12   13   17
16    9   13   13   16   19   19   17
12   10   14   15   18   18   16   14
11    8   10   12   14   13   14   15
 8    6    3    7    9   11   12   12
```

8. Is the histogram equalization operation idempotent? That is, is performing histogram equalization twice the same as doing it just once?

9. Apply histogram equalization to the indices of the image emu.tif.

10. Create a dark image with

```
>> c=imread('cameraman.tif');
>> [x,map]=gray2ind(c);
```

The matrix x, when viewed, will appear as a very dark version of the cameraman image. Apply histogram equalization to it, and compare the result with the original image.

11. Using p and ph from Section 4.3.2, enter the command

```
>> figure,plot(p,ph,'.'),grid on
```

What are you seeing here?

12. Experiment with some other grayscale images.

13. Using LUTs and following the example given in Section 4.4, write a simpler function for performing piecewise stretching than the function described in Section 4.3.1.

CHAPTER FIVE

NEIGHBORHOOD PROCESSING

5.1 Introduction

We have seen in Chapter 4 that an image can be modified by applying a particular function to each pixel value. Neighborhood processing may be considered as an extension of this, where a function is applied to a neighborhood of each pixel.

The idea is to move a mask: a rectangle (usually with sides of odd length) or other shape over the given image. As we do this, we create a new image whose pixels have gray values calculated from the gray values under the mask, as shown in Figure 5.1. The combination of mask and function is called a **filter.** If the function by which the new gray value is calculated is a linear function of all the gray values in the mask, then the filter is called a **linear filter.**

A linear filter can be implemented by multiplying all elements in the mask by corresponding elements in the neighborhood and adding together

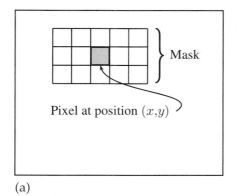

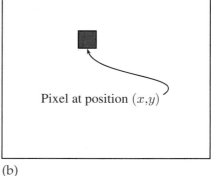

(a)   (b)

FIGURE 5.1 *Using a spatial mask on an image. (a) Original image. (b) Image after filtering.*

all these products. Suppose we have a 3 × 5 mask as illustrated in Figure 5.1. Suppose that the mask values are given by

$m(-1,-2)$	$m(-1,-1)$	$m(-1,0)$	$m(-1,1)$	$m(-1,2)$
$m(0,-2)$	$m(0,-1)$	$m(0,0)$	$m(0,1)$	$m(0,2)$
$m(1,-2)$	$m(1,-1)$	$m(1,0)$	$m(1,1)$	$m(1,2)$

and that corresponding pixel values are

$p(i-1,j-2)$	$p(i-1,j-1)$	$p(i-1,j)$	$p(i-1,j+1)$	$p(i-1,j+2)$
$p(i,j-2)$	$p(i,j-1)$	$p(i,j)$	$p(i,j+1)$	$p(i,j+2)$
$p(i+1,j-2)$	$p(i+1,j-1)$	$p(i+1,j)$	$p(i+1,j+1)$	$p(i+1,j+2)$

We now multiply and add

$$\sum_{s=-1}^{1}\sum_{t=-2}^{2} m(s,t)p(i+s,j+t).$$

A diagram illustrating the process for performing spatial filtering is given in Figure 5.2.

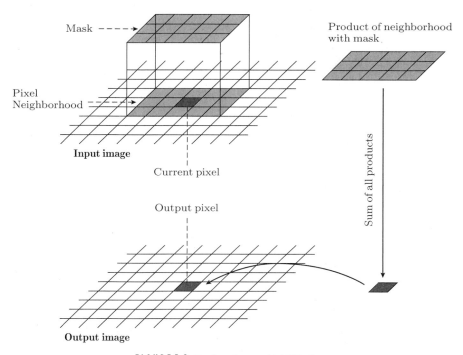

FIGURE 5.2 *Performing spatial filtering.*

Spatial filtering thus requires three steps:

1. Position the mask over the current pixel.
2. Form all products of filter elements with the corresponding elements of the neighborhood.
3. Add all the products.

This must be repeated for every pixel in the image.

Allied to spatial filtering is spatial **convolution.** The method for performing a convolution is the same as that for filtering, except that the filter must be rotated by 180° before multiplying and adding. Using the $m(i, j)$ and $p(i, j)$ notation as before, the output of a convolution with a 3×5 mask for a single pixel is

$$\sum_{s=-1}^{1} \sum_{t=-2}^{2} m(-s, -t)p(i + s, j + t).$$

Note the negative signs on the indices of m. The same result can be achieved with

$$\sum_{s=-1}^{1} \sum_{t=-2}^{2} m(s, t)p(i - s + j - t).$$

Here we have rotated the **image** pixels by 180°; this does not of course affect the result. The importance of convolution will become apparent when we investigate the Fourier transform, and the convolution theorem. Note also that in practice, most filter masks are rotationally symmetric, so that spatial filtering and spatial convolution will produce the same output.

EXAMPLE One important linear filter is to use a 3 × 3 mask and take the average of all nine values within the mask. This value becomes the gray value of the corresponding pixel in the new image. This operation may be described as follows:

$$\begin{array}{|c|c|c|} \hline a & b & c \\ \hline d & e & f \\ \hline g & h & i \\ \hline \end{array} \longrightarrow \frac{1}{9}(a+b+c+d+e+f+g+h+i),$$

where e is gray value of the current pixel in the original image and the average is the gray value of the corresponding pixel in the new image.

To apply this to an image, consider the 5 × 5 image obtained by:

```
>> x=uint8(10*magic(5))

x =

   170   240    10    80   150
   230    50    70   140   160
    40    60   130   200   220
   100   120   190   210    30
   110   180   250    20    90
```

We may regard this array as being made of nine overlapping 3 × 3 neighborhoods. The output of our work will thus consist of only nine values. We will see later how to obtain 25 values in the output.

Consider the top left 3 × 3 neighborhood of our image x.

```
 170   240    10    80   150
 230    50    70   140   160
  40    60   130   200   220
 100   120   190   210    30
 110   180   250    20    90
```

Now we take the average of all these values:

```
>> mean2(x(1:3,1:3))

ans =

   111.1111
```

which can be rounded to 111. Now we can move to the second neighborhood,

```
170   240    10    80   150
230 |  50    70   140| 160
 40 |  60   130   200| 220
100 | 120   190   210|  30
110   180   250    20   90
```

and take its average:

```
>> mean2(x(1:3,2:4))

ans =

   108.8889
```

This can be either rounded down to 108 or to the nearest integer, 109. If we continue in this manner, the following output is obtained:

```
111.1111   108.8889   128.8889
110.0000   130.0000   150.0000
131.1111   151.1111   148.8889
```

This array is the result of filtering x with the 3 × 3 averaging filter.

5.2 Notation

It is convenient to describe a linear filter simply in terms of the coefficients of all the gray values of pixels within the mask. This can be written as a matrix.

The averaging filter above, for example, could have its output written as

$$\frac{1}{9}a + \frac{1}{9}b + \frac{1}{9}c + \frac{1}{9}d + \frac{1}{9}e + \frac{1}{9}f + \frac{1}{9}g + \frac{1}{9}h + \frac{1}{9}i,$$

thus this filter can be described by the matrix

$$\begin{bmatrix} \frac{1}{9} & \frac{1}{9} & \frac{1}{9} \\ \frac{1}{9} & \frac{1}{9} & \frac{1}{9} \\ \frac{1}{9} & \frac{1}{9} & \frac{1}{9} \end{bmatrix} = \frac{1}{9}\begin{bmatrix} 1 & 1 & 1 \\ 1 & 1 & 1 \\ 1 & 1 & 1 \end{bmatrix}.$$

EXAMPLE   The filter

$$\begin{bmatrix} 1 & -2 & 1 \\ -2 & 4 & -2 \\ 1 & -2 & 1 \end{bmatrix}$$

would operate on gray values as

a	b	c
d	e	f
g	h	i

$\longrightarrow a - 2b + c - 2d + 4e - 2d + g - 2h + i.$

5.2.1 Edges of the Image

There is an obvious problem in applying a filter: what happens at the edge of the image, where the mask partly falls outside the image? In such a case, as illustrated in Figure 5.3, there will be a lack of gray values to use in the filter function. There are a number of different approaches to dealing with this problem.

Ignore the edges. The mask is applied only to those pixels in the image for which the mask will lie fully within the image. This means it is applied to all pixels except the edges and results in an output image that is smaller than the original. If the mask is very large, a significant amount

FIGURE 5.3 *A mask at the edge of an image.*

of information may be lost by this method. We applied this method in our example above.

Pad with zeros. We assume that all necessary values outside the image are zero. This assumption gives us all values to work with and will return an output image of the same size as the original, but may have the effect of introducing unwanted artifacts (for example, edges) around the image.

5.3 Filtering in MATLAB

The `filter2` function does the job of linear filtering for us; its use is

```
filter2(filter,image,shape)
```

and the result is a matrix of data type `double`. The parameter `shape` is optional; it describes the method for dealing with the edges.

- `filter2(filter,image,'same')` is the default; it produces a matrix of a size equal to the original `image` matrix. It uses zero padding.

```
>> a=ones(3,3)/9

a =

    0.1111    0.1111    0.1111
    0.1111    0.1111    0.1111
    0.1111    0.1111    0.1111

>> filter2(a,x,'same')

ans =

    76.6667    85.5556    65.5556    67.7778    58.8889
    87.7778   111.1111   108.8889   128.8889   105.5556
    66.6667   110.0000   130.0000   150.0000   106.6667
    67.7778   131.1111   151.1111   148.8889    85.5556
    56.6667   105.5556   107.7778    87.7778    38.8889
```

- `filter2(filter,image,'valid')` applies the mask only to inside pixels. The result will always be smaller than the original.

```
>> filter2(a,x,'valid')

ans =

    111.1111   108.8889   128.8889
    110.0000   130.0000   150.0000
    131.1111   151.1111   148.8889
```

The result of 'same' above may also be obtained by padding with zeros and using 'valid':

```
>> x2=zeros(7,7);
>> x2(2:6,2:6)=x

x2 =

     0      0      0      0      0      0      0
     0    170    240     10     80    150      0
     0    230     50     70    140    160      0
     0     40     60    130    200    220      0
     0    100    120    190    210     30      0
     0    110    180    250     20     90      0
     0      0      0      0      0      0      0

>> filter2(a,x2,'valid')
```

- filter2(filter,image,'full') returns a result larger than the original. It does this by padding with zero and applying the filter at all places on and around the image where the mask intersects the image matrix.

```
>> filter2(a,x,'full')

ans =

    18.8889   45.5556   46.6667   36.6667   26.6667   25.5556   16.6667
    44.4444   76.6667   85.5556   65.5556   67.7778   58.8889   34.4444
    48.8889   87.7778  111.1111  108.8889  128.8889  105.5556   58.8889
    41.1111   66.6667  110.0000  130.0000  150.0000  106.6667   45.5556
    27.7778   67.7778  131.1111  151.1111  148.8889   85.5556   37.7778
    23.3333   56.6667  105.5556  107.7778   87.7778   38.8889   13.3333
    12.2222   32.2222   60.0000   50.0000   40.0000   12.2222   10.0000
```

The shape parameter, being optional, can be omitted, in which case the default value is 'same'.

There is no single best approach; the method must be dictated by the problem at hand, by the filter being used, and by the result required.

We can create our filters by hand or by using the `fspecial` function. This function has many options, which allows easy creation of many different filters. We will use the `average` option, which produces averaging filters of given size. Thus,

```
>> fspecial('average',[5,7])
```

will return an averaging filter of size 5×7; more simply,

```
>> fspecial('average',11)
```

will return an averaging filter of size 11×11. If we leave out the final number or vector, the 3×3 averaging filter is returned.

For example, suppose we apply the 3×3 averaging filter to an image as follows:

```
>> c=imread('cameraman.tif');
>> f1=fspecial('average');
>> cf1=filter2(f1,c);
```

We now have a matrix of data type double. To display this, we can do any of the following:

- Transform it to a matrix of type `uint8` for use with `imshow`.
- Divide its values by 255 to obtain a matrix with values in the 0.1–1.0 range for use with `imshow`.
- Use `mat2gray` to scale the result for display. We will discuss the use of this function later.

Using the second method,

```
>> figure,imshow(c),figure,imshow(cf1/255)
```

will produce the images shown in Figure 5.4(a and b).

The averaging filter blurs the image. The edges in particular are less distinct than in the original. The image can be further blurred by using an averaging filter of larger size. This is shown in Figure 5.4(c), where a 9×9 averaging filter has been used, and in Figure 5.4(d), where a 25×25 averaging filter has been used.

Notice how the zero padding used at the edges has resulted in a dark border appearing around the image. This is especially noticeable when a large filter is being used. If this is an unwanted artifact of the filtering

(a)

(b)

Mathworks

(c)

(d)

FIGURE 5.4 *Average filtering. (a) Original image. (b) Average filtering. (c) Using a 9×9 filter. (d) Using a 25×25 filter.*

(if, for example, it changes the average brightness of the image), then it may be more appropriate to use the `'valid'` shape option.

The resulting image after these filters may appear to be much worse than the original. However, applying a blurring filter to reduce detail in an image may the perfect operation for autonomous machine recognition or if we are only concentrating on the gross aspects of the image, such as numbers of objects, or amount of dark and light areas. In such cases, too much detail may obscure the outcome.

5.3.1 Separable Filters

Some filters can be implemented by the successive application of two simpler filters. For example, since

$$\frac{1}{9} \begin{bmatrix} 1 & 1 & 1 \\ 1 & 1 & 1 \\ 1 & 1 & 1 \end{bmatrix} = \frac{1}{3} \begin{bmatrix} 1 \\ 1 \\ 1 \end{bmatrix} \frac{1}{3} \begin{bmatrix} 1 & 1 & 1 \end{bmatrix},$$

the 3×3 averaging filter can be implemented by first applying a 3×1 averaging filter and then applying a 1×3 averaging filter to the result. The 3×3 averaging filter is thus separable into two smaller filters. Separability can result in great time savings. Suppose an $n \times n$ filter is separable into two filters of size $n \times 1$ and $1 \times n$. The application of an $n \times n$ filter requires n^2 multiplications and $n^2 - 1$ additions for each pixel in the image. But the application of an $n \times 1$ filter requires only n multiplications and $n - 1$ additions. Because this must be done twice, the total number of multiplications and additions are $2n$ and $2n - 2$, respectively. If n is large, the savings in efficiency can be dramatic.

All averaging filters are separable. Another separable filter is the Laplacian

$$\begin{bmatrix} 1 & -2 & 1 \\ -2 & 4 & -2 \\ 1 & -2 & 1 \end{bmatrix} = \begin{bmatrix} 1 \\ -2 \\ 1 \end{bmatrix} \begin{bmatrix} 1 & -2 & 1 \end{bmatrix}.$$

Other examples will be considered below.

5.4 Frequencies: Low- and High-Pass Filters

It will be convenient to have some standard terminology to use to discuss the effects a filter will have on an image and to use to choose the most appropriate filter for a given image-processing task. One important aspect of an image that enables us to do this is the notion of **frequencies.** Roughly speaking, the frequencies of an image are a measure of the amount by which gray values change with distance. This concept will be given a more formal setting in Chapter 7. **High-frequency components** are characterized by large changes in gray values over small distances. Examples of high-frequency components are edges and noise. **Low-frequency components,** on the other hand, are parts of the image characterized by little change in the gray values. These may include backgrounds and skin textures. We then say that a filter is a

high-pass filter if it passes over the high-frequency components and reduces or eliminates low-frequency components; or a

low-pass filter if it passes over the low-frequency components and reduces or eliminates high-frequency components.

For example, the 3×3 averaging filter is low-pass filter, because as it tends to blur edges. The filter

$$\begin{bmatrix} 1 & -2 & 1 \\ -2 & 4 & -2 \\ 1 & -2 & 1 \end{bmatrix}$$

is a high-pass filter.

We note that the sum of the coefficients (that is, the sum of all *e* elements in the matrix) in the high-pass filter is zero. This means that in a low-frequency part of an image, where the gray values are similar, the result of using this filter is that the corresponding gray values in the new image will be close to zero. To see this, consider a 4×4 block of similar pixel values and apply the above high-pass filter to the central four:

150	152	148	149
147	152	151	150
152	148	149	151
151	149	150	148

$\rightarrow$

11	6
−13	−5

.

The resulting values are close to zero, which is the expected result of applying a high-pass filter to a low-frequency component. We will seé how to deal with negative values below.

High-pass filters are of particular value in edge detection and edge enhancement (which we will discuss more in Chapter 9). But we can provide a sneak preview, using the cameraman image.

```
>> f=fspecial('laplacian')

f =

        0.1667      0.6667      0.1667
        0.6667     -3.3333      0.6667
        0.1667      0.6667      0.1667

>> cf=filter2(f,c);
>> imshow(cf/100)
>> f1=fspecial('log')

f1 =

        0.0448      0.0468      0.0564      0.0468      0.0448
        0.0468      0.3167      0.7146      0.3167      0.0468
        0.0564      0.7146     -4.9048      0.7146      0.0564
        0.0468      0.3167      0.7146      0.3167      0.0468
        0.0448      0.0468      0.0564      0.0468      0.0448

>> cf1=filter2(f1,c);
>> figure,imshow(cf1/100)
```

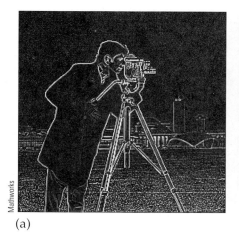

(a)   (b)

FIGURE 5.5 *High-pass filtering. (a) Laplacian filter. (b) Laplacian of Gaussian (log) filtering.*

The images are shown in Figure 5.5, with image (a) the result of the Laplacian filter and image (b) the result of the Laplacian of a Gaussian (log) filter. We discuss Gaussian filters in Section 5.5.

In each case, the sum of all the filter elements is zero.

VALUES OUTSIDE THE RANGE 0–255 We have seen that for image display we would like the gray values of the pixels to be between 0 and 255. However, the result of applying a linear filter may be values that are outside this range. We may need to consider ways of dealing with values outside this displayable range.

Make negative values positive. Making negative values positive will certainly deal with negative values, but not with values greater than 255. Hence, this technique can be used only in specific circumstances, for example, when there are only a few negative values and when these values are themselves close to zero.

Clip values. We apply the following thresholding type operation to the gray values x produced by the filter to obtain a displayable value y:

$$y = \begin{cases} 0 & \text{if } x < 0 \\ x & \text{if } 0 \leq x \leq 255. \\ 255 & \text{if } x > 255 \end{cases}$$

This will produce an image with all pixel values in the required range, but it is not suitable if there are many gray values outside the 0–255 range, in particular, if the gray values are equally spread over a larger range. In such a case this operation will tend to destroy the results of the filter.

Scaling transformation. Suppose the lowest gray value produced by the filter is g_L and the highest value is g_H. We can transform all values in the range g_L–g_H to the range 0–255 by the linear transformation illustrated below:

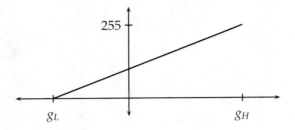

Because the gradient of the line is $255/(g_H - g_L)$, we can write the equation of the line as

$$y = 255 \frac{x - g_L}{g_H - g_L}.$$

Application of this transformation to all gray levels x produced by the filter will result (after any necessary rounding) in an image that can be displayed.

As an example, let's apply the high-pass filter given in this section to the cameraman image:

```
>> f2=[1 -2 1;-2 4 -2;1 -2 1];
>> cf2=filter2(f2,c);
```

Now the maximum and minimum values of the matrix cf2 are 593 and −541, respectively. The mat2gray function automatically scales the matrix elements to displayable values; for any matrix M, it applies a linear transformation to to its elements, with the lowest value mapping to 0.0 and the highest value mapping to 1.0. This means the output of mat2gray is always of type double. The function also requires that the input type is double.

```
>> figure,imshow(mat2gray(cf2));
```

To do this by hand, so to speak, applying the linear transformation above, we can use:

```
>> maxcf2=max(cf2(:));
>> mincf2=min(cf2(:));
>> cf2g=(cf2-mincf2)/(maxcf2-mncf2);
```

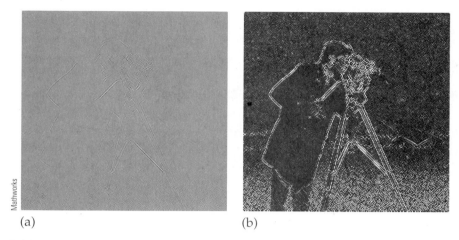

Mathworks

(a)   (b)

FIGURE 5.6 *Using a high-pass filter and displaying the result. (a) Using* `mat2gray`. *(b) Dividing by a constant.*

The result will be a matrix of type `double`, with entries in the range 0.0–1.0. This matrix can be viewed with `imshow`. We can make it a `uint8` image by multiplying by 255 first. The result can be seen in Figure 5.6.

We can generally obtain a better result by dividing the result of the filtering by a constant before displaying it:

```
>> figure,imshow(cf2/60)
```

This is also shown in Figure 5.6.

High-pass filters are often used for edge detection. These can be seen quite clearly in Figure 5.6(b).

5.5 Gaussian Filters

We have seen some examples of linear filters so far: the averaging filter and a high-pass filter. The `fspecial` function can produce many different filters for use with the `filter2` function; we shall look at a particularly important filter here.

Gaussian filters are a class of low-pass filters, all based on the Gaussian probability distribution function

$$f(x) = e^{-\frac{x^2}{2\sigma^2}},$$

FIGURE 5.7 *One-dimensional Gaussians.*

where σ is the standard deviation. A large value of σ produces a flatter curve, and a small value leads to a "pointier" curve. Figure 5.7 shows examples of such one-dimensional Gaussians. Gaussian filters are important for a number of reasons:

1. They are mathematically very well behaved; in particular, the Fourier transform (see Chapter 7) of a Gaussian filter is another Gaussian.

2. They are rotationally symmetric, so are very good starting points for some edge-detection algorithms (see Chapter 9),

3. They are separable, in that a Gaussian filter may be applied by first applying a one-dimensional Gaussian in the x direction, followed by another in the y direction. This can lead to very fast implementations.

4. The convolution of two Gaussians is another Gaussian.

A two-dimensional Gaussian function is given by

$$f(x,y) = e^{-\frac{x^2+y^2}{2\sigma^2}}$$

The command `fspecial('gaussian')` produces a discrete version of this function. We can draw pictures of this with the `surf` function, and to ensure a nice, smooth result, we will create a large filter (size 50×50) with different standard deviations.

```
>> a=50;s=3;
>> g=fspecial('gaussian',[a a],s);
>> surf(1:a,1:a,g)
>> s=9;
>> g2=fspecial('gaussian',[a a],s);
>> figure,surf(1:a,1:a,g2)
```

The surfaces are shown in Figure 5.8.

Gaussian filters have a blurring effect that look very similar to that produced by neighborhood averaging. Let's experiment with the cameraman image and some different Gaussian filters.

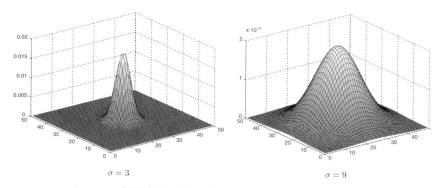

$\sigma = 3$ $\sigma = 9$

FIGURE 5.8 *Two-dimensional Gaussians.*

```
>> g1=fspecial('gaussian',[5,5]);
>> g1=fspecial('gaussian',[5,5],2);
>> g1=fspecial('gaussian',[11,11],1);
>> g1=fspecial('gaussian',[11,11],5);
```

The final parameter is the standard deviation, which, if not given, defaults to 0.5. The second parameter (which is also optional), gives the size of the filter; the default is 3×3. If the filter is to be square, as in all the examples above, we can give just a single number in each case.

Now we can apply the filter to the cameraman image matrix c and view the result.

```
>> imshow(filter2(g1,c)/256)
>> figure,imshow(filter2(g2,c)/256)
>> figure,imshow(filter2(g3,c)/256)
>> figure,imshow(filter2(g4,c)/256)
```

The results are shown in Figure 5.9. Thus, to obtain a spread-out blurring effect, we need a large standard deviation. In fact, if we let the standard deviation grow large without bounds, we obtain the averaging filters as limiting values. For example,

```
>> fspecial('gaussian',3,100)

ans =

    0.1111      0.1111      0.1111
    0.1111      0.1111      0.1111
    0.1111      0.1111      0.1111
```

and we have the 3×3 averaging filter.

5 × 5, σ = 0.5

5 × 5, σ = 2

11 × 11, σ = 1

11 × 11, σ = 5

Mathworks

FIGURE 5.9 *Effects of different Gaussian filters on an image.*

Although the results of Gaussian blurring and averaging look similar, the Gaussian filter has some elegant mathematical properties that make it particularly suitable for blurring.

Other filters will be discussed in future chapters; also check the documentation for `fspecial` for other filters.

5.6 Edge Sharpening

Spatial filtering can be used to make edges in an image slightly sharper and crisper, which generally results in an image more pleasing to the human eye. The operation is variously called **edge enhancement, edge crispening, or unsharp masking.** This last term comes from the printing industry.

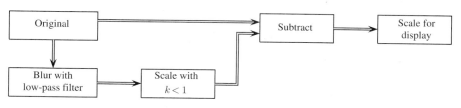

FIGURE 5.10 *Schema for unsharp masking.*

(a)   (b)

FIGURE 5.11 *An example of unsharp masking. (a) Original image. (b) The image after unsharp masking.*

5.6.1 Unsharp Masking

The idea of unsharp masking is to subtract a scaled unsharp version of the image from the original. In practice, we can achieve this affect by subtracting a scaled blurred image from the original. The schema for unsharp masking is shown in Figure 5.10.

Suppose an image x is of type uint8. The unsharp masking can be applied by the following sequence of commands:

```
>> f=fspecial('average');
>> xf=filter2(f,x);
>> xu=double(x)-xf/1.5
>> imshow(xu/70)
```

The last command scales the result so that imshow displays an appropriate image; the value may need to be adjusted according to the input image. Suppose that x is the image shown in Figure 5.11(a), then the result of unsharp masking is given in Figure 5.11(b). The result appears to be a better image than the original; the edges are crisper and more clearly defined.

To see why this works, we may consider the function of gray values as we travel across an edge, as shown in Figure 5.12.

As a scaled blur is subtracted from the original, the result is that the edge is enhanced, as shown in Figure 5.12(c).

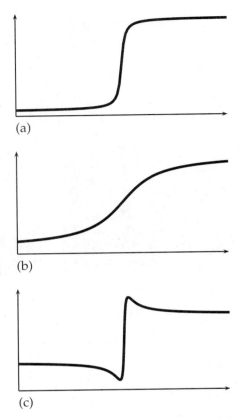

(a)

(b)

(c)

FIGURE 5.12 *Unsharp masking. (a) Pixel values over an edge. (b) The edge blurred.* *(c) (a) − k(b).*

We can, in fact, perform the filtering and subtracting operation in one command, using the linearity of the filter, and the 3×3 filter

$$\begin{bmatrix} 0 & 0 & 0 \\ 0 & 1 & 0 \\ 0 & 0 & 0 \end{bmatrix}$$

is the identity filter.

Hence, unsharp masking can be implemented by a filter of the form

$$f = \begin{bmatrix} 0 & 0 & 0 \\ 0 & 1 & 0 \\ 0 & 0 & 0 \end{bmatrix} - \frac{1}{k} \begin{bmatrix} \frac{1}{9} & \frac{1}{9} & \frac{1}{9} \\ \frac{1}{9} & \frac{1}{9} & \frac{1}{9} \\ \frac{1}{9} & \frac{1}{9} & \frac{1}{9} \end{bmatrix},$$

where k is a constant chosen to provide the best result. Alternatively, the unsharp masking filter may be defined as

$$f = k \begin{bmatrix} 0 & 0 & 0 \\ 0 & 1 & 0 \\ 0 & 0 & 0 \end{bmatrix} - \begin{bmatrix} \frac{1}{9} & \frac{1}{9} & \frac{1}{9} \\ \frac{1}{9} & \frac{1}{9} & \frac{1}{9} \\ \frac{1}{9} & \frac{1}{9} & \frac{1}{9} \end{bmatrix},$$

so that we are in effect subtracting a blur from a scaled version of the original; the scaling factor may also be split between the identity and blurring filters.

The `unsharp` option of `fspecial` produces such filters; the filter created has the form

$$\frac{1}{\alpha + 1} \begin{bmatrix} -\alpha & \alpha - 1 & -\alpha \\ \alpha - 1 & \alpha + 5 & \alpha - 1 \\ -\alpha & \alpha - 1 & -\alpha \end{bmatrix},$$

where α is an optional parameter that defaults to 0.2. If $\alpha = 0.5$, the filter is

$$\frac{1}{3} \begin{bmatrix} -1 & -1 & -1 \\ -1 & 11 & -1 \\ -1 & -1 & -1 \end{bmatrix} = 4 \begin{bmatrix} 0 & 0 & 0 \\ 0 & 1 & 0 \\ 0 & 0 & 0 \end{bmatrix} - 3 \begin{bmatrix} \frac{1}{9} & \frac{1}{9} & \frac{1}{9} \\ \frac{1}{9} & \frac{1}{9} & \frac{1}{9} \\ \frac{1}{9} & \frac{1}{9} & \frac{1}{9} \end{bmatrix}.$$

Figure 5.13 was created using the MATLAB commands

```
>> p=imread('pelicans.tif');
>> u=fspecial('unsharp',0.5);
>> pu=filter2(u,p);
>> imshow(p),figure,imshow(pu/255)
```

Figure 5.13(b) appears much sharper and cleaner than the original. Notice, in particular, the rocks and trees in the background and the ripples on the water.

Although we have used averaging filters above, we can in fact use any low-pass filter for unsharp masking.

5.6.2 High-Boost Filtering

Allied to unsharp masking filters are the **high-boost** filters, which are obtained by

$$\text{high boost} = A(\text{original}) - (\text{low pass}),$$

where A is an amplification factor. If $A = 1$, then the high-boost filter becomes an ordinary high-pass filter. If we take as the low-pass filter the

(a)   (b)

FIGURE 5.13 *Edge enhancement with unsharp masking. (a) The original. (b) After unsharp masking.*

3×3 averaging filter, then a high-boost filter will have the form

$$\frac{1}{9}\begin{bmatrix} -1 & -1 & -1 \\ -1 & z & -1 \\ -1 & -1 & -1 \end{bmatrix},$$

where $z > 8$. If we put $z = 11$, we obtain a filtering very similar to the unsharp filter above, except for a scaling factor. Thus the commands

```
>> f=[-1 -1 -1;-1 11 -1;-1 -1 -1]/9;
>> xf=filter2(x,f);
>> imshow(xf/80)
```

will produce an image similar to that in Figure 5.11. The value 80 was obtained by trial and error to produce an image with an intensity similar to the original.

We can also write the high-boost formula above as

$$\text{high boost} = A(\text{original}) - (\text{low pass})$$
$$= A(\text{original}) - ((\text{original}) - (\text{high pass}))$$
$$= (A - 1)(\text{original}) + (\text{high pass}).$$

Best results for high-boost filtering are obtained if we multiply the equation by a factor w so that the filter values sum to 1; this requires

$$wA - w = 1$$

or

$$w = \frac{1}{A - 1}$$

So a general unsharp masking formula is

$$\frac{A}{A - 1}(\text{original}) - \frac{1}{A - 1}(\text{low pass})$$

Another version of this formula is

$$\frac{A}{2A - 1}(\text{original}) - \frac{1 - A}{2A - 1}(\text{low pass}),$$

where for best results A is taken so that

$$\frac{3}{5} \leq A \leq \frac{5}{6}.$$

If we take $A = \frac{3}{5}$, the formula becomes

$$\frac{\frac{3}{5}}{2\left(\frac{3}{5}\right) - 1}(\text{original}) - \frac{1 - \left(\frac{3}{5}\right)}{2\left(\frac{3}{5}\right) - 1}(\text{low pass}) = 3(\text{original}) - 2(\text{low pass}).$$

If we take $A = \frac{5}{6}$ we obtain

$$\frac{5}{4}(\text{original}) - \frac{1}{4}(\text{low pass}).$$

Using the identity and averaging filters, we can obtain high-boost filters by:

```
>> id=[0 0 0;0 1 0;0 0 0];
>> f=fspecial('average');
>> hb1=3*id-2*f

hb1 =

   -0.2222   -0.2222   -0.2222
   -0.2222    2.7778   -0.2222
   -0.2222   -0.2222   -0.2222

>> hb2=1.25*id-0.25*f

hb2 =

   -0.0278   -0.0278   -0.0278
   -0.0278    1.2222   -0.0278
   -0.0278   -0.0278   -0.0278
```

(a)   (b)

FIGURE 5.14 *High-boost filtering. (a) High-boost filtering with* hb1. *(b) High-boost filtering with* hb2.

If each of the filters hb1 and hb2 are applied to an image with filter2, the result will have enhanced edges. The images in Figure 5.14 show these results; Figure 5.14(a) was obtained with

```
>> x1=filter2(hb1,x);
>> imshow(x1/255)
```

and Figure 5.14(b), similarly.

Of the two filters, hb1 appears to produce the best result; hb2 produces an image not much crisper than the original.

5.7 Nonlinear Filters

Linear filters, as we have seen in the previous sections, are easy to describe and can be applied very quickly and efficiently by MATLAB.

A **nonlinear filter** is obtained by a nonlinear function of the grayscale values in the mask. Simple examples are the **maximum filter,** which has as its output the maximum value under the mask, and the corresponding **minimum filter,** which has as its output the minimum value under the mask.

Both the maximum and minimum filters are examples of **rank-order filters.** In such a filter, the elements under the mask are ordered, and a particular value is returned as output. Thus, if the values are given in increasing order, the minimum filter is a rank-order filter for which the first element is returned, and the maximum filter is a rank-order filter for which the last element is returned

For implementing a general nonlinear filter in MATLAB, the function to use is nlfilter, which applies a filter to an image according to a predefined function. If the function is not already defined, we must create an mfile that defines it.

(a)   (b)

FIGURE 5.15 *Using nonlinear filters. (a) Using a maximum filter. (b) Using a minimum filter.*

Here are some examples. First, to implement a maximum filter over a 3×3 neighborhood:

```
>> cmax=nlfilter(c,[3,3],'max(x(:))');
```

The `nlfilter` function requires three arguments: the image matrix, the size of the filter, and the function to be applied. The function must be a matrix function that returns a scalar value. The result of this operation is shown in Figure 5.15(a).

A corresponding implementation of the minimum filter is

```
>> cmin=nlfilter(c,[3,3],'min(x(:))');
```

and the result is shown in Figure 5.15(b).

Note that in each case the image has lost some sharpness and has been brightened by the maximum filter and darkened by the minimum filter. The `nlfilter` function is very slow; in general, there is little call for nonlinear filters except for a few that are defined by their own commands. We will investigate these filters in later chapters.

Nonlinear filtering using `nlfilter` can be very slow. A faster alternative is to use the `colfilt` function, which rearranges the image into columns first. For example, to apply the maximum filter to the cameraman image, we can use

```
>> cmax=colfilt(c,[3,3],'sliding',@max);
```

The parameter `sliding` indicates that overlapping neighborhoods are being used (which, of course, is the case with filtering). This particular operation is almost instantaneous, as compared with the use of `nlfilter`.

To implement the maximum and minimum filters as rank-order filters, we may use the MATLAB function `ordfilt2`. This requires three inputs: the image, the index value of the ordered results to choose as output, and the definition of the mask. So, to apply the maximum filter on a 3×3 mask, we use

```
>> cmax=ordfilt2(c,9,ones(3,3));
```

and the minimum filter can be applied with

```
>> cmin=ordfilt2(c,1,ones(3,3));
```

A very important rank-order filter is the **median filter,** which takes the central value of the ordered list. We could apply the median filter with

```
>> cmed=ordfilt2(c,5,ones(3,3));
```

However, the median filter has its own command, `medfilt2`, which we discuss in more detail in Chapter 8.

Other nonlinear filters are the **geometric mean filter,** which is defined as

$$\left(\prod_{(i,j)\in M} x(i,j) \right)^{(1/|M|)},$$

where M is the filter mask and $|M|$ its size, and the **alpha-trimmed mean filter,** which first orders the values under the mask, trims off elements at either end of the ordered list, and then takes the mean of the remainder. So, for example, if we have a 3×3 mask, and we order the elements as

$$x_1 \leq x_2 \leq x_3 \leq \cdots \leq x_9$$

and trim off two elements at either end, the result of the filter will be

$$\frac{(x_3 + x_4 + x_5 + x_6 + x_7)}{5}.$$

Both of these filters have uses for image restoration. See Chapter 8. Further examples of nonlinear filters are given in Chapter 16.

Column 406   Column 170

—— Row 58

—— Row 231

FIGURE 5.16 *An image with a ROI.*

5.8 Region of Interest Processing

Often, we may not want to apply a filter to an entire image, but only to a small region within it. A nonlinear filter, for example, may be too computationally expensive to apply to the entire image, or we may only be interested in the small region. Such small regions within an image are called **regions of interest** or **ROIs,** and their processing is called **ROI processing.**

5.8.1 Regions of Interest in MATLAB

Before we can process a ROI, we must define it. There are two way to define a ROI: listing the coordinates of a polygonal region or interactively, using the mouse. For example, suppose we take our image of an iguana peering over a branch

```
>> ig=imread('iguana.tif');
```

and attempt to isolate the head of the animal. If we view the image with pixval on, then the coordinates of a rectangle that enclose the head can be determined to be (58, 406), (58, 600), (231, 406), and (231, 600), as shown in Figure 5.16. We can then define a region of interest using the roipoly function:

```
>> roi=roipoly(ig,[406 600 600 406],[58 58 231 231]);
```

Note that the ROI is defined by two sets of coordinates, first the columns and then the rows, taken in order, as we traverse the ROI from vertex to

FIGURE 5.17 *The mask corresponding to the ROI defined in Figure 5.16.*

vertex. We can view the resulting ROI mask as a binary image; it is shown on the right in Figure 5.17. In general, a ROI mask will be a binary image the same size as the original image, with 1s for the ROI and 0s elsewhere. We can also use the function `roipoly` interactively:

```
>> roi=roipoly(ig);
```

This will bring up the iguana image (if it isn't shown already). Vertices of the ROI can be selected with the mouse: a left click selects a new vertex, backspace or delete removes the most recently chosen vertex, and a right click finishes the selection.

5.8.1 Region of Interest Filtering

One of the simplest operations on a ROI is spatial filtering; this is implemented with the function `roifilt2`. With the iguana image and the ROI found above, we can experiment as follows:

```
>> a=fspecial('average',[15,15]);
>> iga=roifilt2(a,ig,roi);
>> imshow(iga)
>> u=fspecial('unsharp');
>> igu=roifilt2(u,ig,roi);
>> figure,imshow(igu)
>> l=fspecial('log');
>> igl=roifilt2(l,ig,roi);
>> figure,imshow(igl)
```

The images are shown in Figure 5.18.

iga: Average filtering

igu: Unsharp masking

igl: Laplacian of Gaussian

FIGURE 5.18 *Examples of the use of* `roifilt2`.

EXERCISES

1. The array on the next page represents a small grayscale image.
   Compute the images that result when the image is convolved with
   each of the masks (a–h) shown. At the edge of the image use a
   restricted mask. (In other words, pad the image with zeros.)

```
20   20   20   10   10   10   10   10   10
20   20   20   20   20   20   20   20   10
20   20   20   10   10   10   10   20   10
20   20   10   10   10   10   10   20   10
20   10   10   10   10   10   10   20   10
10   10   10   10   20   10   10   20   10
10   10   10   10   10   10   10   10   10
20   10   20   20   10   10   10   20   20
20   10   10   20   10   10   20   10   20
```

$$
\mathbf{a}\quad
\begin{array}{rrr}
-1 & -1 & 0 \\
-1 & 0 & 1 \\
0 & 1 & 1
\end{array}
\qquad
\mathbf{b}\quad
\begin{array}{rrr}
0 & -1 & -1 \\
1 & 0 & -1 \\
1 & 1 & 0
\end{array}
\qquad
\mathbf{c}\quad
\begin{array}{rrr}
-1 & -1 & -1 \\
2 & 2 & 2 \\
-1 & -1 & -1
\end{array}
$$

$$
\mathbf{d}\quad
\begin{array}{rrr}
-1 & 2 & -1 \\
-1 & 2 & -1 \\
-1 & 2 & -1
\end{array}
\qquad
\mathbf{e}\quad
\begin{array}{rrr}
-1 & -1 & -1 \\
-1 & 8 & -1 \\
-1 & -1 & -1
\end{array}
\qquad
\mathbf{f}\quad
\begin{array}{rrr}
1 & 1 & 1 \\
1 & 1 & 1 \\
1 & 1 & 1
\end{array}
$$

$$
\mathbf{g}\quad
\begin{array}{rrr}
-1 & 0 & 1 \\
-1 & 0 & 1 \\
-1 & 0 & 1
\end{array}
\qquad
\mathbf{h}\quad
\begin{array}{rrr}
0 & -1 & 0 \\
-1 & 4 & -1 \\
0 & -1 & 0
\end{array}
$$

2. Check your answers to Question 1 with MATLAB.

3. Describe for what each of the masks Question 1 might be used. If you can't do this, wait until Question 5 below.

4. Devise a 3 × 3 mask for an identity filter, that causes no change in the image.

5. Obtain a grayscale image of a monkey (a mandrill) with the following commands:

```
>> load('mandrill.mat');
>> m=im2uint8(ind2gray(X,map));
```

Apply all the filters listed in Question 1 to this image. Can you now see what each filter does?

6. Apply larger and larger averaging filters to this image. What is the smallest-sized filter for which the whiskers cannot be seen?

7. Repeat the previous question with Gaussian filters with the following parameters:

Size	Standard deviation		
[3,3]	0.5	1	2
[7,7]	1	3	6
[11,11]	1	4	8
[21,21]	1	5	10

At what values do the whiskers disappear?

8. Can you see any observable difference in the results of average filtering and using a Gaussian filter?

9. Read through the help page of the fspecial function, and apply some of the other filters to the cameraman image and to the mandrill image.

10. Apply different Laplacian filters to the mandrill and cameraman images. Which produces the best edge image?

11. Is the 3 × 3 median filter separable? That is, can this filter be implemented by a 3 × 1 filter followed by a 1 × 3 filter?

12. Repeat Question 11 for the maximum and minimum filters.

13. Apply a 3 × 3 averaging filter to the middle nine values of the matrix

$$\begin{bmatrix} a & b & c & d & e \\ f & g & h & i & j \\ k & l & m & n & o \\ p & q & r & s & t \\ u & v & w & x & y \end{bmatrix}$$

and then apply another 3 × 3 averaging filter to the result.

Using your answer, describe a 5 × 5 filter that has the effect of two averaging filters.

Is this filter separable?

14. MATLAB also has an imfilter function, which, if x is an image matrix (of any type) and f is a filter, has the syntax

```
imfilter(x,f);
```

It differs from filter2 in the different parameters it takes (read its help file) and in that the output is always of the same class as the original image.

a. Use imfilter on the mandrill image with the filters listed in Question 1.

b. Apply different-sized averaging filters to the mandrill image using imfilter.

c. Apply different Laplacian filters to the mandrill image using imfilter. Compare the results with those obtained with filter2. Which do you think gives the best results?

15. Display the difference between the cmax and cmin images obtained in Section 5.7. You can do this with

```
>> imshow(imsubtract(cmax,cmin))
```

What are you seeing here? Can you account for the output of these commands?

16. Using the tic and toc timer function, compare the use of nlfilter and colfilt functions.

17. Use colfilt to implement the geometric mean and alpha-trimmed mean filters.

18. Can unsharp masking be used to reverse the effects of blurring? Apply an unsharp masking filter after a 3 × 3 averaging filter and describe the result.

CHAPTER SIX

IMAGE GEOMETRY

There are many situations in which we might want to change the shape, size, or orientation of an image. We may wish to enlarge an image to fit into a particular space or for printing; we also may wish to reduce its size, say for inclusion on a Web page. We might wish to rotate it, maybe to adjust for an incorrect camera angle or simply for effect. Rotation and scaling are examples of **affine transformations,** where lines are transformed to lines and, in particular, parallel lines remain parallel after the transformation. Nonaffine geometrical transformations include warping, which we will not consider here.

6.1 Interpolation of Data

We will start with a simple problem: suppose we have a collection of four values that we wish to enlarge to eight. How do we do this? To start, we have our points x_1, x_2, x_3, and x_4, which we suppose to be evenly spaced, and we have the values at those points $f(x_1)$, $f(x_2)$, $f(x_3)$, and $f(x_4)$. Along the line $x_1 \ldots x_4$, we wish to space eight points x_1', x_2', $\ldots$, x_8'. Figure 6.1 shows how this would be done.

Suppose that the distance between each of the x_i points is 1; thus, the length of the line is 3. Because there are seven increments from x_i' to x_8', the distance between each two points will be $3/7 \approx 0.4286$.

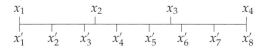

FIGURE 6.1 *Replacing four points with eight.*

FIGURE 6.2 *Figure 6.1 slightly redrawn.*

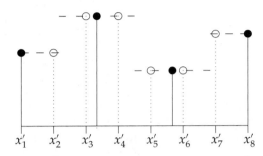

FIGURE 6.3 *Nearest-neighbor interpolation.*

To obtain a relationship between x and x' we draw Figure 6.1 slightly differently, as shown in Figure 6.2. Then

$$x' = \frac{1}{3}(7x - 4),$$

$$x = \frac{1}{7}(3x' + 4).$$

As you see from Figure 6.1, none of the x'_i points coincide exactly with an original x_j, except for the first and last. Thus, we are going to have to estimate function values $f(x'_i)$ based on the known values of nearby $f(x_i)$. Such estimation of function values based on surrounding values is called **interpolation**. Figure 6.3 shows one way of doing this: we assign $f(x'_i) = f(x_j)$, where x_j is the original point closest to x'_i. This is called **nearest-neighbor interpolation**.

The filled circles indicate the original function values $f(x_i)$; the open circles the interpolated values $f(x'_i)$.

Another way is to join the original function values by straight lines and take our interpolated values as the values at those lines. Figure 6.4 shows this approach to interpolation; this is called **linear interpolation.**

To calculate the values required for linear interpolation, consider the diagram shown in Figure 6.5.

In this figure we assume that $x_2 = x_1 + 1$ and that F is the value we require. By considering slopes:

$$\frac{F - f(x_1)}{\lambda} = \frac{f(x_2) - f(x_1)}{1}.$$

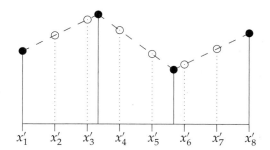

FIGURE 6.4 *Linear interpolation.*

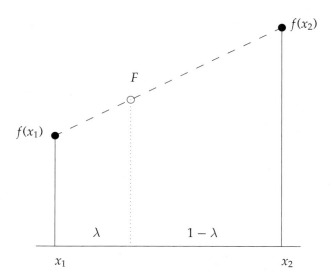

FIGURE 6.5 *Calculating linearly interpolated values.*

Solving this equation for F produces:

$$F = \lambda f(x_2) + (1 - \lambda)f(x_1). \tag{6.1}$$

As an example of how to use this equation, suppose we have the values $f(x_1) = 2$, $f(x_2) = 3$, $f(x_3) = 1.5$, and $f(x_4) = 2.5$. Consider the point x_4'. This point is between x_2 and x_3, and the corresponding value for λ is $2/7$. Thus,

$$f(x_4') = \frac{2}{7}f(x_3) + \frac{5}{7}f(x_2)$$

$$= \frac{2}{7}(1.5) + \frac{5}{7}(3)$$

$$\approx 2.5714.$$

For x_7' we are between x_3 and x_4 with $\lambda = 4/7$. Thus

$$f(x_7') = \frac{4}{7}f(x_4) + \frac{3}{7}f(x_3)$$

$$= \frac{4}{7}(2.5) + \frac{3}{7}(1.5)$$

$$\approx 2.0714.$$

6.2 Image Interpolation

The methods of the previous section can be applied to images. Figure 6.6 shows how a 4×4 image would be interpolated to produce an 8×8 image. Here, the large open circles are the original points, and the smaller filled circles are the new points.

To obtain function values for the interpolated points, consider the diagram shown in Figure 6.7.

We can give a value to $f(x', y')$ by either of the methods above: by setting it equal to the function values of the closest image point or by using linear interpolation. We can apply linear interpolation first along the top row to obtain a value for $f(x, y')$ and then along the bottom row to obtain a value for $f(x+1, y')$. Finally, we can interpolate along the y' column between these new values to obtain $f(x', y')$. Using the formula given by Figure 6.1, then

$$f(x, y') = \mu f(x, y+1) + (1 - \mu)f(x, y)$$

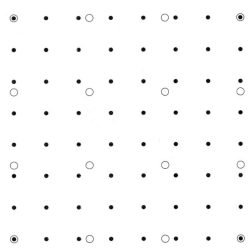

FIGURE 6.6 *Interpolation on an image.*

and

$$f(x+1, y') = \mu f(x+1, y+1) + (1 - \mu) f(x+1, y).$$

Along the y' column we have

$$f(x', y') = \lambda f(x+1, y') + (1 - \lambda) f(x, y'),$$

and substituting with the values just obtained produces

$$
\begin{aligned}
f(x', y') &= \lambda(\mu f(x+1, y+1) + (1 - \mu) f(x+1, y)) \\
&\quad + (1 - \lambda)(\mu f(x, y+1) + (1 - \mu) f(x, y)) \\
&= \lambda\mu f(x+1, y+1) + \lambda(1 - \mu) f(x+1, y) + (1 - \lambda)\mu f(x, y+1) \\
&\quad + (1 - \lambda)(1 - \mu) f(x, y).
\end{aligned}
$$

This last equation is the formula for **bilinear interpolation.**

Now image scaling can be performed easily. Given our image and either a scaling factor (or separate scaling factors for x and y directions) or a size to which we will scale, we first create an array of the required size. In our example above, we had a 4×4 image, given as an array (x, y), and

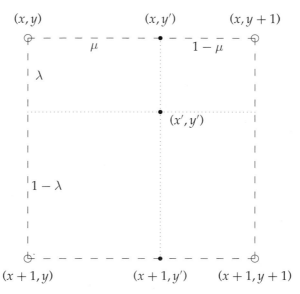

FIGURE 6.7 *Interpolation between four image points.*

a scale factor of two, resulting in an array (x', y') of size 8×8. Going back to Figures 6.1 and 6.2, the relationship between (x, y) and (x', y') is

$$(x', y') = \left(\frac{1}{3}(7x - 4), \frac{1}{3}(7y - 4) \right),$$

$$(x, y) = \left(\frac{1}{7}(3x' + 4), \frac{1}{7}(3y' + 4) \right).$$

Given our (x', y') array, we can step through it point by point and from the corresponding surrounding points from the (x, y) array calculate an interpolated value using either nearest-neighbor or bilinear interpolation.

There is nothing in the above theory that requires the scaling factor be greater than one. We can choose a scaling factor less than one, in which case the resulting image array will be smaller than the original. We can consider Figure 6.6 in this light: the small filled circles are the original image points, and the large open circles the smaller array for which we are to find interpolated values.

MATLAB has the function `imresize` that does all this for us. It can be called with

```
resize(A,k,'method')
```

where `A` is an image of any type, `k` is a scaling factor, and `'method'` is either `'nearest'` or `'bilinear'` (or another method to be described later). Another way of using `imresize` is

```
resize(A,[m,n],'method')
```

where `[m,n]` provide the size of the scaled output. There is another, optional parameter allowing you to choose either the size or type of low-pass filter to be applied to the image before reducing its size—see the help file for details.

Let's try a few examples. We start by taking the head of the cameraman and enlarging it by a factor of four:

```
>> c=imread('cameraman.tif');
>> head=c(33:96,90:153);
>> imshow(head)
>> head4n=imresize(head,4,'nearest');imshow(head4n)
>> head4b=imresize(head,4,'bilinear');imshow(head4b)
```

The head is shown in Figure 6.8, and the results of the scaling are shown in Figure 6.9.

Nearest-neighbor interpolation gives an unacceptable blocky effect; edges in particular appear very jagged. Bilinear interpolation is much smoother, but the trade-off here is a certain blurriness in the result. This is unavoidable. Interpolation can't predict values: we can't create data from nothing! All we can do is to guess at values that fit best with the original data.

FIGURE 6.8 *The head.*

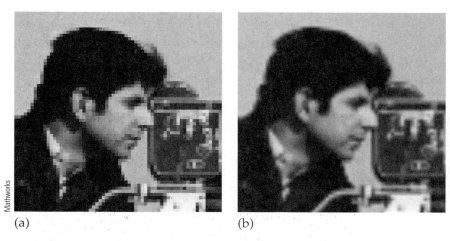

Mathworks

(a)   (b)

FIGURE 6.9 *Scaling by interpolation. (a) Nearest neighbor scaling. (b) Bilinear interpolation.*

6.3 General Interpolation

Although we have presented nearest neighbor and bilinear interpolation as two different methods, they are, in fact, two special cases of a more general approach. The idea is as follows: we wish to interpolate a value $f(x')$ for $x_1 \leq x' \leq x_2$ and suppose $x' - x_1 = \lambda$. We define an interpolation function $R(u)$ and set

$$f(x') = R(-\lambda)f(x_1) + R(1 - \lambda)f(x_2). \tag{6.2}$$

Figure 6.10 shows how this works. The function $R(u)$ is centred at x', so x_1 corresponds with $u = -\lambda$, and x_2 with $u = 1 - \lambda$. Now consider the two functions $R_0(u)$ and $R_1(u)$ shown in Figure 6.11. Both these functions are defined on the interval $-1 \leq u \leq 1$ only. Their formal definitions are:

$$R_0(u) = \begin{cases} 0 & \text{if } u \leq -0.5 \\ 1 & \text{if } -0.5 < u \leq 0.5 \\ 0 & \text{if } u > 0.5 \end{cases}$$

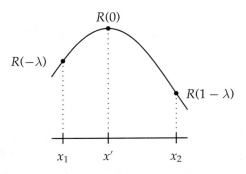

FIGURE 6.10 *Using a general interpolation function.*

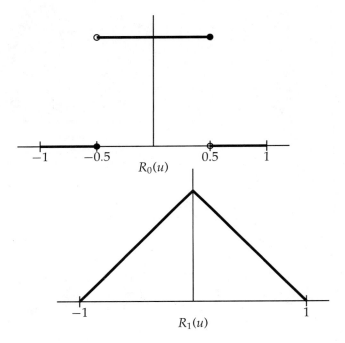

FIGURE 6.11 *Two interpolation functions.*

and

$$R_1(u) = \begin{cases} 1+u & \text{if } u \leq 0 \\ 1-u & \text{if } u \geq 0 \end{cases}.$$

The function $R_1(u)$ can also be written as $1 - |x|$. Now, substituting $R_0(u)$ for $R(u)$ in Equation 6.2 will produce nearest-neighbor interpolation.

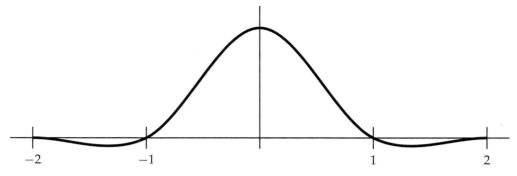

FIGURE 6.12 *The cubic interpolation function $R_3(u)$.*

To see this, consider the two cases $\lambda < 0.5$ and $\lambda \geq 0.5$ separately. If $\lambda < 0.5$, then $R_0(-\lambda) = 1$ and $R_0(1 - \lambda) = 0$. Then

$$f(x') = (1)f(x_1) + (0)f(x_2) = f(x_1).$$

If $\lambda \geq 0.5$, then $R_0(-\lambda) = 0$ and $R_0(1 - \lambda) = 1$. Then

$$f(x') = (0)f(x_1) + (1)f(x_2) = f(x_2).$$

In each case, $f(x')$ is set to the function value of the point closest to x'.

Similarly, substituting $R_1(u)$ for $R(u)$ in Equation 6.2 will produce linear interpolation. We have

$$f(x') = R_1(-\lambda)f(x_1) + R_1(1 - \lambda)f(x_2)$$
$$= (1 - \lambda)f(x_1) + \lambda f(x_2)$$

which is the correct equation.

The functions $R_0(u)$ and $R_1(u)$ are just two members of a family of possible interpolation functions. Another such function provides **cubic interpolation.** Its definition is

$$R_3(u) = \begin{cases} 1.5|u|^3 - 2.5|u|^2 + 1 & \text{if } |u| \leq 1, \\ -0.5|u|^3 + 2.5|u|^2 - 4|u| + 2 & \text{if } 1 < |u| \leq 2. \end{cases}$$

Its graph is shown in Figure 6.12. This function is defined over the interval $-2 \leq u \leq 2$, and its use is slightly different from that of $R_0(u)$ and $R_1(u)$ in that, as well as using the function values $f(x_1)$ and $f(x_2)$ for x_1 and x_2 on either side of x', we use values of x further away. In fact, the formula we use, which extends Equation 6.2, is

$$f(x') = R_3(-1 - \lambda)f(x_1) + R_3(-\lambda)f(x_2) + R_3(1 - \lambda)f(x_3) + R_4(2 - \lambda)f(x_4),$$

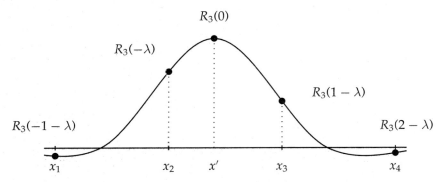

FIGURE 6.13 *Using $R_3(u)$ for interpolation.*

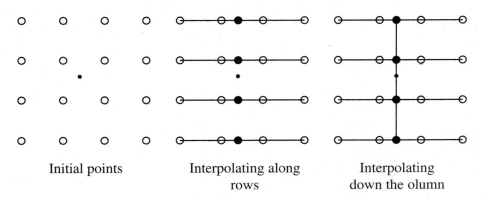

FIGURE 6.14 *How to apply bicubic interpolation.*

where x' is between x_2 and x_3 and $x - x_2 = \lambda$. Figure 6.13 illustrates this. To apply this interpolation to images, we use the 16 known values around our point (x', y'). As for bilinear interpolation, we first interpolate along the rows and then finally down the columns, as shown in Figure 6.14. Alternately, we could first interpolate down the columns and then across the row. This means of image interpolation by applying cubic interpolation in both directions is called **bicubic interpolation.** To perform bicubic interpolation on an image with MATLAB, we use the `'bicubic'` method of the `imresize` function. To enlarge the cameraman's head, we enter

```
>> head4c=imresize(head,4,'bicubic');imshow(head4c)
```

and the result is shown in Figure 6.15.

Mathworks

FIGURE 6.15 *Enlargement using bicubic interpolation.*

6.4 Enlargement by Spatial Filtering

If we merely wish to enlarge an image by a power of two, there is a quick and dirty method that uses linear filtering. We give an example. Suppose we take a simple 4×4 matrix:

```
>> m=magic(4)

m =

    16     2     3    13
     5    11    10     8
     9     7     6    12
     4    14    15     1
```

Our first step is to create a **zero-interleaved** version of this matrix. This is obtained by interleaving rows and columns of zeros between the rows and columns of the original matrix. Such a matrix will be double the size of the original and will contain mostly zeros. If m_2 is the zero-interleaved version of m, then it is defined by

$$m_2(i,j) = \begin{cases} m((i+1)/2, (j+1)/2) & \text{if } i \text{ and } j \text{ are both odd,} \\ 0 & \text{otherwise.} \end{cases}$$

```
function out=zeroint(a)
%
% ZEROINT(A) produces a zero-interleaved version of the matrix A.
% For example:
%
%    a=[1 2 3;4 5 6];
%    zeroint(a)
%
%       1    0    2    0    3
%       0    0    0    0    0
%       4    0    5    0    6
%
[m,n]=size(a);  a2=reshape([a;zeros(m,n)],m,2*n);
out=reshape([a2';zeros(2*n,m)],2*n,2*m)';
```

FIGURE 6.16 *A simple function for implementing zero interleaving.*

This can be implemented with a simple function; one such is shown in Figure 6.16. Applied to our matrix from above:

```
>> m2=zeroint(m)

m2 =

    16     0     2     0     3     0    13     0
     0     0     0     0     0     0     0     0
     5     0    11     0    10     0     8     0
     0     0     0     0     0     0     0     0
     9     0     7     0     6     0    12     0
     0     0     0     0     0     0     0     0
     4     0    14     0    15     0     1     0
     0     0     0     0     0     0     0     0
```

We can now replace the zeros by applying a spatial filter to this matrix. The spatial filters

$$
\begin{bmatrix} 1 & 1 & 0 \\ 1 & 1 & 0 \\ 0 & 0 & 0 \end{bmatrix}, \qquad \frac{1}{4}\begin{bmatrix} 1 & 2 & 1 \\ 2 & 4 & 2 \\ 1 & 2 & 1 \end{bmatrix}
$$

implement nearest-neighbor interpolation and bilinear interpolation, respectively. We can test this with a few commands:

```
>> filter2([1 1 0;1 1 0;0 0 0],m2)

ans =

    16    16     2     2     3     3    13    13
    16    16     2     2     3     3    13    13
     5     5    11    11    10    10     8     8
     5     5    11    11    10    10     8     8
     9     9     7     7     6     6    12    12
     9     9     7     7     6     6    12    12
     4     4    14    14    15    15     1     1
     4     4    14    14    15    15     1     1

>> filter2([1 2 1;2 4 2;1 2 1]/4,m2)

ans =

   16.0000    9.0000    2.0000    2.5000    3.0000    8.0000   13.0000    6.5000
   10.5000    8.5000    6.5000    6.5000    6.5000    8.5000   10.5000    5.2500
    5.0000    8.0000   11.0000   10.5000   10.0000    9.0000    8.0000    4.0000
    7.0000    8.0000    9.0000    8.5000    8.0000    9.0000   10.0000    5.0000
    9.0000    8.0000    7.0000    6.5000    6.0000    9.0000   12.0000    6.0000
    6.5000    8.5000   10.5000   10.5000   10.5000    8.5000    6.5000    3.2500
    4.0000    9.0000   14.0000   14.5000   15.0000    8.0000    1.0000    0.5000
    2.0000    4.5000    7.0000    7.2500    7.5000    4.0000    0.5000    0.2500
```

We can check these with the commands

```
>> m2b=imresize(m,[8,8],'nearest');m2b
>> m2b=imresize(m,[7,7],'bilinear');m2b
```

In the second command we only scaled up to 7×7 to ensure that the interpolation points lie exactly halfway between the original data values. The filter

$$\frac{1}{64} \begin{bmatrix} 1 & 4 & 6 & 4 & 1 \\ 4 & 16 & 24 & 16 & 4 \\ 6 & 24 & 36 & 24 & 6 \\ 4 & 16 & 24 & 16 & 4 \\ 1 & 4 & 6 & 4 & 1 \end{bmatrix}$$

can be used to approximate bicubic interpolation.

We can try all of these with the cameraman's head, doubling its size.

```
>> imshow(hz)
>> imshow(filter2([1 1 0;1 1 0;0 0 0],hz)/255)
>> imshow(filter2([1 2 1;2 4 2;1 2 1]/4,hz)/255)
>> bfilt=[1 4 6 4 1;4 16 24 16 4;6 24 36 24 6;4 16 24 16 4;1 4 6 4 1]/64;
>> imshow(filter2(bfilt,hz)/255)
```

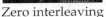

Zero interleaving   Nearest neighbor   Bilinear   Bicubic

FIGURE 6.17 *Enlargement by spatial filtering.*

The results are shown in Figure 6.17. We can enlarge more by simply taking the result of the filter, applying a zero interleave to it, and then apply another filter.

6.5 Scaling Smaller

Making an image smaller is also called **image minimization.** One way to make an image smaller is to delete alternate pixels. If we wished to produce an image one-sixteenth the size of the original, we would take out only those pixels (i, j) for which i and j are both multiples of four. This method is called image **subsampling.** It corresponds to the nearest option of imresize and is very easy to implement.

However, it does not give very good results at high-frequency components of an image. We will give a simple example by constructing a large image consisting of a white square with a single circle on it.

```
>> t=zeros(1024,1024);
>> t=((255.5)^2<(i-512).^2+(j-512).^2) & ((i-512).^2+(j-512).^2<(256.5)^2);
>> t=~t;
```

Now we can resize it by taking out most pixels:

```
>> tr=imresize(t,0.25);
```

This is shown in Figure 6.18(a). Notice that because of the way that pixels were removed, the resulting circle contains gaps. If we were to use one of the other methods,

```
>> trc=imresize(t,0.25,'bicubic');
```

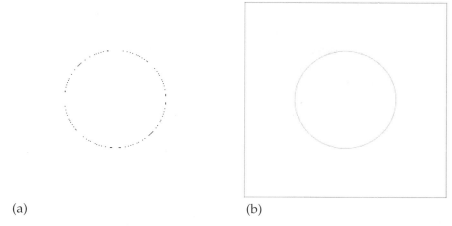

(a)   (b)

FIGURE 6.18 *Minimization. (a) Nearest-neighbor minimization. (b) Bicubic interpolation for minimization.*

a low-pass filter is applied to the image first. The result is shown in Figure 6.18(b). The image in Figure 6.18(b) can be made binary by thresholding (which will be discussed in greater detail in Chapter 9). In this case

```
>> trc=imresize(t,0.25,'bicubic')>0.9;
```

does the trick.

6.6 Rotation

Having done the hard work of interpolation for scaling, we can easily apply the same theory to image rotation. First, recall that the mapping of a point (x, y) to another (x', y') through a counterclockwise rotation of θ as shown in Figure 6.19 is obtained by the matrix product

$$\begin{bmatrix} x' \\ y' \end{bmatrix} = \begin{bmatrix} \cos\theta & -\sin\theta \\ \sin\theta & \cos\theta \end{bmatrix} \begin{bmatrix} x \\ y \end{bmatrix}.$$

Similarly, since the matrix involved is orthogonal (its inverse is equal to its transpose), we have

$$\begin{bmatrix} x \\ y \end{bmatrix} = \begin{bmatrix} \cos\theta & \sin\theta \\ -\sin\theta & \cos\theta \end{bmatrix} \begin{bmatrix} x' \\ y' \end{bmatrix}.$$

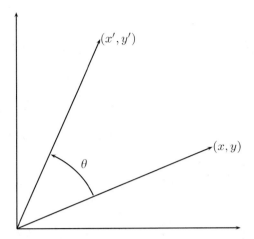

FIGURE 6.19 *Rotating a point through angle θ.*

Now we can rotate an image by considering it as a large collection of points. Figure 6.20 illustrates the idea. In this figure the filled circles indicate the original position, and the open circles point their positions after rotation. However, this approach won't work for images. Since an image grid can be considered as pixels forming a subset of the Cartesian (integer valued) grid, we must ensure that even after rotation, the points remain in that grid. To do this we consider a rectangle that includes the rotated image, as shown in Figure 6.21. Now consider all integer-valued points (x', y') in the dashed rectangle. A point will be in the image if, when rotated back, it lies within the original image limits, that is, if

$$
\begin{aligned}
0 &\le x' \cos\theta + y' \sin\theta \le a \\
0 &\le -x' \sin\theta + y' \cos\theta \le b.
\end{aligned}
$$

If we consider the array of 6×4 points shown in Figure 6.20, then the points after rotation by 30° are shown in Figure 6.22. This technique gives us the position of the pixels in our rotated image, but what about their value? Take a point (x', y') in the rotated image and rotate it back into the original image to produce a point (x'', y''), as shown in Figure 6.23. Now the gray value at (x'', y'') can be found by interpolation, using surrounding gray values. This value is then the gray value for the pixel at (x', y') in the rotated image.

Image rotation in MATLAB is obtained using the command `imrotate`; it has the syntax

```
imrotate(image, angle, 'method')
```

where `method`, as with `imresize`, can be `nearest`, `bilinear`, or `bicubic`. Also as with `imresize`, the `method` parameter may be omitted, in which case nearest-neighbor interpolation is used.

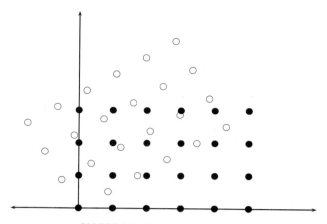

FIGURE 6.20 *Rotating a rectangle.*

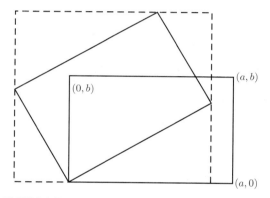

FIGURE 6.21 *A rectangle surrounding a rotated image.*

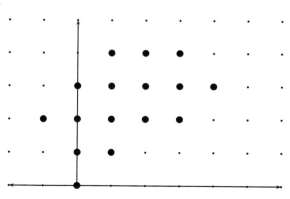

FIGURE 6.22 *The points on a grid after rotation.*

For an example, let's take our old friend the cameraman and rotate him 60°. We will do this twice; once with nearest-neighbor interpolation and once using bicubic interpolation.

```
>> cr=imrotate(c,60);
>> imshow(cr)
>> crc=imrotate(c,60,'bicubic');
>> imshow(crc)
```

The results are shown in Figure 6.24. There is not a great deal of observable difference between the two images; however, nearest-neighbor interpolation produces slightly more jagged edges.

Notice that for angles that are integer multiples of 90°, image rotation can be accomplished far more efficiently with simple matrix

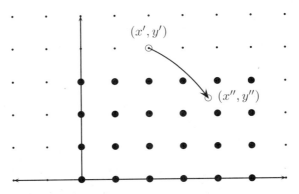

FIGURE 6.23 *Rotating a point back into the original image.*

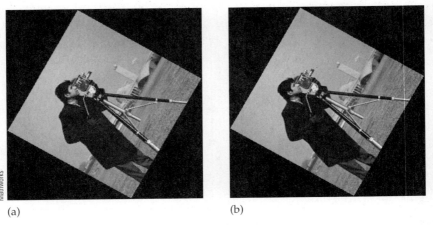

(a)   (b)

FIGURE 6.24 *Rotation with interpolation. (a) Nearest neighbor. (b) Bicubic interpolation.*

transposition and reversing of the order of rows and columns. Using the commands

```
ipud
```

for flipping a matrix in the up or down direction and

```
iplr
```

for flipping a matrix in the left or right direction, we have the following commands for rotations of 90° multiples:

```
 90°   flipud(c');
180°   fliplr(flipud(c));
270°   fliplr(c');
```

In fact, `imrotate` uses these simpler commands for these particular angles.

6.7 Anamorphosis

Anamorphosis refers to the deliberate stretching or distorting of the shape of an object for artistic or dramatic effect. It was popularly used by painters in the 16th and 17th centuries. Figure 6.25 shows a painting by Hans Holbein called *The Ambassadors*. The odd shape at the bottom of the painting is, in

FIGURE 6.25 The Ambassadors *(1533) by Hans Holbein.*

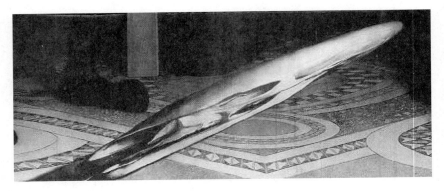

FIGURE 6.26 *The skull alone.*

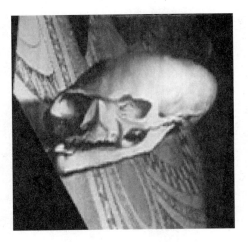

FIGURE 6.27 *The corrected skull.*

fact, an anamorphic skull; this can only be seen properly when the painting is viewed from a certain angle. In MATLAB:

```
>> a=imread('AMBASSADORS.JPG');
>> a=rgb2gray(a);
```

By a judicious use of `pixval` we can isolate the skull:

```
>> skull=a(566:743,157:586);
```

This is shown in Figure 6.26. To undo the effects of the anamorphosis, we must rotate the skull slightly clockwise and then stretch it vertically. This can be done with one command:

```
>> skull2=imresize(imrotate(skull,-22,'bicubic'),[500,150],'bicubic');
```

The angle of rotation and size of the scaling were determined using trial and error. After much fiddling and experimentation, these techniques seem to produce the best output.

Finally, we shall view the portion of skull2 that contains the corrected skull:

```
>> imshow(skull2(200:350,:))
```

this is shown in Figure 6.27.

EXERCISES

1. By hand, enlarge the list

   1 4 7 4 3 6

   to lengths
   a. 9
   b. 11
   c. 2

   by using nearest-neighbor interpolation and linear interpolation. Check your answers with MATLAB.

2. By hand, enlarge the matrix

$$\begin{bmatrix} 8 & 6 & 13 & 9 \\ 1 & 13 & 1 & 15 \\ 5 & 4 & 7 & 7 \\ 5 & 10 & 3 & 7 \end{bmatrix}$$

   to sizes
   a. 7×7,
   b. 8×8,
   c. 10×10

   by using nearest-neighbor interpolation and bilinear interpolation. Check your answers with MATLAB.

3. Use zero interleaving and spatial filtering to enlarge the cameraman's head by a factor of four in each dimension, using the three filters given. Use the following sequence of commands

```
>> head2=zeroint(head);
>> head2n=filter2(filt,head2);
>> head4=zeroint(head2n);
>> head4n=filter2(filt,head4);
>> imshow(head4n/255)
```

where `filt` is a filter. Compare your results with those given by `imresize`. Are there any observable differences?

4. Take another small part of an image, say the head of the girl in `pout.tif`. This can be obtained with:

```
>> p=imread('pout.tif');
>> ph=histeq(p);
>> head=ph(10:129,60:179);
```

Enlarge the head to four times as big using both `imresize` with the different parameters and the zero interleave method with the different filters. As above, compare the results.

5. Suppose an image is enlarged by some amount k, and the result is decreased by the same amount. Should this result be exactly the same as the original? If not, why not?

6. What happens if the image is decreased first and the result enlarged?

7. Create an image consisting of a white square with a black background. Rotate the image 30° and 45°. Use

   a. `imrotate` with the `nearest` option,
   b. `imrotate` with `bilinear`.

   Compare the results.

8. For the rotated squares in Question 7, rotate back to the original orientation. How close is the result to the original square?

9. In general, suppose an image is rotated and then the result rotated back. Should this result be exactly the same as the original? If not, why not?

10. Write a MATLAB function to implement image enlargement using zero interleaving and spatial filtering. The function should have the syntax

```
imenlarge(image,n,filt)
```

where n is the number of times the interleaving is to be done and `filt` is the filter to use. For example, the command

```
>> imenlarge(head,2,bfilt);
```

would enlarge an image to four times its size, using the 5 × 5 filter described in Section 6.4.

11. Consider the image `ic.tif`. By trial and error, find an angle by which the image can be rotated so that its lines are all horizontal and vertical.

CHAPTER SEVEN

THE FOURIER TRANSFORM

7.1 Introduction

The Fourier transform is of fundamental importance to image processing. It allows us to perform tasks that would be impossible to perform any other way; its efficiency allows us to perform other tasks more quickly. The Fourier transform provides, among other things, a powerful alternative to linear spatial filtering. It is more efficient to use the Fourier transform than a spatial filter for a large filter. The Fourier transform also allows us to isolate and process particular image frequencies and thus perform low-pass and high-pass filtering with a great degree of precision.

Before we discuss the Fourier transform of images, we will investigate the one-dimensional Fourier transform and a few of its properties.

7.2 Background

Our starting place is the observation that a periodic function may be written as the sum of sines and cosines of varying amplitudes and frequencies. For example, in Figure 7.1 we plot a function and its decomposition into sine functions.

Some functions will require only a finite number of functions in their decomposition; others will require an infinite number. For example, a square wave, such as is shown in Figure 7.2, has the decomposition

$$f(x) = \sin x + \frac{1}{3}\sin 3x + \frac{1}{5}\sin 5x + \frac{1}{7}\sin 7x + \frac{1}{9}\sin 9x + \cdots \tag{7.1}$$

In Figure 7.2 we take the first four terms only to provide the approximation. The more terms of the series we take, the closer the sum will

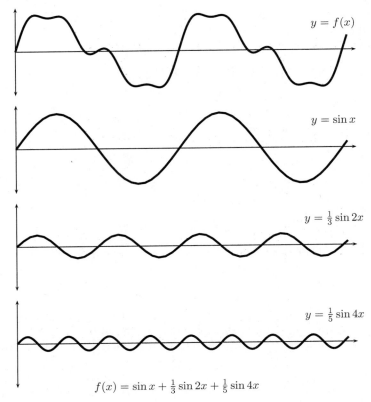

$$f(x) = \sin x + \tfrac{1}{3}\sin 2x + \tfrac{1}{5}\sin 4x$$

FIGURE 7.1 *A function and its trigonometric decomposition.*

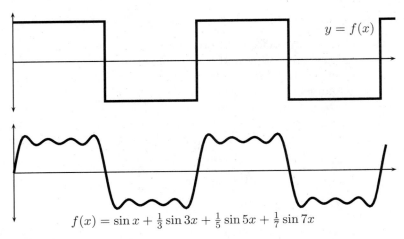

$$f(x) = \sin x + \tfrac{1}{3}\sin 3x + \tfrac{1}{5}\sin 5x + \tfrac{1}{7}\sin 7x$$

FIGURE 7.2 *A square wave and its trigonometric approximation.*

approach the original function. This can be formalized. If $f(x)$ is a function of period $2T$, then we can write

$$f(x) = a_0 + \sum_{n=1}^{\infty} \left(a_n \cos \frac{n\pi x}{T} + b_n \sin \frac{n\pi x}{T} \right)$$

where

$$a_0 = \frac{1}{2T} \int_{-T}^{T} f(x)\, dx$$

$$a_n = \frac{1}{T} \int_{-T}^{T} f(x) \cos \frac{n\pi x}{T}\, dx, \quad n = 1, 2, 3, \ldots$$

$$b_n = \frac{1}{T} \int_{-T}^{T} f(x) \sin \frac{n\pi x}{T}\, dx, \quad n = 1, 2, 3, \ldots$$

These are the equations for the **Fourier series expansion** of $f(x)$, and they can be expressed in complex form:

$$f(x) = \sum_{n=-\infty}^{\infty} c_n \exp \left(\frac{in\pi x}{T} \right) dx,$$

where

$$c_n = \frac{1}{2T} \int_{-T}^{T} f(x) \exp \left(\frac{-in\pi x}{T} \right) dx.$$

If the function is nonperiodic, we can obtain similar results by letting $T \to \infty$, in which case

$$f(x) = \int_{0}^{\infty} [a(\omega) \cos \omega x + b(\omega) \sin \omega x]\, d\omega$$

where

$$a(\omega) = \frac{1}{\pi} \int_{-\infty}^{\infty} f(x) \cos \omega x\, dx,$$

$$b(\omega) = \frac{1}{\pi} \int_{-\infty}^{\infty} f(x) \sin \omega x\, dx.$$

These equations can be written again in complex form:

$$f(x) = \int_{-\infty}^{\infty} F(\omega)e^{i\omega x}\, d\omega,$$

$$F(\omega) = \frac{1}{2\pi} \int_{-\infty}^{\infty} f(x)e^{i\omega x}\, dx.$$

In this last form the functions $f(x)$ and $F(\omega)$ form a **Fourier transform pair.** Further details can be found, for example, in James [18].

7.3 The One-Dimensional Discrete Fourier Transform

When we deal with a **discrete** function, as we will for images, the situation changes slightly from the previous section. Because we have to obtain only a finite number of values, we need only a finite number of functions to do it.

Consider for example the discrete sequence

$$1,\quad 1,\quad 1,\quad 1,\quad -1,\quad -1,\quad -1,\quad -1,$$

which we may take as a discrete approximation to the square wave of Figure 7.2. This can be expressed as the sum of only two sine functions, which is shown in Figure 7.3. We will see below how to obtain those sequences.

The Fourier transform allows us to obtain those individual sine waves that compose a given function or sequence. Because we will be concerned with discrete sequences and, of course, images, we will investigate only the **discrete Fourier transform,** abbreviated DFT.

7.3.1 Definition of the One-Dimensional DFT

Suppose

$$\mathbf{f} = [f_0, f_1, f_2, \ldots, f_{N-1}]$$

is a sequence of length N. We define its DFT to be the sequence

$$\mathbf{F} = [F_0, F_1, F_2, \ldots, F_{N-1}],$$

where

$$F_u = \frac{1}{N} \sum_{x=0}^{N-1} \exp\left[-2\pi i \frac{xu}{N}\right] f_x. \tag{7.2}$$

Note the similarity between this equation and the equations for the Fourier series expansion discussed in the previous section. Instead of an integral,

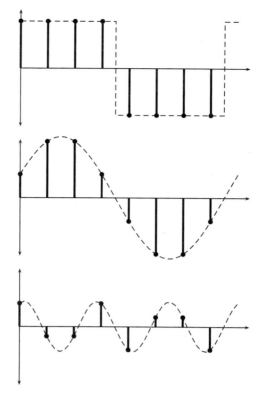

FIGURE 7.3 *Expressing a discrete function as the sum of sines.*

we now have a finite sum. This definition can be expressed as a matrix multiplication:

$$F = \mathcal{F}f,$$

where $\mathcal{F}$ is an $N \times N$ matrix defined by

$$\mathcal{F}_{m,n} = \frac{1}{N} \exp\left[-2\pi i \frac{mn}{N}\right].$$

Given N, we shall define

$$\omega = \exp\left[\frac{-2\pi i}{N}\right]$$

so that

$$\mathcal{F}_{m,n} = \frac{1}{N}\omega^{mn}.$$

Then we can write

$$\mathcal{F} = \frac{1}{N} \begin{bmatrix} 1 & 1 & 1 & 1 & 1 & \cdots & 1 \\ 1 & \omega^1 & \omega^2 & \omega^3 & \omega^4 & \cdots & \omega^{N-1} \\ 1 & \omega^2 & \omega^4 & \omega^6 & \omega^8 & \cdots & \omega^{2(N-1)} \\ 1 & \omega^3 & \omega^6 & \omega^9 & \omega^{12} & \cdots & \omega^{3(N-1)} \\ 1 & \omega^4 & \omega^8 & \omega^{12} & \omega^{16} & \cdots & \omega^{4(N-1)} \\ \vdots & \vdots & \vdots & \vdots & \vdots & \ddots & \vdots \\ 1 & \omega^{N-1} & \omega^{2(N-1)} & \omega^{3(N-1)} & \omega^{4(N-1)} & \cdots & \omega^{(N-1)^2} \end{bmatrix}.$$

EXAMPLE 7.3.1   Suppose $f = [1, 2, 3, 4]$ so that $N = 4$. Then

$$\omega = \exp\left[\frac{-2\pi i}{4}\right]$$

$$= \exp\left[-\frac{\pi i}{2}\right]$$

$$= \cos\left(-\frac{\pi}{2}\right) + i\sin\left(-\frac{\pi}{2}\right)$$

$$= -i.$$

Then we have

$$\mathcal{F} = \begin{bmatrix} 1 & 1 & 1 & 1 \\ 1 & -i & (-i)^2 & (-i)^3 \\ 1 & (-i)^2 & (-i)^4 & (-i)^6 \\ 1 & (-i)^3 & (-i)^6 & (-i)^9 \end{bmatrix} = \begin{bmatrix} 1 & 1 & 1 & 1 \\ 1 & -i & -1 & i \\ 1 & -1 & 1 & -1 \\ 1 & i & -1 & -i \end{bmatrix}$$

and so

$$F = \frac{1}{4} \begin{bmatrix} 1 & 1 & 1 & 1 \\ 1 & -i & -1 & i \\ 1 & -1 & 1 & -1 \\ 1 & i & -1 & -i \end{bmatrix} \begin{bmatrix} 1 \\ 2 \\ 3 \\ 4 \end{bmatrix} = \frac{1}{4} \begin{bmatrix} 10 \\ -2 + 2i \\ -2 \\ -2 - 2i \end{bmatrix}.$$

THE INVERSE DFT   The formula for the inverse DFT is very similar to the forward transform:

$$x_u = \sum_{x=0}^{N-1} \exp\left[2\pi i \frac{xu}{N}\right] F_u. \tag{7.3}$$

If you compare Equation (7.3) with Equation 7.2 you will see that there are really only two differences:

1. There is no scaling factor $1/N$.
2. The sign inside the exponential function has been changed to positive.
3. The index of the sum is u, instead of x.

As with the forward transform, we can express this as a matrix product:

$$f = \mathcal{F}^{-1}F$$

with

$$\mathcal{F}^{-1} = \begin{bmatrix} 1 & 1 & 1 & 1 & 1 & \cdots & 1 \\ 1 & \overline{\omega}^1 & \overline{\omega}^2 & \overline{\omega}^3 & \overline{\omega}^4 & \cdots & \overline{\omega}^{N-1} \\ 1 & \overline{\omega}^2 & \overline{\omega}^4 & \overline{\omega}^6 & \overline{\omega}^8 & \cdots & \overline{\omega}^{2(N-1)} \\ 1 & \overline{\omega}^3 & \overline{\omega}^6 & \overline{\omega}^9 & \overline{\omega}^{12} & \cdots & \overline{\omega}^{3(N-1)} \\ 1 & \overline{\omega}^4 & \overline{\omega}^8 & \overline{\omega}^{12} & \overline{\omega}^{16} & \cdots & \overline{\omega}^{4(N-1)} \\ \vdots & \vdots & \vdots & \vdots & \vdots & \ddots & \vdots \\ 1 & \overline{\omega}^{N-1} & \overline{\omega}^{2(N-1)} & \overline{\omega}^{3(N-1)} & \overline{\omega}^{4(N-1)} & \cdots & \overline{\omega}^{(N-1)^2} \end{bmatrix}$$

where

$$\overline{\omega} = \frac{1}{\omega} = \exp\left[\frac{2\pi i}{N}\right].$$

In MATLAB, we can calculate the forward and inverse transforms with
`fft` and `ifft`. Here `fft` stands for **fast Fourier transform,** which is a
fast and efficient method of performing the DFT (see below for details).
For example:

```
a =

     1     2     3     4     5     6

>> fft(a')

ans =

   21.0000
   -3.0000 + 5.1962i
   -3.0000 + 1.7321i
   -3.0000
   -3.0000 - 1.7321i
   -3.0000 - 5.1962i
```

We note that to apply a DFT to a single vector in MATLAB we should use a
column vector.

7.4 Properties of the One-Dimensional DFT

The one-dimensional DFT satisfies many useful and important properties. We will investigate some of them here. A more complete list can be found in Jain, for example [17].

LINEARITY   This is a direct consequence of the definition of the DFT as a matrix product. Suppose f and g are two vectors of equal length, and p and q are scalars, with h = pf + qg. If F, G, and H are the DFT's of f, g, and h, respectively, we have

$$H = pF + qG.$$

This follows from the definitions of

$$F = \mathcal{F}f, \quad G = \mathcal{F}g, \quad H = \mathcal{F}h$$

and the linearity of the matrix product.

SHIFTING   Suppose we multiply each element x_n of a vector x by $(-1)^n$. In other words, we change the sign of every second element. Let the resulting vector be denoted x′. The DFT X′ of x′ is equal to the DFT X of x with the swapping of the left and right halves.
Let's do a quick MATLAB example:

```
>> x = [2 3 4 5 6 7 8 1];

>> x1=(-1).^[0:7].*x

x1 =

     2    -3     4    -5     6    -7     8    -1

>> X=fft(x')

  36.0000
  -9.6569 + 4.0000i
  -4.0000 - 4.0000i
   1.6569 - 4.0000i
   4.0000
   1.6569 + 4.0000i
  -4.0000 + 4.0000i
  -9.6569 - 4.0000i
```

```
>> X1=fft(x1')

X1 =

    4.0000
    1.6569 + 4.0000i
   -4.0000 + 4.0000i
   -9.6569 - 4.0000i
   36.0000
   -9.6569 + 4.0000i
   -4.0000 - 4.0000i
    1.6569 - 4.0000i
```

Notice that the first four elements of X are the last four elements of X1 and vice versa.

CONJUGATE SYMMETRY   If x is real and of length N, then its DFT X satisfies the condition that

$$X_k = \overline{X_{N-k}},$$

where $\overline{X_{N-k}}$ is the complex conjugate of X_{N-k} for all $k = 1, 2, 3, \ldots, N-1$. Thus, in our example of length 8, we have

$$X_1 = \overline{X_7}, \quad X_2 = \overline{X_6}, \quad X_3 = \overline{X_5}.$$

In this case we also have $X_4 = \overline{X_4}$, which means X_4 must be real. In fact, if N is even, then $X_{N/2}$ will be real. Examples can be seen above.

CONVOLUTION   Suppose x and y are two vectors of the same length N. If so, we define their **convolution** (or more properly, their **circular convolution**) to be the vector

$$z = x * y,$$

where

$$z_k = \frac{1}{n} \sum_{n=0}^{N-1} x_n y_{k-n}.$$

For example, if $N = 4$, then

$$z_0 = \frac{1}{4}(x_0 y_0 + x_1 y_{-1} + x_2 y_{-2} + x_3 y_{-3})$$

$$z_1 = \frac{1}{4}(x_0 y_1 + x_1 y_0 + x_2 y_{-1} + x_3 y_{-2})$$

$$z_2 = \frac{1}{4}(x_0 y_2 + x_1 y_1 + x_2 y_0 + x_3 y_{-1})$$

$$z_3 = \frac{1}{4}(x_0 y_3 + x_2 y_1 + x_2 y_1 + x_3 y_0).$$

The negative indices can be interpreted by imagining the y vector to be periodic and can be indexed backward from 0, as well as forward:

$$
\begin{array}{ccccccccc}
\cdots & y_0 & y_1 & y_2 & y_3 & y_0 & y_1 & y_2 & y_3 & \cdots \\
= & \cdots & y_0 & y_{-3} & y_{-2} & y_{-1} & y_0 & y_1 & y_2 & y_3 & \cdots
\end{array}
$$

Thus $y_{-1} = y_3$, $y_{-2} = y_2$, and $y_{-3} = y_1$.

It can be checked from the definition that convolution is commutative (the order of the operands is irrelevant):

$$x * y = y * x.$$

Circular convolution as defined looks like a messy operation. However, it can be defined in terms of polynomial products. Suppose $p(u)$ is the polynomial in u whose coefficients are the elements of x. And let $q(u)$ be the polynomial whose coefficients are the elements of y. Form the product $p(u)q(u)(1+u^N)$, and extract the coefficients of u^N to u^{2N-1}. These coefficients will be our required circular convolution.

For example, suppose we have:

$$x = [1, 2, 3, 4], \qquad y = [5, 6, 7, 8].$$

Then we have

$$p(u) = 1 + 2u + 3u^2 + 4u^3$$

and

$$q(u) = 5 + 6u + 7u^2 + 8u^3.$$

We expand

$$p(u)q(u)(1 + u^4) = 5 + 16x + 34u^2 + 60u^3 + 66u^4 + 68u^5 + 66u^6$$
$$+ 60u^7 + 61u^8 + 52u^9 + 32u^{10}.$$

Extracting the coefficients of $u^4, u^5, \ldots, u^7$, we obtain

$$x * y = [66, 68, 66, 60].$$

```
function out=cconv(a,b)

if length(a)~=length(b)
   error('Vectors must be the same length')
end;
la=length(a);
temp=conv([a a],b);
out=temp(la+1:2*la);
```

FIGURE 7.4 *A function to calculate the circular convolution of two vectors.*

MATLAB has a conv function, which produces the coefficients of the polynomial $p(u)q(u)$ as defined above:

```
>> a=[1 2 3 4]

a =

     1     2     3     4

>> b=[5 6 7 8]

b =

     5     6     7     8

>> conv(a,b)

ans =

     5    16    34    60    61    52    32
```

We can write a simple function cconv to perform circular convolution. We first notice that the polynomial $p(u)(1 + u^N)$ can be obtained by simply repeating the coefficients of x. This leads to the function given in Figure 7.4. For example,

```
>> cconv(a,b)

ans =

    66    68    66    60
```

which is exactly what we obtained above.

The importance of convolution is the **convolution theorem,** which states:

> Suppose x and y are vectors of equal length. Then the DFT of their circular convolution x * y is equal to the element-by-element product of the DFT's of x and y.

So if Z, X, and Y are the DFT's of z = x * y, x, and y, respectively, then

Z = X.Y.

We can check this with our vectors above:

```
>> fft(cconv(a,b)')

ans =

   1.0e+02 *

   2.6000
        0 - 0.0800i
   0.0400
        0 + 0.0800i

>> fft(a').*fft(b');

ans =

   1.0e+02 *

   2.6000
        0 - 0.0800i
   0.0400
        0 + 0.0800i
```

Note that in each case the results are the same. The convolution theorem thus provides us with another way of performing convolution: multiply the DFT's of our two vectors and invert the result.

```
>> fft(a').*fft(b');
>> ifft(ans)'

ans =

   66    68    66    60
```

TABLE 7.1   *Comparison of FFT and direct arithmetic.*

2^n	Direct Arithmetic	FFT	Increase in Speed
4	16	8	2.0
8	84	24	2.67
16	256	64	4.0
32	1024	160	6.4
64	4096	384	10.67
128	16384	896	18.3
256	65536	2048	32.0
512	262144	4608	56.9
1024	1048576	10240	102.4

A formal proof of the convolution theorem for the DFT is given by Petrou [25].

THE FAST FOURIER TRANSFORM   One of the many aspects that make the DFT so attractive for image processing is the existence of very fast algorithms to compute it. There are a number of extremely fast and efficient algorithms for computing a DFT; such an algorithm is called a **fast Fourier transform, or FFT**. The use of an FFT vastly reduces the time needed to compute a DFT.

One FFT method works recursively by dividing the original vector into two halves, computing the FFT of each half, and then putting the results together. This means that the FFT is most efficient when the vector length is a power of two. This method is discussed in Appendix B.

Table 7.1 shows the advantage gained by using the FFT algorithm, as opposed to the direct arithmetic definition of Equations 7.2 and 7.3 (see Section 7.3.1) by comparing the number of multiplications required for each method. For a vector of length 2^n, the direct method takes $(2^n)^2 = 2^{2n}$ multiplications, the FFT only $n2^n$. The savings in time is thus of an order of $\frac{2^n}{n}$. Clearly the advantage of using an FFT algorithm becomes greater as the size of the vector increases.

Because of this computational advantage, any implementation of the DFT will use an FFT algorithm.

7.5 The Two-Dimensional DFT

In two dimensions, the DFT takes a matrix as input and returns another matrix of the same size as output. If the original matrix values are $f(x, y)$, where x and y are the indices, then the output matrix values are $F(u, v)$. We call the matrix F the **Fourier transform of** f and write

$$F = \mathcal{F}(f).$$

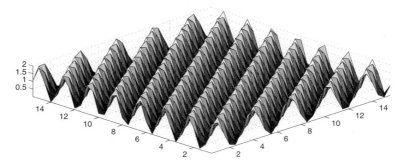

FIGURE 7.5 *A "corrugation" function.*

The original matrix f is the **inverse Fourier transform of F,** and we write

$$f = \mathcal{F}^{-1}(F).$$

We have seen that a (one-dimensional) function can be written as a sum of sines and cosines. Given that an image may be considered as a two-dimensional function $f(x, y)$, it seems reasonable to assume that f can be expressed as sums of corrugation functions that have the general form

$$z = a \sin (bx + cy).$$

A sample of such a function is shown in Figure 7.5. This is, in fact, exactly what the two-dimensional Fourier transform does: it rewrites the original matrix in terms of sums of corrugations.

The definition of the two-dimensional DFT is very similar to that with one dimension. The forward and inverse transforms for an $M \times N$ matrix, where for notational convenience we assume that the x indices are from 0 to $M - 1$ and the y indices are from 0 to $N - 1$, are:

$$F(u, v) = \sum_{x=0}^{M-1} \sum_{y=0}^{N-1} f(x, y) \exp \left[-2\pi i \left(\frac{xu}{M} + \frac{yv}{N} \right) \right]. \tag{7.4}$$

$$f(x, y) = \frac{1}{MN} \sum_{u=0}^{M-1} \sum_{v=0}^{N-1} F(u, v) \exp \left[2\pi i \left(\frac{xu}{M} + \frac{yv}{N} \right) \right]. \tag{7.5}$$

These are horrendous-looking formulas, but if we spend a bit of time pulling them apart, we will see that they aren't as bad as they look.

Before we do this, we note that the formulas given in Equations 7.4 and 7.5 are not used by all authors. The main change is the position of the scaling factor $\frac{1}{MN}$. Some people put it in front of the sums in the forward formula. Others put a factor of $\frac{1}{\sqrt{MN}}$ in front of both sums. The point is that the sums by themselves would produce a result (after both forward and inverse transforms) that is too large by a factor of MN. Thus somewhere in the forward inverse formulas a corresponding $\frac{1}{MN}$ must exist; it doesn't really matter where.

7.5.1 Some Properties of the Two-Dimensional Fourier Transform

All the properties of the one-dimensional DFT transfer into two dimensions. But there are some further properties not previously mentioned that are of particular use for image processing.

SIMILARITY   First note that the forward and inverse transforms are very similar, with the exception of the scale factor $\frac{1}{MN}$ in the inverse transform and the negative sign in the exponent of the forward transform. This similarity means that the same algorithm, only very slightly adjusted, can be used for both the forward and inverse transforms.

THE DFT AS A SPATIAL FILTER   Note that the values

$$\exp\left[\pm 2\pi i \left(\frac{xu}{M} + \frac{yv}{N}\right)\right]$$

are independent of the values f or F. This independence means that they can be calculated in advance and only then put into the formulas above. It also means that every value $F(u, v)$ is obtained by multiplying every value of $f(x, y)$ by a fixed value and adding up all the results. But this is precisely what a linear spatial filter does: it multiplies all elements under a mask with fixed values and adds them all up. Thus, we can consider the DFT as a linear spatial filter that is as big as the image. To deal with the problem of edges, we assume that the image is tiled in all directions so that the mask always has image values to use.

SEPARABILITY   Note that the Fourier transform filter elements can be expressed as products:

$$\exp\left[2\pi i \left(\frac{xu}{M} + \frac{yv}{N}\right)\right] = \exp\left[2\pi i \frac{xu}{M}\right] \exp\left[2\pi i \frac{yv}{N}\right].$$

The first product value

$$\exp\left[2\pi i \frac{xu}{M}\right]$$

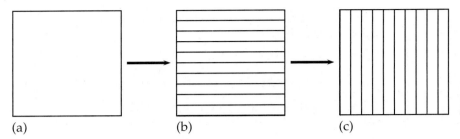

(a)   (b)   (c)

FIGURE 7.6 *Calculating a two-dimensional DFT. (a) Original image. (b) DFT of each row of (a). (c) DFT of each column of (b).*

depends only on x and u, and is independent of y and v. Conversely, the second product value

$$\exp\left[2\pi i \frac{yv}{N}\right]$$

depends only on y and v and is independent of x and u. This means that we can break down our formulas above to simpler formulas that work on single rows or columns:

$$F(u) = \sum_{x=0}^{M-1} f(x) \exp\left[-2\pi i \frac{xu}{M}\right] \qquad (7.6)$$

$$f(x) = \frac{1}{M} \sum_{u=0}^{M-1} F(u) \exp\left[2\pi i \frac{xu}{M}\right]. \qquad (7.7)$$

If we replace x and u with y and v, we obtain the corresponding formulas for the DFT of matrix columns. These are the same equations as Equations 7.2 and 7.3, except that here we are using functional notation for $f(x)$ and $F(u)$, rather than the subscript series notation.

The two-dimensional DFT can be calculated by using this property of separability. To obtain the two-dimensional DFT of a matrix, we first calculate the DFT of all the rows and then calculate the DFT of all the columns of the result, as shown in Figure 7.6. Since a product is independent of the order, we can equally well calculate a two-dimensional DFT by calculating the DFT of all the columns first, then calculating the DFT of all the rows of the result.

LINEARITY   An important property of the DFT is its linearity; the DFT of a sum is equal to the sum of the individual DFTs, and the same goes for scalar multiplication

$$\mathcal{F}(f + g) = \mathcal{F}(f) + \mathcal{F}(g)$$
$$\mathcal{F}(kf) = k\mathcal{F}(f),$$

where k is a scalar and f and g are matrices. This follows directly from the definition given in Equation (7.4).

This property is very useful in dealing with image degradation such as noise, which can be modeled as a sum

$$d = f + n,$$

where f is the original image, n is the noise, and d is the degraded image. Because

$$\mathcal{F}(d) = \mathcal{F}(f) + \mathcal{F}(n),$$

we may be able to remove or reduce n by modifying the transform. As we shall see, some noise appears on the DFT in a way that makes it particularly easy to remove.

THE CONVOLUTION THEOREM   This result provides one of the most powerful advantages of using the DFT. Suppose we wish to convolve an image M with a spatial filter S. Our method has been to place S over each pixel of M in turn, calculate the product of all corresponding gray values of M and elements of S, and add the results. The result is called the **digital convolution** of M and S and is denoted

$$M * S.$$

This method of convolution can be very slow, especially if S is large. The convolution theorem states that the result $M * S$ can be obtained by the following sequence of steps:

1. Pad S with zeroes so that it is the same size as M; denote this padded result by S'.
2. Form the DFTs of both M and S to obtain $\mathcal{F}(M)$ and $\mathcal{F}(S')$.
3. Form the element-by-element product of these two transforms:

   $$\mathcal{F}(M) \cdot \mathcal{F}(S').$$

4. Take the inverse transform of the result:

   $$\mathcal{F}^{-1}(\mathcal{F}(M) \cdot \mathcal{F}(S')).$$

Put simply, the convolution theorem states

$$M * S = \mathcal{F}^{-1}(\mathcal{F}(M) \cdot \mathcal{F}(S')),$$

or equivalently that

$$\mathcal{F}(M * S) = \mathcal{F}(M) \cdot \mathcal{F}(S').$$

Although this might seem like an unnecessarily clumsy and roundabout way of computing something as simple as a convolution, it can have enormous speed advantages if S is large.

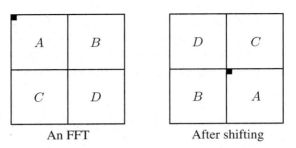

FIGURE 7.7 *Shifting a DFT.*

For example, suppose we wish to convolve a 512 × 512 image with a 32 × 32 filter. To do this directly would require $32^2 = 1,024$ multiplications for each pixel, of which there are 512 × 512 = 262,144. Thus, there will be a total of 1,024 × 262,144 = 268,435,456 multiplications needed. Now look at applying the DFT (using an FFT algorithm). Each row requires 4,608 multiplications according to Table 7.1; there are 512 rows, so a total of 4,608 × 512 = 2,359,296 multiplications are required. The same must be done again for the columns. Thus, to obtain the DFT of the image requires 4,718,592 multiplications. We need the same amount to obtain the DFT of the filter and for the inverse DFT. We also require 512 × 512 multiplications to perform the product of the two transforms.

Thus, the total number of multiplications needed to perform convolution using the DFT is

$$4,718,592 \times 3 + 262,144 = 14,417,920,$$

which is an enormous savings compared with the direct method.

THE DC COEFFICIENT   The value $F(0,0)$ of the DFT is called the **DC coefficient.** If we put $u = v = 0$ in the definition given in Equation (7.4), then

$$F(0,0) = \sum_{x=0}^{M-1}\sum_{y=0}^{N-1} f(x,y) \exp(0) = \sum_{x=0}^{M-1}\sum_{y=0}^{N-1} f(x,y).$$

That is, this term is equal to the sum of all terms in the original matrix.

SHIFTING   For purposes of display, it is convenient to have the DC coefficient in the center of the matrix. This will happen if all elements $f(x,y)$ in the matrix are multiplied by $(-1)^{x+y}$ before the transform. Figure 7.7 demonstrates how the matrix is shifted by this method. In each diagram the DC coefficient is the top left-hand element of submatrix A and is shown as a black square.

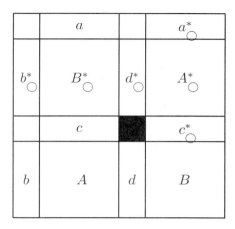

FIGURE 7.8 *Conjugate symmetry in the DFT.*

CONJUGATE SYMMETRY   An analysis of the Fourier transform definition leads to a symmetry property; if we make the substitutions $u = -u$ and $v = -v$ in Equation 7.4, then

$$\mathcal{F}(u,v) = \mathcal{F}^*(-u + pM, -v + qN)$$

for any integers p and q. This means that half of the transform is a mirror image of the conjugate of the other half. We can think of the top and bottom halves, or the left and right halves, being mirror images of the conjugates of each other.

Figure 7.8 demonstrates this symmetry in a shifted DFT. As with Figure 7.7, the black square shows the position of the DC coefficient. The symmetry means that its information is given in just half of a transform, and the other half is redundant.

DISPLAYING TRANSFORMS   Having obtained the Fourier transform $F(u,v)$ of an image $f(x,y)$, we would like to see what it looks like. Because the elements $F(u,v)$ are complex numbers, we can't view them directly, but we can view their magnitude $|F(u,v)|$. Since these will be numbers of type `double`, generally with large range, we have two approaches:

1. Find the maximum value m of $|F(u,v)|$ (this will be the DC coefficient), and use `imshow` to view $|F(u,v)|/m$.

2. Use `mat2gray` to view $|F(u,v)|$ directly.

One problem is that the DC coefficient is generally very much larger than all other values. This has the effect of showing a transform as a single white dot surrounded by black. One way of stretching out the values is to take the logarithm of $|F(u,v)|$ and to display

$$\log(1 + |F(u,v)|).$$

The display of the magnitude of a Fourier transform is called the **spectrum** of the transform. We will see some examples later.

7.6 Fourier Transforms in MATLAB

The relevant MATLAB functions for us are:

- fft, which takes the DFT of a vector,
- ifft, which takes the inverse DFT of a vector,
- fft2, which takes the DFT of a matrix,
- ifft2, which takes the inverse DFT of a matrix, and
- fftshift, which shifts a transform as shown in Figure 7.7.

We have seen the first two listed functions.

Before attacking a few images, let's take the Fourier transform of a few small matrices to get more of an idea what the DFT does.

EXAMPLE 7.6.1   Suppose we take a constant matrix $f(x, y) = 1$. Going back to the idea of a sum of corrugations, then no corrugations are required to form a constant. Thus, we would hope that the DFT consists of a DC coefficient and zeroes everywhere else. We will use the ones function, which produces an $n \times n$ matrix consisting of ones, where n is an input to the function.

```
>> a=ones(8);
>> fft2(a)
```

The result is indeed as we expected:

```
ans =
      64     0     0     0     0     0     0     0
       0     0     0     0     0     0     0     0
       0     0     0     0     0     0     0     0
       0     0     0     0     0     0     0     0
       0     0     0     0     0     0     0     0
       0     0     0     0     0     0     0     0
       0     0     0     0     0     0     0     0
       0     0     0     0     0     0     0     0
```

Note that the DC coefficient is indeed the sum of all the matrix values.

EXAMPLE 7.6.2   Now we'll take a matrix consisting of a single corrugation:

```
>> a = [100 200; 100 200];
>> a = repmat(a,4,4)

ans =
       100    200    100    200    100    200    100    200
       100    200    100    200    100    200    100    200
       100    200    100    200    100    200    100    200
       100    200    100    200    100    200    100    200
       100    200    100    200    100    200    100    200
       100    200    100    200    100    200    100    200
       100    200    100    200    100    200    100    200
       100    200    100    200    100    200    100    200

>> af = fft2(a)

ans =
      9600      0      0      0  -3200      0      0      0
         0      0      0      0      0      0      0      0
         0      0      0      0      0      0      0      0
         0      0      0      0      0      0      0      0
         0      0      0      0      0      0      0      0
         0      0      0      0      0      0      0      0
         0      0      0      0      0      0      0      0
         0      0      0      0      0      0      0      0
```

What we have here is really the sum of two matrices: a constant matrix, each element of which is 150, and a corrugation, which alternates −50 and 50 from left to right. The constant matrix alone would produce (as in Example 7.6.1) a DC coefficient of value 64 × 150 = 9,600; the corrugation is a single value. By linearity, the DFT will consist of just the two values.

EXAMPLE 7.6.3   We will take here a single-step edge:

```
>> a = [zeros(8,4) ones(8,4)]
a =
        0      0      0      0      1      1      1      1
        0      0      0      0      1      1      1      1
        0      0      0      0      1      1      1      1
        0      0      0      0      1      1      1      1
        0      0      0      0      1      1      1      1
        0      0      0      0      1      1      1      1
        0      0      0      0      1      1      1      1
        0      0      0      0      1      1      1      1
```

Now we shall perform the Fourier transform with a shift to place the DC coefficient in the center, and because it contains some complex values, for simplicity we will show just the rounded absolute values:

```
>> af=fftshift(fft2(a));
>> round(abs(af))

ans =
```

0	0	0	0	0	0	0	0
0	0	0	0	0	0	0	0
0	0	0	0	0	0	0	0
0	0	0	0	0	0	0	0
0	9	0	21	32	21	0	9
0	0	0	0	0	0	0	0
0	0	0	0	0	0	0	0
0	0	0	0	0	0	0	0

The DC coefficient is, of course, the sum of all values of a; the other values may be considered to be the coefficients of the necessary sine functions required to form an edge, as given in Equation (7.1). The mirroring of values about the DC coefficient is a consequence of the symmetry of the DFT.

7.7 Fourier Transforms of Images

We will create a few simple images, and see what the Fourier transform produces.

EXAMPLE 7.7.1   We will produce a simple image consisting of a single edge:

```
>> a=[zeros(256,128)  ones(256,128)];
```

(see Figure 7.10). Now we will take its DFT and shift it:

```
>> af=fftshift(fft2(a));
```

To view its spectrum, we have the choice of two commands:

1. ```afl=log(1+abs(af));
   imshow(afl/afl(129,129))```
   This works because after shifting, the DC coefficient is at position $x = 129, y = 129$. We stretch the transform using log and divide the

```
function fftshow(f,type)

% Usage:   FFTSHOW(F,TYPE)
%
% Displays the fft matrix F using imshow, where TYPE must be one of
% 'abs' or 'log'.   If TYPE='abs', then then abs(f) is displayed; if
% TYPE='log' then log(1+abs(f)) is displayed.   If TYPE is omitted, then
% 'log' is chosen as a default.
%
%   Example:
%      c=imread('cameraman.tif');
%      cf=fftshift(fft2(c));
%      fftshow(cf,'abs')
%

if nargin<2,
   type='log';
end

if (type=='log')
   fl = log(1+abs(f));
   fm = max(fl(:));
   imshow(im2uint8(fl/fm))
elseif (type=='abs')
   fa=abs(f);
   fm=max(fa(:));
   imshow(fa/fm)
else
   error('TYPE must be abs or log.');
end;
```

FIGURE 7.9 *A function to display a Fourier transform.*

result by the middle value to obtain a matrix of type `double` with values in the range 0.0–1.0. This can then be viewed directly with `imshow`.

2. `imshow(mat2gray(log(1+abs(af))))`
   The `mat2gray` function automatically scales a matrix for display as an image, as we have seen in Chapter 5.

It is, in fact, convenient to write a small function for viewing transforms. One such is shown in Figure 7.9. Then, for example,

```
>> fftshow(af,'log')
```

will show the logarithm of the absolute values of the transform and

```
>> fftshow(af,'abs')
```

will show the absolute values of the transform without any scaling.

FIGURE 7.10 *A single edge and its DFT.*

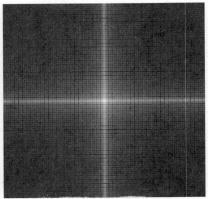

FIGURE 7.11 *A box and its DFT.*

The result is shown on the right in Figure 7.10. We observe immediately that the result is similar (although larger) to Example 7.6.3.

EXAMPLE 7.7.2   Now we'll create a box and its Fourier transform:

```
>> a=zeros(256,256);
>> a(78:178,78:178)=1;
>> imshow(a)
>> af=fftshift(fft2(a));
>> figure,fftshow(af,'abs')
```

The box is shown on the left in Figure 7.11, and its Fourier transform is shown on the right.

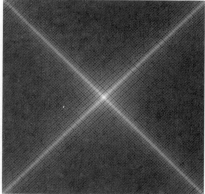

FIGURE 7.12 *A rotated box and its DFT.*

EXAMPLE 7.7.3   Now we will look at a box rotated 45°.

```
>> [x,y]=meshgrid(1:256,1:256);
>> b=(x+y<329)&(x+y>182)&(x-y>-67)&(x-y<73);
>> imshow(b)
>> bf=fftshift(fft2(b));
>> figure,fftshow(bf)
```

The results are shown in Figure 7.12. Note that the transform of the rotated box is the rotated transform of the original box.

EXAMPLE 7.7.4   We will create a small circle and then transform it:

```
>> [x,y]=meshgrid(-128:217,-128:127);
>> z=sqrt(x.^2+y.^2);
>> c=(z<15);
```

The result is shown on the left in Figure 7.13. Now we will create its Fourier transform and display it:

```
>> cf=fft2shift(fft2(z));
>> fftshow(cf,'log')
```

This is shown in Figure 7.13b. Note the ringing in the Fourier transform. This is an artifact associated with the sharp cutoff of the circle. As we have seen from both the edge and box images in the previous examples, an edge appears in the transform as a line of values at right angles to the edge. We may

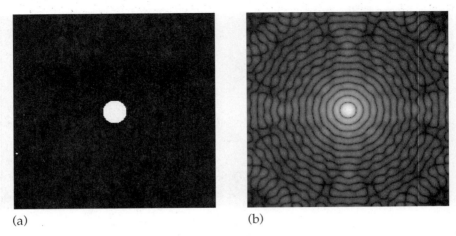

(a)   (b)

FIGURE 7.13 *(a) A circle and (b) its DFT.*

consider the values on the line as being the coefficients of the appropriate corrugation functions that sum to the edge. With the circle, we have lines of values radiating out from the circle; these values appear as circles in the transform.

A circle with a gentle cutoff, so that its edge appears blurred, will have a transform with no ringing. Such a circle can be made with the command (given z above):

```
b=1./(1+(z./15).^2);
```

This image appears as a blurred circle, and its transform is very similar—check them out!

7.8 Filtering in the Frequency Domain

We have seen in Section 7.5 that one of the reasons for the use of the Fourier transform in image processing is due to the convolution theorem: a spatial convolution can be performed by element-wise multiplication of the Fourier transform by a suitable filter matrix. In this section we will explore some filtering using this method.

7.8.1 Ideal Filtering

LOW-PASS FILTERING Suppose we have a Fourier transform matrix F shifted so that the DC coefficient is in the center. Because the low-frequency components are toward the center, we can perform low-pass filtering by multiplying the transform by a matrix in such a way that center values are

Mathworks

FIGURE 7.14 *The "cameraman" image and its DFT.*

maintained and values away from the center are either removed or minimized. One way to do this is to multiply by an **ideal low-pass matrix,** which
is a binary matrix m defined by:

$$m(x, y) = \begin{cases} 1 & \text{if } (x, y) \text{ is closer to the center than some value } D, \\ 0 & \text{if } (x, y) \text{ is further from the center than } D. \end{cases}$$

The circle c displayed in Figure 7.13 is just such a matrix, with $D = 15$. Then
the inverse Fourier transform of the element-wise product of F and m is the
result we require:

$$\mathcal{F}^{-1}(F \cdot m).$$

Let's see what happens if we apply this filter to an image. First we obtain an
image and its DFT.

```
>> cm=imread('cameraman.tif');
>> cf=fftshift(fft2(cm));
>> figure,fftshow(cf,'log')
```

The cameraman image and its DFT are shown in Figure 7.14. Now we can
perform a low-pass filter by multiplying the transform matrix by the circle matrix (recall that "dot asterisk" is the MATLAB syntax for element-wise
multiplication of two matrices):

```
>> cfl=cf.*c;
>> figure,fftshow(cfl,'log')
```

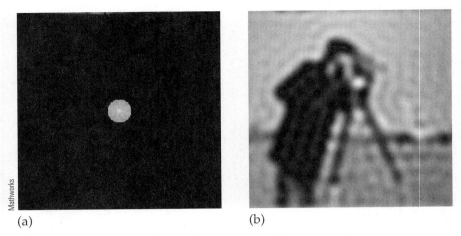

(a)   (b)

FIGURE 7.15 *Applying ideal low-pass filtering. (a) Ideal filtering on the DFT. (b) After inversion.*

This is shown in Figure 7.15(a). Now we can take the inverse transform and display the result:

```
>> cfli=ifft2(cfl);
>> figure,fftshow(cfli,'abs')
```

This is shown in Figure 7.15(b). Note that even though `cfli` is supposedly a matrix of real numbers, we are still using `fftshow` to display it. This is because the `fft2` and `fft2` functions, being numeric, will not produce mathematically perfect results, but rather very close numeric approximations. So using `fftshow` with the `'abs'` option rounds out any errors obtained during the transform and its inverse. Note the ringing around the edges in this image. This is a direct result of the sharp cutoff of the circle. The ringing as shown in Figure 7.13 is transferred to the image.

We would expect that the smaller the circle, the more blurred the image, and the larger the circle, the less blurred. Figure 7.16 demonstrates this, using cutoffs of 5 and 30. Notice that ringing is still present and clearly visible in Figure 7.16(b).

HIGH-PASS FILTERING Just as we can perform low-pass filtering by keeping the center values of the DFT and eliminating the others, so can high-pass filtering be performed by the opposite: eliminating center values and keeping the

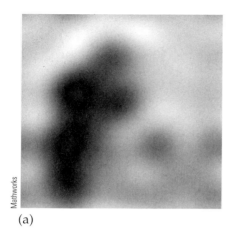

(a)   (b)

FIGURE 7.16 *Ideal low-pass filtering with different cutoffs. (a) Cutoff of 5. (b) Cutoff of 30.*

others. This can be done with a minor modification of the preceding method of low-pass filtering. First we create the circle

```
>> [x,y]=meshgrid(-128:127,-128:127);
>> z=sqrt(x.^2+y.^2);
>> c=(z>15);
```

and multiply it by the DFT of the image:

```
>> cfh=cf.*c;
>> figure,fftshow(cfh,'log')
```

This is shown in Figure 7.17(a). The inverse DFT can be easily produced and displayed:

```
>> cfhi=ifft2(cfh);
>> figure,fftshow(cfhi,'abs')
```

This is shown in Figure 7.17(b). As with low-pass filtering, the size of the circle influences the information available to the inverse DFT, hence the final result. Figure 7.18 shows some results of ideal high-pass filtering with different cutoffs. If the cutoff is large, then more information is removed from the transform, leaving only the highest frequencies. This can be observed in Figure 7.18(c and d); only the edges of the image remain. If we have a small cutoff, such as in Figure 7.18(a), we are removing only a small amount

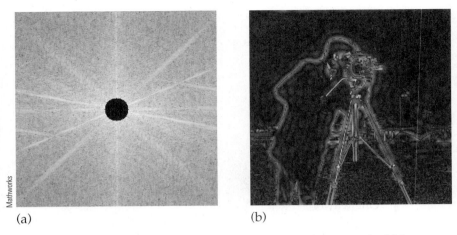

(a)   (b)

FIGURE 7.17 *Applying an ideal high-pass filter to an image. (a) The DFT after high-pass filtering. (b) The resulting image.*

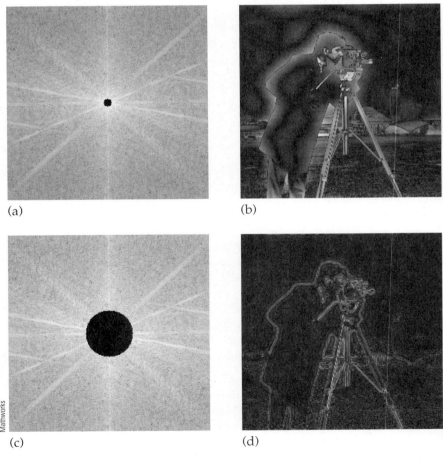

(a)   (b)

(c)   (d)

FIGURE 7.18 *Ideal high-pass filtering with different cutoffs. (a) Cutoff of 5. (b) The resulting image. (c) Cutoff of 30. (d) The resulting image.*

of the transform. We would thus expect that only the lowest frequencies of the image would be removed. This is indeed true, as seen in Figure 7.18(b). There is some grayscale detail in the final image, but large areas of low frequency are close to zero.

7.8.2 Butterworth Filtering

Ideal filtering simply cuts off the Fourier transform at some distance from the center. This cutoff is very easy to implement, as we have seen, but it has the disadvantage of introducing unwanted artifacts (ringing) into the result. One way of avoiding these artifacts is to use as a filter matrix a circle with a cutoff that is less sharp. A popular choice is to use **Butterworth filters.**

Before we describe these filters, we will look again at the ideal filters. Because these are radially symmetric about the center of the transform, they can be described simply in terms of their cross sections. That is, we can describe the filter as a function of the distance x from the center. For an ideal low-pass filter, this function can be expressed as

$$f(x) = \begin{cases} 1 & \text{if } x < D, \\ 0 & \text{if } x \geq D \end{cases}$$

where D is the cutoff radius. The ideal high-pass filters can be described similarly:

$$f(x) = \begin{cases} 1 & \text{if } x > D, \\ 0 & \text{if } x \leq D \end{cases}$$

These functions are illustrated in Figure 7.19. Butterworth filter functions are based on the following functions for low-pass filters,

$$f(x) = \frac{1}{1 + (x/D)^{2n}}$$

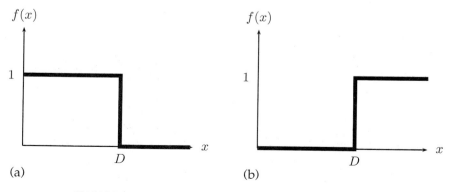

FIGURE 7.19 *Ideal filter functions. (a) Low pass. (b) High pass.*

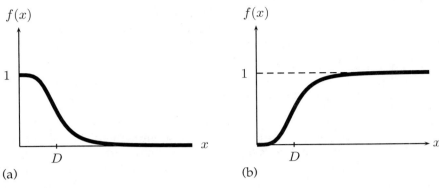

(a)   (b)

FIGURE 7.20 *Butterworth filter functions with n = 2. (a) Low pass. (b) High pass.*

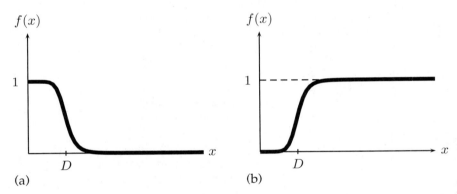

(a)   (b)

FIGURE 7.21 *Butterworth filter functions with n = 4. (a) Low pass. (b) High pass.*

and for high-pass filters,

$$f(x) = \frac{1}{1 + (D/x)^{2n}}$$

where in each case the parameter n is called the **order** of the filter. The size of n dictates the sharpness of the cutoff. These functions are illustrated in Figures 7.20 and 7.21.

It is easy to implement these functions in MATLAB; here are the commands to produce a Butterworth low-pass filter of size 256×256 with $D = 15$ and order $n = 2$:

```
>> [x,y]=meshgrid(-128:217,-128:127));
>> bl=1./(1+((x.^2+y.^2)/15).^2);
```

Since a Butterworth high-pass filter can be obtained by subtracting a low-pass filter from 1, we can write general MATLAB functions to

```
function out=lbutter(im,d,n)
% LBUTTER(IM,D,N) creates a low-pass Butterworth filter
% of the same size as image IM, with cutoff D, and order N
%
% Use:
%    x=imread('cameraman.tif');
%    l=lbutter(x,25,2);
%
height=size(im,1);
width=size(im,2);
[x,y]=meshgrid(-floor(width/2):floor((width-1)/2),-floor(height/2): ...
        floor((height-1)/2));
out=1./(1+(sqrt(2)-1)*((x.^2+y.^2)/d^2).^n);
```

FIGURE 7.22 *A function to generate a low-pass Butterworth filter.*

```
function out=hbutter(im,d,n)
% HBUTTER(IM,D,N) creates a high-pass Butterworth filter
% of the same size as image IM, with cutoff D, and order N
%
% Use:
%    x=imread('cameraman.tif');
%    l=hbutter(x,25,2);
%

out=1-lbutter(im,d,n);
```

FIGURE 7.23 *A function to generate a high-pass Butterworth filter.*

generate Butterworth filters of general sizes. These are shown in Figures 7.22 and 7.23.

So, to apply a Butterworth low-pass filter to the DFT of the cameraman image,

```
>> bl=lbutter(c,15,1);
>> cfbl=cf.*bl;
>> figure,fftshow(cfbl,'log')
```

and this is shown in Figure 7.24(a). Note that there is no sharp cutoff as seen in Figure 7.15 and that the outer parts of the transform are not equal to zero, although they are dimmed considerably. Performing the inverse transform and displaying it as we have done previously produces Figure 7.24(b). This is certainly a blurred image, but the ringing seen in Figure 7.15 is completely absent. Compare the transform after multiplying with a Butterworth filter [Figure 7.24(a)] with the original transform (Figure 7.14). The Butterworth filter causes an attenuation of values away from the center, even

(a)   (b)

FIGURE 7.24 *Butterworth low-pass filtering. (a) The DFT after Butterworth low-pass filtering. (b) The resulting image.*

if they don't become suddenly zero, as with the ideal low-pass filter in Figure 7.15.

We can apply a Butterworth high-pass filter similarly, first by creating the filter and applying it to the image transform,

```
>> bh=hbutter(cm,15,1);
>> cfbh=cf.*bh;
>> figure,fftshow(cfbh,'log')
```

and then inverting and displaying the result:

```
>> cfbhi=ifft2(cfbh);
>> figure,fftshow(cfbhi,'abs')
```

The images are shown in Figure 7.25.

7.8.3 Gaussian Filtering

We have been introduced to Gaussian filters in Chapter 5, and we saw that they could be used for low-pass filtering. However, we can also use Gaussian filters in the frequency domain. As with ideal and Butterworth filters, the implementation is very simple: create a Gaussian filter, multiply it by the image transform, and invert the result. Since Gaussian filters have the very nice mathematical property that a Fourier transform of a Gaussian is always a Gaussian, we should get exactly the same results as when using a linear Gaussian spatial filter.

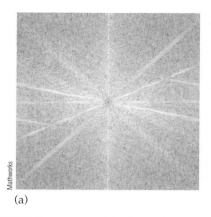
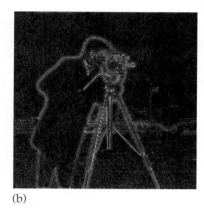

(a)   (b)

FIGURE 7.25 *Butterworth high-pass filtering. (a) The DFT after Butterworth high-pass filtering. (b) The resulting image.*

Gaussian filters may be considered to be the smoothest of all the filters we have discussed so far, with ideal filters the least smooth and Butterworth filters in the middle.

We can create Gaussian filters using the `fspecial` function and apply them to our transform.

```
>> g1=mat2gray(fspecial('gaussian',256,10));
>> cg1=cf.*g1;
>> fftshow(cg1,'log')
>> g2=mat2gray(fspecial('gaussian',256,30));
>> cg2=cf.*g2;
>> figure,fftshow(cg2,'log')
```

Note the use of the `mat2gray` function. The `fspecial` function on its own produces a low-pass Gaussian filter with a very small maximum:

```
>> g=fspecial('gaussian',256,10);
>> format long, max(g(:)), format

ans =

   0.00158757552679
```

This occurs because `fspecial` adjusts its output to always keep the volume under the Gaussian function 1. This means that a wider function, with a large standard deviation, will have a low maximum. Thus, we need to scale the result so that the central value will be 1, and `mat2gray` does that automatically.

The transforms are shown in Figure 7.26(a and c). In each case, the final parameter of the `fspecial` function is the standard deviation; it controls

(a)   (b)

(c)   (d)

Mathworks

FIGURE 7.26 *Applying a Gaussian low-pass filter in the frequency domain. (a)* $\sigma = 10$. *(b) Resulting image. (c)* $\sigma = 30$. *(d) Resulting image.*

the width of the filter. Clearly, the larger the standard deviation, the wider the function, and thus the greater amount of the transform is preserved.

The results of the transform on the original image can be produced using the usual sequence of commands:

```
>> cgi1=ifft2(cg1);
>> cgi2=ifft2(cg2);
>> fftshow(cgi1,'abs');
>> fftshow(cgi2,'abs');
```

The results are shown in Figure 7.26(b and d).

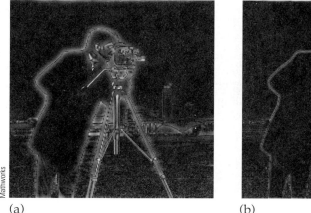 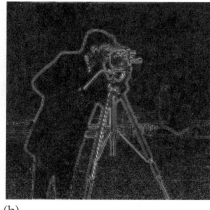

Mathworks

(a)   (b)

FIGURE 7.27 *Applying a Gaussian high-pass filter in the frequency domain. (a) Using* $\sigma = 10$. *(b) Using* $\sigma = 30$.

We can apply a high-pass Gaussian filter easily; we create a high-pass filter by subtracting a low-pass filter from 1.

```
>> h1=1-g1;
>> h2=1-g2;
>> ch1=cf.*h1;
>> ch2=cf.*h2;
>> ch1i=ifft2(ch1);
>> chi1=ifft2(ch1);
>> chi2=ifft2(ch2);
>> fftshow(chi1,'abs')
>> figure,fftshow(chi2,'abs')
```

The images are shown in Figure 7.27. As with ideal and Butterworth filters, the wider the high-pass filter, the more of the transform we are reducing and the less of the original image will appear in the result.

7.9 Homomorphic Filtering

If we have an image that suffers from variable illumination (dark in some sections, light in others), we may wish to enhance the contrast locally and, in particular, to enhance the dark regions. Such an image may be obtained if we are recording a scene with high-intensity range (say, an outdoor scene on a sunny day, which includes shadows) onto a medium with a smaller intensity range. The resulting image will contain very bright regions (those well illuminated). On the other hand, regions in shadow may appear very dark indeed.

In such a case histogram equalization won't be of much help, because the image already has high contrast. We need to reduce the intensity range and at the same time increase the local contrast. We first note that the intensity of an object in an image may be considered to be a combination of two factors: the amount of light falling on it and the amount of light reflected by the object. In fact, if $f(x,y)$ is the intensity of a pixel at position (x,y) in our image, we may write

$$f(x,y) = i(x,y)r(x,y),$$

where $i(x,y)$ is the **illumination** and $r(x,y)$ is the **reflectance.** These satisfy

$$0 < i(x,y) < \infty$$

and

$$0 < r(x,y) < 1.$$

There is no (theoretical) limit as to the amount of light that can fall on an object, but reflectance is strictly bounded.

To reduce the intensity range we need to reduce the illumination and to increase the local contrast we need to increase the reflectance. However, this means we need to separate $i(x,y)$ and $r(x,y)$. We can't do this directly, because the image is formed from their product. However, if we take the logarithm of the image

$$\log f(x,y) = \log i(x,y) + \log r(x,y),$$

we can then separate the logarithms of $i(x,y)$ and $r(x,y)$. The basis of homomorphic filtering is working with the logarithm of the image, rather than with the image directly. A schema for homomorphic filtering is given in Figure 7.28.

The exp in the second to the last box simply reverses the effect of the original logarithm. We assume that the logarithm of illumination will vary slowly, and the logarithm of reflectance will vary quickly so that the filtering processes given in Figure 7.28 will have the desired effects.

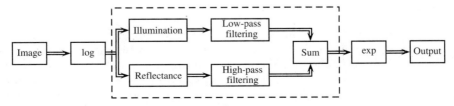

FIGURE 7.28 *A schema for homomorphic filtering.*

Clearly, this schema will be unworkable in practice: given a value $\log f(x,y)$, we can't determine the values of its summands $\log i(x,y)$ and $\log r(x,y)$. A simpler way is to replace the dashed box in Figure 7.28 with a high-boost filter of the Fourier transform. This gives the simpler schema shown in Figure 7.29.

A simple function to apply homomorphic filtering to an image (using a Butterworth high-boost filter) is given in Figure 7.30.

To see this filter in action, suppose we take an image of type `double` (so that its pixel values are between 0.0 and 1.0) and multiply it by a trigonometric function scaled to between 0.1 and 1. If, for example, we use $\sin x$, then the function

$$y = 0.5 + 0.4 \sin x$$

satisfies $0.1 \leq y \leq 1.0$. The result will be an image with varying illumination.

Suppose we take an image i of size 256×256. Then we can superimpose a sine function with:

```
>> r=[1:256]'*ones(1,256);
>> x=i.*(0.5+0.4*sin((r-32)/16));
```

The transformation `(r-32)/16` was chosen by trial and error to produce bands of suitable width and on such places as to obscure detail in our image.

FIGURE 7.29 *A simpler schema for homomorphic filtering.*

```
function res=homfilt(im,cutoff,order,lowgain,highgain)

% HOMFILT(IMAGE,FILTER) applies homomorphic filtering to the image IMAGE
% with the given parameters

u=im2uint8(im);

u(find(u==0))=1;
l=log(double(u));
ft=fftshift(fft2(l));
f=hb_butter(im,cutoff,order,lowgain,highgain);
b=f.*ft;
ib=abs(ifft2(b));
res=exp(ib);
```

FIGURE 7.30 *A function to apply homomorphic filtering.*

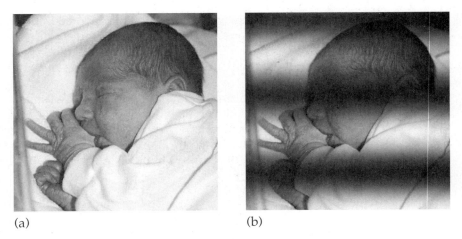

(a)   (b)

FIGURE 7.31 *Varying illumination across an image. (a) The "newborn" image. (b) Altering the illumination with a sine function.*

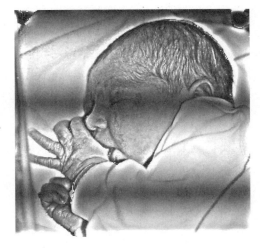

FIGURE 7.32 *The result of homomorphic filtering.*

If the original image is in Figure 7.31(a), then the result of this is shown in Figure 7.31(b).

If we apply homomorphic filtering with

```
>> xh=homfilt(x,10,2,0.5,2);
>> imshow(xh/16)
```

the result is shown in Figure 7.32.

(a)   (b)

FIGURE 7.33 *Applying homomorphic filtering to an image. (a) The arch. (b) After homomorphic filtering.*

The result shows that details originally unobservable in the original image—especially in regions of poor illumination—are now clear. Even though the dark bands have not been completely removed, they do not obscure underlying detail as they did originally.

Figure 7.33(a) shows a picture of a ruined archway. Due to the bright light through the archway, much of the details are too dark to be seen clearly. Given this image x, we can perform homomorphic filtering and display the result with:

```
>> ah=homfilt(a,128,2,0.5,2);
>> imshow(xh/14)
```

This is shown in Figure 7.33(b).

Note that the arch details are now much clearer, and it is even possible to make out the figure of a person standing at its base.

EXERCISES

1. By hand, compute the DFT of each of the following sequences:
   a. $[2, 3, 4, 5]$
   b. $[2, -3, 4, -5]$
   c. $[-9, -8, -7, -6]$
   d. $[-9, 8, -7, 6]$

   Compare your answers with those given by MATLAB's `fft` function.

2. For each of the transforms you computed in Question 1, compute the inverse transform by hand.

3. By hand, verify the convolution theorem for each of the following pairs of sequences:

   a. $[2, \quad 4, \quad 6, \quad 8]$ and $[-1, \quad 2 \quad -3, \quad 4]$

   b. $[4, \quad 5, \quad 6, \quad 7]$ and $[3, \quad 1 \quad 5, \quad -1]$

4. Using MATLAB, verify the convolution theorem for the following pairs of sequences:

   a. $[2, \quad -3, \quad 5, \quad 6, \quad -2, \quad -1, \quad 3, \quad 7]$ and $[-1, \quad 5, \quad 6, \quad 4, \quad -3, \quad -5, \quad 1, \quad 2]$

   b. $[7, \quad 6, \quad 5, \quad 4, \quad -4, \quad -5, \quad -6, \quad -7]$ and $[2, \quad 2, \quad -5, \quad -5, \quad 6, \quad 6, \quad -7, \quad -7]$

5. Consider the following matrix:

$$\begin{bmatrix} 4 & 5 & -9 & -5 \\ 3 & -7 & 1 & 2 \\ 6 & -1 & -6 & 1 \\ 3 & -1 & 7 & -5 \end{bmatrix}$$

Using MATLAB, calculate the DFT of each row. You can do this with the commands:

```
>> a=[4 5 -9 -5;3 -7 1 2;6 -1 -6 1;3 -1 7 -5];
>> a1=fft(a')'
```

(The fft function, applied to a matrix, produces the individual DFTs of all the columns. Here we transpose first, so that the rows become columns, then transpose back afterward.)

   a. Use similar commands to calculate the DFT of each column of a1.

   b. Compare the result with the output of the command fft2(a).

6. Perform similar calculations as in Question 5 with the matrices produced by the commands magic(4) and hilb(6).

7. a. How do you think filtering with an averaging filter will affect the output of a Fourier transform?

   b. Compare the DFTs of the cameraman image and of the image after filtering with a 5 × 5 averaging filter.

   c. Can you account for the result?

   d. What happens if the averaging filter increases in size?

8. What is the result of two DFTs performed in succession? Apply a DFT to an image, and then another DFT to the result. Can you account for what you see?

9. Open up the image `engineer.tif`:

```
>> en=imread('engineer.tif');
```

Experiment with applying the Fourier transform to this image and the following filters:

a. Ideal filters (both low and high pass)
b. Butterworth filters
c. Gaussian filters

What is the smallest radius of a low-pass ideal filter for which the face is still recognizable?

10. If you have access to a digital camera or a scanner, produce a digital image of the face of somebody you know and perform the same calculations as in Question 9.

CHAPTER EIGHT

IMAGE RESTORATION

8.1 Introduction

Image restoration concerns the removal or reduction of degradations that have occurred during the acquisition of the image. Such degradations may include noise, which are errors in the pixel values, or optical effects such as out-of-focus blurring or blurring due to camera motion. We will see that some restoration techniques can be performed very successfully using neighborhood operations, while others require the use of frequency domain processes. Image restoration remains one of the most important areas of image processing, but in this chapter the emphasis will be on the techniques for dealing with restoration, rather than with the degradations themselves, or the properties of electronic equipment that give rise to image degradation.

8.1.1 A Model of Image Degradation

In the spatial domain, we might have an image $f(x, y)$ and a spatial filter $h(x, y)$ for which convolution with the image results in some form of degradation. For example, if $h(x, y)$ consists of a single line of ones, the result of the convolution will be a motion blur in the direction of the line. Thus we may write

$$g(x, y) = f(x, y) * h(x, y)$$

for the degraded image, where the symbol $*$ represents convolution. However, this is not all. We must consider noise, which can be modeled as an additive function to the convolution. Thus, if $n(x, y)$ represents random errors that may occur, we have as our degraded image:

$$g(x, y) = f(x, y) * h(x, y) + n(x, y).$$

We can perform the same operations in the frequency domain, where convolution is replaced by multiplication and addition remains as addition because of the linearity of the Fourier transform. Thus,

$$G(i,j) = F(i,j)H(i,j) + N(i,j)$$

represents a general image degradation, where, of course, F, H, and N are the Fourier transforms of f, h, and n, respectively.

If we knew the values of H and N, we could recover F by writing the above equation as

$$F(i,j) = (G(i,j) - N(i,j))/H(i,j).$$

However, as we shall see, this approach may not be practical. Even though we may have some statistical information about the noise, we will not know the value of $n(x,y)$ or $N(i,j)$ for all, or even any, values. As well, dividing by $H(i,j)$ will cause difficulties if there are values that are close to, or equal to, zero.

8.2 Noise

We may define **noise** to be any degradation in the image signal caused by external disturbance. If an image is being sent electronically from one place to another, via satellite or wireless transmission or through networked cables, we may expect errors to occur in the image signal. These errors will appear on the image output in different ways depending on the type of disturbance in the signal. Usually we know what type of errors to expect and the type of noise on the image; hence, we can choose the most appropriate method for reducing the effects. Cleaning an image corrupted by noise is thus an important area of image restoration.

In this chapter we will investigate some of the standard noise forms and the different methods of eliminating or reducing their effects on the image.

We will look at four different noise types, and how they appear on an image.

8.2.1 Salt and Pepper Noise

Also called impulse noise, shot noise, or binary noise, salt and pepper degradation can be caused by sharp, sudden disturbances in the image signal; its appearance is randomly scattered white or black (or both) pixels over the image.

To demonstrate its appearance, we will first generate a grayscale image, starting with a color image:

```
>> tw=imread('twins.tif');
>> t=rgb2gray(tw);
```

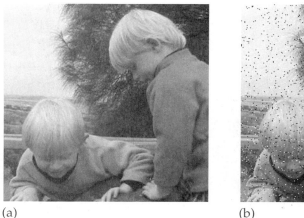

(a)   (b)

FIGURE 8.1 *Noise on an image. (a) Original image. (b) With added salt and pepper noise.*

To add noise, we use the MATLAB function `imnoise`, which takes a number of different parameters. To add salt and pepper noise:

```
>> t_sp=imnoise(t,'salt & pepper');
```

The amount of noise added defaults to 10%; to add more or less noise we include an optional parameter, being a value between 0 and 1 indicating the fraction of pixels to be corrupted. Thus, for example,

```
>> imnoise(t,'salt & pepper',0.2);
```

would produce an image with 20% of its pixels corrupted by salt and pepper noise.

The twins image is shown in Figure 8.1(a) and the image with noise is shown in Figure 8.1(b).

8.2.2 Gaussian Noise

Gaussian noise is an idealized form of **white noise,** which is caused by random fluctuations in the signal. We can observe white noise by watching a television slightly mistuned to a particular channel. Gaussian noise is white noise that is normally distributed. If the image is represented as I, and the Gaussian noise by N, then we can model a noisy image by simply adding the two:

$$I + N.$$

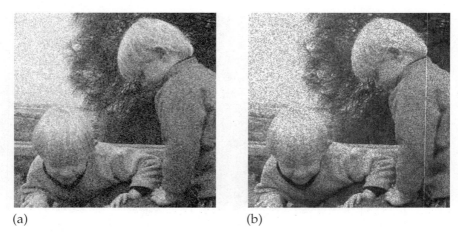

(a)   (b)

FIGURE 8.2 *The twins image corrupted by Gaussian and speckle noise. (a) Gaussian noise. (b) Speckle noise.*

Here we may assume that I is a matrix whose elements are the pixel values of our image, and N is a matrix whose elements are normally distributed. It can be shown that this is an appropriate model for noise. The effect can again be demonstrated by the imnoise function:

```
>> t_ga=imnoise(t,'gaussian');
```

As with salt and pepper noise, the "gaussian" parameter also can take optional values, giving the mean and variance of the noise. The default values are 0 and 0.01, and the result is shown in Figure 8.2(a).

8.2.3 Speckle Noise

Whereas Gaussian noise can be modeled by random values added to an image; **speckle** noise (or more simply just speckle) can be modeled by random values multiplied by pixel values; hence, it is also called **multiplicative noise.** Speckle noise is a major problem in some radar applications. As above, imnoise can produce speckle:

```
>> t_spk=imnoise(t,'speckle');
```

The result is shown in Figure 8.2(b). In MATLAB, speckle noise is implemented as

$$I(1 + N)$$

FIGURE 8.3 *The twins image corrupted by periodic noise.*

where I is the image matrix, and N consists of normally distributed values with mean 0. An optional parameter gives the variance of N; its default value is 0.04.

Although Gaussian noise and speckle noise appear superficially similar, they are formed by two totally different methods and thus require different approaches for their removal.

8.2.4 Periodic Noise

If the image signal is subject to a periodic, rather than a random disturbance, we might obtain an image corrupted by **periodic noise.** The effect is of bars over the image. The function `imnoise` does not have a periodic option, but it is quite easy to create our own by adding a periodic matrix (using a trigonometric function), to our image:

```
>> s=size(t);
>> [x,y]=meshgrid(1:s(1),1:s(2));
>> p=sin(x/3+y/5)+1;
>> t_pn=(im2double(t)+p/2)/2;
```

and the resulting image is shown in Figure 8.3.

Salt and pepper noise, Gaussian noise, and speckle noise can all be cleaned by using spatial filtering techniques. Periodic noise, however, requires the use of frequency domain filtering. This is because whereas the other forms of noise can be modeled as local degradations, periodic noise is a global effect.

8.3 Cleaning Salt and Pepper Noise

8.3.1 Low-Pass Filtering

Given that pixels corrupted by salt and pepper noise are high-frequency components of an image, we should expect a low-pass filter should reduce them. We might try filtering with an average filter:

```
>> a3=fspecial('average');
>> t_sp_a3=filter2(a3,t_sp);
```

The result is shown in Figure 8.4(a). Notice, however, that the noise is not so much removed as "smeared" over the image; the result is not noticeably better than the noisy image. The effect is even more pronounced if we use a larger averaging filter:

```
>> a7=fspecial('average',[7,7]);
>> t_sp_a7=filter2(a7,t_sp);
```

The result is shown in Figure 8.4(b).

8.3.2 Median Filtering

Median filtering seems almost tailor-made for removal of salt and pepper noise. Recall that the median of a set is the middle value when values are sorted. If there are an even number of values, the median is the mean of the

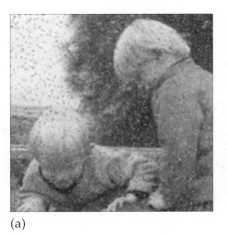
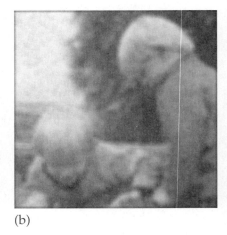

(a)   (b)

FIGURE 8.4 *Attempting to clean salt and pepper noise with average filtering. (a) 3×3 averaging. (b) 7×7 averaging.*

middle two. A median filter is an example of a nonlinear spatial filter; using a 3 × 3 mask, the output value is the median of the values in the mask. For example:

50	65	52
63	255	58
61	60	57

$\longrightarrow$ 50 52 57 58 $\boxed{60}$ 61 63 65 255 $\longrightarrow$ 60

The operation of obtaining the median means that very large or very small values—noisy values—will end up at the top or bottom of the sorted list. Thus, the median will, in general, replace a noisy value with one closer to its surroundings.

In MATLAB, median filtering is implemented by the medfilt2 function:

```
>> t_sp_m3=medfilt2(t_sp);
```

and the result is shown in Figure 8.5. The result is a vast improvement on using averaging filters. As with most functions, medfilt2 takes an optional parameter; in this case a 2 element vector giving the size of the mask to be used.

FIGURE 8.5 *Cleaning salt and pepper noise with a median filter.*

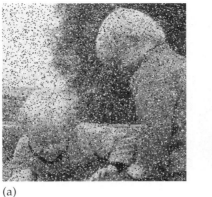

(a)   (b)

FIGURE 8.6 *Using a* 3×3 *median filter on more noise. (a) 20% salt and pepper noise. (b) After median fitering.*

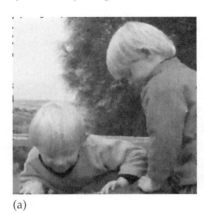
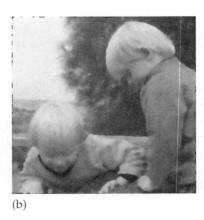

(a)   (b)

FIGURE 8.7 *Cleaning 20% salt and pepper noise with median filtering. (a) Using* `medfilt2` *twice. (b) Using a* 5×5 *median filter.*

If we corrupt more pixels with noise:

```
>> t_sp2=imnoise(t,'salt & pepper',0.2);
```

then `medfilt2` still does a remarkably good job, as shown in Figure 8.6. To remove noise completely, we can either try a second application of the 3×3 median filter, the result of which is shown in Figure 8.7(a), or try a 5×5 median filter on the original noisy image:

```
>> t_sp2_m5=medfilt2(t_sp2,[5,5]);
```

the result of which is shown in Figure 8.7(b).

8.3.3 Rank-Order Filtering

Median filtering is a special case of a more general process called **rank-order filtering.** Rather than take the median of a set, we order the set and take the nth value for some predetermined value of n. Thus, median filtering using a 3×3 mask is equivalent to rank-order filtering with $n = 5$. Similarly, median filtering using a 5×5 mask is equivalent to rank-order filtering with $n = 13$. MATLAB implements rank-order filtering with the `ordfilt2` function; in fact, the procedure for `medfilt2` is really just a wrapper for a procedure that calls `ordfilt2`. There is only one reason for using rank-order filtering instead of median filtering, and that is that it allows us to choose the median of nonrectangular masks. For example, if we decided to use as a mask a 3×3 cross shape:

then the median would be the third of these values when sorted. The command to do this is:

```
>> ordfilt2(t_sp,3,[0 1 0;1 1 1;0 1 0]);
```

In general, the second argument of `ordfilt2` gives the value of the ordered set to take, and the third element gives the **domain;** the nonzero values of which specify the mask. If we wish to use a cross with size and width 5 (so containing nine elements), we can use:

```
>> ordfilt2(t_sp,5,[0 0 1 0 0;0 0 1 0 0;1 1 1 1 1;0 0 1 0 0;0 0 1 0 0])
```

8.3.4 An Outlier Method

Applying the median filter can in general be a slow operation: each pixel requires the sorting of at least nine values.[1] To overcome this difficulty, Pratt [26] has proposed the use of cleaning salt and pepper noise by treating noisy pixels as **outliers,** that is, pixels whose gray values are significantly

---

[1] In fact, this is not the case with MATLAB, which uses a highly optimized method. Nonetheless, we introduce a different method to show that there are other ways of cleaning salt and pepper noise.

```
function res=outlier(im,d)
% OUTLIER(IMAGE,D) removes salt and pepper noise using an outlier method.
% This is done by using the following algorithm:
%
% For each pixel in the image, if the difference between its gray value
% and the average of its eight neighbors is greater than D, it is
% classified as noisy, and its grey value is changed to that of the
% average of its neighbors.
%
% IMAGE can be of type UINT8 or DOUBLE; the output is of type
% UINT8.    The threshold value D must be chosen to be between 0 and 1.

f=[0.125 0.125 0.125; 0.125 0 0.125; 0.125 0.125 0.125];
imd=im2double(im);
imf=filter2(f,imd);
r=abs(imd-imf)-d>0;
res=im2uint8(r.*imf+(1-r).*imd);
```

FIGURE 8.8 *A* MATLAB *function for cleaning salt and pepper noise using an outlier method.*

different from those of their neighbors. This leads to the following approach for noise cleaning:

1. Choose a threshold value D.
2. For a given pixel, compare its value p with the mean m of the values of its eight neighbors.
3. If $|p - m| > D$, then classify the pixel as noisy, otherwise not.
4. If the pixel is noisy, replace its value with m; otherwise leave its value unchanged.

There is no MATLAB function for doing this, but it is very easy to write one. First, we can calculate the average of a pixel's eight neighbors by convolving with the linear filter

$$\frac{1}{8} \begin{bmatrix} 1 & 1 & 1 \\ 1 & 0 & 1 \\ 1 & 1 & 1 \end{bmatrix} = \begin{bmatrix} 0.125 & 0.125 & 0.125 \\ 0.125 & 0 & 0.125 \\ 0.125 & 0.125 & 0.125 \end{bmatrix}.$$

We can then produce a matrix r consisting of 1s at only those places where the difference of the original and the filter are greater than D, that is, where pixels are noisy. $1 - r$ will then consist of 1s at only those places where pixels are not noisy. Multiplying r by the filter replaces noisy values with averages; multiplying $1 - r$ with original values gives the rest of the output.

A MATLAB function for implementing this is shown in Figure 8.8. An immediate problem with the outlier method is that it is not completely automatic—the threshold D must be chosen. An appropriate way to use the outlier method is to apply it, using several different thresholds, and choose the value that provides the best results. Suppose we attempt to use the outlier method to clean the noise from Figure 8.1(b), that is, the twins image with 10% salt and pepper noise. Choosing $D = 0.2$ gives the image in

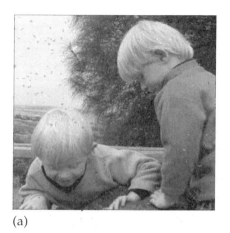
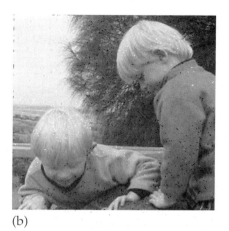

(a)   (b)

FIGURE 8.9 *Applying the outlier method to 10% salt and pepper noise. (a) D = 0.2.
(b) D = 0.4.*

Figure 8.9(a). This is not as good a result as using a median filter: the effect of the noise has been lessened, but there are still noise artifacts over the image. In this case we have chosen a threshold that is too small. If we choose $D = 0.4$, we obtain the image in Figure 8.9(b), which still has some noise artifacts, although in different places. We can see that a lower value of D tends to remove noise from dark areas, and a higher value of D tends to remove noise from light areas. A midway value, about $D = 0.3$, does in fact produce an acceptable result, although one not quite as good as median filtering.

Clearly using an appropriate value of D is essential for cleaning salt and pepper noise by this method. If D is too small, then too many non-noisy pixels will be classified as noisy and their values changed to the average of their neighbors. This will result in a blurring effect, similar to that obtained by using an averaging filter. If D is chosen to be too large, then not enough noisy pixels will be classified as noisy, and there will be little change in the output.

The outlier method is not particularly suitable for cleaning large amounts of noise. For such situations the median filter is preferred. The outlier method may thus be considered to be a "quick and dirty" method for cleaning salt and pepper noise when the median filter proves too slow. A further method for cleaning salt and pepper noise will be discussed in Chapter 10.

8.4 Cleaning Gaussian Noise

8.4.1 Image Averaging

It may sometimes happen that instead of just one image corrupted with Gaussian noise, we have many different copies of it. An example is satellite imaging; if a satellite passes over the same spot many times, we will obtain many different images of the same place. Another example is in microscopy: we might take many different images of the same object. In such a case a very simple approach to cleaning Gaussian noise is to simply take the average—the mean—of all the images.

To see why this works, suppose we have 100 copies of our image, each with noise; then the ith noisy image will be:

$$M + N_i$$

where M is the matrix of original values, and N_i is a matrix of normally distributed random values with mean 0. We can find the mean M' of these images by the usual add and divide method:

$$M' = \frac{1}{100} \sum_{i=1}^{100} (M + N_i)$$

$$= \frac{1}{100} \sum_{i=1}^{100} M + \frac{1}{100} \sum_{i=1}^{100} N_i$$

$$= M + \frac{1}{100} \sum_{i=1}^{100} N_i.$$

Because N_i is normally distributed with mean 0, it can be readily shown that the mean of all the N_i's will be close to zero—the greater the number of N_i's; the closer to zero. Thus,

$$M' \approx M,$$

and the approximation is closer for larger number of images $M + N_i$.

We can demonstrate this with the twins image. We first need to create different versions with Gaussian noise and then take the average of them. We will create 10 versions. One way to do this is to create an empty three-dimensional array of depth 10 and fill each level with a noisy image:

```
>> s=size(t);
>> t_ga10=zeros(s(1),s(2),10);
>> for i=1:10 t_ga10(:,:,i)=imnoise(t,'gaussian'); end
```

Note here that the gaussian option of imnoise calls the random number generator randn, which creates normally distributed random numbers. Each time randn is called, it creates a different sequence of numbers. Thus, we may be sure that all levels in our three-dimensional array do indeed contain different images. Now we can take the average:

```
>> t_ga10_av=mean(t_ga10,3);
```

(a)   (b)

FIGURE 8.10 *Image averaging to remove Gaussian noise. (a) 10 images. (b) 100 images.*

The optional parameter 3 here indicates that we are taking the mean along the third dimension of our array. The result is shown in Figure 8.10(a). This is not quite clear, but is a vast improvement on the noisy image of Figure 8.2(a). An even better result is obtained by taking the average of 100 images; this can be done by replacing 10 with 100 in the commands above. The result is shown in Figure 8.10(b). Note that this method works only if the Gaussian noise has mean 0.

8.4.2 Average Filtering

If the Gaussian noise has mean 0, then we would expect that an average filter would average the noise to zero. The larger the size of the filter mask, the closer to zero. Unfortunately, averaging tends to blur an image, as we have seen in Chapter 5. However, if we are prepared to trade off blurring for noise reduction, then we can reduce noise significantly by this method.

Suppose we take the 3 × 3 and 5 × 5 averaging filters and apply them to the noisy image t_ga.

```
>> a3=fspecial('average');
>> a5=fspecial('average',[5,5]);
>> tg3=filter2(a3,t_ga);
>> tg5=filter2(a5,t_ga);
```

The results are shown in Figure 8.11. The results are not really particularly pleasing. Although there has been some noise reduction, the "smeary" nature of the resulting images is unattractive.

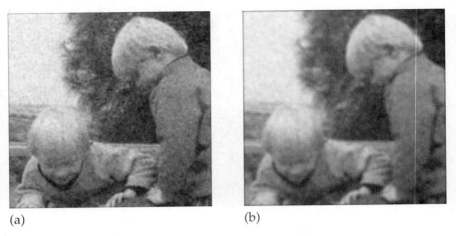

(a)   (b)

FIGURE 8.11 *Using averaging filtering to remove Gaussian noise. (a) 4×3 averaging.*
(b) 5×5 averaging.

8.4.3 Adaptive Filtering

Adaptive filters are a class of filters that change their characteristics according to the values of the grayscales under the mask; they may act more like median filters, or more like average filters, depending on their position within the image. Such a filter can be used to clean Gaussian noise by using local statistical properties of the values under the mask.

One such filter is the **minimum mean-square error filter.** This is a nonlinear spatial filter, and as with all spatial filters, it is implemented by applying a function to the gray values under the mask.

Since we are dealing with additive noise, our noisy image M' can be written as

$$M' = M + N,$$

where M is the original correct image and N is the noise, which we assume to be normally distributed with mean 0. However, within our mask, the mean may not be zero. Suppose the mean is m_f and the variance in the mask is σ_f^2. Suppose also that the variance of the noise over the entire image is known to be σ_g^2. Then the output value can be calculated as

$$m_f + \frac{\sigma_f^2}{\sigma_f^2 + \sigma_g^2}(g - m_f),$$

where g is the current value of the pixel in the noisy image. Note that if the local variance σ_f^2 is high, then the fraction will be close to 1, and the output close to the original image value g. This is appropriate, because high-variance implies high detail such as edges, which should be preserved.

Conversely, if the local variance is low, such as in a background area of the image, the fraction is close to zero, and the value returned is close to the mean value m_f. See Lim [22] for details.

Another version of this filter [37] has output defined by

$$g - \frac{\sigma_g^2}{\sigma_f^2}(g - m_f),$$

and again the filter returns a value close to either g or m_f depending on whether the local variance is high or low.

In practice, m_f can be calculated by simply taking the mean of all gray values under the mask and σ_f^2 by calculating the variance of all gray values under the mask. The value σ_g^2 may not necessarily be known, so a slight variant of the first filter may be used:

$$m_f + \frac{\max\{0, \sigma_f^2 - n\}}{\max\{\sigma_f^2, n\}}(g - m_f),$$

where n is the computed noise variance and is calculated by taking the mean of all values of σ_f^2 over the entire image. This particular filter is implemented in MATLAB with the function `wiener2`. The name reflects the fact that this filter attempts to minimize the square of the difference between the input and output images; such filters are in general known as **Wiener filters.** However, Wiener filters are more usually applied in the frequency domain; see Section 8.7.

Suppose we take the noisy image shown in Figure 8.2(a) and attempt to clean this image with adaptive filtering. We will use the `wiener2` function, which can take an optional parameter indicating the size of the mask to be used. The default size is 3×3. We will create four images:

```
>> t1=wiener2(t_ga);
>> t2=wiener2(t_ga,[5,5]);
>> t3=wiener2(t_ga,[7,7]);
>> t4=wiener2(t_ga,[9,9]);
```

These are shown in Figure 8.12. Being a low-pass filter, adaptive filtering tends to blur edges and high-frequency components of the image. However, it does a far better job than using a low-pass blurring filter.

We can achieve very good results for noise where the variance is not as high as that in our current image.

```
>> t2=imnoise(t,'gaussian',0,0.005);
>> imshow(t2)
>> t2w=wiener2(t2,[7,7]);
>> figure,imshow(t2w)
```

(a)   (b)

(c)   (d)

FIGURE 8.12 *Examples of adaptive filtering to remove Gaussian noise. (a) 3 × 3 filtering. (b) 5 × 5 filtering. (c) 7 × 7 filtering. (d) 9 × 9 filtering.*

The image and its appearance after adaptive filtering is shown in Figure 8.13. The result is a great improvement over the original noisy image. Notice in each case that there may be some blurring of the background, but the edges are preserved well, as predicted by our analysis of the adaptive filter formulas above.

8.5 Removal of Periodic Noise

Periodic noise may occur if the imaging equipment (the acquisition or networking hardware) is subject to electronic disturbance of a repeating nature, such as may be caused by an electric motor. We can easily create periodic noise by overlaying an image with a trigonometric function:

FIGURE 8.13 *Using adaptive filtering to remove Gaussian noise with low variance.*

```
>> [x,y]=meshgrid(1:256,1:256);
>> p=1+sin(x+y/1.5);
>> tp=(double(t)/128+p)/4;
```

where cm is the cameraman image from previous sections. The second line simply creates a sine function and adjusts its output to be in the range 0–2. The last line first adjusts the cameraman image to be in the same range, adds the sine function to it, and divides by 4 to produce a matrix of type double with all elements in the range 0.0–1.0. This can be viewed directly with imshow, and it is shown in Figure 8.14(a). We can produce its shifted DFT, and this is shown in Figure 8.14(b). The extra two spikes away from the center correspond to the noise just added. In general, the tighter the period of the noise, the further from the center the two spikes will be. This is because a small period corresponds to a high frequency (large change over a small distance) and is therefore further away from the center of the shifted transform.

We will now remove these extra spikes and invert the result. If we put pixval on and move around the image, we find that the spikes have row and column values of (156, 170) and (102, 88). These have the same distance from the center: 49.0918. We can check this by:

```
>> z=sqrt((x-129).^2+(y-129).^2);
>> z(156,170)
>> z(102,88)
```

There are two methods we can use to eliminate the spikes.

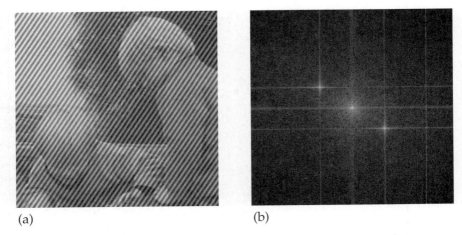

(a)   (b)

FIGURE 8.14 *The twins image (a) with periodic noise, and (b) its transform.*

BAND REJECT FILTERING We create a filter consisting of 1s with a ring of 0s, the 0s lying at a radius of 49 from the center:

```
>> br=(z < 47 | z > 51);
```

where z is the matrix consisting of distances from the origin. This particular ring will have a thickness large enough to cover the spikes. Then as before, we multiply this by the transform:

```
>> tbr=tf.*br;
```

This is shown in Figure 8.15(a). The result is that the spikes have been blocked out by this filter. Taking the inverse transform produces the image shown in Figure 8.15(b). Note that not all the noise has gone, but a significant amount has, especially in the center of the image.

NOTCH FILTERING With a notch filter we simply make the rows and columns of the spikes 0:

```
>> tf(156,:)=0;
>> tf(102,:)=0;
>> tf(:,170)=0;
>> tf(:,88)=0;
```

The result is shown in Figure 8.16(a). The image after inversion is shown in Figure 8.16(b). As before, much of the noise in the center has been removed.

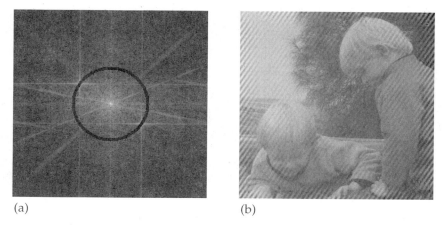

(a)   (b)

FIGURE 8.15 *Removing periodic noise with a band-reject filter. (a) A band-reject filter. (b) After inversion.*

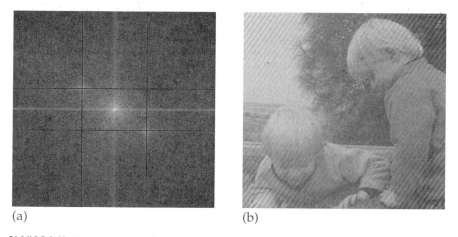

(a)   (b)

FIGURE 8.16 *Removing periodic noise with a notch filter. (a) A notch filter. (b) After inversion.*

Making more rows and columns of the transform 0 would result in a larger reduction of noise.

8.6 Inverse Filtering

We have seen that we can perform filtering in the Fourier domain by multiplying the DFT of an image by the DFT of a filter, which is a direct use of the convolution theorem. We thus have

$$Y(i,j) = X(i,j)F(i,j),$$

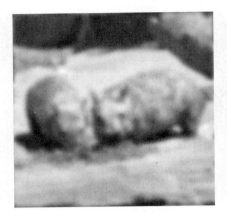

FIGURE 8.17 *An attempt at inverse filtering.*

where X is the DFT of the image, F is the DFT of the filter, and Y is the DFT of the result. If we are given Y and F, then we should be able to recover the DFT of the original image X simply by dividing by F:

$$X(i,j) = \frac{Y(i,j)}{F(i,j)}. \tag{8.1}$$

Suppose, for example, we take the wombats image `wombats.tif` and blur it using a low-pass Butterworth filter:

```
>> w=imread('wombats.tif');
>> wf=fftshift(fft2(w));
>> b=lbutter(w,15,2);
>> wb=wf.*b;
>> wba=abs(ifft2(wb));
>> wba=uint8(255*mat2gray(wba));
>> imshow(wba)
```

The result is shown on the left in Figure 8.17. We can attempt to recover the original image by dividing by the filter:

```
>> w1=fftshift(fft2(wba))./b;
>> w1a=abs(ifft2(w1));
>> imshow(mat2gray(w1a))
```

The result is shown on the right in Figure 8.17. This is no improvement! The trouble is that some elements of the Butterworth matrix are very small, so dividing produces very large values that dominate the output. We can deal with this problem in two ways:

1. We can apply a low-pass filter L to the division:

$$X(i,j) = \frac{Y(i,j)}{F(i,j)} L(i,j).$$

This should eliminate very low (or zero) values.

2. We can use constrained division, where we choose a threshold value d, and if $|F(i,j)| < d$, we don't perform a division, but just keep our original value. Thus:

$$X(i,j) = \begin{cases} \dfrac{Y(i,j)}{F(i,j)} & \text{if } |F(i,j)| \geq d \\[2ex] Y(i,j) & \text{if } |F(i,j)| < d. \end{cases}$$

We can apply the first method by multiplying a Butterworth low-pass filter to the matrix `c1` above:

```
>> wbf=fftshift(fft2(wba));
>> w1=(wbf./b).*lbutter(w,40,10);
>> w1a=abs(ifft2(w1));
>> imshow(mat2gray(w1a))
```

Figure 8.18 shows the results obtained by using a different cutoff radius of the Butterworth filter each time: Figure 8.18(a) uses 40 (as in the MATLAB commands just given); Figure 8.18(b) uses 60; Figure 8.18(c) uses 80, and Figure 8.18(d) uses 100. It seems that using a low-pass filter with a cutoff of approximately 60 will yield the best results. After we use larger cutoffs, the result degenerates.

We can try the second method. To implement it we simply make all values of the filter that are too small equal to 1:

```
>> d=0.01;
>> b=lbutter(w,15,2);b(find(b<d))=1;
>> w1=fftshift(fft2(wba))./b;
>> w1a=abs(ifft2(w1));
>> imshow(mat2gray(w1a))
```

Figure 8.19 shows the results obtained by using a different cutoff radius of the Butterworth filter each time: Figure 8.19(a) uses $d = 0.01$ (as in the MATLAB commands just given); Figure 8.19(b) uses $d = 0.005$; Figure 8.19(c) uses $d = 0.002$, and Figure 8.19(d) uses $d = 0.001$. It seems that using a threshold d in the range $0.002 \leq d \leq 0.005$ produces reasonable results.

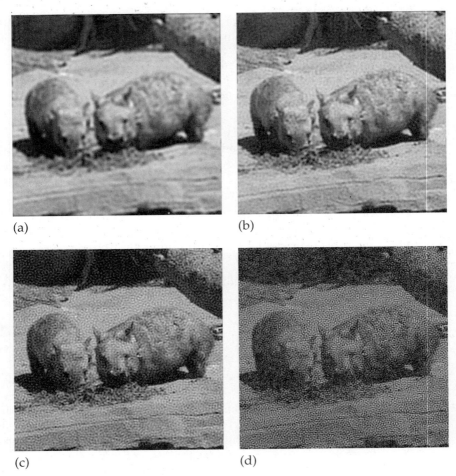

(a)   (b)

(c)   (d)

FIGURE 8.18 *Inverse filtering using low-pass filtering to eliminate zeros.*

8.6.1 Motion Deblurring

We can consider the removal of blur caused by motion to be a special case of inverse filtering. Suppose we take an image and blur it by a small amount.

```
>> bc=imread('board.tif');
>> bg=im2uint8(rgb2gray(bc));
>> b=bg(100:355,50:305);
>> imshow(b)
```

These commands simply take the color image of a circuit board (the image board.tif), make a grayscale version of data type uint8, and pick out a

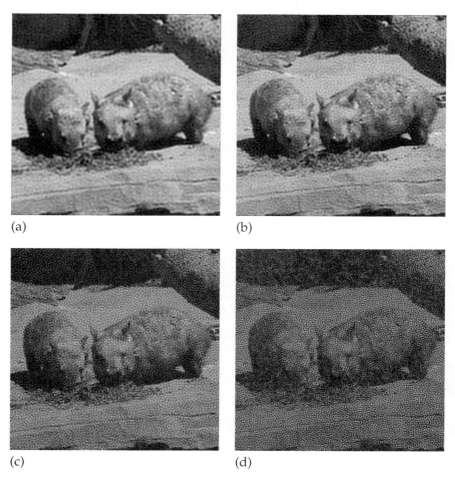

(a)   (b)

(c)   (d)

FIGURE 8.19 *Inverse filtering using constrained division.*

square subimage. The result is shown as Figure 8.20(a). To blur it, we can use the `blur` parameter of the `fspecial` function.

```
>> m=fspecial('motion',7,0);
>> bm=imfilter(b,m);
>> imshow(bm)
```

The result is shown as Figure 8.20(b). The result of the blur has effectively obliterated the text on the image.

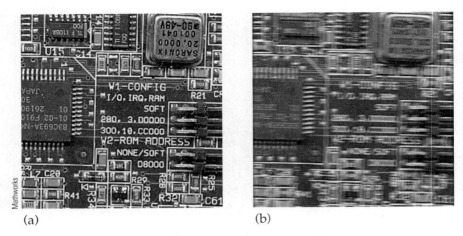

(a)   (b)

FIGURE 8.20 *The result of motion blur.*

To deblur the image, we need to divide its transform by the transform corresponding to the blur filter. This means that we first must create a matrix corresponding to the transform of the blur:

```
>> m2=zeros(256,256);
>> m2(1,1:7)=m;
>> mf=fft2(m2);
```

Now we can attempt to divide by this transform.

```
>> bmi=ifft2(fft2(bm)./mf);
>> fftshow(bmi,'abs')
```

The result is shown in Figure 8.21(a). As with inverse filtering, the result is not particularly good, because the values close to 0 in the matrix mf have tended to dominate the result. As above, we can constrain the division by dividing only by values that are above a certain threshold,

```
>> d=0.02;
>> mf=fft2(m2);mf(find(abs(mf)<d))=1;
>> bmi=ifft2(fft2(bm)./mf);
>> imshow(mat2gray(abs(bmi))*2)
```

where the last multiplication by 2 just brightens the result, which is shown in Figure 8.21(b). The writing, especially in the center of the image, is now quite legible.

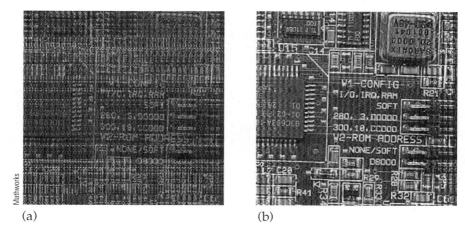

(a)   (b)

FIGURE 8.21 *Attempts at removing motion blur. (a) Straight division. (b) Constrained division.*

8.7 Wiener Filtering

As we have seen from the previous section, inverse filtering does not necessarily produce particularly pleasing results. The situation is even worse if the original image has been corrupted by noise. Here we would have an image X filtered with a filter F and corrupted by noise N. If the noise is additive (for example, Gaussian noise), then the linearity of the Fourier transform gives us

$$Y(i,j) = X(i,j)F(i,j) + N(i,j)$$

and so

$$X(i,j) = \frac{Y(i,j) - N(i,j)}{F(i,j)},$$

as we have seen in the introduction to this chapter. So not only do we have the problem of dividing by the filter, we have the problem of dealing with noise. In such a situation the presence of noise can have a catastrophic effect on the inverse filtering: the noise can completely dominate the output, making direct inverse filtering impossible.

To introduce Wiener filtering, we will discuss a more general question: given a degraded image M' of some original image M and a restored version R, what measure can we use to say whether our restoration has done a good job? Clearly, we would like R to be as close as possible to the correct image

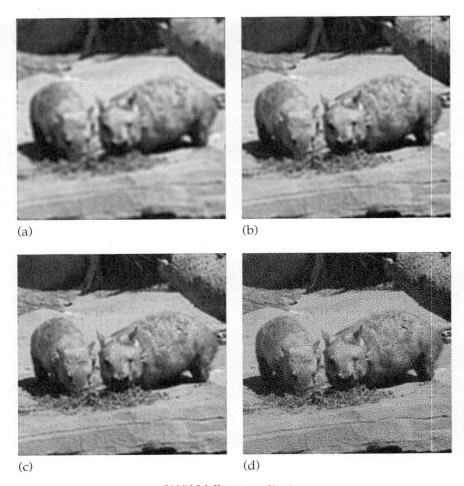

(a)   (b)

(c)   (d)

FIGURE 8.22 *Wiener filtering.*

M. One way of measuring the closeness of R to M is by adding the squares of all differences:

$$\sum (m_{i,j} - r_{i,j})^2,$$

where the sum is taken over all pixels of R and M (which we assume to be of the same size). This sum can be taken as a measure of the closeness of R to M. If we can minimize this value, we may be sure that our procedure has done as good a job as possible. Filters that operate on this principle of least squares are called Wiener filters. We can obtain X by

$$X(i,j) \approx \left[\frac{1}{F(i,j)} \frac{|F(i,j)|^2}{|F(i,j)|^2 + K} \right] Y(i,j), \tag{8.2}$$

where K is a constant [7]. This constant can be used to approximate the amount of noise: if the variance σ^2 of the noise is known, then $K = 2\sigma^2$ can be used. Otherwise, K can be chosen interactively (in other words, by trial and error) to yield the best result. Note that if $K = 0$, then Equation 8.2 reduces to Equation 8.1.

We can easily implement Equation 8.2:

```
>> K=0.01;
>> wbf=fftshift(fft2(wba));
>> w1=wbf.*(abs(b).^2./(abs(b).^2+K)./b); % This is the equation
>> w1a=abs(ifft2(w1));
>> imshow(mat2gray(w1a))
```

The result is shown in Figure 8.22(a). Figure 8.22(b–d) show the results with $K = 0.001$, $K = 0.0001$, and $K = 0.00001$, respectively. Thus, as K becomes very small, noise starts to dominate the image.

EXERCISES

1. The arrays below represent small grayscale images. Compute the 4×4 image that would result in each case if the middle 16 pixels were transformed using a 3×3 median filter:

8	17	4	10	15	12
10	12	15	7	3	10
15	10	50	5	3	12
4	8	11	4	1	8
16	7	4	3	0	7
16	24	19	3	20	10

1	1	2	5	3	1
3	20	5	6	4	6
4	6	4	20	2	2
4	3	3	5	1	5
6	5	20	2	20	2
6	3	1	4	1	2

7	8	11	12	13	9
8	14	0	9	7	10
11	23	10	14	1	8
14	7	11	8	9	11
13	13	18	10	7	12
9	11	14	12	13	10

2. Using the same images as in Question 1, transform them by using a 3×3 averaging filter.

3. Use the outlier method to find noisy pixels in each of the images given in Question 1. What are the reasonable values to use for the difference between the gray value of a pixel and the average of its 8 neighbors?

4. Pratt [26] has proposed a pseudomedian filter to overcome some of the speed disadvantages of the median filter. For example, given a five-element sequence $\{a, b, c, d, e\}$, its pseudomedian is defined as

$$\text{psmed}(a, b, c, d, e) = \tfrac{1}{2} \max \left[\min(a, b, c) + \min(b, c, d) + \min(c, d, e) \right]$$
$$+ \tfrac{1}{2} \min \left[\max(a, b, c) + \max(b, c, d) + \max(c, d, e) \right]$$

So for a sequence of length 5, we take the maxima and minima of all subsequences of length three. In general, for an odd-length sequence L of length $2n + 1$, we take the maxima and minima of all subsequences of length $n + 1$.

We can apply the pseudomedian to 3×3 neighborhoods of an image, or cross-shaped neighborhoods containing 5 pixels, or any other neighborhood with an odd number of pixels.

Apply the pseudomedian to the images in Question 1, using 3×3 neighborhoods of each pixel.

5. Write a MATLAB function to implement the pseudomedian and apply it to the images above with the `nlfilter` function. Does it produce a good result?

6. Produce a gray subimage of the colour image `flowers.tif` by

```
>> f=imread('flowers.tif');
>> fg=rgb2gray(f);
>> f=im2uint8(f(30:285,60:315));
```

Add 5% salt and pepper noise to the image. Attempt to remove the noise with

a. Average filtering.
b. Median filtering.
c. The outlier method.
d. Pseudomedian filtering.

Which method gives the best results?

7. Repeat Question 6, but with 10% and then 20% noise.

8. For 20% noise, compare the results with a 5×5 median filter and two applications of a 3×3 median filter.

9. Add Gaussian noise to the grayscale flowers image with the following parameters:

a. Mean 0, variance 0.01 (the default).
b. Mean 0, variance 0.02.
c. Mean 0, variance 0.05.
d. Mean 0, variance 0.1.

In each case, attempt to remove the noise with average filtering and with Wiener filtering.

Can you produce satisfactory results with the last two noisy images?

10. Gonzalez and Woods [7] mention the use of a midpoint filter for cleaning Gaussian noise. This is defined by

$$g(x,y) = \frac{1}{2} \left(\max_{(x,y) \in B} f(x,y) + \min_{(x,y) \in B} f(x,y) \right),$$

where the maximum and minimum are taken over all pixels in a neighborhood B of (x, y). Use `ordfilt2` to find maxima and minima, and experiment with this approach to cleaning Gaussian noise using different variances. Visually, how do the results compare with spatial Wiener filtering or a blurring filter?

11. In Chapter 5 we defined the alpha-trimmed mean filter and the geometric mean filter. Using either `nlfilter` or `ordfilt2`, write MATLAB functions to implement these filters and apply them to images corrupted with Gaussian noise.
    How well do they compare to average filtering, image averaging, or adaptive filtering?

12. a. Experiment with low-pass filtering for removing speckle noise.
    b. Experiment with averaging of multiple images for speckle noise.
    c. What happens if you average the logs of the images, and take the exponential of the result?

13. Add the sine waves to the engineer face using the same commands as for the cameraman:

```
>> [x,y]=meshgrid(1:256,1:256);
>> s=1+sin(x+y/1.5);
>> ep=(double(en)/128+s)/4;
```

Now attempt to remove the noise using band-reject filtering or notch filtering. Which one gives the best result?

14. For each of the following sine commands:
    a. s=1+sin(x/3+y/5);
    b. s=1+sin(x/5+y/1.5);
    c. s=1+sin(x/6+y/6);

    add the sine wave to the image as shown in Question 12 and attempt to remove the resulting periodic noise using band-reject filtering or notch filtering.
    Which of the three is easiest to clean up?

15. Apply a 5×5 blurring filter with `imfilter` to the cameraman image. Attempt to deblur the result using inverse filtering with constrained division. Which threshold gives the best results?

16. Repeat Question 15 using a 7×7 blurring filter.

17. Work through the motion deblurring example, experimenting with different values of the threshold. What gives the best results?

CHAPTER NINE

Image Segmentation

9.1 Introduction

Segmentation refers to the operation of partitioning an image into component parts or into separate objects. In this chapter, we will investigate two very important topics: thresholding and edge detection.

9.2 Thresholding

9.2.1 Single Thresholding

A grayscale image is turned into a binary (black and white) image by first choosing a gray level T in the original image and then turning every pixel black or white according to whether its gray value is greater than or less than T:

$$\text{A pixel becomes } \begin{cases} \text{white if its gray level is} > T, \\ \text{black if its gray level is} \leq T. \end{cases}$$

Not only is thresholding important for fundamental segmentation problems, such as isolating particular objects from an image, it is also an important component of robot vision.

Thresholding can be done very simply in MATLAB. Suppose we have an 8-bit image stored as the variable X. Then the command

```
X > T
```

will perform the thresholding. We can view the result with `imshow`. For example, the commands

```
>> r=imread('rice.tif');
>> imshow(r),figure,imshow(r>110)
```

CRC Press

FIGURE 9.1 *Thresholded image of rice grains.*

will produce the images shown in Figure 9.1. The resulting image can then be further processed to find the number or average size of the grains.

To see how this works, recall that in MATLAB an operation on a single number, when applied to a matrix, is interpreted as being applied simultaneously to all elements of the matrix; this is called vectorization, which we discuss in Appendix A. The command X>T will thus return 1 (for true) for all those pixels for which the gray values are greater than T and 0 (for false) for all those pixels for which the gray values are less than or equal to T. We thus end up with a matrix of 0s and 1s, which can be viewed as a binary image.

The rice image in Figure 9.1 has light grains on a dark background. An image with dark objects over a light background may be treated the same,

```
>> b=imread('bacteria.tif');
>> imshow(b),figure,imshow(b>100)
```

will produce the images shown in Figure 9.2.

As well as the above method, MATLAB has the im2bw function, which thresholds an image **of any data type,** using the general syntax

```
im2bw(image,level)
```

where level is a value between 0 and 1 (inclusive), indicating the fraction of gray values to be turned white. This command will work on grayscale, colored, and indexed images of data type uint8, uint16, or double. For example, the thresholded rice and bacteria images could be obtained using

```
>> im2bw(r,0.43);
>> im2bw(b,0.39);
```

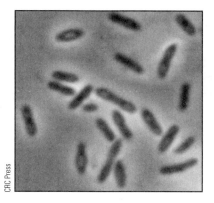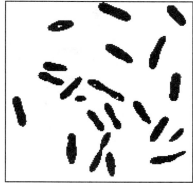

CRC Press

FIGURE 9.2 *Thresholded image of bacteria.*

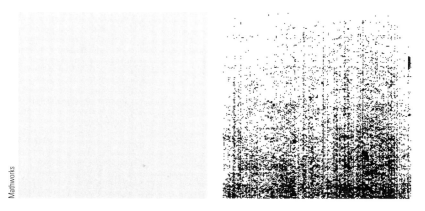

Mathworks

FIGURE 9.3 *The paper image and result after thresholding.*

The `im2bw` function automatically scales the value `level` to a gray value appropriate to the image type and then performs a thresholding by our first method.

As well as isolating objects from the background, thresholding provides a very simple way of showing hidden aspects of an image. For example, the image `paper.tif` appears all white because nearly all the gray values are very high. However, thresholding at a high level produces an image of far greater interest. We can use the commands

```
>> p=imread('paper1.tif');
>> imshow(p),figure,imshow(p>241)
```

to provide the images shown in Figure 9.3.

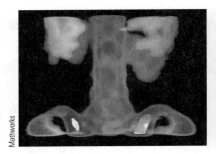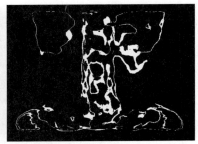

FIGURE 9.4 *The image* `spine.tif` *as the result after double thresholding.*

9.2.2 Double Thresholding

Here we choose two values T_1 and T_2 and apply a thresholding operation as:

$$\text{a pixel becomes} \begin{cases} \text{white if its gray level is between } T_1 \text{ and } T_2, \\ \text{black if its gray level is otherwise.} \end{cases}$$

We can implement this by a simple variation on the above method:

```
X>T1 & X<T2
```

Since the ampersand acts as a logical "and," the result will produce only a 1 where both inequalities are satisfied. Consider the following sequence of commands, which start by producing an 8-bit gray version of the indexed image `spine.tif`:

```
>> [x,map]=imread('spine.tif');
>> s=uint8(256*ind2gray(x,map));
>> imshow(s),figure,imshow(s>115 & s<125)
```

The output is shown in Figure 9.4. Note how double thresholding brings out subtle features of the spine that single thresholding would be unable to do. We can obtain similar results using `im2bw`,

```
imshow(im2bw(x,map,0.45)&~{}im2bw(x,map,0.5))}
```

but this is somewhat slower because of all the extra computation involved when dealing with an indexed image.

9.3 Applications of Thresholding

We have seen that thresholding can be useful

1. when we want to remove unnecessary detail from an image to concentrate on essentials. Examples of this were given in the rice and bacteria images. By removing all gray level information, the rice and bacteria were reduced to binary blobs. But this information may be all we need to investigate sizes, shapes, or number of blobs.

2. to bring out hidden detail. This situation was illustrated with paper and spine images. In both, the detail was obscured because of the similarity of the gray levels involved.
   Thresholding can be vital for other purposes. It can be useful

3. when we want to remove a varying background from text or a drawing. We can simulate a varying background by taking the image `text.tif` and placing it on a random background. This can be easily implemented with some simple MATLAB commands:

```
>> r=rand(256)*128+127;
>> t=imread('text.tif');
>> tr=uint8(r.*double(not(t)));
>> imshow(tr)
```

The first command simply uses the `rand` function (which produces matrices of uniformly generated random numbers between 0.0 and 1.0) and scales the result so the random numbers are between 127 and 255. We then read in the text image, which shows white text on a dark background.

The third command does several things at once: `not(t)` reverses the text image to have black text on a white background; `double` changes the numeric type so that the matrix can be used with arithmetic operations; finally the result is multiplied into the random matrix, and the whole thing converted to `uint8` for display. The result is shown on the left in Figure 9.5.

If we threshold this image and display the result with

```
>> imshow(tr>100)
```

we achieve the result shown on the right in Figure 9.5, and the background has been completely removed.

CRC Press

FIGURE 9.5 *Text on a varying background and thresholding.*

9.4 Choosing an Appropriate Threshold Value

We have seen that one of the important uses of thresholding is to isolate objects from their background. We can then measure the sizes of the objects or count them. Clearly, the success of these operations depends very much on choosing an appropriate threshold level. If we choose a value too low, we may decrease the size of some of the objects or reduce their number. Conversely, if we choose a value too high, we may begin to include extraneous background material.

Consider for example the image nodules1.tif, and suppose we try to threshold using the im2bw function and various threshold values *t* for $0 < t < 1$.

```
>> n=imread('nodules1.tif');
>> imshow(n);
>> n1=im2bw(n,0.35);
>> n2=im2bw(n,0.75);
>> figure,imshow(n1),figure,imshow(n2)
```

All the images are shown in Figure 9.6. One approach is to investigate the histogram of the image to see if there is a clear spot to break it up. Sometimes this can work well, but not always.

Figure 9.7 shows various histograms. In each case the image consists of objects on a background. But only for some histograms is it easy to see where we can split it. In both the coin and nodule images we could split the histograms about halfway, but for the rice and bacteria images, the choice is not as clear.

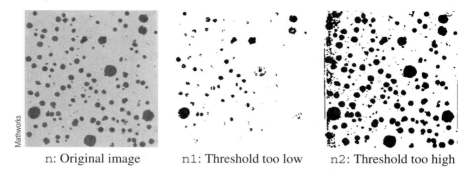

n: Original image   n1: Threshold too low   n2: Threshold too high

FIGURE 9.6 *Attempts at thresholding.*

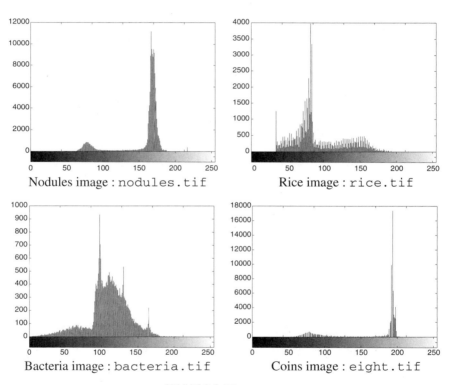

Nodules image : `nodules.tif`   Rice image : `rice.tif`

Bacteria image : `bacteria.tif`   Coins image : `eight.tif`

FIGURE 9.7 *Histograms.*

The trouble is that in general the individual histograms of the objects and background will overlap, and without prior knowledge of the individual histograms it may be difficult to find a splitting point. Figure 9.8 illustrates this, assuming in each case that the histograms for the objects and backgrounds are those of a normal distribution. We then choose the threshold values to be the place where the two histograms cross over.

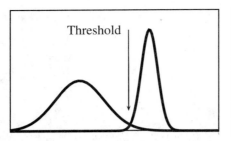 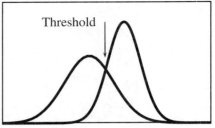

FIGURE 9.8 *Splitting up a histogram for thresholding.*

In practice, though, the histograms won't be as clearly defined as those in Figure 9.8, so we need some sort of automatic method for choosing a best threshold. One method is to describe the image histogram as a probability distribution, so that

$$p_i = n_i/N,$$

where n_i is the number of pixels with gray level i, N is the total number of pixels, so that p_i is the probability of a pixel having gray level i. If we threshold at level k, we define

$$\omega(k) = \sum_{i=0}^{k} p_i$$

$$\mu(k) = \sum_{i=k+1}^{L-1} p_i,$$

where L is the number of grayscales, so that $L-1$ is the largest. By definition,

$$\omega(k) + \mu(k) = \sum_{i=0}^{L-1} p_i = 1.$$

We would like to find k to maximize the difference between $\omega(k)$ and $\mu(k)$. This can be done by first defining the image average as

$$\mu_T = \sum_{i=0}^{L-1} ip_i,$$

and then finding k, which maximizes

$$\frac{\left(\mu_T\omega(k) - \mu(k)\right)^2}{\omega(k)\mu(k)}.$$

This method of finding an optimal threshold is called **Otsu's method** after its developer and is implemented by the MATLAB function graythresh. We can try this on our four images: nodules, rice, bacteria, and coins.

```
>> tn=graythresh(n)

tn =

     0.5804

>> r=imread('rice.tif');
>> tr=graythresh(r)

tr =

     0.4902

>> b=imread('bacteria.tif');
>> tb=graythresh(b)

tb =

     0.3765

>> e=imread('eight.tif');
>> te=graythresh(e)

te =

     0.6490
```

Now we can apply them to the images using im2bw.

```
>> imshow(im2bw(n,tn))
>> figure,imshow(im2bw(r,tr))
>> figure,imshow(im2bw(b,tb))
>> figure,imshow(im2bw(e,te))
```

The results are shown in Figure 9.9. Note that for each image the result given is quite satisfactory.

9.5 Adaptive Thresholding

Sometimes it is not possible to obtain a single threshold value that will isolate an object completely. This may happen if both the object and its background vary. For example, suppose we take the circles image and adjust it so that both the circles and the background vary in brightness across the image.

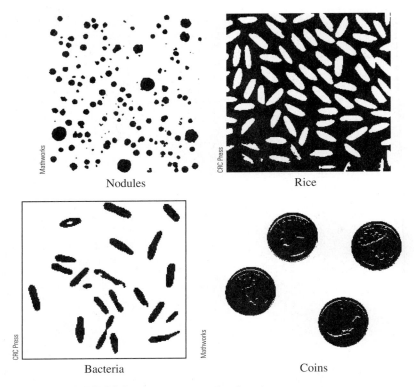

FIGURE 9.9 *Thresholding with values from* `graythresh`.

```
>> c=imread('circles.tif');
>> x=ones(256,1)*[1:256];
>> c2=double(c).*(x/2+50)+(1-double(c)).*x/2;
>> c3=uint8(255*mat2gray(c2));
```

Figure 9.10 shows an attempt at thresholding using `graythresh`.

```
>> t=graythresh(c3)

t =

    0.4196

>> ct=im2bw(c3,t);
```

As you see, the result is not particularly good; not all of the object has been isolated from its background. Even if different thresholds are used, the

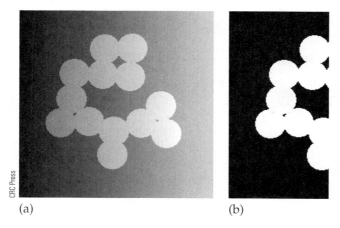

(a)   (b)

FIGURE 9.10 *An attempt at thresholding. (a) Circles image:* c3. *(b) Thresholding attempt:* ct.

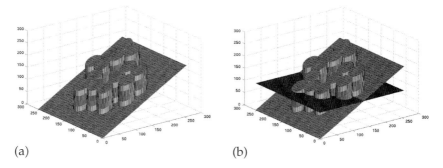

(a)   (b)

FIGURE 9.11 *An attempt at thresholding—functional version. (a) The image as a function. (b) Thresholding attempt.*

results are similar. Figure 9.11 illustrates the reason why a single threshold cannot work. In this figure the image is being shown as a function; the threshold is shown on the right as a horizontal plane. It can be seen that no position of the plane can cut off the circles from the background.

In a situation like this we can cut the image into small pieces and apply thresholding to each piece individually. Because in this particular example the brightness changes from left to right, we cut up the image into four pieces:

```
>> p1=c3(:,1:64);
>> p2=c3(:,65:128);
>> p3=c3(:,129:192);
>> p4=c3(:,193:256);
```

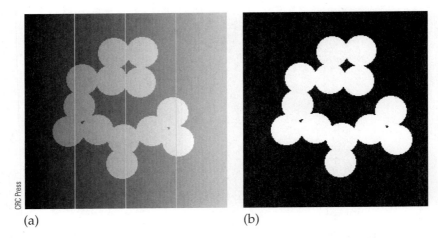

(a)   (b)

FIGURE 9.12 *Adaptive thresholding. (a) Cutting up the image. (b) Thresholding each part separately.*

Figure 9.12(a) shows how the image is sliced up. Now we can threshold each piece

```
>> g1=im2bw(p1,graythresh(p1));
>> g2=im2bw(p2,graythresh(p2));
>> g3=im2bw(p3,graythresh(p3));
>> g4=im2bw(p4,graythresh(p4));
```

and display them as a single image:

```
>> imshow([g1 g2 g3 g4])
```

The result is shown in Figure 9.12(b). These commands can be done much more simply by using the command `blkproc`, which applies a particular function to each block of the image. We can define our function with

```
>> fun=inline('im2bw(x,graythresh(x))');
```

Notice that this is the same as the commands used above to create g1, g2, g3, and g4 except now x is used to represent a general input variable.

The function can then be applied it to the image t3 with

```
>> t4=blkproc(t3,[256,64],fun);
```

51	52	53	59
54	52	53	62
50	52	53	68
55	52	53	55

(a)

50	53	155	160
51	53	160	170
52	53	167	190
51	53	162	155

(b)

FIGURE 9.13 *Blocks of pixels.*

What this command means is that we apply our function fun to each distinct 256×64 block of our image.

9.6 Edge Detection

Edges contain some of the most useful information in an image. We may use edges to measure the size of objects in an image, to isolate particular objects from their background, and to recognize or classify objects. There are a large number of edge-finding algorithms in existence, and we will look at some of the more straightforward of them. The general MATLAB command for finding edges is

```
edge(image, 'method', parameters . . . )
```

where the parameters available depend on the method used. In this chapter, we show how to create edge images using basic filtering methods and discuss the MATLAB edge function.

An **edge** may be loosely defined as a local discontinuity in the pixel values that exceeds a given threshold. More informally, an edge is an observable difference in pixel values. For example, consider both four blocks of pixels shown in Figure 9.13.

In Figure 9.13(a), there is a clear difference between the gray values in the second and third columns, and for these values the differences exceed 100. This would be easily discernible in an image—the human eye can pick out gray differences of this magnitude with relative ease. Our aim is to develop methods that will enable us to pick out the edges of an image.

9.7 Derivatives and Edges

9.7.1 Fundamental Definitions

Consider the image in Figure 9.14. Suppose we plot the gray values as we traverse the image from left to right. Two types of edges are illustrated here: a **ramp edge,** where the gray values change slowly, and a **step edge,** or an **ideal edge,** where the gray values change suddenly.

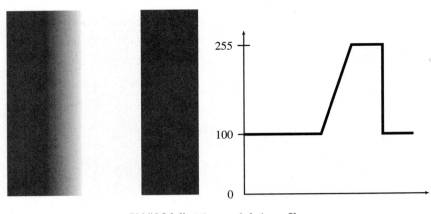

FIGURE 9.14 *Edges and their profiles.*

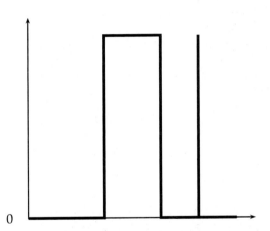

FIGURE 9.15 *The derivative of the edge profile.*

Suppose the function that provides the profile in Figure 9.14 is $f(x)$; then its derivative $f'(x)$ can be plotted. This is shown in Figure 9.15. The derivative, as expected, returns zero for all constant sections of the profile and is nonzero (in this example) only in those parts of the image in which differences occur.

Many edge-finding operators are based on differentiation; to apply the continuous derivative to a discrete image, first recall the definition of the derivative:

$$\frac{df}{dx} = \lim_{h \to 0} \frac{f(x+h) - f(x)}{h}.$$

Since in an image, the smallest possible value of h is 1, being the difference between the index values of two adjacent pixels, a discrete version of the derivative expression is

$$f(x+1) - f(x).$$

Other expressions for the derivative are

$$\lim_{h \to 0} \frac{f(x) - f(x-h)}{h}, \quad \lim_{h \to 0} \frac{f(x+h) - f(x-h)}{2h}$$

with discrete counterparts

$$f(x) - f(x-1), \quad \frac{(f(x+1) - f(x-1))}{2}.$$

For an image with two dimensions, we use partial derivatives. An important expression is the **gradient,** which is the vector defined by

$$\left[\frac{\partial f}{\partial x} \quad \frac{\partial f}{\partial y} \right],$$

which for a function $f(x,y)$ points in the direction of its greatest increase. The direction of that increase is given by

$$\tan^{-1} \left(\frac{\partial f / \partial y}{\partial f / \partial x} \right),$$

and its magnitude by

$$\sqrt{ \left(\frac{\partial f}{\partial x} \right)^2 + \left(\frac{\partial f}{\partial y} \right)^2 }.$$

Most edge-detection methods are concerned with finding the magnitude of the gradient and then applying a threshold to the result.

9.7.2 Some Edge Detection Filters

Using the expression $f(x+1) - f(x-1)$ for the derivative, leaving the scaling factor out produces horizontal and vertical filters

$$\begin{bmatrix} -1 & 0 & 1 \end{bmatrix} \quad \text{and} \quad \begin{bmatrix} -1 \\ 0 \\ 1 \end{bmatrix}.$$

These filters will find vertical and horizontal edges in an image and produce a reasonably bright result. However, the edges in the result can be a bit jerky.

This can be overcome by smoothing the result in the opposite direction by using the filters

$$\begin{bmatrix}1\\1\\1\end{bmatrix} \quad \text{and} \quad \begin{bmatrix}1 & 1 & 1\end{bmatrix}.$$

Both filters can be applied at once, using the combined filter

$$P_x = \begin{bmatrix}-1 & 0 & 1\\-1 & 0 & 1\\-1 & 0 & 1\end{bmatrix}.$$

This filter, and its companion for finding horizontal edges,

$$P_y = \begin{bmatrix}-1 & -1 & -1\\0 & 0 & 0\\1 & 1 & 1\end{bmatrix}$$

are the **Prewitt** filters for edge detection.

If p_x and p_y are the gray values produced by applying P_x and P_y to an image, then the magnitude of the gradient is obtained with

$$\sqrt{p_x^2 + p_y^2}.$$

In practice, however, its is more convenient to use either

$$\max\{|p_x|, |p_y|\}$$

or

$$|p_x| + |p_y|.$$

For example, let us take the image of the integrated circuit shown in Figure 9.16, which can be read into MATLAB with

```
>> ic=imread('ic.tif');
```

Applying each of P_x and P_y individually provides the results shown in Figure 9.17. Figure 9.17(a) was produced with the MATLAB commands

```
>> px=[-1 0 1;-1 0 1;-1 0 1];
>> icx=filter2(px,ic);
>> figure,imshow(icx/255)
```

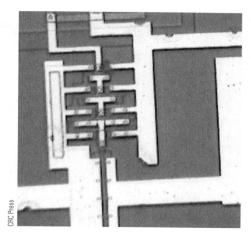

CRC Press

FIGURE 9.16 *An integrated circuit.*

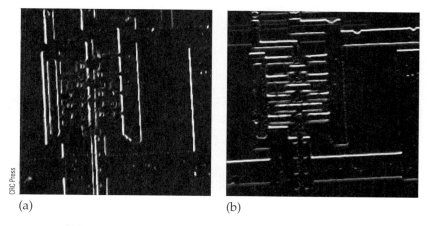

CRC Press

(a)   (b)

FIGURE 9.17 *The circuit after filtering with the Prewitt filters.*

and Figure 9.17(b) with

```
>> py=px';
>> icy=filter2(py,ic);
>> figure,imshow(icy/255)
```

Note that the filter P_x highlights vertical edges and P_y horizontal edges. We can create a figure containing all the edges with:

```
>> edge_p=sqrt(icx.^2+icy.^2);
>> figure,imshow(edge_p/255)
```

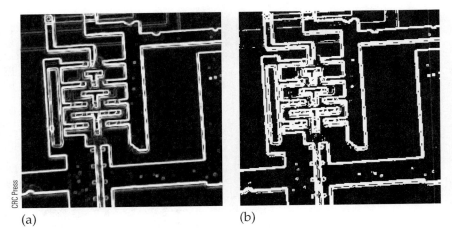

(a)   (b)

FIGURE 9.18 *All the edges of the circuit.*

The result is shown in Figure 9.18(a). This is a grayscale image; a binary image containing edges only can be produced by thresholding. Figure 9.18(b) shows the result after the command

```
>> edge_t=im2bw(edge_p/255,0.3);
```

We can obtain edges by the Prewitt filters directly by using the command

```
>> edge_p=edge(ic,'prewitt');
```

and the `edge` function takes care of all the filtering and choosing a suitable threshold level. See its help text for more information. The result is shown in Figure 9.19. Note that Figures 9.18(b) and 9.19 seem different from one another. This is because the `edge` function does some extra processing over and above taking the square root of the sum of the squares of the filters.

Slightly different edge-finding filters are the **Roberts cross-gradient filters**

$$\begin{bmatrix} 1 & 0 & 0 \\ 0 & -1 & 0 \\ 0 & 0 & 0 \end{bmatrix} \quad \text{and} \quad \begin{bmatrix} 0 & 1 & 0 \\ -1 & 0 & 0 \\ 0 & 0 & 0 \end{bmatrix}$$

and the **Sobel filters:**

$$\begin{bmatrix} -1 & 0 & 1 \\ -2 & 0 & 2 \\ -1 & 0 & 1 \end{bmatrix} \quad \text{and} \quad \begin{bmatrix} -1 & -2 & 1 \\ 0 & 0 & 0 \\ 1 & 2 & 1 \end{bmatrix}.$$

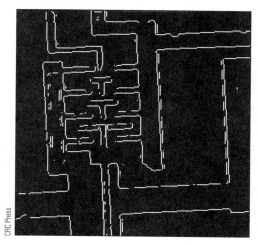

FIGURE 9.19 *The* `prewitt` *option of edge.*

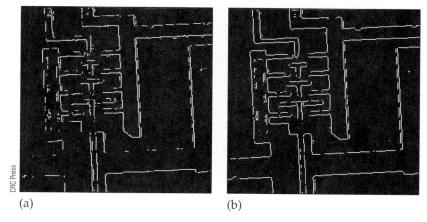

(a)   (b)

FIGURE 9.20 *Results of the Roberts and Sobel filters. (a) Roberts edge detection. (b) Sobel edge detection.*

The Sobel filters are similar to the Prewitt filters in that they apply a smoothing filter in the direction opposite to the central difference filter. In the Sobel filters, the smoothing takes the form

$$\begin{bmatrix} 1 & 2 & 1 \end{bmatrix},$$

which gives slightly more prominence to the central pixel. Figure 9.20 shows the respective results of the MATLAB commands

```
>> edge_r=edge(ic,'roberts');
>> figure,imshow(edge_r)
```

and

```
>> edge_s=edge(ic,'sobel');
>> figure,imshow(edge_s)
```

The appearance of each of these images can be changed by specifying a threshold level.

Of the three filters, the Sobel filters are probably the best; they provide good edges, and they perform reasonably well in the presence of noise.

9.8 Second Derivatives

9.8.1 The Laplacian

Another class of edge-detection methods is obtained by considering the second derivatives.

The sum of second derivatives in both directions is called the **Laplacian.** It is written as

$$\nabla^2 f = \frac{\partial^2 f}{\partial x^2} + \frac{\partial^2 f}{\partial y^2}$$

and can be implemented by the filter

$$\begin{bmatrix} 0 & 1 & 0 \\ 1 & -4 & 1 \\ 0 & 1 & 0 \end{bmatrix}.$$

This is known as a **discrete Laplacian.** The Laplacian has the advantage over first-derivative methods in that it is an **isotropic filter** [30]; this means it is invariant under rotation. That is, if the Laplacian is applied to an image and the image is then rotated, the same result would be obtained if the image were rotated first and the Laplacian applied second. This would appear to make this class of filters ideal for edge detection. However, a major problem with all second-derivative filters is that they are very sensitive to noise.

To see how the second derivative affects an edge, take the derivative of the pixel values as plotted in Figure 9.14; the results are shown schematically in Figure 9.21.

The Laplacian (after taking an absolute value, or squaring) gives double edges. To see an example, suppose we enter the MATLAB commands

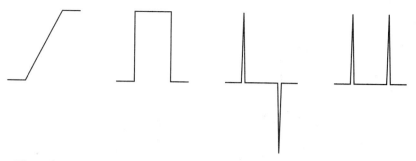

The edge   First derivative   Second derivative   Absolute values

FIGURE 9.21 *Second derivatives of an edge function.*

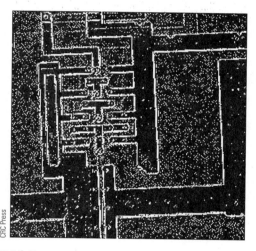

FIGURE 9.22 *Result after filtering with a discrete Laplacian.*

```
>> l=fspecial('laplacian',0);
>> ic_l=filter2(l,ic);
>> figure,imshow(mat2gray(ic_l))
```

the result of which is shown in Figure 9.22.

Although the result is adequate, it is very messy when compared with the results of the Prewitt and Sobel methods discussed earlier. Other Laplacian masks can be used, for example,

$$\begin{bmatrix} 1 & 1 & 1 \\ 1 & -8 & 1 \\ 1 & 1 & 1 \end{bmatrix} \quad \text{and} \quad \begin{bmatrix} -2 & 1 & -2 \\ 1 & 4 & 1 \\ -2 & 1 & -2 \end{bmatrix}.$$

50	50	50	50	50	50	50	50	50	50
50	50	50	50	50	50	50	50	50	50
50	50	200	200	200	200	200	200	50	50
50	50	200	200	200	200	200	200	50	50
50	50	200	200	200	200	200	200	50	50
50	50	200	200	200	200	200	200	50	50
50	50	50	50	200	200	200	200	50	50
50	50	50	50	200	200	200	200	50	50
50	50	50	50	50	50	50	50	50	50
50	50	50	50	50	50	50	50	50	50

(a)

-100	-50	-50	-50	-50	-50	-50	-50	-50	-100
-50	0	150	150	150	150	150	150	0	-50
-50	150	-300	-150	-150	-150	-150	-300	150	-50
-50	150	-150	0	0	0	0	-150	150	-50
-50	150	-150	0	0	0	0	-150	150	-50
-50	150	-300	-150	0	0	0	-150	150	-50
-50	0	150	300	-150	0	0	-150	150	-50
-50	0	0	150	-300	-150	-150	-300	150	-50
-50	0	0	0	150	150	150	150	0	-50
-100	-50	-50	-50	-50	-50	-50	-50	-50	-100

(b)

FIGURE 9.23 *Locating zero crossings in an image. (a) A simple image. (b) After laplace filtering.*

In MATLAB, Laplacians of all sorts can be generated using the `fspecial` function, in the form

```
fspecial('laplacian',ALPHA)
```

which produces the Laplacian

$$\frac{1}{\alpha + 1} \begin{bmatrix} \alpha & 1 - \alpha & \alpha \\ 1 - \alpha & -4 & 1 - \alpha \\ \alpha & 1 - \alpha & \alpha \end{bmatrix}.$$

If the parameter `ALPHA` (which is optional) is omitted, it is assumed to be 0.2. The value 0 gives the Laplacian developed earlier.

9.8.2 Zero Crossings

A more appropriate use for the Laplacian is to find the position of edges by locating zero crossings. From Figure 9.21, the position of the edge is given by the place where the value of the filter takes on a zero value. In general, these are places where the result of the filter changes sign. For example, consider the simple image given in Figure 9.23(a) and the result after filtering with a Laplacian mask in Figure 9.23(b).

We define the **zero crossings** in such a filtered image to be pixels that satisfy either of the following:

1. They have a negative gray value and are orthogonally adjacent to a pixel whose gray value is positive.
2. They have a value of zero and are between negative- and positive-valued pixels.

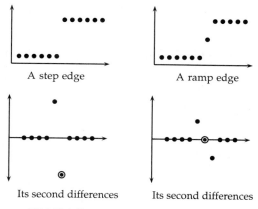

A step edge   A ramp edge

Its second differences   Its second differences

FIGURE 9.24 *Edges and second differences.*

To give an indication of the way zero crossings work, look at the edge plots and their second differences in Figure 9.24.

In each case the zero crossing is circled. The important point to note is that across any edge there can be only one zero crossing. Thus an image formed from zero crossings has the potential to be very neat.

In Figure 9.23(b) the zero crossings are shaded. We now have an additional method of edge detection: take the zero crossings after a Laplace filtering. This is implemented in MATLAB with the `zerocross` option of `edge`, which takes the zero crossings after filtering with a given filter:

```
>> l=fspecial('laplace',0);
>> icz=edge(ic,'zerocross',l);
>> imshow(icz)
```

The result is shown in Figure 9.25(a). This is not, in fact, a very good result—far too many gray level changes have been interpreted as edges by this method. To eliminate them, we may first smooth the image with a Gaussian filter. This leads to the following sequence of steps for edge detection, the **Marr-Hildreth** method:

1. Smooth the image with a Gaussian filter.
2. Convolve the result with a Laplacian filter.
3. Find the zero crossings.

This method was designed to provide a edge detection method to be as close as possible to biological vision. The first two steps can be combined into one to produce a Laplacian of Gaussian or LoG filter. These filters can be created with the `fspecial` function. If no extra parameters are provided

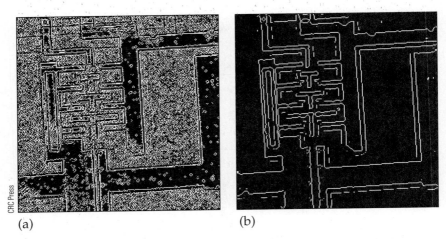

(a)   (b)

FIGURE 9.25 *Edge detection using zero crossings. (a) Zero crossings. (b) Using an LoG filter first.*

to the `zerocross` edge option, then the filter is chosen to be the LoG filter found by:

```
>> fspecial('log',13,2)
```

This means that the following command

```
>> edge(ic,'log');
```

produces exactly the same result as the commands:

```
>> log=fspecial('log',13,2);
>> edge(ic,'zerocross',log);
```

In fact the LoG and `zerocross` options implement the same edge-finding method, the difference being that the `zerocross` option allows you to specify your own filter. The result after applying a LoG filter and finding its zero crossings is given in Figure 9.25(b).

9.9 The Canny Edge Detector

The `edge` function has another option, `canny`, which implements the **Canny edge detector,** named after John Canny, who described this method in 1986 [3]. It was designed to meet three criteria for edge detection:

1. Low error rate of detection. It should find all edges and nothing but edges.

2. Localization of edges. The distance between actual edges in the image and edges found by this algorithm should be minimized.

3. Single response. The algorithm should not return multiple edge pixels when only a single edge exists.

Canny showed that the best filter to use for beginning his algorithm was a Gaussian (for smoothing), followed by the derivative of the Gaussian, which in one dimension is

$$\left(-\frac{x}{\sigma^2}\right) e^{-\frac{x^2}{2\sigma^2}}. \tag{9.1}$$

These filters have the effect of both smoothing noise and finding possible candidate pixels for edges. Because this filter is separable, it can be applied first to the columns as a column filter, and next to the rows as a row filter. We can then put the two results together to form an edge image. Recall from Chapter 5 that this is more efficient computationally than applying a two-dimensional filter.

Thus, at this stage we have the following sequence of steps:

1. Take our image x.
2. Create a one-dimensional Gaussian filter g.
3. Create a one-dimensional filter dg corresponding to the expression given in Equation 9.1.
4. Convolve g with dg to obtain gdg.
5. Apply gdg to x producing x1.
6. Apply gdg' to x producing x2.

We can now form an edge image with

$$xe = \sqrt{x1^2 + x2^2}.$$

So far, we have not achieved much more than we would with a standard edge detection using a filter.

The next step is that of **non-maximum suppression.** We want to threshold the edge image xe from above to keep only edge pixels and remove the others. However, thresholding alone will not produce acceptable results. The idea is that every pixel p has a direction ϕ_p (an edge gradient) associated with it, and to be considered as an edge pixel, a p must have a greater magnitude than its neighbors in direction ϕ_p.

Just as we computed the magnitude xe above, we can compute the edge gradient using the inverse tangent function:

$$xg = \tan^{-1}\left(\frac{x2}{x1}\right).$$

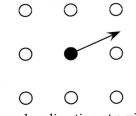

The edge direction at a pixel

FIGURE 9.26 *Nonmaximum suppression in the Canny edge detector.*

In general that direction will point between pixels in its 3×3 neighborhood, as shown in Figure 9.26. There are two approaches here. We can compare the gradient of the current (center) pixel with the value obtained from linear interpolation (see Chapter 6); we just take the weighted average of the gradients of the two pixels. In Figure 9.26 we take the weighted average of the upper two pixels on the right.

The second approach is to quantize the gradient to one of the values $0°$, $45°$, $90°$, or $135°$ and compare the original gradient to the gradient of the pixel to which the quantized gradient points. That is, suppose the gradient at position (x, y) was $\phi(x, y)$. We quantize this to one of the four angles given to obtain $\phi'(x, y)$. Consider the two pixels in direction $\phi'(x, y)$ and $\phi'(x, y) + 180°$ from (x, y). If the edge magnitude of either of those is greater than the magnitude of the current pixel, we mark the current pixel for deletion. After we have passed over the entire image, we delete all marked pixels.

We can, in fact, compute the quantized gradients without using the inverse tangent: we simply compare the values in the two filter results x1 and x2. Depending on the relative values of x1(x, y) and x2(x, y), we can place the gradient at (x, y) into one of the four gradient classes. Figure 9.27 shows how this is done. We divide the image plane into eight regions separated by lines at $45°$, as shown, with the x axis positive to the right and the y axis positive down. We can then assign regions and degrees to pixel values according to this table:

Region	Degree	Pixel Location
1	$0°$	$y \leq 0$ and $x > -y$
(1)	$0°$	$y \geq 0$ and $x < -y$
2	$45°$	$x > 0$ and $x \leq -y$
(2)	$45°$	$x < 0$ and $x \geq -y$
3	$90°$	$x \leq 0$ and $x > y$
(3)	$90°$	$x \geq 0$ and $x < y$
4	$135°$	$y < 0$ and $x \leq y$
(4)	$135°$	$y > 0$ and $x \geq y$

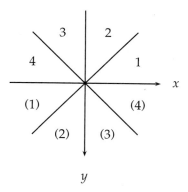

FIGURE 9.27 *Using pixel locations to quantize the gradient.*

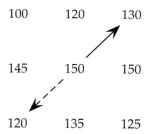

FIGURE 9.28 *Quantizing in non-maximum suppression.*

Suppose we had a neighborhood for a pixel whose gradient had been quantized to 45°, as shown in Figure 9.28. The dashed arrow indicates the direction opposite to the current gradient. In this figure both magnitudes at the ends of the arrows are smaller than the center magnitude, so we keep the center pixel as an edge pixel. If, however, one of those two values was greater than 150, we would mark the central pixel for deletion.

After performing nonmaximum suppression, we can threshold to obtain a binary edge image. Canny proposed that rather than using a single threshold, a technique called **hysteresis thresholding,** be used, which uses two threshold values: a low value t_L and a high value t_H. Any pixel with a value greater than t_H is assumed to be an edge pixel. Also, any pixel with a value p where $t_L \leq p \leq t_H$ that is adjacent to an edge pixel is also considered to be an edge pixel.

The Canny edge detector is implemented by the `canny` option of the `edge` function. We can enter the threshold values, or they will be chosen automatically.

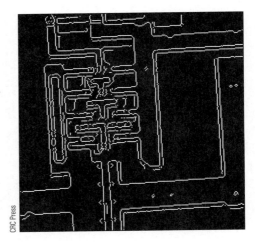

FIGURE 9.29 *Canny edge detection.*

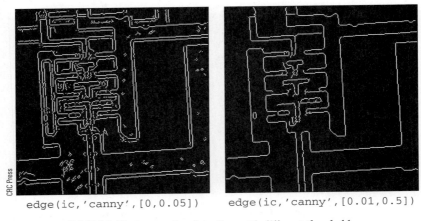

edge(ic,'canny',[0,0.05])   edge(ic,'canny',[0.01,0.5])

FIGURE 9.30 *Canny edge detection with different thresholds.*

```
>> [icc,t]=edge(ic,'canny');
>> t

t =

    0.0500    0.1250

>> imshow(icc)
```

The result is shown in Figure 9.29. Two other results with different thresholds are given in Figure 9.30. The higher we make the upper threshold, the fewer edges will be shown. We can also vary the standard deviation of the original Gaussian filter.

The Canny edge detector is the most complex of the edge detectors we have discussed; however, it is not the last word in edge detectors. A good account of edge detectors is given by Parker [23], and an interesting account of some advanced edge-detection techniques can be found in Heath et al. [11].

9.10 The Hough Transform

If the edge points found by the above edge-detection methods are sparse, the resulting edge image may consist of individual points, rather than straight lines or curves. Thus, in order to establish a boundary between the regions, it might be necessary to fit a line to those points. This can be a time-consuming and computationally inefficient process, especially if there are many such edge points. One way of finding such boundary lines is by use of the Hough transform.

The **Hough transform**[1] is designed to find lines in images, but it can be easily varied to find other shapes. The idea is simple. Suppose (x, y) is a point in the image (which we shall assume to be binary). We can write $y = ax + b$, and consider all pairs (a, b) that satisfy this equation, plotting them into an **accumulator array.** The (a, b) array is the **transform array.**

For example, take $(x, y) = (1, 1)$. Since the equation relating a and b is

$$1 = a.1 + b,$$

we can write

$$b = -a + 1.$$

Thus the line $b = -a + 1$ consists of all pairs of points relating to the single point $(1, 1)$. This is shown in Figure 9.31.

Each point in the image is mapped onto a line in the transform. The points in the transform corresponding to the greatest number of intersections correspond to the strongest line in the image.

---

[1] Hough is pronounced *Huff.*

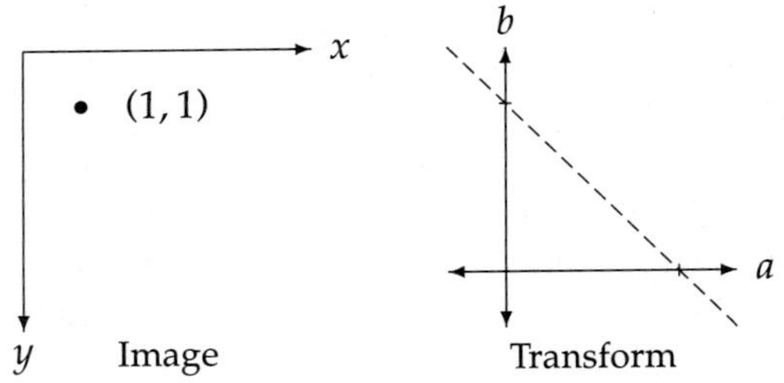

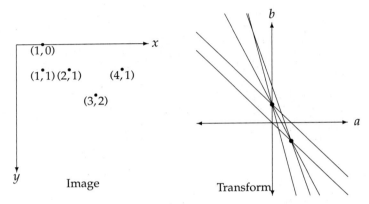

FIGURE 9.31 *A point in an image and its corresponding line in the transform.*

FIGURE 9.32 *An image and its corresponding lines in the transform.*

For example, suppose we consider an image with five points: $(1, 0)$, $(1, 1)$, $(2, 1)$, $(4, 1)$, and $(3, 2)$. Each of these points corresponds to a line as follows:

$(1, 0) \rightarrow b = -a$

$(1, 1) \rightarrow b = -a + 1$

$(2, 1) \rightarrow b = -2a + 1$

$(4, 1) \rightarrow b = -4a + 1$

$(3, 2) \rightarrow b = -3a + 2.$

Each of these lines appears in the transform as shown in Figure 9.32.

The dots in the transform indicate places where there are maximum intersections of lines: at each dot three lines intersect. The coordinates of these dots are $(a, b) = (1, 0)$ and $(a, b) = (1, -1)$. These values correspond to the lines

$$y = 1.x + 0$$

and

$$y = 1.x + (-1)$$

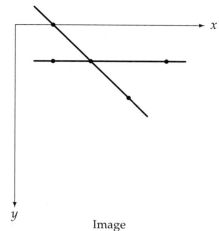

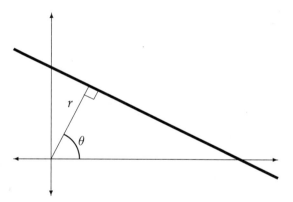

FIGURE 9.33 *Lines found by the Hough transform.*

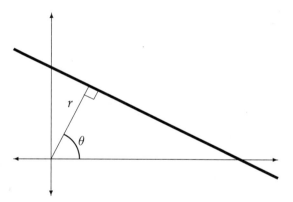

FIGURE 9.34 *A line and its parameters.*

or $y = x$ and $y = x - 1$. These lines are shown on the image in Figure 9.33.

These are indeed the strongest lines in the image in that they contain the greatest number of points.

There is a problem with this implementation of the Hough transform and that is that it cannot find vertical lines. We cannot express a vertical line in the form $y = mx + c$, because m represents the gradient and a vertical line has infinite gradient. We need another parameterization of lines.

Consider a general line, as shown in Figure 9.34. Clearly, any line can be described in terms of the two parameters r and θ: r is the perpendicular distance from the line to the origin, and θ is the angle of the line's perpendicular to the x axis. In this parameterization, vertical lines are simply those that have $\theta = 0$. If we allow r to have negative values, we can restrict θ to the range

$$-90 < \theta \le 90.$$

Given this parameterization, we need to be able to find the equation of the line. First, note that the point (p, q) where the perpendicular to the line meets the line is $(p, q) = (r \cos \theta, r \sin \theta)$. Also note that the gradient of the perpendicular is $\tan \theta = \sin \theta / \cos \theta$. Now let (x, y) be any point on the line. The gradient of the line is

$$\frac{\text{rise}}{\text{run}} = \frac{y - q}{x - p}$$

$$= \frac{y - r \sin \theta}{x - r \cos \theta}.$$

But because the gradient of the line's perpendicular is $\tan \theta$, the gradient of the line itself must be

$$-\frac{1}{\tan \theta} = -\frac{\cos \theta}{\sin \theta}.$$

Putting these two expressions for the gradient together produces:

$$\frac{y - r \sin \theta}{x - r \cos \theta} = -\frac{\cos \theta}{\sin \theta}.$$

If we now multiply these fractions we obtain:

$$y \sin \theta - r \sin^2 \theta = -x \cos \theta + r \cos^2 \theta,$$

and this equation can be rewritten as

$$y \sin \theta + x \cos \theta = r \sin^2 \theta + r \cos^2 \theta$$

$$= r(\sin^2 \theta + \cos^2 \theta)$$

$$= r.$$

We finally have the required equation for the line as

$$x \cos \theta + y \sin \theta = r.$$

The Hough transform can then be implemented as follows. We start by choosing a discrete set of values of r and θ to use. For each pixel (x, y) in the image, we compute

$$x \cos \theta + y \sin \theta$$

for each value of θ and place the result in the appropriate position in the (r, θ) array. At the end, the values of (r, θ) with the highest values in the array will correspond to strongest lines in the image.

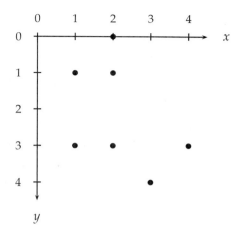

FIGURE 9.35 *A small image.*

An example will clarify this: Consider the image shown in Figure 9.35. We will discretize θ to use only the values

$$-45°, \quad 0°, \quad 45°, \quad 90°.$$

We can start by making a table containing all values $x \cos \theta + y \sin \theta$ for each point and for each value of θ:

(x, y)	$-45°$	$0°$	$45°$	$90°$
$(2, 0)$	1.4	2	1.4	0
$(1, 1)$	0	1	1.4	1
$(2, 1)$	0.7	2	2.1	1
$(1, 3)$	-1.4	1	2.8	3
$(2, 3)$	-0.7	2	3.5	3
$(4, 3)$	0.7	4	4.9	3
$(3, 4)$	-0.7	3	4.9	4

The accumulator array contains the number of times each value of (r, θ) appears in the above table:

	-1.4	-0.7	0	0.7	1	1.4	2	2.1	2.8	3	3.5	4	4.9
$-45°$	1	2	1	2		1							
$0°$					2		3			1		1	
$45°$					2			1	1		1		2
$90°$			1		2					3		2	

In practice this array will be very large and can be displayed as an image. In this example the two equal, largest values occur at $(r, \theta) = (2, 0°)$ and

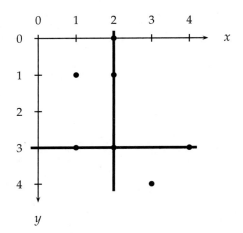

FIGURE 9.36 *Lines found by the Hough Transform.*

$(r, \theta) = (3, 90°)$. The lines then are

$$x \cos 0 + y \sin 0 = 2$$

or $x = 2$, and

$$x \cos 90 + y \sin 90 = 3$$

or $y = 3$. These lines are shown in Figure 9.36.

9.11 Implementing the Hough Transform in MATLAB

The Image Processing Toolbox does not contain a hough routine, and although the Hough transform can be obtained by other means, it is a pleasant programming exercise to write our own. Following the procedure outlined above, we will

1. decide on a discrete set of values of θ and r to use,
2. calculate for each foreground pixel (x, y) in the image the values of $r = x \cos \theta + y \sin \theta$ for all of our chosen values of θ,
3. create an accumulator array whose sizes are the numbers of angles θ and values r in our chosen discretizations from Step 1, and
4. step through all of our r values, updating the accumulator array as we go.

We will consider each step in turn.

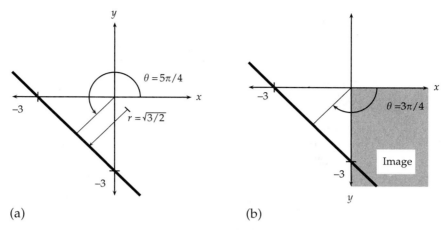

FIGURE 9.37 *A line parameterized with r and θ. (a) Using ordinary Cartesian axes. (b) Using matrix axes.*

9.11.1 Discretizing r and θ

We observe that even though a particular pair (r, θ) corresponds to only one line, a given line can be parameterized in different ways. For example, the line $x + y = -3$ can be parameterized using $\theta = 5\pi/4$ and $r = \sqrt{3/2}$ as shown in Figure 9.37(a).

Ҋ However, the same line can be parameterized using $\theta = \pi/4$ and $r = -\sqrt{3/2}$. We have a choice: we may restrict the values of θ, say to the range $-\pi/2 < \theta \leq \pi/2$, and let r have both positive and negative values, or we may let θ take any value chosen from the range $0 \leq \theta < 2\pi$ and restrict r to non-negative values. Because we are going to use the values of θ and r as indices into the accumulator array, it is simplest to take the second option. However, consider Figure 9.37(a) slightly redrawn to take into account the directions of x and y as column and row indices of a matrix, as shown in Figure 9.37(b). Because our image, for which both x and y will be positive, will sit in the bottom right quadrant, we will only have positive r values for $-90 \leq \theta \leq 180$. For if θ is outside that range, the perpendicular will point into the second (upper-left) quadrant, which would require a negative value of r if the line were to intersect the image.

Ҋ We can choose any discrete set of values we like, but let us take all the integer degree values in the given range and convert them to radians for the purposes of calculation:

```
>> angles=[-90:180]*pi/180;
```

9.11.2 Calculating the r Values

Suppose that the image is binary. We can then find the positions of all the foreground pixels with a simple application of the `find` function:

```
>> [x,y]=find(im);
```

If the image is not binary, we can create a binary edge image by use of the edge function. Now we can calculate all the r values with one simple command,

```
>> r=floor(x*cos(angles)+y*sin(angles));
```

where we use `floor` so as to obtain only integer values.

9.11.3 Forming the Accumulator Array

If the image is of size $m \times n$ pixels, then supposing the origin to be at the upper-left corner, the maximum value of r will be $\sqrt{m^2 + n^2}$. The size of the accumulator array can then be set at $\sqrt{m^2 + n^2} \times 270$. However, we are only interested in positive values of r: given our choice of range of θ, negative values can be discarded. We can first find the largest positive value of r and use that as one dimension of the array:

```
>> rmax=max(r(find(r>0)));
>> acc=zeros(rmax+1,270);
```

The `rmax+1` allows us to have values of $r = 0$.

9.11.4 Updating the Accumulator Array

We now must step through the array of r values, and for each value (r, θ) increase the corresponding accumulator value by one. First notice that the array r, as defined above, has size $N \times 360$, where N is the number of foreground pixels. Hence, the second index of both r and `acc` corresponds to the angle.

This can be done with nested loops, at the heart of which will be the command

```
if r(i,j)>=0, acc(r(i,j)+1,i)=acc(r(i,j)+1,i)+1;
```

Note that this is not a very efficient method of creating the accumulator array, but it does have the advantage of following the theory very closely. The entire program is shown in Figure 9.38.

```
function res=hough(image)

%
% HOUGH(IMAGE) creates the Hough transform corresponding to the image IMAGE
%

if ~isbw(image)
   edges=edge(image,'canny');
else
   edges=image;
end;
[x,y]=find(edges);
angles=[-90:180]*pi/180;
r=floor(x*cos(angles)+y*sin(angles));
rmax=max(r(find(r>0)));
acc=zeros(rmax+1,270);
for i=1:length(x),
   for j=1:270,
      if r(i,j)>=0
         acc(r(i,j)+1,j)=acc(r(i,j)+1,j)+1;
      end;
   end;
end;
res=acc;
```

FIGURE 9.38 *A simple* MATLAB *function for implementing the Hough transform.*

EXAMPLE   Let us take the cameraman image and apply our Hough transform procedure to it:

```
>> c=imread('cameraman.tif');
>> hc=hough(c);
```

This last command may take some time, because of the inefficient nested loops. The first thing we may do is to view the result,

```
>> imshow(mat2gray(hc)*1.5)
```

where the extra 1.5 at the end is there just to brighten up the image. The result is shown in Figure 9.39.

What we are viewing here is the accumulator array. It is what we should expect: a series of curves, with some bright points indicating places of maximum intersection. Because of the use of sines and cosines in the construction of the transform, we can expect the curves to be of a sinusoidal nature.

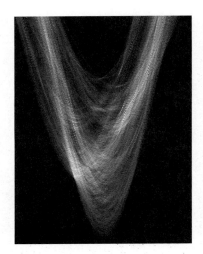

FIGURE 9.39 *The result of a Hough Transform.*

What now? Let us find the maximum value of the transform:

```
>> max(hc(:))

ans =

    91
```

We can now find the *r* and *θ* values corresponding to the maximum:

```
>> [r,theta]=find(hc==91)

r =

    138


theta =

    181
```

However, because we are using the pixel coordinates as Cartesian coordinates, our *x* and *y* axes have been rotated counterclockwise 90°. Thus we are measuring *θ* in a clockwise direction from the left vertical edge of our image. Figure 9.40 shows how this works.

FIGURE 9.40 *A line from the Hough Transform.*

We can easily create a small function to draw lines for us, given their perpendicular distance from the origin and the angle of the perpendicular from the *x* axis. The tool for this will be the `line` function, which in the form

```
>> line([x1,x2],[y1,y2])
```

draws a line between coordinates (x1, y1) and (x2, y2) over the current image. The only difficulty here is that `line` takes the *x* axis to be on the top and the *y* on the left. This is easily dealt with by replacing θ with $\pi/2 - \theta$. A simple function for drawing lines is shown in Figure 9.41.

Note the expression `181-theta` in the line

```
angle=pi*(181-theta)/180;
```

This can be interpreted as $180 + 1 - \theta$. The initial 180 swaps between Cartesian and matrix coordinates and the extra 1 counters the accumulation of r+1 in the function `hough.m`.

```
function houghline(image,r,theta)
%
% Draws a line at perpendicular distance R from the upper left corner of the
% current figure, with perpendicular angle THETA to the left vertical axis.
% THETA is assumed to be in degrees.
%
[x,y]=size(image);
angle=pi*(181-theta)/180;
X=[1:x];
if sin(angle)==0
   line([r r],[0,y],'Color','black')
else
   line([0,y],[r/sin(angle),(r-y*cos(angle))/sin(angle)],'Color','black')
end;
```

FIGURE 9.41 *A simple* MATLAB *function for drawing lines on an image.*

Mathworks

(a)   (b)

FIGURE 9.42 *The* houghline *function in action.*

We can use this as follows:

```
>> c2=imadd(imdivide(cm,4),192);
>> imshow(c2)
>> houghline(c2,r,theta)
```

The idea of using c2 is simply to lighten the image to show the line more clearly. The result is shown in Figure 9.42(a). To draw other lines, we can extract some more points from the transform:

```
>> [r,theta]=find(hc>80)
r =
    148
    138
    131
     85
     90
```

```
theta =

     169
     181
     182
     204
     204
```

Then the command

```
>> houghline(c,r(1),theta(1))
```

will place the line as shown on the right in Figure 9.42(b). Clearly, we can use these functions to find any lines we like.

The Hough transform can be generalized to finding other shapes in images, for example circles or ellipses. For an account of these generalizations (as well as very good discussions of the basic Hough transform), see Leavers [21] or Sonka et al. [35].

EXERCISES

Thresholding

1. Suppose you thresholded an image at value t_1 and thresholded the result at value t_2. Describe the result if:

   a. $t_1 > t_2$.
   b. $t_1 < t_2$.

2. Create a simple image with

```
>> [x,y]=meshgrid(1:256,1:256);
>> z=sqrt((x-128).^2+(y-128).^2);
>> z2=1-mat2gray(z);
```

   Using im2bw, threshold z2 at different values and comment on the results. What happens to the amount of white as the threshold value increases? Can you state and prove a general result?

3. Repeat Question 2, but with the image cameraman.tif.

4. Can you create a small image that produces an X shape when thresholded at one level, and a cross shape (+) when thresholded at another level? If not, why not?

5. Superimpose the image `text.tif` onto the image `cameraman.tif`. You can do this with:

```
>> t=imread('text.tif');}
>> c=imread('cameraman.tif');}
>> m=uint8(double(c)+255*double(t));}
```

Can you threshold this new image `m` to isolate the text?

6. Try the same problem as above, but define `m` as:

```
>> m=uint8(double(c).*double(~t));
```

7. Create a version of the circles image with:

```
>> t=imread('circles.tif');
>> [x,y]=meshgrid(1:256,1:256);
>> t2=double(t).*((x+y)/2+64)+x+y;
>> t3=uint8(255*mat2gray(t2));
```

Attempt to threshold the image `t3` to obtain the circles alone, using adaptive thresholding and the `blkproc` function. What size blocks produce the best result?

Edge Detection

8. Enter the following matrix into MATLAB:

201	195	203	203	199	200	204	190	198	203
201	204	209	197	210	202	205	195	202	199
205	198	46	60	53	37	50	51	194	205
208	203	54	50	51	50	55	48	193	194
200	193	50	56	42	53	55	49	196	211
200	198	203	49	51	60	51	205	207	198
205	196	202	53	52	34	46	202	199	193
199	202	194	47	51	55	48	191	190	197
194	206	198	212	195	196	204	204	199	200
201	189	203	200	191	196	207	203	193	204

and use `imfilter` to apply each of the Roberts, Prewitt, Sobel, Laplacian, and zero-crossing edge-finding methods to the image. In the case of applying two filters (such as with Roberts, Prewitt, or Sobel), apply each filter separately and join the results.

Apply thresholding if necessary to obtain a binary image showing only the edges. Which method seems to produce the best results?

9. Now with the same matrix as above, use the `edge` function with all possible parameters. Which method seems to produce the best results?

10. Open up the image `cameraman.tif` in MATLAB, and apply each of the following edge-finding techniques in turn:
    a. Roberts.
    b. Prewitt.
    c. Sobel.
    d. Laplacian.
    e. Zero-crossings of a Laplacian.
    f. the Marr-Hildreth method.
    g. Canny.

    Which seems to you to provide the best-looking result?

11. Repeat the above exercise, but use the image `tire.tif`.

12. Obtain a grayscale flower image with:

```
fl=imread('flowers.tif');
f=im2uint8(rgb2gray(fl));
```

Now repeat Question 10.

13. Pick a grayscale image, and add some noise to it, say with

```
c=imread('cameraman.tif');
c1=imnoise(c,'salt & pepper',0.1);
c2=imnoise(c,'gaussian',0,0.02);
```

Now apply the edge-finding techniques to each of the noisy images `c1` and `c2`.

Which technique seems to give:
a. The best results in the presence of noise?
b. The worst results in the presence of noise?

The Hough Transform

14. Write the lines $y = x - 2$, $y = 1 - x/2$ in (r, θ) form.

15. Use the Hough transform to detect the strongest line in the binary image shown below. Use the form $x \cos \theta + y \sin \theta = r$ with θ in steps of $45°$ from $-45°$ to $90°$ and place the results in an accumulator array.

x

y	-3	-2	-1	0	1	2	3
-3	0	0	0	0	0	1	0
-2	0	0	0	0	0	0	0
-1	0	1	0	1	0	1	0
0	0	0	1	0	0	0	0
1	0	0	0	0	0	0	0
2	1	0	0	0	0	1	0
3	0	0	0	0	0	0	0

16. Repeat Question 15 with the images:

x

y	-3	-2	-1	0	1	2	3
-3	0	0	0	0	1	0	0
-2	0	0	0	0	0	0	0
-1	0	0	1	0	0	0	1
0	0	1	0	0	1	0	0
1	1	0	0	0	0	0	1
2	0	0	0	0	1	0	0
3	0	0	0	1	1	0	0

x

y	-3	-2	-1	0	1	2	3
-3	0	0	0	1	0	0	0
-2	1	0	0	0	1	0	0
-1	0	0	0	0	0	0	0
0	0	0	1	0	0	1	0
1	0	1	0	1	0	0	0
2	1	0	0	0	0	0	1
3	0	0	1	0	0	1	0

17. Find some more lines on the cameraman image, and plot them with houghline.

18. Read and display the image alumgrns.tif.

    a. Where does it appear that the strongest lines will be?

    b. Using hough and houghline, plot the five strongest lines.

19. Experiment with the two routines by changing the initial edge detection of hough. Can you affect the lines found by the Hough transform?

CHAPTER TEN

MATHEMATICAL MORPHOLOGY

10.1 Introduction

Mathematical morphology, or *morphology* for short, is a branch of image processing that is particularly useful for analyzing shapes in images. We will develop basic morphological tools for investigation of binary images and then show how to extend these tools to grayscale images. MATLAB has many tools for binary morphology in the Image Processing Toolbox, most of which can be used for grayscale morphology as well.

10.2 Basic Ideas

The theory of mathematical morphology can be developed in many different ways. We will adopt one standard method that uses operations on sets of points. A very solid and detailed account can be found in Haralick and Shapiro [11].

10.2.1 Translation

Suppose that A is a set of pixels in a binary image and $w = (x, y)$ is a particular coordinate point. Then A_w is the set A translated in direction (x, y). That is,

$$A_w = \{(a, b) + (x, y) : (a, b) \in A\}.$$

For example, in Figure 10.1, A is the cross-shaped set, and $w = (2, 2)$. The set A has been shifted in the x and y directions by the values given in w. Note that here we are using matrix coordinates rather than Cartesian coordinates, thus the origin is at the top left, x goes down, and y goes across.

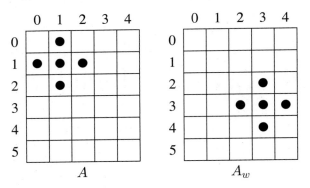

FIGURE 10.1 *Translation.*

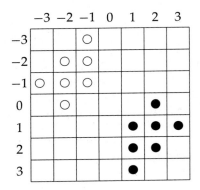

FIGURE 10.2 *Reflection.*

10.2.2 Reflection

If A is set of pixels, then its **reflection,** denoted $\hat{A}$, is obtained by reflecting A in the origin:

$$\hat{A} = \{(-x, -y) : (x, y) \in A\}.$$

For example, in Figure 10.2, the open and closed circles form sets that are reflections of each other.

10.3 Dilation and Erosion

The following are the basic operations of morphology in the sense that all other operations are built from a combination of these two.

10.3.1 Dilation

Suppose A and B are sets of pixels. Then the **dilation of** A by B, denoted $A \oplus B$, is defined as

$$A \oplus B = \bigcup_{x \in B} A_x.$$

This means that for every point $x \in B$, we translate A by those coordinates. We then take the union of all these translations.

An equivalent definition is that

$$A \oplus B = \{(x, y) + (u, v) : (x, y) \in A, (u, v) \in B\}.$$

From this last definition, dilation is seen to be commutative, that

$$A \oplus B = B \oplus A.$$

An example of a dilation is given in Figure 10.3. In the translation diagrams, the gray squares show the original position of the object. Note that $A_{(0,0)}$ is, of course, just A itself. In this example, we have

$$B = \{(0,0), (1,1), (-1,1), (1,-1), (-1,-1)\},$$

and these are the coordinates by which we translate A.

In general, $A \oplus B$ can be obtained by replacing every point (x, y) in A with a copy of B, placing the $(0, 0)$ point of B at (x, y). Equivalently, we can replace every point (u, v) of B with a copy of A.

Dilation is also known as **Minkowski addition**; see Haralick and Shapiro [9] for more information.

As you see in Figure 10.3, dilation has the effect of increasing the size of an object. However, it is not necessarily true that the original object A will lie within its dilation $A \oplus B$. Depending on the coordinates of B, $A \oplus B$ may end up quite a long way from A. Figure 10.4 gives an example of this: A is the same as in Figure 10.3, and B has the same shape but a different position. In this figure, we have

$$B = \{(7,3), (6,2), (6,4), (8,2), (8,4)\}$$

so that

$$A \oplus B = A_{(7,3)} \cup A_{(6,2)} \cup A_{(6,4)} \cup A_{(8,2)} \cup A_{(8,4)}.$$

For dilation, we generally assume that A is the image being processed and B is a small set of pixels. In this case B is referred to as a **structuring element** or as a **kernel.**

Dilation in MATLAB is performed with the command:

```
>> imdilate(image,kernel)
```

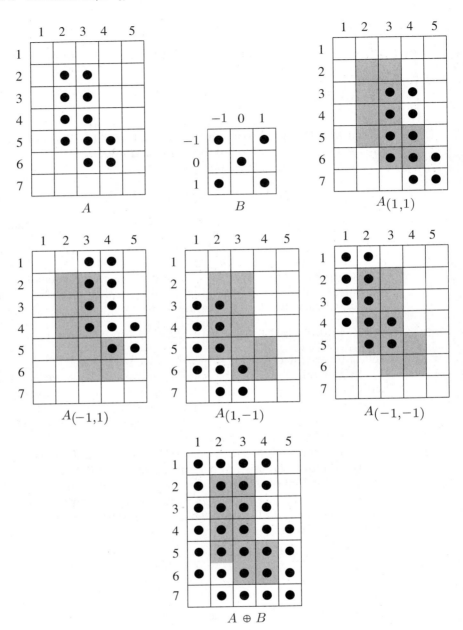

FIGURE 10.3 *Dilation.*

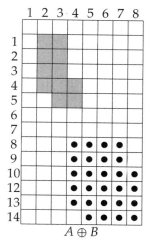

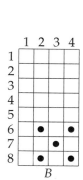

B

$A \oplus B$

FIGURE 10.4 *A dilation for which $A \not\subseteq A \oplus B$.*

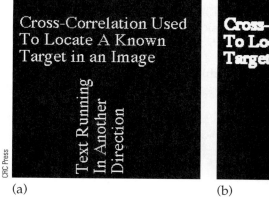

(a)   (b)

FIGURE 10.5 *Dilation of a binary image. (a) Text image. (b) Result of dilation.*

To see an example of dilation, consider the commands:

```
>> t=imread('text.tif');
>> sq=ones(3,3);
>> td=imdilate(t,sq);
>> subplot(1,2,1),imshow(t)
>> subplot(1,2,2),imshow(td)
```

The result is shown in Figure 10.5(b). Notice how the image has been thickened. This thickening is really what dilation does, hence its name.

10.3.2 Erosion

Given sets A and B, the erosion of A by B, written $A \ominus B$, is defined as:

$$A \ominus B = \{w : B_w \subseteq A\}.$$

In other words the erosion of A by B consists of all points $w = (x, y)$ for which B_w is in A. To perform an erosion, we can move B over A, find all the places it will fit, and for each such place mark down the corresponding $(0, 0)$ point of B. The set of all such points will form the erosion.

An example of erosion is given in Figure 10.6.

Note that in the example, the erosion $A \ominus B$ was a subset of A. This is not necessarily the case; it depends on the position of the origin in B. If B contains the origin (as it did in Figure 10.6), then the erosion will be a subset of the original object.

Figure 10.7 shows an example where B does not contain the origin. In this figure, the open circles in Figure 10.7(b) form the erosion.

Note that in Figure 10.7, the shape of the erosion is the same as that in Figure 10.6; however, its position is different. Since the origin of B in Figure 10.7 is translated by $(-4, -3)$ from its position in Figure 10.6, we can assume that the erosion will be translated by the same amount. And if we compare Figures 10.6 and 10.7, we can see that the second erosion has indeed been shifted by $(-4, -3)$ from the first.

For erosion, as for dilation, we generally assume that A is the image being processed and B is a small set of pixels—the structuring element or kernel.

Erosion is related to **Minkowski subtraction:** the Minkowski subtraction of B from A is defined as

$$A - B = \bigcap_{b \in B} A_b.$$

Erosion in MATLAB is performed with the following command:

```
>> imerode(image,kernel)
```

We will give an example, using a different binary image:

```
>> c=imread('circbw.tif');
>> ce=imerode(c,sq);
>> subplot(1,2,1),imshow(c)
>> subplot(1,2,2),imshow(ce)
```

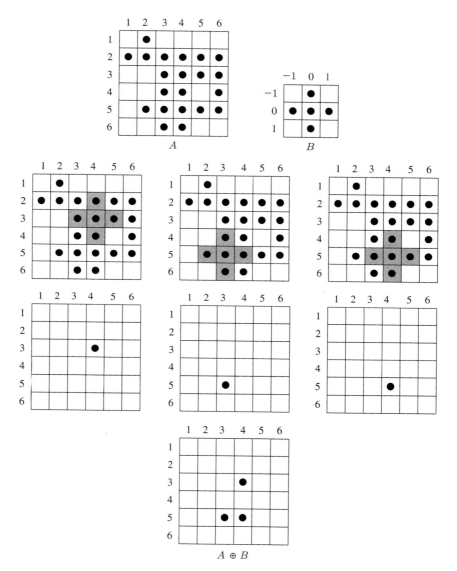

FIGURE 10.6 *Erosion with a cross-shaped structuring element.*

The result is shown in Figure 10.8(b). Notice how the image has been thinned. This is the expected result of an erosion, hence its name. If we continued to erode the image, we would end up with a completely black result.

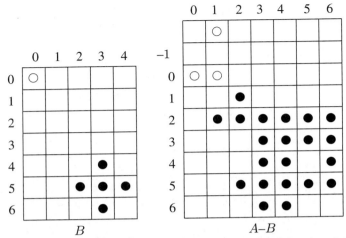

FIGURE 10.7 *Erosion with a structuring element not containing the origin.*

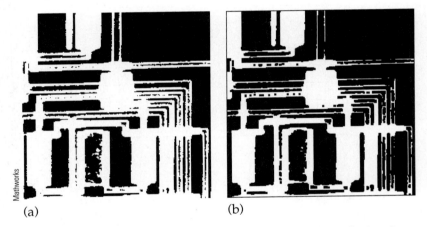

Mathworks

(a)   (b)

FIGURE 10.8 *Erosion of a binary image. (a) Original image. (b) Result of erosion.*

RELATIONSHIP BETWEEN EROSION AND DILATION   It can be shown that erosion and dilation are inverses of each other. More precisely, the complement of an erosion is equal to the dilation of the complement. Thus,

$$\overline{A \ominus B} = \overline{A} \oplus \hat{B}.$$

A proof of this can be found in Haralick and Shapiro [9].

It can be similarly shown that the same relationship holds if erosion and dilation are interchanged, that

$$\overline{A \oplus B} = \overline{A} \ominus \hat{B}.$$

We can demonstrate the truth of this using MATLAB commands. All we need to know is that the complement of a binary image

```
b
```

is obtained using

```
>> ~b
```

and that given two images a and b, their equality is determined with

```
>> all(a(:)==b(:))
```

To demonstrate the equality

$$\overline{A \ominus B} = \overline{A} \oplus \hat{B},$$

pick a binary image, say the text image, and a structuring element. The left-hand side of this equation is then produced with

```
>> lhs=~imerode(t,sq);
```

and the right-hand side with

```
>> rhs=imdilate(~t,sq);
```

Finally, the command

```
>> all(lhs(:)==rhs(:))
```

should return 1, for true.

10.3.3 An Application: Boundary Detection

If A is an image and B a small structuring element consisting of points symmetrically placed about the origin, we can then define the boundary of A by any of the following methods:

(i) $A - (A \ominus B)$ internal boundary
(ii) $(A \oplus B) - A$ external boundary
(iii) $(A \oplus B) - (A \ominus B)$ morphological gradient

In each definition the minus sign refers to a set difference. For some examples, see Figure 10.9. Note that the internal boundary consists of those pixels

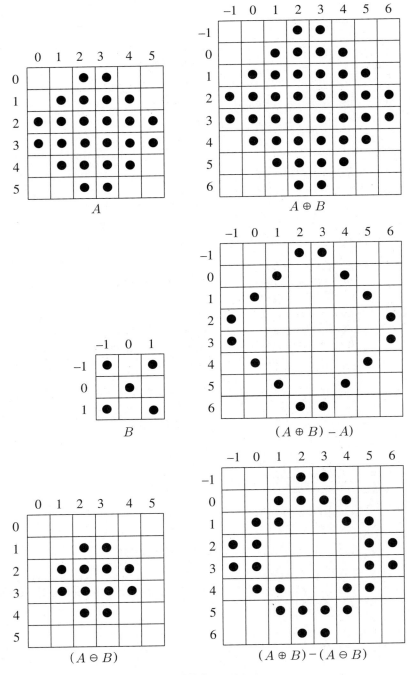

FIGURE 10.9 *Boundaries.*

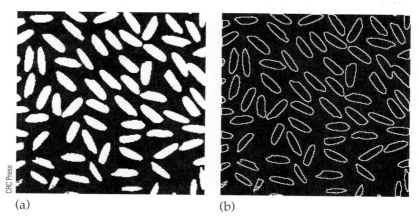

(a)   (b)

FIGURE 10.10 *Morphological edge detection. (a) The rice grains image. (b) The internal boundary.*

in A that are at its edge; the external boundary consists of pixels outside A that are just next to it. Note also that the morphological gradient is a combination of both the internal and external boundaries.

To see some examples, choose the image rice.tif and threshold it to obtain a binary image:

```
>> rice=imread('rice.tif');
>> r=rice>110;
```

The internal boundary is then obtained with:

```
>> re=imerode(r,sq);
>> r_int=r&~re;
>> subplot(1,2,1),imshow(r)
>> subplot(1,2,2),imshow(r_int)
```

The result is shown in Figure 10.10(b). The external boundary and morphological gradients can be obtained similarly:

```
>> rd=imdilate(r,sq);
>> r_ext=rd&~r;
>> r_grad=rd&~re;
>> subplot(1,2,1),imshow(r_ext)
>> subplot(1,2,2),imshow(r_grad)
```

The results are shown in Figure 10.11.

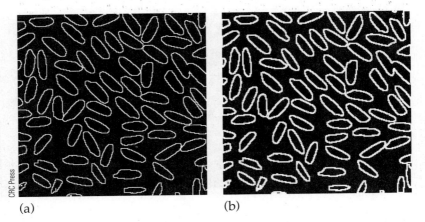

(a)   (b)

FIGURE 10.11 *More morphological edge detection. (a) External boundary. (b) Morphological gradient.*

Note that the external boundaries are larger than the internal boundaries. This is because the internal boundaries show the outer edge of the image components, whereas the external boundaries show the pixels just outside the components. The morphological gradient is thicker than either and is, in fact, the union of both.

10.4 Opening and Closing

These operations may be considered as second-level operations in that they build on the basic operations of dilation and erosion. They are also, as we shall see, better behaved mathematically.

10.4.1 Opening

Given A and a structuring element B, the **opening** of A by B, denoted $A \circ B$, is defined as

$$A \circ B = (A \ominus B) \oplus B.$$

Thus an opening consists of an erosion followed by a dilation. An equivalent definition is

$$A \circ B = \cup \{B_w : B_w \subseteq A\}.$$

That is, $A \circ B$ is the union of all translations of B that fit inside A. Note the difference with erosion: the erosion consists only of the $(0,0)$ point of B for those translations that fit inside A. The opening consists of all of B. An example of opening is given in Figure 10.12.

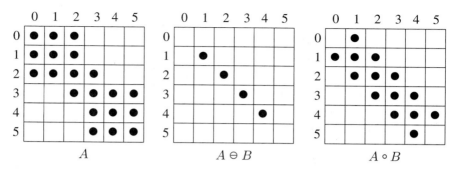

FIGURE 10.12 *Opening.*

The opening operation satisfies the following properties:

1. $(A \circ B) \subseteq A$. Note that this is not the case with erosion. As we have seen, an erosion may not necessarily be a subset.

2. $(A \circ B) \circ B = A \circ B$. That is, an opening can never be done more than once. This property is called **idempotence**. Again, this is not the case with erosion. You can keep on applying a sequence of erosions to an image until nothing is left.

3. If $A \subseteq C$, then $(A \circ B) \subseteq (C \circ B)$.

4. Opening tends to smooth an image, to break narrow joins, and to remove thin protrusions.

10.4.2 Closing

Analogous to opening, **closing,** may be considered as a dilation followed by an erosion and is denoted $A \bullet B$:

$$A \bullet B = (A \oplus B) \ominus B.$$

Another definition of closing is that $x \in A \bullet B$ if all translations B_w that contain x have nonempty intersections with A. An example of closing is given in Figure 10.13. The closing operation satisfies the following properties:

1. $A \subseteq (A \bullet B)$.

2. $(A \bullet B) \bullet B = A \bullet B$; that is, closing, like opening, is idempotent.

3. If $A \subseteq C$, then $(A \bullet B) \subseteq (C \bullet B)$.

4. Closing also tends to smooth an image, but it fuses narrow breaks and thin gulfs and eliminates small holes.

Opening and closing are implemented by the `imopen` and `imclose` functions, respectively. We can see the effects on a simple image using the square and cross-structuring elements.

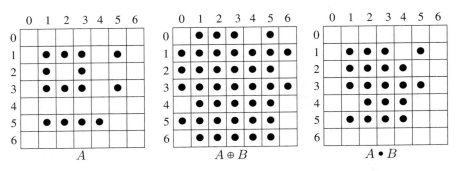

FIGURE 10.13 *Closing.*

```
>> cr=[0 1 0;1 1 1;0 1 0];
>> >> test=zeros(10,10);test(2:6,2:4)=1;test(3:5,6:9)=1;
      test(8:9,4:8)=1;test(4,5)=1
test =
      0     0     0     0     0     0     0     0     0     0
      0     1     1     1     0     0     0     0     0     0
      0     1     1     1     0     1     1     1     1     0
      0     1     1     1     1     1     1     1     1     0
      0     1     1     1     0     1     1     1     1     0
      0     1     1     1     0     0     0     0     0     0
      0     0     0     0     0     0     0     0     0     0
      0     0     0     1     1     1     1     1     0     0
      0     0     0     1     1     1     1     1     0     0
      0     0     0     0     0     0     0     0     0     0
>> imopen(test,sq)
ans =
      0     0     0     0     0     0     0     0     0     0
      0     1     1     1     0     0     0     0     0     0
      0     1     1     1     0     1     1     1     1     0
      0     1     1     1     0     1     1     1     1     0
      0     1     1     1     0     0     0     0     0     0
      0     0     0     0     0     0     0     0     0     0
      0     0     0     0     0     0     0     0     0     0
      0     0     0     0     0     0     0     0     0     0
      0     0     0     0     0     0     0     0     0     0
      0     0     0     0     0     0     0     0     0     0
>> imopen(test,cr)
ans =
      0     0     0     0     0     0     0     0     0     0
      0     0     1     0     0     0     0     0     0     0
      0     1     1     1     0     1     1     1     0     0
      0     1     1     1     1     1     1     1     1     0
      0     1     1     1     0     1     1     1     0     0
      0     0     1     0     0     0     0     0     0     0
      0     0     0     0     0     0     0     0     0     0
      0     0     0     0     0     0     0     0     0     0
      0     0     0     0     0     0     0     0     0     0
      0     0     0     0     0     0     0     0     0     0
```

Note that in each case the image has been separated into distinct components and the lower part has been removed completely.

```
>> imclose(test,sq)

ans =
```

1	1	1	1	0	0	0	0	0	0
1	1	1	1	0	0	0	0	0	0
1	1	1	1	1	1	1	1	1	1
1	1	1	1	1	1	1	1	1	1
1	1	1	1	1	1	1	1	1	1
1	1	1	1	1	1	1	1	0	0
0	0	0	1	1	1	1	1	0	0
0	0	0	1	1	1	1	1	0	0
0	0	0	1	1	1	1	1	0	0
0	0	0	1	1	1	1	1	0	0

```
>> imclose(test,cr)

ans =
```

0	0	1	0	0	0	0	0	0	0
0	1	1	1	0	0	0	0	0	0
1	1	1	1	1	1	1	1	1	0
1	1	1	1	1	1	1	1	1	1
1	1	1	1	1	1	1	1	1	0
0	1	1	1	1	1	1	1	0	0
0	0	1	1	1	1	1	0	0	0
0	0	0	1	1	1	1	1	0	0
0	0	0	1	1	1	1	1	0	0
0	0	0	0	1	1	1	0	0	0

With closing, the image is now fully "joined up." We can obtain a joining up effect with the text image, using a diagonal structuring element.

```
>> diag=[0 0 1;0 1 0;1 0 0]

diag =

         0     0     1
         0     1     0
         1     0     0

>> tc=imclose(t,diag);
>> imshow(tc)
```

The result is shown in Figure 10.14.

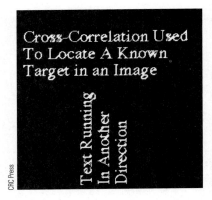

FIGURE 10.14 *An example of closing.*

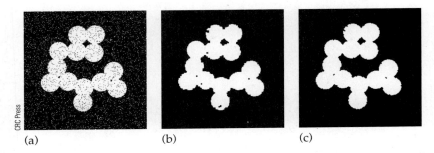

(a)   (b)   (c)

FIGURE 10.15 *A noisy binary image and results after morphological filtering with different structuring elements. (a) Binary noise. (b) Using the square kernel. (c) Using the cross kernel.*

AN APPLICATION: NOISE REMOVAL Suppose A is a binary image corrupted by impulse noise—some of the black pixels are white, and some of the white pixels are black. An example is given in Figure 10.15. $A \ominus B$ will remove the single black pixels, but will enlarge the holes. We can fill the holes by dilating twice:

$$((A \ominus B) \oplus B) \oplus B.$$

The first dilation returns the holes to their original size; the second dilation removes them. This will enlarge the objects in the image, however. To reduce them to their correct size, perform a final erosion:

$$(((A \ominus B) \oplus B) \oplus B) \ominus B.$$

The inner two operations constitute an opening, the outer two operations a closing. Thus, this noise-removal method is, in fact, an opening followed by a closing:

$$((A \circ B) \bullet B).$$

This is called **morphological filtering**.

Suppose we take an image and apply 10% shot noise to it:

```
>> c=imread('circles.tif');
>> x=rand(size(c));
>> d1=find(x<=0.05);
>> d2=find(x>=0.95);
>> c(d1)=0;
>> c(d2)=1;
>> imshow(c)
```

The result is shown in Figure 10.15(a). The filtering process can be implemented with

```
>> cf1=imclose(imopen(c,sq),sq);
>> figure,imshow(cf1)
>> cf2=imclose(imopen(c,cr),cr);
>> figure,imshow(cf2)
```

The results are shown in Figure 10.15(b and c). The results are rather blocky, although less so with the cross-structuring element.

RELATIONSHIP BETWEEN OPENING AND CLOSING   Opening and closing share a relationship very similar to that of erosion and dilation. The complement of an opening is equal to the closing of a complement, and the complement of a closing is equal to the opening of a complement. Specifically,

$$\overline{A \bullet B} = \overline{A} \circ \hat{B}$$

and

$$\overline{A \circ B} = \overline{A} \bullet \hat{B}.$$

Again, see Haralick and Shapiro [11] for a formal proof.

10.5 The Hit-or-Miss Transform

The hit-or-miss transform is a powerful method for finding shapes in images. As with all other morphological algorithms, it can be defined entirely in terms of dilation and erosion; in this case, erosion only.

Suppose we wish to locate 3×3 square shapes, such as is in the center of the image A in Figure 10.16. If we performed an erosion $A \ominus B$ with B being the square structuring element, we would obtain the result given in

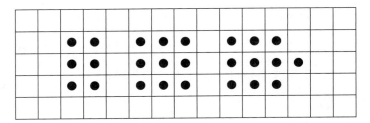

FIGURE 10.16 *An image A containing a shape to be found.*

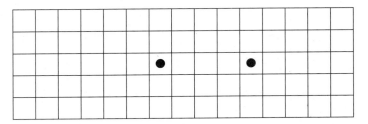

FIGURE 10.17 *The erosion $A \ominus B$.*

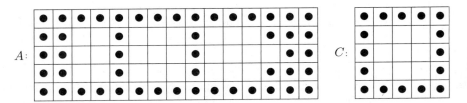

FIGURE 10.18 *The complement and the second structuring element.*

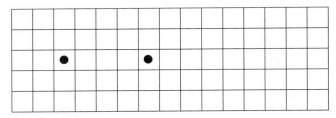

FIGURE 10.19 *The erosion $\overline{A} \ominus C$.*

Figure 10.17. The result contains two pixels, because there are exactly two places in A where B will fit. Now suppose we also erode the complement of A with a structuring element C, which fits exactly around the 3×3 square. $\overline{A}$ and C are shown in Figure 10.18. [We assume that $(0, 0)$ is at the center of C.]

If we now perform the erosion $\overline{A} \ominus C$, we would obtain the result shown in Figure 10.19.

The intersection of the two erosion operations would produce just one pixel at the position of the center of the 3×3 square in A, which is just what we want. If A had contained more than one square, the final result would have been single pixels at the positions of the centers of each. This combination of erosions forms the hit-or-miss transform.

In general, if we are looking for a particular shape in an image, we design two structuring elements: B_1, which is the same shape, and B_2, which fits around the shape. We then write $B = (B_1, B_2)$ and

$$A \circledast B = (A \ominus B_1) \cap (\overline{A} \ominus B_2)$$

for the hit-or-miss transform.

As an example, we will attempt to find the hyphen in "Cross-Correlation" in the text image shown in Figure 10.5. This is, in fact, a line of pixels of length 6. We thus can create our two structuring elements as

```
>> b1=ones(1,6);
>> b2=[1 1 1 1 1 1 1 1;1 0 0 0 0 0 0 1; 1 1 1 1 1 1 1 1];
>> tb1=erode(t,b1);
>> tb2=erode(~t,b2);
>> hit_or_miss=tb1&tb2;
>> [x,y]=find(hit_or_miss==1)
```

and this returns a coordinate of $(41, 76)$, which is right in the middle of the hyphen. Note that the command

```
>> tb1=erode(t,b1);
```

is not sufficient, because there are quite a few lines of length 6 in this image. We can see this by viewing the image tb1, which is given in Figure 10.20.

10.6 Some Morphological Algorithms

In this section we shall investigate some simple algorithms that use some of the morphological techniques we have discussed in previous sections.

10.6.1 Region Filling

Suppose in an image we have a region bounded by an 8-connected boundary, as shown in Figure 10.21. Given a pixel p within the region, we wish to fill up the entire region. To do this, we start with p and dilate as many times as necessary with the cross-shaped structuring element B (as used in

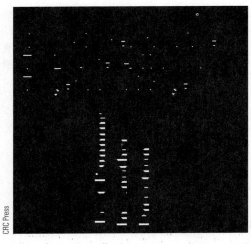

CRC Press

FIGURE 10.20 *Text eroded by a hyphen-shaped structuring element.*

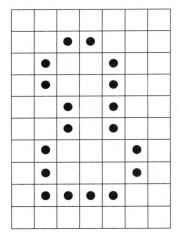

FIGURE 10.21 *An 8-connected boundary of a region to be filled.*

Figure 10.6), each time taking an intersection with $\overline{A}$ before continuing. We thus create a sequence of sets

$$\{p\} = X_0, X_1, X_2, \ldots, X_k = X_{k+1},$$

for which

$$X_n = (X_{n-1} \oplus B) \cap \overline{A}.$$

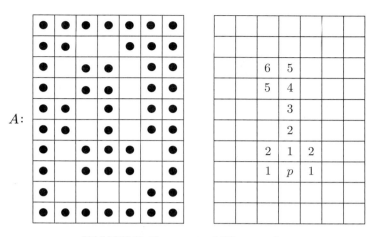

FIGURE 10.22 *The process of filling a region.*

Finally, $X_k \cup A$ is the filled region. Figure 10.22 shows how this is done. In Figure 10.22(b) we have

$$X_0 = \{p\}, \quad X_1 = \{p, 1\}, \quad X_2 = \{p, 1, 2\}, \ldots$$

Note that the use of the cross-shaped structuring element means that we never cross the boundary.

10.6.2 Connected Components

We use a very similar algorithm to fill a connected component. We use the cross-shaped structuring element for 4-connected components and the square structuring element for 8-connected components.[*] Starting with a pixel p, we fill up the rest of the component by creating a sequence of sets

$$X_0 = \{p\}, X_1, X_2, \ldots,$$

such that

$$X_n = (X_{n-1} \oplus B) \cap A$$

until $X_k = X_{k-1}$. Figure 10.23 shows an example. In each case we are starting in the center of the square in the lower left. Because this square is itself a 4-connected component, the cross-structuring element cannot go beyond it.

Both of these algorithms can be very easily implemented by MATLAB functions. To implement region filling, we keep track of two images, current and previous, and stop when there is no difference between

---

[*] The terms 4-connected and 8-connected are defined in Chapter 11.

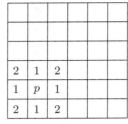

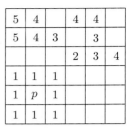

Using the cross   Using the square

FIGURE 10.23 *Filling connected components.*

```
function out=regfill(im,pos,kernel)
% REGFILL(IM,POS,KERNEL) performs region filling of binary
% image IMAGE,with kernel KERNEL, starting at point with
% coordinates given by POS.
% Example:
%              n=imread('nicework.tif');
%              nb=n&~imerode(n,ones(3,3));
%              nr=regfill(nb,[74,52],ones(3,3));
%
current=zeros(size(im));
last=zeros(size(im));
last(pos(1),pos(2))=1;
current=imdilate(last,kernel)&~im;
while any(current(:)~=last(:)),
   last=current;
   current=imdilate(last,kernel)&~im;
end;
out=current;
```

FIGURE 10.24 *A simple program for filling regions.*

them. We start with `previous` being the single point p in the region and `current` the dilation $(p \oplus B) \cap \overline{A}$. At the next step we set

previous $\leftarrow$ current,

current $\leftarrow$ (current $\oplus B) \cap \overline{A}$.

Given B, we can implement the last step in MATLAB by

```
imdilate(current,B)&~A.
```

The function is shown in Figure 10.24. We can use this to fill a particular region delineated by a boundary.

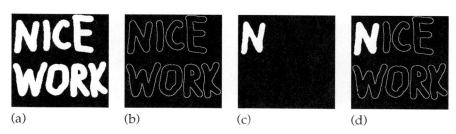

(a)　　　　　(b)　　　　　(c)　　　　　(d)

FIGURE 10.25 *Region filling.*

```
>> n=imread('nicework.tif');
>> imshow(n),pixval on
>> nb=n&~imerode(n,sq);
>> figure,imshow(nb)
>> nf=regfill(nb,[74,52],sq);
>> figure,imshow(nf)
```

The results are shown in Figure 10.25. Figure 10.25(a) is the original, Figure 10.25(b) the boundary, and Figure 10.25(c) the result of a region fill. Figure 10.25(d) shows a variation on the region filling; we just include all boundaries. This was obtained with

```
>> figure,imshow(nf|nb)
```

The function for connected components is almost exactly the same as that for region filling, except whereas for region filling we took an intersection with the complement of our image, for connected components we take the intersection with the image itself. Thus, we need only change one line, and the resulting function is shown in Figure 10.26. We can experiment with this function with the "nice work" image. We will use the square-structuring element and also a larger structuring element of size 11×11.

```
>> sq2=ones(11,11);
>> nc=components(n,[57,97],sq);
>> imshow(nc)
>> nc2=components(n,[57,97],sq2);
>> figure,imshow(nc2)
```

The results are shown in Figure 10.27. Figure 10.27(a) uses the 3×3 square, and Figure 10.27(b) uses the 11×11 square.

```
function out=components(im,pos,kernel)
% COMPONENTS(IM,POS,KERNEL) produces the connected component
% of binary image IMAGE which nicludes the point with coordinates given
% by POS, using kernel KERNEL.
%
% Example:
%              n=imread('nicework.tif');
%              nc=components(nb,[74,52],ones(3,3));
%
current=zeros(size(im));
last=zeros(size(im));
last(pos(1),pos(2))=1;
current=imdilate(last,kernel)&im;
while any(current(:)~=last(:)),
   last=current;
   current=imdilate(last,kernel)&im;
end;
out=current;
```

FIGURE 10.26 *A simple program for connected components.*

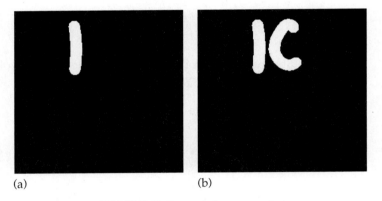

(a)   (b)

FIGURE 10.27 *Connected components.*

10.6.3 Skeletonization

The skeleton of a binary object is a collection of lines and curves that encapsulate the size and shape of the object. There are in fact many different methods of defining a skeleton, and for a given object, there are many possible different skeletons. We shall look at some of these in Chapter 11. However, a skeleton can be obtained quite simply using morphological methods.

Consider the table of operations as shown in Table 10.1.

Here we use the convention that a sequence of k erosions using the same structuring element B is denoted $A \ominus kB$. We continue the table until $(A \ominus kB) \circ B$ is empty. The skeleton is then obtained by taking the unions of all the set differences. An example is given in Figure 10.28, using the cross-structuring element.

Since $(A \ominus 2B) \circ B$ is empty, we stop here. The skeleton is the union of all the sets in the third column; it is shown in Figure 10.29. This method of skeletonization is called **Lantuéjoul's method.** For details see Serra [33].

TABLE 10.1   *Operations used to construct the skeleton.*

Erosions	Openings	Set differences
A	$A \circ B$	$A - (A \circ B)$
$A \ominus B$	$(A \ominus B) \circ B$	$(A \ominus B) - ((A \ominus B) \circ B)$
$A \ominus 2B$	$(A \ominus 2B) \circ B$	$(A \ominus 2B) - ((A \ominus 2B) \circ B)$
$A \ominus 3B$	$(A \ominus 3B) \circ B$	$(A \ominus 3B) - ((A \ominus 3B) \circ B)$
$\vdots$	$\vdots$	$\vdots$
$A \ominus kB$	$(A \ominus kB) \circ B$	$(A \ominus kB) - ((A \ominus kB) \circ B)$

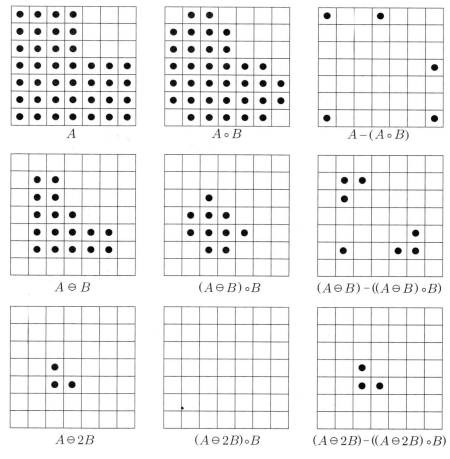

FIGURE 10.28 *Skeletonization.*

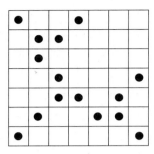

FIGURE 10.29 *The final skeleton.*

```
function skel = imskel(image,str)
% IMSKEL(IMAGE,STR) - Calculates the skeleton of binary image IMAGE using
% structuring element STR.  This function uses Lantejoul's algorithm.
%
skel=zeros(size(image));
e=image;
while (any(e(:))),
    o=imopen(e,str);
    skel=skel | (e&~o);
    e=imerode(e,str);
end
```

FIGURE 10.30 *A simple program for computing skeletons.*

This algorithm again can be implemented very easily; a function to do so is shown in Figure 10.30. We will experiment with the "nice work" image.

```
>> nk=imskel(n,sq);
>> imshow(nk)
>> nk2=imskel(n,cr);
>> figure,imshow(nk2)
```

The result is shown in Figure 10.31. Figure 10.31(a) is the result using the square-structuring element; Figure 10.31(b) is the result using the cross-structuring element.

10.7 A Note on Matlab's bwmorph Function

The theory of morphology developed so far uses versions of erosion and dilation sometimes called **generalized erosion and dilation,** so called because the definitions allow for general structuring elements. This is the method used in the imerode and imdilate functions. However, the bwmorph

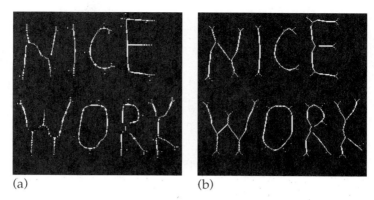

(a)   (b)

FIGURE 10.31 *Skeletonization of a binary image.*

function actually uses a different approach to morphology, that based on lookup tables. We will discuss the use of lookup tables for binary operations in Chapter 11. They can be just as easily applied to implement morphological algorithms.

The idea is simple. Consider the 3×3 neighborhood of a pixel. Since each pixel in the neighborhood can have only two values, there are $2^9 = 512$ different possible neighborhoods. We define a morphological operation to be a function that maps these neighborhoods to the values 0 and 1. Each possible neighborhood state can be associated with a numeric value from 0 (all pixels have value 0) to 511 (all pixels have value 1). The lookup table is then a binary vector of length 512. Its kth element is the value of the function for state k.

With this approach, we can define dilation as follows: a 0-valued pixel is changed to 1 if at least one of its eight neighbors is black and has value 1. Conversely, we may define erosion as changing a 1-valued pixel to 0 if at least one of its eight neighbors has value 0.

Many other operations can be defined by this method (see the help file for `bwmorph`). The advantage is that any operation can be implemented extremely easily simply by listing the lookup table. Moreover, the use of a lookup table allows us to satisfy certain requirements; the skeleton, for example, can be connected and have exactly one pixel thickness. This is not necessarily true of the algorithm presented in Section 10.6.3. The disadvantage of lookup tables is that we are restricted to using 3×3 neighborhoods. For more details, see Pratt [26].

10.8 Grayscale Morphology

The operations of erosion and dilation can be generalized to be applied to grayscale images. But before we do, we will reconsider binary erosion and dilation. We have defined binary erosion, $A \ominus B$, to be the union of the $(0, 0)$ positions of all translations B_x for which $B_x \subseteq A$.

```
0  0  0  0  0  0  0  0
0  1  1  1  1  0  0  0
0  1  1  1  1  1  0  0
0  1  1  1  1  1  1  0
0  1  1  1  1  1  1  0               0  0  0
0  0  1  1  1  1  1  0               0  0  0
0  0  0  1  1  1  1  0               0  0  0
0  0  0  0  0  0  0  0                  B
           A
```

FIGURE 10.32 *An example for erosion.*

Suppose we take B to be a 3×3 square consisting entirely of zeros. Let A be the image as shown in Figure 10.32. Now suppose we move over the image A, and for each point p we perform the following steps:

1. Find the 3×3 neighborhood N_p of p.
2. Compute the matrix $N_p - B$.
3. Find the minimum of that result.

We note that since B consists of all 0s, the second and third items could be reduced to finding the minimum of N_p. However, we shall see that for generalization it will be more convenient to have this expanded form. An immediate consequence of these steps is that if a neighborhood contains at least one 0, the output will be 0. The output is 1 only if the neighborhood contains all 1s. For example:

```
0  0  0
0  1  1        ⟶        0
0  1  1
```

If we perform this operation, we will obtain

```
0  0  0  0  0  0  0
0  0  0  0  0  0  0
0  0  1  1  0  0  0
0  0  1  1  1  0  0
0  0  1  1  1  0  0
0  0  0  1  1  0  0
0  0  0  0  0  0  0
0  0  0  0  0  0  0
```

which you can verify is exactly the erosion $A \ominus B$.

For dilation, we perform a sequence of steps very similar to those for erosion:

1. Find the 3×3 neighborhood N_p of p.
2. Compute the matrix $N_p + B$.
3. Find the maximum of that result.

We note again that since B consists of all 0s, the second and third items could be reduced to finding the maximum of N_p. If the neighborhood contains at least one 1, then the output will be 1. The output will be 0 only if the neighborhood contains all 0s.

Suppose A to be surrounded by 0s, so that neighborhoods are defined for all points in A above. Applying these steps produces

```
1  1  1  1  1  1  0  0
1  1  1  1  1  1  1  0
1  1  1  1  1  1  1  1
1  1  1  1  1  1  1  1
1  1  1  1  1  1  1  1
1  1  1  1  1  1  1  1
0  1  1  1  1  1  1  1
0  0  1  1  1  1  1  1
```

which again can be verified to be the dilation $A \oplus B$.

If A is a grayscale image and B is a structuring element, which will be an array of integers, we define grayscale erosion by using the steps above for each pixel p in the image:

1. Position B so that $(0, 0)$ lies over p.
2. Find the neighborhood N_p of p corresponding to the shape of B.
3. Find the value $\min(N_p - B)$.

We note that there is nothing in this definition that requires B to be any particular shape or size or that the elements of B be positive. As for binary dilation, B does not have to contain the origin $(0, 0)$.

We can define this more formally. Let B be a set of points with associated values. For example, for our square of 0s we would have:

Point	Value
$(-1, -1)$	0
$(-1, 0)$	0
$(-1, 1)$	0
$(0, -1)$	0
$(0, 0)$	0
$(0, 1)$	0
$(1, -1)$	0
$(1, 0)$	0
$(1, 1)$	0

The set of points forming B is called the domain of B and is denoted D_B. Now we can define

$$(A \ominus B)(x, y) = \min\{A(x + s, y + t) - B(s, t), (s, t) \in D_B\},$$
$$(A \oplus B)(x, y) = \max\{A(x + s, y + t) + B(s, t), (s, t) \in D_B\}.$$

$$
\begin{array}{c|ccccc}
 & \multicolumn{5}{c}{y} \\
 & 1 & 2 & 3 & 4 & 5 \\
\hline
1 & 10 & 20 & 20 & 20 & 30 \\
2 & 20 & 30 & 30 & 40 & 50 \\
x \quad 3 & 20 & 30 & 30 & 50 & 60 \\
4 & 20 & 40 & 50 & 50 & 60 \\
5 & 30 & 50 & 60 & 60 & 70 \\
\end{array}
\qquad
\begin{array}{c|ccc}
 & \multicolumn{3}{c}{t} \\
 & -1 & 0 & 1 \\
\hline
-1 & 1 & 2 & 3 \\
s \quad 0 & 4 & 5 & 6 \\
1 & 7 & 8 & 9 \\
\end{array}
$$

$$A \qquad\qquad\qquad\qquad\qquad\qquad B$$

FIGURE 10.33 *An example for grayscale erosion and dilation.*

We note that some published definitions use $s - x$ and $t - y$ instead of $x + s$ and $y + t$. This just requires that the structuring element be rotated $180°$.

EXAMPLE Suppose we take A and B as given in Figure 10.33. In this example $(0, 0) \in D_B$. Consider $(A \ominus B)(1, 1)$. By the definition, we have

$$(A \ominus B)(1, 1) = \min\{A(1 + s, 1 + t) - B(s, t), (s, t) \in D_B\}.$$

Since $D_B = \{(s, t) : -1 \le s \le 1; -1 \le t \le 1\}$, we have

$$(A \ominus B)(1, 1) = \min\{A(1 + s, 1 + t) - B(s, t) : -1 \le s \le 1; -1 \le t \le 1\}.$$

To ensure we don't require matrix indices that move outside A, we simply cut off the structuring element so that we restrict it to elements in A.

The values of $A(1 + s, 1 + t) - B(s, t)$ can then be obtained by matrix arithmetic,

$$
\begin{bmatrix} 10 & 20 \\ 20 & 30 \end{bmatrix} - \begin{bmatrix} 5 & 6 \\ 8 & 9 \end{bmatrix} = \begin{bmatrix} 5 & 14 \\ 12 & 21 \end{bmatrix}
$$

and the minimum of the result is 5. Note that to create the matrices we ensure that the $(0, 0)$ point of B sits over the current point of A, in this case the point $(1, 1)$. Another example is

$$(A \ominus B)(3, 4) = \min \left\{ \begin{bmatrix} 30 & 40 & 50 \\ 30 & 50 & 60 \\ 50 & 50 & 60 \end{bmatrix} - \begin{bmatrix} 1 & 2 & 3 \\ 4 & 5 & 6 \\ 7 & 8 & 9 \end{bmatrix} \right\}$$

$$= \min \left\{ \begin{bmatrix} 29 & 38 & 47 \\ 26 & 45 & 54 \\ 43 & 42 & 51 \end{bmatrix} \right\} = 26.$$

Finally, we have

$$A \ominus B = \begin{matrix} 5 & 6 & 14 & 15 & 16 \\ 8 & 9 & 17 & 18 & 19 \\ 12 & 13 & 25 & 26 & 39 \\ 15 & 16 & 28 & 29 & 46 \\ 18 & 19 & 39 & 48 & 49 \end{matrix}$$

Dilation is very similar to erosion, except that we add B and take the maximum of the result. As for erosion, we restrict the structuring element so that it doesn't go outside A. For example:

$$(A \oplus B)(1, 1) = \max \left\{ \begin{bmatrix} 10 & 20 \\ 20 & 30 \end{bmatrix} + \begin{bmatrix} 5 & 6 \\ 8 & 9 \end{bmatrix} \right\} = \max \left\{ \begin{bmatrix} 15 & 26 \\ 28 & 39 \end{bmatrix} \right\} = 39,$$

$$(A \oplus B)(3, 4) = \max \left\{ \begin{bmatrix} 30 & 40 & 50 \\ 30 & 50 & 60 \\ 50 & 50 & 60 \end{bmatrix} + \begin{bmatrix} 1 & 2 & 3 \\ 4 & 5 & 6 \\ 7 & 8 & 9 \end{bmatrix} \right\}$$

$$= \max \left\{ \begin{bmatrix} 31 & 42 & 53 \\ 34 & 55 & 66 \\ 57 & 58 & 69 \end{bmatrix} \right\} = 69.$$

After all the calculations, we have

$$A \oplus B = \begin{matrix} 39 & 39 & 49 & 59 & 58 \\ 39 & 39 & 59 & 69 & 68 \\ 49 & 59 & 59 & 69 & 68 \\ 59 & 69 & 69 & 79 & 78 \\ 56 & 66 & 66 & 76 & 75 \end{matrix}$$

Note that an erosion may contain negative values or a dilation value greater than 255. To render the result suitable for display, we have the same choices as for spatial filtering: we may apply a linear transformation, or we may clip values.

In general, and this can be seen from the examples, erosion will tend to decrease and darken objects in an image, and dilation will tend to enlarge and lighten objects.

RELATIONSHIP BETWEEN GRAYSCALE EROSION AND DILATION   By definition of maximum and minimum we have, if X and Y are two matrices,

$$\max\{X + Y\} = -\min\{-X - Y\}.$$

Since $\max\{X + Y\}$ corresponds to $A \oplus B$ and $\min\{X - Y\}$ to $A \ominus B$, we have

$$A \oplus B = -(-A \ominus B)$$
$$A \ominus B = -(-A \oplus B)$$

or

$$-(A \oplus B) = -A \ominus B$$
$$-(A \ominus B) = -A \oplus B.$$

We can use the `imerode` and `imdilate` functions for grayscale erosion and dilation, but we have to be more careful about the structuring element. To create a structuring element for use with grayscale morphology, we must provide both the neighborhood D_B and the values. To do this we need to use the `strel` function.

For example, we will use MATLAB with the previous examples. First we need to create the structuring element.

```
>> str=strel('arbitrary',ones(3,3),[1 2 3;4 5 6;7 8 9])

str =

Nonflat STREL object containing 9 neighbors.

Neighborhood:
        1       1       1
        1       1       1
        1       1       1


Height:
        1       2       3
        4       5       6
        7       8       9
```

Here we use the `arbitrary` parameter of `strel`. This allows us to create a structuring element containing any values we like. The first matrix, `ones(3,3)`, provides the neighborhood; the second matrix provides the values. Now we can test it.

```
>> A=[10 20 20 20 30;20 30 30 40 50;20 30 30 50 60;20 40 50 50 60;30 50 60 60 70];
>> imerode(A,str)

ans =
        5       6      14      15      16
        8       9      17      18      19
       12      13      25      26      39
       15      16      28      29      46
       18      19      39      48      49
```

For dilation, MATLAB implements the convention of the structuring element being rotated 180°. Thus, to obtain the result we produced above, we need to rotate `str` to obtain `str2`.

```
>> str2=strel('arbitrary',ones(3,3),[9 8 7;6 5 4;3 2 1])
str2 =
Nonflat STREL object containing 9 neighbors.

Neighborhood:
       1       1       1
       1       1       1
       1       1       1

Height:
       9       8       7
       6       5       4
       3       2       1

>> imdilate(A,str2)

ans =

      39      39      49      59      58
      39      39      59      69      68
      49      59      59      69      68
      59      69      69      79      78
      56      66      66      76      75
```

Now we can experiment with an image. We would expect that dilation would increase light areas in an image and erosion would decrease them.

```
>> c=imread('caribou.tif');
>> str=strel('square',5)

str =

Flat STREL object containing 25 neighbors.
Decomposition: 2 STREL objects containing a total of 10 neighbors

Neighborhood:
       1       1       1       1       1
       1       1       1       1       1
       1       1       1       1       1
       1       1       1       1       1
       1       1       1       1       1

>> cd=imdilate(c,str);
>> ce=imerode(c,str);
>> imshow(cd),figure,imshow(ce)
```

The results are shown in Figure 10.34. Figure 10.34(a) is the dilation and image Figure 10.34(b) the erosion.

(a)   (b)

FIGURE 10.34 *Morphology. (a) Dilation. (b) Erosion.*

(a)   (b)

FIGURE 10.35 *Grayscale opening and closing. (a) Opening. (b) Closing.*

OPENING AND CLOSING   Opening and closing are defined exactly as for binary morphology: opening is an erosion followed by a dilation, and closing is a dilation followed by an erosion. The imopen and imclose functions can be applied to grayscale images if a structuring element has been created with strel.

Using the caribou image and the same 5×5 square-structuring element as above:

```
>> co=imopen(c,str);
>> cc=imclose(c,str);
>> imshow(co),figure,imshow(cc)
```

The results are shown in Figure 10.35, Figure 10.35(a) being the opening and Figure 10.35(b) the closing.

10.9 Applications of Grayscale Morphology

Almost all the applications we saw for binary images can be carried over directly to grayscale images.

10.9.1 Edge Detection

We can use the morphological gradient

$$(A \oplus B) - (A \ominus B)$$

for grayscale edge detection. We can try this with two different structuring elements.

```
>> str1=strel('square',3);
>> str2=strel('square',5);
>> ce1=imerode(c,str1);
>> ce2=imerode(c,str2);
>> cd1=imdilate(c,str1);
>> cd2=imdilate(c,str2);
>> cg1=imsubtract(cd1,ce1);
>> cg2=imsubtract(cd2,ce2);
>> imshow(cg1),figure,imshow(cg2)
```

The results are shown in Figure 10.36. Figure 10.36(a) uses the 3×3 square and Figure 10.36(b) the 5×5 square.

10.9.2 Noise Removal

As before, we can attempt to remove noise with morphological filtering: an opening followed by a closing.

```
>> cn=imnoise(c,'salt & pepper');
>> cf=imclose(imopen(cn,str),str);
>> imshow(cn),figure,imshow(cf)
```

These are shown in Figure 10.37. The result is reasonable, if slightly blurry. Morphological filtering does not perform particularly well on Gaussian noise.

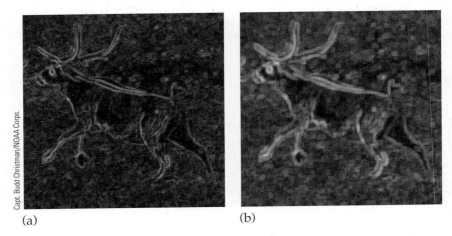

(a)   (b)

FIGURE 10.36 *Use of the morphological gradient.*

(a)   (b)

FIGURE 10.37 *Use of morphological filtering to remove noise.*

EXERCISES

1. For each of the following images A and structuring elements B:

$A =$

```
0 0 0 0 0 0 0 0    0 0 0 0 0 0 0 0    0 0 0 0 0 0 0 0
0 0 0 1 1 1 1 0    0 1 1 1 1 1 1 0    0 0 0 0 0 1 1 0
0 0 0 1 1 1 1 0    0 1 1 1 1 1 1 0    0 1 1 1 0 1 1 0
0 1 1 1 1 1 1 0    0 1 1 0 0 1 1 0    0 1 1 1 0 1 1 0
0 1 1 1 1 1 1 0    0 1 1 0 0 1 1 0    0 1 1 1 0 1 1 0
0 1 1 1 1 0 0 0    0 1 1 1 1 1 1 0    0 1 1 1 0 0 0 0
0 1 1 1 1 0 0 0    0 1 1 1 1 1 1 0    0 1 1 1 0 0 0 0
0 0 0 0 0 0 0 0    0 0 0 0 0 0 0 0    0 0 0 0 0 0 0 0
```

$B =$

```
0   1   0     1   1   1     1   0   0
1   1   1     1   1   1     0   0   0
0   1   0     1   1   1     0   0   1
```

calculate the erosion $A \ominus B$, the dilation $A \oplus B$, the opening $A \circ B$ and the closing $A \bullet B$.

Check your answers with MATLAB.

2. Suppose a square object was eroded by a circle whose radius was about one quarter the side of the square. Draw the result.

3. Repeat the Question 2 with dilation.

4. Using the binary images `circbw.tif`, `circles.tif`, `circlesm.tif`, `logo.tif` and `testpat2.tif`, view the erosion and dilation with both the square- and the cross-structuring elements. Can you see any differences?

5. Read in the image `circlesm.tif`.

   a. Erode with squares of increasing size until the image starts to split into disconnected components.
   b. Use `pixval` on and find the coordinates of a pixel in one of the components.
   c. Use the `components` function to isolate that particular component.

6. a. With your disconnected image from Question 5, compute its boundary.
   b. Again with `pixval` on, find a pixel inside one of the boundaries.
   c. Use the `regfill` function to fill that region.
   d. Display the image as a boundary with one of the regions filled in.

7. Using the 3 × 3 square-structuring element, compute the skeletons of
   a. A 7 square.
   b. A 5 × 9 rectangle.
   c. An L-shaped figure formed from an 8 × 8 square with a 3 × 3 square taken from a corner.
   d. An H-shaped figure formed from a 15 × 15 square with 5 × 5 squares taken from the centers of the top and bottom.
   e. A cross formed from an 11 × 11 square with 3 × 3 squares taken from each corner.

   In each case check your answer with MATLAB

8. Repeat Question 7, but use the cross-structuring element.

9. For the images listed in Question 4, obtain their skeletons by both the `bwmorph` function and by using the function given in Figure 10.30. Which seems to provide the best result?

10. Use the hit-or-miss transform with appropriate structuring elements to find the dot on the *i* in the word *in* in the image `text.tif`.

11. Let A be the matrix obtained with the MATLAB command

```
>> A=magic(6)
```

By hand, compute the grayscale erosions and dilations with the structuring elements
$B =$

10	10	10
10	10	10
10	10	10

	5	20	5
	20	5	20
	5	20	5

In each case, check your answers with MATLAB.

12. Perform grayscale erosions, dilations, openings, and closings on the cameraman image using the above structuring elements.

13. a. Obtain the grayscale version of the twins image as was used in Chapter 8.
    b. Apply salt and pepper noise to the image.
    c. Attempt to remove the noise using morphological techniques.
    d. Compare the results to median filtering.

14. Repeat Question 13, but use Gaussian noise.

15. Use morphological methods to find the edges of the image `ic.tif`. Do this in two ways:

    a. By thresholding first and using binary morphology.
    b. By using grayscale morphology and thresholding second.

    Which seems to give the best results?

16. Compare the results of Question 15 with standard edge-detection techniques.

CHAPTER ELEVEN

Image Topology

11.1 Introduction

We are often interested in only the very basic aspects of an image: the number of occurrences of a particular object, whether or not there are holes, and so on. The investigation of these fundamental properties of an image is called **digital topology** or **image topology,** and in this chapter we will investigate some of the more elementary aspects of this subject.

For example, consider an image thresholded and cleaned up with a morphological opening to show a collection of blobs.

```
>> n=imread('nodules1.tif');
>> nt=~im2bw(e,0.5);
>> n2=imopen(nt,strel('disk',5));
```

The image n2 is shown in Figure 11.1. The number of blobs can be determined by morphological methods. However, the study of image topology provides alternative and very powerful methods for such tasks as object counting. Topology provides very rigorous definitions for concepts such as adjacency and distance. As we shall see, skeletonization can be performed very efficiently using topological methods.

11.2 Neighbors and Adjacency

A first task is to define the concept of adjacency: under what conditions a pixel may be regarded as being next to another pixel. For this chapter, the concern will be with binary images only, and thus we will be dealing only with positions of pixels.

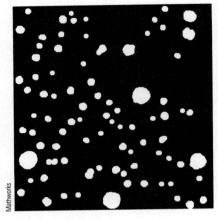

FIGURE 11.1 *How many blobs?*

A pixel P has four 4-neighbors:

and eight 8-neighbors:

Two pixels P and Q are **4-adjacent** if they are 4-neighbors of one another and **8-adjacent** if they are 8-neighbors of one another.

11.3 Paths and Components

Suppose that P and Q are any two (not necessarily adjacent) pixels, and suppose that P and Q can be joined by a sequence of pixels as shown:

If the path contains only 4-adjacent pixels, as the path does in the above diagram, then P and Q are **4-connected.** If the path contains 8-adjacent pixels, then P and Q are **8-connected.** The following picture shows an example of 8-connected pixels.

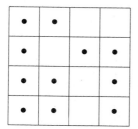

A set of pixels, all of which are 4-connected to each other, is called a **4-component.** If all the pixels are 8-connected, the set is an **8-component.**

For example, the following image has two 4-components (one component containing all the pixels in the left two columns, and the other component containing all the pixels in the right two columns), but only one 8-component.

We can define **path** more formally as follows:

A 4-path from P to Q is a sequence of pixels

$$P = p_0, p_1, p_2, \ldots, p_n = Q$$

such that for each $i = 0, 1, \ldots, n - 1$, pixel p_i is 4-adjacent to pixel p_{i+1}.

An 8-path is where the pixels in the sequence connecting P and Q are 8-adjacent.

11.4 Equivalence Relations

A relation $x \sim y$ between two objects x and y is an equivalence relation if the relation is

1. **reflexive,** $x \sim x$ for all x,
2. **symmetric,** $x \sim y \iff y \sim x$ for all x and y,
3. **transitive,** if $x \sim y$ and $y \sim z$, then $x \sim z$ for all x, y, and z.

For some examples, see the following:

1. For numeric equality, $x \sim y$ if x and y are two numbers for which $x = y$.
2. For divisors, $x \sim y$ if x and y are two numbers that have the same remainder when divided by 7.
3. For set cardinality, $S \sim T$ if S and T are two sets with the same number of elements.
4. For connectedness, $P \sim Q$ if P and Q are two connected pixels.

Here are some relations that are not equivalence relations.

1. Personal relations: define $x \sim y$ if x and y are two people who are related to each other. This is not an equivalence relation. It is reflexive (a person is certainly related to himself or herself) and symmetric, but not transitive (can you give an example?).
2. Pixel adjacency: this is not transitive.
3. Subset relation: define $S \sim T$ if $S \subseteq T$. This is reflexive (a set is a subset of itself) and transitive, but not reflexive. If $S \subseteq T$ then it is not necessarily true that $T \subseteq S$.

The importance of the equivalence relation concept is that it allows us a very neat way of dealing with issues of connectedness. We need another definition. An **equivalence class** is the set of all objects equivalent to each other.

We can now define the components of a binary image as being the equivalence classes of the connectedness equivalence relation.

11.5 Component Labeling

In this section we give an algorithm for labeling all the 4-components of a binary image, starting at the top left and working across and down. If p is the current pixel, let u be its upper 4-neighbor, and l its left-hand 4-neighbor:

	u	
l	p	

We will scan the image row by row, moving across from left to right. We will assign labels to pixels in the image, and these labels will be the numbers of the components of the image.

For descriptive purposes, a pixel in the image will be called a **foreground pixel.** A pixel not in the image will be called a **background pixel.** And now for the algorithm:

1. Check the state of p. If it is a background pixel, move on to the next scanning position. If it is a foreground pixel, check the state of u and l. If they are both background pixels, assign a new label to p. (This is the case when a new component has been encountered.)

- If just one of u or l is a foreground pixel, then assign its label to p.
- If both u and l are foreground pixels and have the same label, assign that label to p.
- If both u and l are foreground pixels, but have different labels, assign either of those labels to p and make a note that those two labels are equivalent (since u and l belong to the same 4-component connected through p).

2. At the end of the scan, all foreground pixels have been labeled, but some labels may be equivalent. We now sort the labels into equivalence classes and assign a different label to each class.

3. Do a second pass through the image, replacing the label on each foreground pixel with the label assigned to its equivalence class in the previous step.

We now give an example of this algorithm in practice, on the binary image, which has two 4-components: one the three pixels in the top left, the other the five pixels in the bottom right.

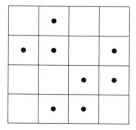

Step 1. We start moving along the top row. The first foreground pixel is the bullet in the second place, and since its upper and left neighbors are either background pixels or nonexistent, we assign it the label 1.

	•1		
•	•		•
		•	•
	•	•	

In the second row, the first (foreground) pixel again has its upper or left neighbors as either background or nonexistent, so we assign it a new label—2.

	•1		
•2	•		•
		•	•
	•	•	

The second (foreground) pixel in the second row now has both its upper and left neighbors being foreground pixels. However, they have different labels. We thus assign either of these labels to this second pixel, say label 1, and make a note that labels 1 and 2 are equivalent.

	•1		
•2	•1		•
		•	•
	•	•	

The third foreground pixel in the second row has both its upper and left neighbors being background pixels, so we assign it a new label—3.

	•1		
•2	•1		•3
		•	•
	•	•	

In the third row, the first foreground pixel has both its upper and left neighbors being background pixels, so we assign it a new label—4. The second (foreground) pixel in the third row now has both its upper and left neighbors being foreground pixels. However, they have different labels. We thus assign either of these labels to this second pixel, say label 3, and make a note that labels 3 and 4 are equivalent.

	•1		
•2	•1		•3
		•4	•3
	•	•	

In the fourth row, the first foreground pixel has both its upper and left neighbors being background pixels, so we assign it a new label—5. The second (foreground) pixel in the fourth row now has both its upper and left neighbors being foreground pixels. However, they have different labels. We thus assign either of these labels to this second pixel, say label 4, and make a note that labels 4 and 5 are equivalent.

	•1		
•2	•1		•3
		•4	•3
	•5	•4	

This completes Step 1.

Step 2. We have the following equivalence classes of labels:

$$\{1, 2\} \quad \text{and} \quad \{3, 4, 5\}.$$

Assign label 1 to the first class and label 2 to the second class.

Step 3. Each pixel with labels 1 or 2 from the first step will be assigned label 1, and each pixel with labels 3, 4, or 5 from the first step will be assigned label 2.

	•1		
•1	•1		•2
		•2	•2
	•2	•2	

This completes the algorithm.

The algorithm can be modified to label 8-components of an image, but in Step 1 we need to consider diagonal elements of p:

d	u	e
l	p	

The algorithm is similar to the previous algorithm. Step 1 is changed as follows:

Step 1. If p is a background pixel, move on to the next scanning position. If it is a foreground pixel, check d, u, e, and l. If they are all background pixels, assign a new label to p. If just one is a foreground pixel, assign its label to p. If two or more are foreground pixels, assign any of their labels to p and make a note that all their labels are equivalent.

Steps 2 and 3 are as before.

This algorithm is implemented by the bwlabel function. We will give an example on a small image:

```
>> i=zeros(8,8);
>> i(2:4,3:6)=1;
>> i(5:7,2)=1;
>> i(6:7,5:8)=1;
>> i(8,4:5)=1;
>> i
```

and the result is:

```
0    0    0    0    0    0    0    0
0    0    1    1    1    1    0    0
0    0    1    1    1    1    0    0
0    0    1    1    1    1    0    0
0    1    0    0    0    0    0    0
0    1    0    0    1    1    1    1
0    1    0    0    1    1    1    1
0    0    0    1    1    0    0    0
```

This image can be seen to have two 8-components and three 4-components. To see these, we can enter

```
>> bwabel(i,4)
```

which produces

```
0    0    0    0    0    0    0    0
0    0    2    2    2    2    0    0
0    0    2    2    2    2    0    0
0    0    2    2    2    2    0    0
0    1    0    0    0    0    0    0
0    1    0    0    3    3    3    3
0    1    0    0    3    3    3    3
0    0    0    3    3    0    0    0
```

and

```
>> bwlabel(i,8)
```

which produces

```
0    0    0    0    0    0    0    0
0    0    1    1    1    1    0    0
0    0    1    1    1    1    0    0
0    0    1    1    1    1    0    0
0    1    0    0    0    0    0    0
0    1    0    0    2    2    2    2
0    1    0    0    2    2    2    2
0    0    0    2    2    0    0    0
```

To experiment with a real image, let's try to count the number of bacteria in the image bacteria.tif. The image must first be thresholded to obtain a binary image showing only the bacteria and then bwlabel applied to the result. We can find the number of objects simply by finding the largest label produced.

```
>> b=imread('bacteria.tif');
>> bt=b<100;
>> bl=bwlabel(bt);
>> max(bl(:))
```

The result is given as

```
>> 21
```

which is the required number.

11.6 Lookup Tables

Lookup tables provide a very neat and efficient method of binary image processing. Consider the 3×3 neighborhood of a pixel. Since there are 9 pixels in this neighborhood, each with two possible states, the total number of different neighborhoods is $2^9 = 512$. Since the output of any binary operation will be either zero or one, a lookup table is a binary vector of length 512, each element representing the output from the corresponding neighborhoods. Note that this is slightly different from the lookup tables discussed in Section 4.4. In that section lookup tables were applied to single-pixel gray values; here they are applied to neighborhoods.

The trick is to be able to order all the neighborhoods so that we have a one-one correspondence between neighborhoods and output values. This is done by giving each pixel in the neighborhood a weight.

1	8	64
2	16	128
4	32	256

The value of the neighborhood is obtained by adding the weights of one-valued pixels. That value is then the index to the lookup table. For example, the following show neighborhoods and their values.

0	1	0
1	1	0
0	0	1

Value $= 2 + 8 + 16 + 256 = 282$

1	0	0
0	1	1
1	1	1

Value $= 1 + 4 + 16 + 32 + 128 + 256 = 437$

To apply a lookup table, we must first make it. It would be tedious to create a lookup table element by element, so we use the `makelut` function, which defines a lookup table according to a rule. Its syntax is

```
makelut(function, n, P1, P2, ...)
```

where `function` is a string defining a MATLAB matrix function, n is either 2 or 3, and `P1`, `P2`, and so on are optional parameters to be passed to the function. We note that `makelut` allows for lookup tables on 2×2 neighborhoods. In this case the lookup table has only $2^4 = 16$ elements.

Suppose we wish to find the 4-boundary of an image. We define a pixel to be a boundary pixel, if it is a foreground pixel, which is 4-adjacent to a background pixel. So the function to be used in `makelut` is a function that returns one if and only if the central pixel of the 3×3 neighborhood is a boundary pixel:

```
>> f=inline('x(5)&~(x(2)*x(4)*x(6)*x(8))');
```

Note that for this function we are using the single-value matrix indexing scheme, so that `x(5)` is the central pixel of a 3×3 matrix x, and `x(2)`, `x(4)`, `x(6)`, `x(8)` are the pixels 4-adjacent to the center.

Now we can make the lookup table:

```
>> lut=makelut(f,3);
```

and apply it to an image.

```
>> c=imread('circles.tif');
>> cw=applylut(c,lut);
>> imshow(c),figure,imshow(cw)
```

The result is shown in Figure 11.2.

FIGURE 11.2 *The circles image and its boundary.*

FIGURE 11.3 *The 8-boundary of the circles image.*

We can easily adjust the function to find the 8-boundary pixels, these being foreground pixels that are 8-adjacent to background pixels.

```
>> f8=inline('x(5)&~(x(1)*x(2)*x(3)*x(4)*x(6)*x(7)*x(8)*x(9))');
>> lut=makelut(f8,3);
>> cw=applylut(c,lut);
>> imshow(cw)
```

The result is shown in Figure 11.3. Note that this is a stronger boundary, since more pixels are classified as boundary pixels.

As we will see in Section 11.8, lookup tables can be used to great effect in performing skeletonization.

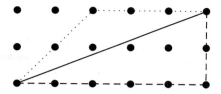

FIGURE 11.4 *Comparison of three metrics.*

11.7 Distances and Metrics

It is necessary to define a function that provides a measure of distance between two points x and y on a grid. A distance function $d(x,y)$ is called a **metric** if it satisfies the following:

1. $d(x,y) = d(y,x)$ (symmetry).
2. $d(x,y) \geq 0$ and $d(x,y) = 0$ if and only if $x = y$ (positivity).
3. $d(x,y) + d(y,z) \leq d(x,z)$ (the triangle inequality).

A standard distance metric is provided by **Euclidean distance,** where if $x = (x_1, x_2)$ and $y = (y_1, y_2)$ then

$$d(x,y) = \sqrt{(x_1 - y_1)^2 + (x_2 - y_2)^2}.$$

This is just the length of the straight line between the points x and y. It is easy to see that the first two properties are satisfied by this metric: it is always positive and is zero only when $x_1 = y_1$ and $x_2 = y_2$; that is, when $x = y$. The third property may be proved very easily; it simply says that given three points x, y, and z, it is shorter to go from x to z directly than via y.

However, if we are constrained to points on a grid, then the Euclidean metric may not be applicable. Figure 11.4 shows the shortest paths for the Euclidean metric and for 4-connected and 8-connected paths. In this figure, the Euclidean distance is $\sqrt{5^2 + 2^2} \approx 5.39$, and the 4-path (the dashed line) and 8-path (dotted line) have length, measured by the number of line segments in each, of 7 and 5, respectively.

Metrics for measuring distance by 4-paths and 8-paths are given by the following two functions:

$$d_4(x,y) = |x_1 - y_1| + |x_2 - y_2|$$
$$d_8(x,y) = \max\{|x_1 - y_1|, |x_2 - y_2|\}$$

As with the Euclidean distance, the first two properties are immediate; to prove the triangle inequality takes a little effort. The metric d_4 is sometimes known as the **taxicab metric,** because it gives the length of the shortest taxicab route through a rectangular grid of streets.

11.7.1 The Distance Transform

In many applications, it is necessary to find the distance of every pixel from a region R. Finding this distance can be done using the standard Euclidean distance defined above. However, this means that to calculate the distance of (x, y) to R, we need to determine all possible distances from (x, y) to pixels in R and take the smallest value as our distance. This is very computationally inefficient: if R is large, then we must compute many square roots. A savings can be obtained since, because the square root function is increasing, we can write the minimum distance as

$$md(x, y) = \sqrt{\min_{(p, q) \in R} \left((x - p)^2 + (y - q)^2\right)},$$

which involves only one square root. But even this definition is slow to compute. There is a great deal of arithmetic involved, and the finding of a smallest value.

The **distance transform** is a computationally efficient method of finding such distance. We will describe it in a sequence of steps:

Step 1. Attach to each pixel (x, y) in the image a label $d(x, y)$, giving its distance from R. Start with labeling each pixel in R with 0 and each pixel not in R with ∞.

Step 2. We now travel through the image pixel by pixel. For each pixel (x, y) replace its label with

$$\min\{d(x, y), d(x + 1, y) + 1, d(x - 1, y) + 1, d(x, y - 1) + 1, d(x, y + 1) + 1\}$$

using $\infty + 1 = \infty$.

Step 3. Repeat Step 2 until all labels have been converted to finite values.

To give some examples of Step 2, suppose we have this neighborhood:

$$
\begin{array}{ccc}
\infty & \infty & \infty \\
2 & \infty & \infty \\
\infty & 3 & \infty
\end{array}
$$

We are only interested in the center pixel (whose label we are about to change) and the four pixels above, below, and to the left and right. To these four pixels we add 1:

$$
\begin{array}{ccc}
 & \infty & \\
3 & \infty & \infty \\
 & 4 &
\end{array}
$$

The minimum of these five values is 3, thus that is the new label for the center pixel.

Suppose we have this neighborhood:

2   ∞   ∞
∞   ∞   ∞
3   ∞   5

Again, we add 1 to each of the four pixels above, below, to the left and right, and keep the center value:

```
        ∞
  ∞   ∞   ∞
        ∞
```

The minimum of these values is ∞, so at this stage the pixel's label is not changed.

Suppose we take an image whose labels after Step 1 are given below

∞	∞	∞	∞	∞	∞
∞	∞	0	0	∞	∞
∞	∞	∞	0	∞	∞
∞	∞	∞	0	∞	∞
∞	∞	∞	0	0	∞
∞	∞	∞	∞	∞	∞

Step 1

∞	∞	1	1	∞	∞
∞	1	0	0	1	∞
∞	∞	1	0	1	∞
∞	∞	1	0	1	∞
∞	∞	1	0	0	1
∞	∞	∞	1	1	∞

Step 2 (first pass)

∞	2	1	1	2	∞
2	1	0	0	1	2
∞	2	1	0	1	2
∞	2	1	0	1	2
∞	2	1	0	0	1
∞	∞	2	1	1	2

Step 2 (second pass)

3	2	1	1	2	3
2	1	0	0	1	2
3	2	1	0	1	2
3	2	1	0	1	2
3	2	1	0	0	1
∞	3	2	1	1	2

Step 2 (third pass)

3	2	1	1	2	3
2	1	0	0	1	2
3	2	1	0	1	2
3	2	1	0	1	2
3	2	1	0	0	1
4	3	2	1	1	2

Step 2 (final pass)

At this stage we stop, because all label values are finite.

An immediate observation is that the distance values given are not, in fact, a very good approximation of real distances. To provide better accuracy, we need to generalize the above transform. One way to do this is to use the concept of a mask. The mask used above was

```
    1
1   0   1
    1
```

Step two in the transform then consists of adding the corresponding mask elements to labels of the neighboring pixels and taking the minimum. To obtain good accuracy with simple arithmetic, the mask will generally consist of integer values, but the final result may require scaling.

Suppose we apply the mask

```
4  3  4
3  0  3
4  3  4
```

to the above image. Step 1 is as above; Step 2 is

∞	4	3	3	4	∞		7	4	3	3	4	7		7	4	3	3	4	7
∞	3	0	0	3	∞		6	3	0	0	3	6		6	3	0	0	3	6
∞	4	3	0	3	∞		7	4	3	0	3	6		7	4	3	0	3	6
∞	∞	3	0	3	∞		8	6	3	0	3	6		8	6	3	0	3	6
∞	∞	3	0	0	3		∞	6	3	0	0	3		9	6	3	0	0	3
∞	∞	4	3	3	4		∞	7	4	3	3	4		10	7	4	3	3	4

Step 2 (first pass)   Step 2 (second)   Step 2 (third)

at which point we stop, and divide all values by three:

2.3	1.3	1	1	1.3	2.3
2	1	0	0	1	2
2.3	1.3	1	0	1	2
2.7	2	1	0	1	2
3	2	1	0	0	1
3.3	2.3	1.3	1	1	1.3

These values are much closer to the Euclidean distances than those provided by the first transform.

Even better accuracy can be obtained by using the mask

```
      11      11
11   7   5   7   11
      5   0   5
11   7   5   7   11
      11      11
```

and dividing the final result by 5:

11	7	5	5	7	11		2.2	1.4	1	1	1.4	2.2
10	5	0	0	5	10		2	1	0	0	1	2
11	7	5	0	5	10		2.2	1.4	1	0	1	2
14	10	5	0	5	7		2.8	2	1	0	1	1.4
16	10	5	0	0	5		3.2	2	1	0	0	1
16	11	7	5	5	7		3.2	2.2	1.4	1	1	1.4

Result of transform   After division by 5

The method we have described can, in fact, be very slow. For a large image we may require many passes before all distance labels become finite. A quicker method requires two passes only: the first pass starts at the top left of the image and moves left to right, top to bottom. The second pass starts at the bottom right of the image and moves right to left, from bottom to top. For this method we break the mask up into two halves; one-half inspects only values to the left and above (this is used for the first pass), and the other half inspects only values to the right and below (this is used for the second pass).

Such pairs of masks are shown in Figure 11.5, and the solid lines show how the original mask is broken up into its two halves.

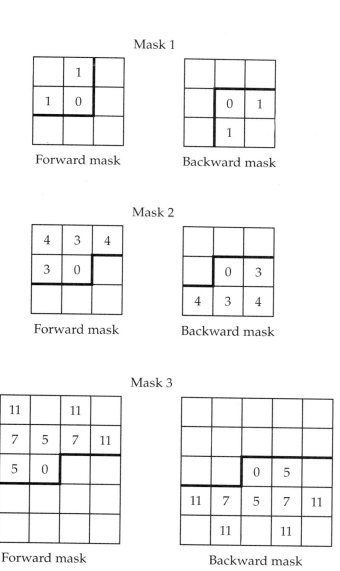

FIGURE 11.5 *Pairs of masks for the two-pass distance transform.*

We apply these masks as follows: first surround the image with zeros (such as for spatial filtering), so that at the edges of the image the masks have values to work with. For the forward pass, for each pixel at position (i, j), add the values given in the forward mask to its neighbors. Take the minimum and replace the current label with it. This is similar to Step 2 in the original algorithm, except we are using fewer pixels. We do the same for the backward pass, except we use the backward mask and start at the bottom right.

If we apply forward masks 1 and 2 to our image, the results of the forward passes are:

∞	∞	∞	∞	∞	∞		∞	∞	∞	∞	∞	∞
∞	∞	0	0	1	2		∞	∞	0	0	3	6
∞	∞	1	0	1	2		∞	4	3	0	3	6
∞	∞	2	0	1	2		8	7	5	0	3	6
∞	∞	3	0	0	1		11	8	4	0	0	3
∞	∞	4	1	1	2		12	8	4	3	3	4

Use of mask 1   Use of mask 2

After applying the backward masks, we will obtain the distance transforms as above.

IMPLEMENTATION IN MATLAB   We can easily write a function to perform the distance transform using the second method as above. Our function will implement the transform as follows:

1. Using the size of the mask, pad the image with an appropriate number of 0s.

2. Change each 0 to infinity, and each 1 to 0.

3. Create forward and backward masks.

4. Perform a forward pass. Replace each label with the minimum of its neighborhood plus the forward mask.

5. Perform a backward pass. Replace each label with the minimum of its neighborhood plus the backward mask.

Let's consider each of these steps separately:

1. Suppose the image is of size $r \times c$ and the mask is of size $r_m \times c_m$, where both mask dimensions are odd numbers. We need to add, on each side of the image, a number of columns equal to $(c_m - 1)/2$, and we need to add, on both top and bottom of the image, a number of rows equal to $(r_m - 1)/2$. In other words, we can embed the image in a larger array of size $(r + r_m - 1) \times (c + c_m - 1)$:

```
>> [r,c]=size(image);
>> [mr,mc]=size(mask);
>> nr=(mr-1)/2;
>> nc=(mc-1)/2;
>> image2=zeros(r+mr-1,c+mc-1);
>> image2(nr+1:r+nr,nc+1:c+nc)=image;
```

2. This can be easily done using the find function. First, change all 0s to infinity. Next change all 1s to 0s:

```
>> image2(find(image2)==0)=Inf;
>> image2(find(image2)==1)=0;
```

3. Suppose we are given a forward mask. We can do this most simply by making all blank entries in the masks shown in Figure 11.5 infinity; this means that pixels in these positions will have no effect on the final minimum. The backward mask can be obtained by two 90° rotations. For example:

```
>> mask1=[Inf 1 Inf;1 0 Inf;Inf Inf Inf];
>> backmask=rot90(rot90(mask1));
```

4. We can implement the forward mask with nested loops:

```
>> for i=nr+1:r+nr,
     for j=nc+1:c+nc,
        image2(i,j)=min(min(image2(i-nr:i+nr,j-nc:j+nc)+mask));
     end;
   end;
```

5. The backward pass is done similarly:

```
>> for i=r+nr:-1:nr+1,
     for j=c+nc:-1:nc+1,
       image2(i,j)=min(min(image2(i-nr:i+nr,j-nc:j+nc)+backmask));
     end;
   end;
```

The full function is shown in Figure 11.6.

```
function res=disttrans(image,mask)
%
% This function implements the distance transform by
% applying MASK to IMAGE, using the two step algorithm
% with "forward" and "backwards" masks.
backmask=rot90(rot90(mask));
[mr,mc]=size(mask);
if ((floor(mr/2)==ceil(mr/2)) | (floor(mc/2)==ceil(mc/2))) then
    error('The mask must have odd dimensions.')
    end;
[r,c]=size(image);
nr=(mr-1)/2;
nc=(mc-1)/2;
image2=zeros(r+mr-1,c+mc-1);
image2(nr+1:r+nr,nc+1:c+nc)=image;
%
% This is the first step; replacing R values with 0 and other
% values with infinity
%
image2(find(image2==0))=Inf;
image2(find(image2==1))=0;
%
% Forward pass
%
for i=nr+1:r+nr,
  for j=nc+1:c+nc,
    image2(i,j)=min(min(image2(i-nr:i+nr,j-nc:j+nc)+mask));
  end;
end;
%
% Backward pass
%
for i=r+nr:-1:nr+1,
  for j=c+nc:-1:nc+1,
    image2(i,j)=min(min(image2(i-nr:i+nr,j-nc:j+nc)+backmask));
  end;
end;

res=image2(nr+1:r+nr,nc+1:c+nc);
```

FIGURE 11.6 *A function for computing the distance transform.*

Let's try it out, first creating our image and the three masks:

```
>> im=[0 0 0 0 0 0;...
0 0 1 1 0 0;...
0 0 0 1 0 0;...
0 0 0 1 0 0;...
0 0 0 1 1 0;...
0 0 0 0 0 0]

im =

      0      0      0      0      0      0
      0      0      1      1      0      0
```

(continued)

```
        0       0       0       1       0       0
        0       0       0       1       0       0
        0       0       0       1       1       0
        0       0       0       0       0       0

>> mask1=[Inf 1 Inf;1 0 Inf;Inf Inf Inf]

mask1 =

    Inf      1    Inf
      1      0    Inf
    Inf    Inf    Inf

>> mask2=[4 3 4;3 0 Inf;Inf Inf Inf]

mask2 =

      4      3      4
      3      0    Inf
    Inf    Inf    Inf

>> mask3=[Inf 11 Inf 11 Inf;...
11 7 5 7 11;...
Inf 5 0 Inf Inf;...
Inf Inf Inf Inf Inf;...
Inf Inf Inf Inf Inf]

mask3 =

    Inf     11    Inf     11    Inf
     11      7      5      7     11
    Inf      5      0    Inf    Inf
    Inf    Inf    Inf    Inf    Inf
    Inf    Inf    Inf    Inf    Inf
```

Now we can apply the transform:

```
>> disttrans(im,mask1)

ans =

      3      2      1      1      2      3
      2      1      0      0      1      2
      3      2      1      0      1      2
      3      2      1      0      1      2
      3      2      1      0      0      1
```

(continued)

```
        4        3        2        1        1        2

>> disttrans(im,mask2)

ans =

        7        4        3        3        4        7
        6        3        0        0        3        6
        7        4        3        0        3        6
        8        6        3        0        3        4
        9        6        3        0        0        3
       10        7        4        3        3        4

>> disttrans(im,mask3)

ans =

       11        7        5        5        7       11
       10        5        0        0        5       10
       11        7        5        0        5       10
       14       10        5        0        5        7
       15       10        5        0        0        5
       16       11        7        5        5        7
```

Now the results of the transforms using masks 2 and 3 should be divided by appropriate values to get approximations to the true distances.

We can, of course, apply the distance transform to a large image, say circles.tif:

```
>> c=~imread('circles.tif');
>> imshow(c)
>> cd=disttrans(c,mask1);
>> figure,imshow(mat2gray(cd))
```

Note that we invert the circles image to produce black circles on a white background. This means that our transform will find distances toward the inside of the original circles. The only reason for doing this is because it is easier to make sense of the resulting image. The circles image is shown in Figure 11.7(a) and the distance transform in Figure 11.7(b).

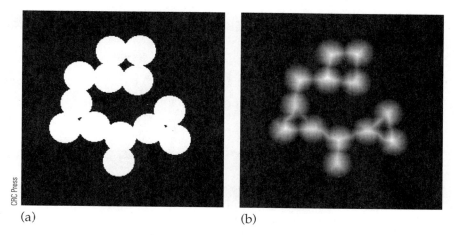

CRC Press

(a)   (b)

FIGURE 11.7 *An example of a distance transform.*

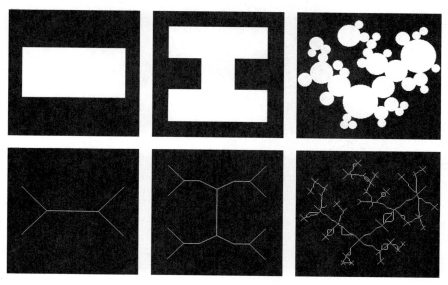

FIGURE 11.8 *Examples of skeletonization.*

11.8 Skeletonization

As we have seen in chapter 10, a skeleton consists of lines and curves which provide information about the size and shape of an object. Figure 11.8 shows some further examples. In this section we investigate some of the properties a skeleton may have, and provide formal methods for determining whether or not a pixel is in the object's skeleton. We will also discuss methods for obtaining a skeleton.

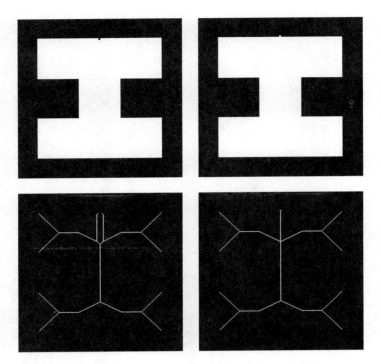

FIGURE 11.9 *Skeletons after small changes to an object.*

A problem with skeletonization is that very small changes to an object can result in large changes to the skeleton. Figure 11.9 shows what happens if we subtract from or add to the central image of Figure 11.8.

One very popular way of defining a skeleton is by the **medial axis** of an object. A pixel is on the medial axis if it is equidistant from at least two pixels on the boundary of the object. To implement this definition directly requires a quick and efficient method of obtaining approximate distances. One way is to use the distance transform. Other ways of approaching the medial axis are the following:

- Imagine the object to be burning up by a fire that advances at a constant rate from the boundary. The places where two lines of fire meet form the medial axis.
- Consider the set of all circles within the object that touch at least two points on the boundary. The centers of all such circles form the medial axis. Figure 11.10 shows this in action.

A very good account of the medial axis (and of skeletonization, in general), is given by Parker [23].

Topological methods provide some powerful methods of skeletonization because we can directly define those pixels that are to be deleted to

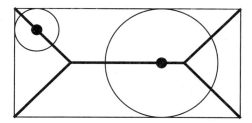

FIGURE 11.10 *The medial axis of an object.*

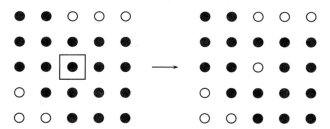

FIGURE 11.11 *A nondeletable pixel creates a hole.*

obtain the final skeleton. In general, we want to delete pixels that can be deleted without changing the **connectivity** of an object, those that do not change the number of components, change the number of holes, or change the relationship of objects and holes. For example, Figure 11.11 shows a nondeletable pixel. Deleting the center (boxed) pixel introduces a hole into the object. In Figure 11.12 there is another example of a nondeletable pixel; in this case deletion removes a hole, because the hole and the exterior become joined. In Figure 11.13 there is another example of a nondeletable pixel. In this case, deletion breaks the object into two separate components. Sometimes we need to consider whether the object is 4-connected or 8-connected. In the previous examples this wasn't a problem. However, look at the examples in Figure 11.14. In Figure 11.14(a), the central point cannot be deleted without changing both the 4-connectivity and the 8-connectivity. In Figure 11.14(b) deleting the central pixel will change the 4-connectivity, but not the 8-connectivity. A pixel that can be deleted without changing the 4-connectivity of the object is called **4-simple.** Similarly, a pixel that can be deleted without changing the 8-connectivity of the object is called **8-simple.** Thus the central pixel in Figure 11.14(a) is neither 4-simple nor 8-simple, but the central pixel in Figure 11.14(b) is 8-simple but not 4-simple.

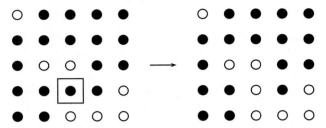

FIGURE 11.12 *A nondeletable pixel removes a hole.*

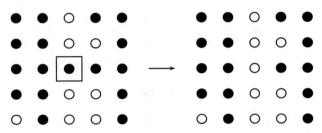

FIGURE 11.13 *A nondeletable pixel disconnects an object.*

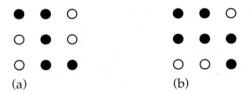

(a)   (b)

FIGURE 11.14 *Simple points.*

A pixel can be tested for deletability by checking its 3×3 neighborhood. Look again at Figure 11.14(a). Suppose the central pixel is deleted. There are two options:

1. The top two pixels and the bottom two pixels become separated, in effect breaking up the object.

2. The top two pixels and the bottom two pixels are joined by a chain of pixels outside the shown neighborhood. In this case all pixels will encircle a hole, and removing the central pixel will remove the hole, as in Figure 11.12.

To check whether a pixel is 4-simple or 8-simple, we introduce some numbers associated with the neighborhood of a foreground pixel p. First define N_p to

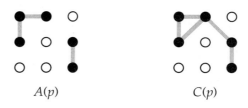

$A(p)$ $C(p)$

FIGURE 11.15 *Components of N_p^*.*

be the 3×3 neighborhood of p and N_p^* to be the 3×3 neighborhood excluding p. Then,

$A(p) =$ the number of 4-components in N_p^*

$C(p) =$ the number of 8-components in N_p^*

$B(p) =$ the number of foreground pixels in N_p^*.

For example, in Figure 11.14(a), we have

$A(p) = 2$

$C(p) = 2$

$B(p) = 4.$

and in Figure 11.14(b) we have

$A(p) = 2$

$C(p) = 1$

$B(p) = 5.$

We can see the last example by deleting the central pixel and enumerating the components of the remaining foreground pixels. This is shown in Figure 11.15. The importance of simple points for deletion can now be stated:

> A foreground pixel p is 4-simple if and only if $A(p) = 1$ and is 8-simple if and only if $C(p) = 1$.

Returning again to Figure 11.14(b), since $C(p) = 1$, the central pixel p is 8-simple and thus can be deleted without affecting the 8-connectivity of the object. But since $A(p) \neq 1$, the central pixel p is not 4-simple and thus cannot be deleted without affecting the 4-connectivity of the object. This is exemplified in Figure 11.15.

11.8.1 Calculating $A(p)$ and $C(p)$

To implement any algorithm involving the values $A(p)$ and $C(p)$, we need an efficient method of calculating them. For $A(p)$ we are only interested in the case where $A(p) = 1$, and this can be determined by calculating the **crossing number** $X(p)$ of a foreground pixel.

> The crossing number $X(p)$ of a foreground pixel p is defined to be the number of times a 0 is followed by a 1 as we traverse the 8-neighbors of p in a clockwise direction.

Suppose we label the neighbors of p as follows:

$$
\begin{array}{ccc}
p_1 & p_2 & p_3 \\
p_8 & p & p_4 \\
p_7 & p_6 & p_5
\end{array}
$$

Consider the sequence

$$p_1, \quad p_2, \quad p_3, \quad p_4, \quad p_5, \quad p_6, \quad p_7, \quad p_8, \quad p_1.$$

The number of times the subsequence

$$0, \quad 1$$

occurs is the crossing number. The importance of the crossing number is that

1. it is easy to compute, and
2. if $X(p) = 1$, then $A(p) = 1$ and thus p is 4-simple.

Consider the neighborhoods in Figure 11.14, but this time using 0s and 1s for background and foreground pixels:

$$
\begin{array}{ccc}
1 & 1 & 0 \\
0 & p & 0 \\
0 & 1 & 1
\end{array}
\qquad\qquad
\begin{array}{ccc}
1 & 1 & 0 \\
1 & p & 1 \\
0 & 0 & 1
\end{array}
$$

Reading the neighbors of p from the left-hand neighborhood produces

$$1, \quad 1, \quad 0, \quad 0, \quad 1, \quad 1, \quad 0, \quad 0, \quad 1.$$

The subsequence 0, 1 occurs twice, so $X(p) = 2$.

For the right hand neighborhood, we have

$$1, \quad 1, \quad 0, \quad 1, \quad 1, \quad 0, \quad 0, \quad 1, \quad 1.$$

Again the subsequence 0, 1 occurs twice, so $X(p) = 2$.

Here are two more:

```
1  1  1              1  1  0
1  p  1              0  p  0
1  0  0              1  0  1
```

For the left neighborhood, the sequence is

$$1, \quad 1, \quad 1, \quad 1, \quad 0, \quad 0, \quad 1, \quad 1, \quad 1.$$

The subsequence 0, 1 occurs only once, so $X(p) = 1$.
　For the right neighborhood, the sequence is

$$1, \quad 1, \quad 0, \quad 0, \quad 1, \quad 0, \quad 1, \quad 0, \quad 1.$$

The subsequence 0, 1 occurs three times, so $X(p) = 3$.
　To implement the crossing number in MATLAB, we first note that a 3×3 matrix a in MATLAB can be indexed using single indexing as

```
a(1)    a(4)    a(7)
a(2)    a(5)    a(8)
a(3)    a(6)    a(9)
```

We can now create two sequences: the neighboring pixels in clockwise order

```
>> p=[a(1) a(4) a(7) a(8) a(9) a(6) a(3) a(2)];
```

and the neighboring pixels starting at a(4)

```
>> pp=[p(2:8) p(1)];
```

Thus, pp(i)=p(i+1) with pp(8)=p(1). A 0, 1 is counted if for any i with $1 \le i \le 8$ we have p(i)=0 and pp(i)=1. This will occur if and only if

```
(1-p(i))*pp(i)
```

is equal to 1.
　Now we can calculate the crossing number as the sum:

```
>> crossnum=sum((1-p).*pp)
```

Calculating $C(p)$ can be done with this simple function:

$$C(p) = [\overline{p_2} \wedge (p_3 \vee p_4)] + [\overline{p_4} \wedge (p_5 \vee p_6)] + [\overline{p_7} \wedge (p_8 \vee p_9)] + [\overline{p_8} \wedge (p_1 \vee p_2)]$$

where

$\overline{p_i} = $ complement of p_i ($= 1 - p_i$)

$\wedge, \vee = $ usual boolean AND, OR

$+ = $ arithmetic addition.

For discussion of this method of calculating $C(p)$ see Hall, et al. [8].

Again, look at the neighborhoods from Figure 11.14 given above as 0s and 1s. For the left-hand neighborhood we have

$$
\begin{aligned}
C(p) &= [\overline{1} \wedge (0 \vee 0)] + [\overline{0} \wedge (1 \vee 1)] + [\overline{1} \wedge (0 \vee 0)] + [\overline{0} \wedge (1 \vee 1)] \\
&= [0 \wedge 0] + [1 \wedge 1] + [0 \wedge 0] + [1 \wedge 1] \\
&= 0 + 1 + 0 + 1 \\
&= 2
\end{aligned}
$$

and this is indeed the number of 8-components in N_p^*. For the right-hand neighborhood (which is shown in Figure 11.15) we have

$$
\begin{aligned}
C(p) &= [\overline{1} \wedge (0 \vee 1)] + [\overline{1} \wedge (1 \vee 0)] + [\overline{0} \wedge (0 \vee 1)] + [\overline{1} \wedge (1 \vee 1)] \\
&= [0 \wedge 1] + [0 \wedge 1] + [1 \wedge 1] + [0 \wedge 1] \\
&= 0 + 0 + 0 + 1 \\
&= 1,
\end{aligned}
$$

which is the number of 8-components in N_p^*.

11.8.2 How Not To Do Skeletonization

Now we know how to check if a pixel can be deleted without affecting the connectivity of the object. In general, a skeletonization algorithm works by an iteration process, at each step identifying deletable pixels and deleting them all. The algorithm will continue until no further deletions are possible.

One way to remove pixels is as follows:

At each step, find all foreground pixels that are 4-simple and delete them all.

Sounds good? Let's try it on a small rectangle of size 2×4:

$$
\begin{array}{cccccc}
0 & 0 & 0 & 0 & 0 & 0 \\
0 & 1 & 1 & 1 & 1 & 0 \\
0 & 1 & 1 & 1 & 1 & 0 \\
0 & 0 & 0 & 0 & 0 & 0
\end{array}
$$

If we check the pixels in this object carefully, we will find that they are all 4-simple. Deleting them all will thus remove the object completely, a very undesirable result. Clearly, we need to be a bit more careful about which pixels we can delete and when. We need to add an extra test for deletability so that we don't delete too many pixels.

We have two options here:

1. We can provide a stepwise algorithm and change the test for deletability at each step.
2. We can apply a different test for deletability according to where the pixel lies on the image grid.

Algorithms that work according to the first option are called **subiteration algorithms;** algorithms that work according to the second option are called **subfield algorithms.**

11.8.3 The Zhang-Suen Skeletonization Algorithm

This algorithm has attained the status of a modern classic; it has some faults (as we shall see), but it works fairly fast and most of the time produces acceptable results. It is an example of a subiteration algorithm in that we apply a slightly different deletablity test for different steps of the algorithm.

Step N Flag a foreground pixel $p = 1$ to be deletable if

1. $2 \leq B(p) \leq 6$,
2. $X(p) = 1$,
3. If N is odd, then

$$
p_2 \cdot p_4 \cdot p_6 = 0
$$
$$
p_4 \cdot p_6 \cdot p_8 = 0.
$$

If N is even, then

$$
p_2 \cdot p_4 \cdot p_8 = 0
$$
$$
p_2 \cdot p_6 \cdot p_8 = 0.
$$

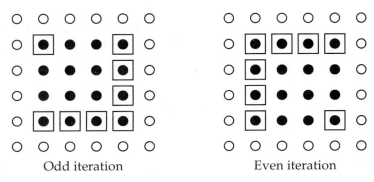

Odd iteration   Even iteration

FIGURE 11.16 *Deletion in the Zhang-Suen algorithm.*

Item 3 can be written alternatively as:

3. If N is odd, then

$$p_4 = 0, \quad \text{or} \quad p_6 = 0, \quad \text{or} \quad p_2 = p_8 = 0$$

If N is even, then

$$p_2 = 0, \quad \text{or} \quad p_8 = 0, \quad \text{or} \quad p_4 = p_6 = 0.$$

If we check the diagram for the neighbors of a foreground pixel p, we see that we can rephrase this item as follows:

> For odd iterations, delete only pixels that are on the right-hand side, or bottom of an object, or on a northwest corner.

> For even iterations, delete only pixels that are on the left-hand side, or top of an object, or on a southeast corner.

Figure 11.16 shows pixels that may be considered for deletion at different iterations. Item 1 in the algorithm ensures that we don't delete pixels that have only one neighbor or have seven or more. If a pixel has only one neighbor, it would be at the end of a skeletal line and we would not want it to be deleted. If a pixel has seven neighbors, then deleting it would start an unacceptable erosion into the object's shape. This item thus ensures that the basic shape of the object is kept by the skeleton. Item 2 is our standard connectivity condition.

A major fault with this algorithm is that there are objects that will be deleted completely. Consider a 2×2 square:

```
0  0  0  0
0  1  1  0
0  1  1  0
0  0  0  0
```

We can check carefully that every item is satisfied by every pixel, and hence every pixel will be deleted.

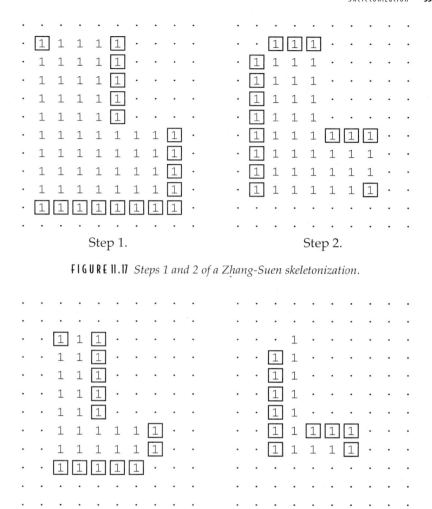

Step 1.   Step 2.

FIGURE 11.17 *Steps 1 and 2 of a Zhang-Suen skeletonization.*

Step 3.   Step 4.

FIGURE 11.18 *Steps 3 and 4 of a Zhang-Suen skeletonization.*

EXAMPLE Consider the L shape shown in Figure 11.17, where for ease of viewing we have replaced all the zeros (background pixels) with dots. The boxed pixels show those that will be deleted by steps 1 and 2 of the algorithm. Figure 11.18 shows steps 3 and 4 of the skeletonization. After step 4, no more deletions are possible, and so the skeleton consists of the unboxed foreground pixels in the right-hand diagram of Figure 11.18. Note that the skeleton does not include the corners of the original object.

We can implement this algorithm easily in MATLAB. We use lookup tables, one for the odd iterations and one for the even. We then apply these lookup

```
function out=zsodd(nbhd);
s=sum(nbhd(:))-nbhd(5);
temp1=(2<=s)&(s<=6);
p=[nbhd(1) nbhd(4) nbhd(7) nbhd(8) nbhd(9) nbhd(6) nbhd(3) nbhd(2)];
pp=[p(2:8) p(1)];
xp=sum((1-p).*pp);
temp2=(xp==1);
prod1=nbhd(4)*nbhd(8)*nbhd(6);
prod2=nbhd(8)*nbhd(6)*nbhd(2);
temp3=(prod1==0)&(prod2==0);
if temp1&temp2&temp3&nbhd(5)==1
   out=0;
else
   out=nbhd(5);
end;
```

FIGURE 11.19 *A* MATLAB *function for Zhang-Suen odd iterations.*

```
function out=zseven(nbhd);
s=sum(nbhd(:))-nbhd(5);
temp1=(2<=s)&(s<=6);
p=[nbhd(1) nbhd(4) nbhd(7) nbhd(8) nbhd(9) nbhd(6) nbhd(3) nbhd(2)];
pp=[p(2:8) p(1)];
xp=sum((1-p).*pp);
temp2=(xp==1);
prod1=nbhd(4)*nbhd(8)*nbhd(2);
prod2=nbhd(4)*nbhd(6)*nbhd(2);
temp3=(prod1==0)&(prod2==0);
if temp1&temp2&temp3&nbhd(5)==1
   out=0;
else
   out=nbhd(5);
end;
```

FIGURE 11.20 *A* MATLAB *function for Zhang-Suen even iterations.*

tables alternately until there is no change in the image for two successive iterations. We manage this by keeping three images at any given time: the current image, the previous image, and the last (that is, before the previous) image. If the current and last images are equal, we stop. Otherwise, push the images back: the previous image becomes last and the current image become previous. We then apply whichever lookup table is appropriate to the current image to create the new current image. That is,

$$last \leftarrow previous$$

$$previous \leftarrow current$$

$$current \leftarrow \text{applylut}(current, \text{lut})$$

The functions for creating the lookup tables are given in Figures 11.19 and 11.20

```
function out=zs(im)
%
% ZS(IM) applises the Zhang-Suen skeletonization algorithm to image IM.  IM
% must be binary.
%
luteven=makelut('zseven',3);
lutodd=makelut('zsodd',3);
done=0;
N=2;
last=im;
previous=applylut(last,lutodd);
current=applylut(previous,luteven);
while done==0,
  if all(current(:)==last(:)),
    done=1;
  end;
  N=N+1;
  last=previous;
  previous=current;
  if mod(N,2)==0,
    current=applylut(current,luteven);
  else
    current=applylut(current,lutodd);
  end;
end;

out=current;
```

FIGURE 11.21 *A* MATLAB *function implementing Zhang-Suen skeletonization.*

Now we create a function that is applied as described above; it is shown in Figure 11.21 We can test this first on our L shape above.

```
>> L=zeros(12,10);L(2:11,2:6)=1;L(7:11,7:9)=1

L =

     0     0     0     0     0     0     0     0     0     0
     0     1     1     1     1     1     0     0     0     0
     0     1     1     1     1     1     0     0     0     0
     0     1     1     1     1     1     0     0     0     0
     0     1     1     1     1     1     0     0     0     0
     0     1     1     1     1     1     0     0     0     0
     0     1     1     1     1     1     1     1     1     0
     0     1     1     1     1     1     1     1     1     0
     0     1     1     1     1     1     1     1     1     0
     0     1     1     1     1     1     1     1     1     0
     0     0     0     0     0     0     0     0     0     0

>> Ls=zs(L)

Ls =

     0     0     0     0     0     0     0     0     0     0
     0     0     0     0     0     0     0     0     0     0
     0     0     0     0     0     0     0     0     0     0
```

(continued)

FIGURE 11.22 *Examples of the Zhang-Suen skeletonization.*

0	0	0	1	0	0	0	0	0	0
0	0	0	1	0	0	0	0	0	0
0	0	0	1	0	0	0	0	0	0
0	0	0	1	0	0	0	0	0	0
0	0	0	1	0	0	0	0	0	0
0	0	0	1	1	1	0	0	0	0
0	0	0	0	0	0	0	0	0	0
0	0	0	0	0	0	0	0	0	0
0	0	0	0	0	0	0	0	0	0

This result is exactly the same as that obtained previously.

We have two more examples, the circle image and the "nice work" image. Both the images and their skeletonizations are shown in Figure 11.22.

```
                Step 1                                    Step 2

 .  [1]  2  [1]  2  [1]  .   .   .   .   .    [2]  .  [2]  .   .   .   .
 .   2   1   2   1   2   .   .   .        .   [2]  1  [2]  1   2   .   .   .
 .  [1]  2   1   2  [1]  .   .   .        .   [2]  1  [2]  .   .   .   .
 .   2   1   2   1   2   .   .   .        .   [2]  1   2   1  [2]  .   .   .
 .  [1]  2   1   2  [1]  .   .        .   .   [2]  1  [2]  .   .   .   .
 .   2   1   2   1   2  [1]  2  [1]  .   .    [2]  1   2   1  [2]  .  [2]  .   .
 .  [1]  2   1   2   1   2   1   2   .   .  . [2]  1   2   1  [2]  1  [2]  .
 .   2   1   2   1   2   1   2  [1]  .   .    [2]  1   2   1   2   1  [2]  .
 .  [1]  2   1   2   1   2   1   2   .   .  .  2   1  [2]  1  [2]  1  [2]  .
 .   2  [1]  2  [1]  2  [1]  2  [1]  .   .    2   .  [2]  .  [2]  .  [2]  .   .
```

FIGURE 11.23 *Steps 1 and 2 of a Guo-Hall skeletonization.*

11.8.4 The Guo-Hall Skeletonization Algorithm

There are, in fact, a number of Guo-Hall algorithms. We will investigate one that has the advantages of being simple to describe, easy to implement, and fast to run, while giving good results. What could be better?

The Guo-Hall algorithm is an example of a subfield algorithm. We imagine the image grid being labeled with 1s and 2s in a chessboard configuration:

$$
\begin{array}{cccc}
1 & 2 & 1 & 2 \quad \cdots \\
2 & 1 & 2 & 1 \quad \cdots \\
1 & 2 & 1 & 2 \quad \cdots \\
2 & 1 & 2 & 1 \quad \cdots \\
\vdots & \vdots & \vdots & \vdots \quad \ddots
\end{array}
$$

At step one, we only consider foreground pixels whose labels are 1. At step two, we only consider foreground pixels whose labels are 2. We continue alternating between pixels labeled 1 and pixels labeled 2 from step to step until no more deletions are possible. Here is the algorithm:

Flag a foreground pixel p as deletable if $C(p) = 1$ and $B(p) > 1$, and then delete all flagged pixels. This is done, in parallel, at alternate iterations for each of the two subfields. Continue until no deletions are possible in two successive iterations.

```
.   .   .   .   .   .   .   .   .   .   .   .   .   .   .   .   .   .   .

.   .   .   .   .   .   .   .   .   .   .   .   .   .   .   .   .   .   .

.   .   1   .  [1]  .   .   .   .   .   .   1   .   1   .   .   .   .   .

.   .   .   1   .   .   .   .   .   .   .   1   .   .   .   .   .   .   .

.   . [1]  2  [1]  .   .   .   .   .   .   2   .   .   .   .   .   .   .

.   .   .   1   .   .   .   .   .   .   .   1   .   .   .   .   .   .   .

.   . [1]  2  [1]  .   .   .   .   .   .   2   .   .   .   .   .   .   .

.   .   . [1]  2  [1]  .   1   .   .   .   .   2   .   .   1   .   .   .

.   . [1]  2   1   2   1   .   .   .   .   2   .   2   1   .   .   .   .

.   .   2  [1]  .  [1]  .   1   .   .   2   .   .   .   1   .   .

.   2   .   .   .   .   .   .   .   2   .   .   .   .   .   .

.   .   .   .   .   .   .   .   .   .   .   .   .   .   .   .

            Step 3                          Step 4
```

FIGURE 11.24 *Steps 3 and 4 of a Guo-Hall skeletonization.*

Consider our L example from above. We first superimpose a chessboard of 1s and 2s. In step 1 we consider 1s only. Step 1 shown in Figure 11.23 illustrates the first step: we delete only those 1s satisfying the Guo-Hall deletablity conditions. These pixels are shown in squares. Having deleted them, we now consider 2s only; the deletable 2s are shown in step 2.

Steps 3 and 4 continue the work; by step 4 there are no more deletions to be done, and we stop. We notice two aspects of the Guo-Hall algorithm as compared with Zhang-Suen:

1. More pixels may be deleted at each step, so we would expect the algorithm to work faster.

2. The final result includes more corner information than the Zhang-Suen algorithm.

We can implement this in MATLAB using very similar means to our implementation of Zhang-Suen. We have a base program, almost identical to zs.m, which applies odd and even iterations until no more deletions occur after two iterations.

We then require three supplementary programs: the deletions at odd iterations, the deletions at even iterations, and the program to compute $C(p)$. To perform our deletions, we first place a chessboard pattern over the image. For odd deletions, we move over the image pixel by pixel. If the pixel has value 1, we consider if for deletion, and if it is deletable, we replace its value with 3. This does not change the deletablity of neighboring pixels. After we have tested all pixels, we change all the 3s to 0s. Even iterations are similar, except that here we check only pixels whose value is 2 for deletability.

Figure 11.25 shows the base program, and Figures 11.26 and 11.27 the programs for dealing with odd and even iterations, respectively. Figure 11.28 is the program for testing if $C(p) = 1$.

```
function out=gh(a)

a1=ceil(size(a,1)/2);
a2=ceil(size(a,2)/2);
aa=repmat([1 2;2 1],a1,a2);
aa=aa(1:size(a,1),1:size(a,2)).*a;

done=0;
N=2;
last=aa;
previous=gh_odd(last);
current=gh_even(previous);
while done==0,
  if all(current(:)==last(:)),
    done=1;
  end;
  N=N+1;
  last=previous;
  previous=current;
  if mod(N,2)==0,
    current=gh_even(current);
  else
    current=gh_odd(current);
  end;
end;

current(find(current>0))=1;
out=current;
```

FIGURE 11.25 *A* MATLAB *function for Guo-Hall skeletonization.*

Having done all this hard work, we can now test the algorithm, first on the L shape

```
>> gh(L)

ans =

      0      0      0      0      0      0      0      0      0      0
      0      0      0      0      0      0      0      0      0      0
      0      0      1      0      1      0      0      0      0      0
      0      0      0      1      0      0      0      0      0      0
      0      0      0      1      0      0      0      0      0      0
      0      0      0      1      0      0      0      0      0      0
      0      0      0      1      0      0      0      0      0      0
      0      0      0      0      1      0      0      1      0      0
      0      0      0      1      0      1      1      0      0      0
      0      0      1      0      0      0      0      1      0      0
      0      1      0      0      0      0      0      0      0      0
      0      0      0      0      0      0      0      0      0      0
```

```
function out=gh_odd(a)

height=size(a,1);
width=size(a,2);
out=a;

for i=2:height-1,
  for j=2:width-1,
    if a(i,j)==1,
      nbhd=a(i-1:i+1,j-1:j+1);
      nbhd(find(nbhd>0))=1;
      b=sum(nbhd(:))-1;
      if eight_comps(nbhd)==1 & b>1,
        out(i,j)=3;
      end;
    end;
  end;
end;

out(find(out==3))=0;
```

FIGURE 11.26 *A* MATLAB *function for Guo-Hall odd iterations.*

```
function out=gh_even(a)

height=size(a,1);
width=size(a,2);
out=a;

for i=2:height-1,
  for j=2:width-1,
    if a(i,j)==2,
      nbhd=a(i-1:i+1,j-1:j+1);
      nbhd(find(nbhd>0))=1;
      b=sum(nbhd(:))-1;
      if eight_comps(nbhd)==1 & b>1,
        out(i,j)=3;
      end;
    end;
  end;
end;

out(find(out==3))=0;
```

FIGURE 11.27 *A* MATLAB *function for Guo-Hall even iterations.*

```
function out=eight_comps(a)

  out=min(1-a(4),max(a(7),a(8)))+...
      min(1-a(8),max(a(9),a(6)))+...
      min(1-a(6),max(a(3),a(2)))+...
      min(1-a(2),max(a(1),a(4)));
```

FIGURE 11.28 *A* MATLAB *function for testing if* $C(p) = 1$.

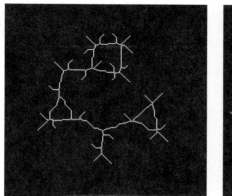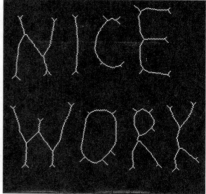

FIGURE 11.29 *Examples of Guo-Hall skeletonization.*

and then on the circles and "nice work" images, for which the results are shown in Figure 11.29. Note the differences between these skeletons and those produced by the Zhang-Suen algorithm as shown in Figure 11.22.

Although the Guo-Hall algorithm is faster than that of Zhang-Suen, our implementation is, in fact, slower. It is slower because we were able to use lookup tables in our program zs.m, but the nature of subfields does not allow the use of lookup tables for gh.m. Full accounts of both the Zhang-Suen and Guo-Hall algorithms, with extensive analysis, can be found in Hall [9].

11.8.5 Skeletonization Using the Distance Transform

The distance transform can be used to provide the skeleton of a region R. We apply the distance transform, using mask 1, to the image negative, just as we did for the circles image previously. Then the skeleton consists of those pixels (i, j) for which

$$d(i,j) \geq \max\{d(i - 1, j), d(i + 1, j), d(i, j - 1), d(i, j + 1)\}.$$

For example, suppose we take a small region consisting of a single rectangle and find the distance transform of its negative:

```
>> c=zeros(7,9);c(2:6,2:8)=1

c =

     0     0     0     0     0     0     0     0     0

>> cd2=ordfilt2(cd,5,[0 1 0;1 1 1;0 1 0])

cd2 =

     0     1     1     1     1     1     1     1     0
     1     1     2     2     2     2     2     1     1
     1     2     2     3     3     3     2     2     1
     1     2     3     3     3     3     3     2     1
     1     2     2     3     3     3     2     2     1
     1     1     2     2     2     2     2     1     1
     0     1     1     1     1     1     1     1     0

>> cd2<=cd

ans =

     1     0     0     0     0     0     0     0     1
     0     1     0     0     0     0     0     1     0
     0     0     1     0     0     0     1     0     0
     0     0     0     1     1     1     0     0     0
     0     0     1     0     0     0     1     0     0
     0     1     0     0     0     0     0     1     0
     1     0     0     0     0     0     0     0     1
```

We can obtain the skeleton using a double loop:

```
>> skel=zeros(size(c));
>> for i=2:6,
     for j=2:8,
       if cd(i,j)>=max([cd(i-1,j),cd(i+1,j),cd(i,j-1),cd(i,j+1)])
         skel(i,j)=1;
       end;
     end;
   end;

>> skel

skel =

     0     0     0     0     0     0     0     0     0
     0     1     0     0     0     0     0     1     0
     0     0     1     0     0     0     1     0     0
     0     0     0     1     1     1     0     0     0
     0     0     1     0     0     0     1     0     0
     0     1     0     0     0     0     0     1     0
     0     0     0     0     0     0     0     0     0
```

In fact, we can produce the skeleton more efficiently by using MATLAB's `ordfilt2` function, which was introduced in Chapter 5. This can be used to find the largest value in a neighborhood, and the neighborhood can be very precisely defined:

```
>> cd2=ordfilt2(cd,5,[0 1 0;1 1 1;0 1 0])

cd2 =

     0     1     1     1     1     1     1     1     0
     1     1     2     2     2     2     2     1     1
     1     2     2     3     3     3     2     2     1
     1     2     3     3     3     3     3     2     1
     1     2     2     3     3     3     2     2     1
     1     1     2     2     2     2     2     1     1
     0     1     1     1     1     1     1     1     0

>> cd2<=cd

ans =

     1     0     0     0     0     0     0     0     1
     0     1     0     0     0     0     0     1     0
     0     0     1     0     0     0     1     0     0
     0     0     0     1     1     1     0     0     0
     0     0     1     0     0     0     1     0     0
     0     1     0     0     0     0     0     1     0
     1     0     0     0     0     0     0     0     1
```

We can easily restrict the image so as not to obtain the extra 1s in the corners of the result. Now let's do the same thing with our circles image:

```
>> c=imread('circles.tif');
>> cd=disttrans(c,mask1);
>> cd2=ordfilt2(cd,5,[0 1 0;1 1 1;0 1 0]);
>> imshow((cd2<=cd)&~c)
```

The result is shown in Figure 11.30. The use of the command `(cd2<=cd)&~c` blocks out the outside of the circles so that just the skeleton is left. We saw in Chapter 10 how to thicken this skeleton and also other ways of obtaining the skeleton.

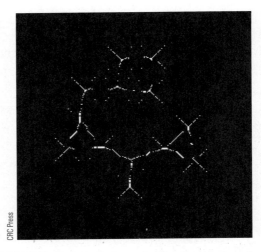

FIGURE 11.30 *Skeletonization using the distance transform.*

EXERCISES

1. What are the coordinates of the 4-neighbors of the pixel (i, j)? What are the coordinates of its 8-neighbors?

2. Find the length of the shortest 4-path from
   a. Pixel $(1, 1)$ to pixel $(5, 4)$.
   b. Pixel $(3, 1)$ to pixel $(1, 6)$.
   c. Pixel (i, j) to pixel (l, m).

   For this question define the length of a path by the number of pixels in it.

3. Find the shortest 8-paths between each pair of pixels in Question 2.

4. Consider the two images

Find the 4-components and 8-components of each image.

5. The above matrices were obtained with the MATLAB commands

```
>> A=magic(10)>50
>> B=magic(10)>60
```

Check your answers for Question 4 with the `bwlabel` function.

6. We can define the 6-neighbors of a pixel p with coordinates (x, y) to be the pixels with coordinates $(x + 1, y)$, $(x - 1, y)$, $(x, y + 1)$, $(x, y - 1)$, $(x + 1, y + 1)$, and $(x - 1, y - 1)$. Draw a diagram showing the six 6-neighbors of a pixel.

7. Prove the triangle inequality for the Euclidean distance metric and for the 4-path and 8-path metrics d_4 and d_8.

8. Define the relation 6-connectedness as:
   p is 6-connected to q if there is a path $p = p_1, p_2, \ldots, p_n = q$ such that for each $i = 1, 2, \ldots, n - 1$, p_i is 6-adjacent to p_{i+1}.
   Show that this is an equivalence relation.

9. Find the lengths of the shortest 6-paths between pixels with the following coordinates:
   a. $(0, 0)$ and $(2, 2)$.
   b. $(1, 2)$ and $(5, 4)$.
   c. $(2, 1)$ and $(6, 8)$.
   d. $(3, 1)$ and $(7, 4)$.

   Can you develop an expression for a 6-path metric?

10. Show how to refine the algorithms for component labeling to label the 6-components of a binary image.

11. For the following image:

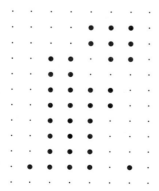

   use your algorithm developed in Question 10 to label the 6-components.

12. Use `bwlabel` to determine the number of blobs in the example given at the beginning of this chapter. Is there any difference between the results using 4- and 8-adjacency? Can you account for your answer?

13. Obtain the 6-components of the images A and B given in Question 4.

14. Let C be the image:

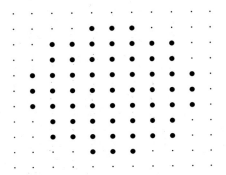

Obtain the 4-boundary and 8-boundary of this image.

15. The image in Question 14 was obtained with the MATLAB commands:

```
>> [x,y]=meshgrid(-5:5,-5:5);
>> C=(x.^2+y.^2)<20
```

Check your answers to Question 14 with the `bwperim` function.

16. Determine if each of the following foreground pixels is:

a. 4-simple.
b. 8-simple.

17. Calculate $C_S(p)$ for each configuration in Question 16, and show that the result is equal to $C(p)$ in each case.

18. Find configurations of pixels surrounding p for which

a. $C(p) = A(p) - 2$.
b. $C(p) = A(p) - 3$.
c. $C(p) = A(p) - 4$.

19. Show that $C(p) \leq A(p)$ for every configuration of pixels.

20. Skeletonize each of the following images using

a. the Zhang-Suen algorithm.
b. the Guo-Hall algorithm.

21. Consider the cross shape formed by starting with an 11 × 11 square and removing a 3 × 3 square from each corner. Skeletonize it by each of the algorithms.

22. Check your answers to Questions 20 and 21 with MATLAB.

23. Which of the algorithms seems to be the fastest by requiring the least number of iterations or removing the greatest number of pixels at each step?

24. Sketch the skeletons of:

    a. a 2 × 1 rectangle.
    b. a triangle.

25. Apply both algorithms to the image `circbw.tif`.

    a. Which one works faster?
    b. Which gives the best-looking results?

26. Repeat Question 25 on some other binary images.

27. For each of the following images,

0	0	0	0	0	0	0	0
0	0	0	0	1	0	0	0
0	1	1	1	1	0	0	0
0	0	1	1	1	1	0	0
0	0	0	1	1	1	1	1
0	1	1	1	1	0	0	0
0	0	0	0	1	0	0	0
0	0	0	0	0	0	0	0

0	0	0	0	0	0	0	0
0	1	1	1	1	1	1	0
0	1	0	0	0	0	1	0
0	1	0	0	0	0	1	0
0	1	0	0	0	0	1	0
0	1	0	0	0	0	1	0
0	1	1	1	1	1	1	0
0	0	0	0	0	0	0	0

0	0	0	0	0	0	0	0
0	0	0	1	1	0	0	0
0	0	0	1	1	0	0	0
0	0	1	1	1	1	0	0
0	1	1	1	1	1	1	0
0	1	0	0	0	0	1	0
0	1	0	0	0	0	1	0
0	0	0	0	0	0	0	0

apply the distance transform to approximate distances from the region containing 1s to all other pixels in the image, using the masks:

a.
$$\begin{matrix} & 1 & \\ 1 & 0 & 1 \\ & 1 & \end{matrix}$$

b.
$$\begin{matrix} 1 & 1 & 1 \\ 1 & 0 & 1 \\ 1 & 1 & 1 \end{matrix}$$

c.
$$\begin{matrix} 4 & 3 & 4 \\ 3 & 0 & 3 \\ 4 & 3 & 4 \end{matrix}$$

d.
$$\begin{matrix} & & 11 & & 11 & & \\ & 11 & 7 & 5 & 7 & 11 & \\ & & 5 & 0 & 5 & & \\ & 11 & 7 & 5 & 7 & 11 & \\ & & 11 & & 11 & & \end{matrix}$$

and applying any necessary scaling at the end.

28. Apply the distance transform and use it to find the skeleton in the images `circlesm.tif` and `nicework.tif`.

29. Compare the result of Question 28 with the results given by the Zhang-Suen and Guo-Hall methods. Which method produces the most visually appealing results? Which method seems fastest?

CHAPTER TWELVE

SHAPES AND BOUNDARIES

12.1 Introduction

In this chapter we will investigate tools for examining image shapes. Some tools have already been discussed in Chapter 10; now we look at specific methods for examining shapes of objects. Questions we might ask about shapes include the following:

- How do we tell if two objects have the same shape?
- How can we classify shape?
- How can we describe the shape of an object?

Formal means of describing shapes are called **shape descriptors.** Shape descriptors may include size, symmetry, and length of perimeter. A precise definition of the exact shape in some efficient manner is a **shape representation.**

In this chapter we will be concerned with the boundary of objects. A boundary differs from an edge in that whereas an edge is an example of a local property of an image, a boundary is a global property.

12.2 Chain Codes and Shape Numbers

The idea of a chain code is quite straightforward; we walk around the boundary of an object, taking note of the direction we take. The resulting list of directions is the chain code.

We need to consider two types of boundaries: 4-connected and 8-connected (see Chapter 11). If the boundary is 4-connected, there are four possible directions in which to walk. If the boundary is 8-connected, there are eight possible directions. These directions are shown in Figure 12.1.

To see how they work, consider the object and its boundary shown in Figure 12.2.

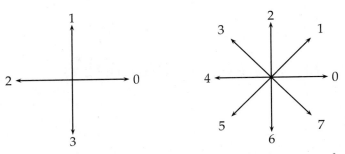

Directions for 4-connectedness   Directions for 8-connectedness

FIGURE 12.1 *Directions for chain codes.*

0	1	1	1	0
0	1	1	1	1
0	1	1	1	1
1	1	1	1	1
1	1	1	1	1
1	1	1	1	0

FIGURE 12.2 *A 4-connected object and its boundary.*

Suppose we walk along the boundary in a clockwise direction starting at the leftmost point in the bottom row and list the directions as we go. This is shown in Figure 12.3.

We can thus read off the chain code as:

3 3 3 2 3 3 0 0 0 1 0 1 1 1 2 1 2 2

If we treat the object in Figure 12.2 as being 8-connected, then its boundary and chain code are generated as in the right-hand diagram in Figure 12.3. In this case, the resulting chain code is:

6 6 5 6 6 0 0 0 1 5 5 5 3 4 4

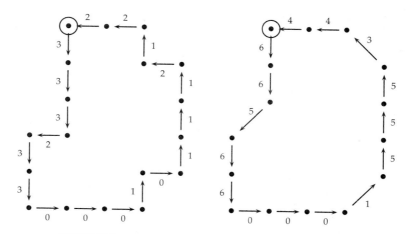

FIGURE 12.3 *Obtaining the chain code from the object in Figure 12.2.*

To obtain the chain code in MATLAB, we must write a small function to do the job for us. We must first be able to trace the boundary of our object, and once we can do that, we can write down our directions to form the chain code. A simple boundary-following algorithm has been given by Sonka et al. [35]. For simplicity, we will give just the version for 4-connected boundaries:

Step 1. Start by finding the pixel in the object that has the left-most value in the topmost row; call this pixel P_0. Define a variable `dir` (for direction), and set it equal to 3. (Since P_0 is the top left pixel in the object, the direction to the next pixel must be 3.)

Step 2. Traverse the 3×3 neighborhood of the current pixel in a counter-clockwise direction, beginning the search at the pixel in direction

```
dir+3 (mod 4)
```

This simply sets the current direction to the first direction counterclockwise from `dir`:

dir		0	1	2	3
dir + 3 (mod 4)		3	0	1	2

The first foreground pixel will be the new boundary element. Update `dir`.

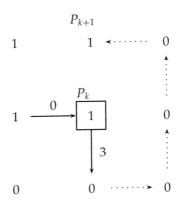

FIGURE 12.4 *Traversing a neighborhood.*

Step 3. Stop when the current boundary element P_n is equal to the second element P_1 and the previous boundary pixel P_{n-1} is equal to the first boundary element P_0.

Suppose we have a binary image im consisting of a single object. We can find the top-left pixel with the following MATLAB commands:

```
>> [x,y]=find(im==1);
>> x=min(x)
>> imx=im(x,:);
>> y=min(imx)
```

The first command simply finds the coordinates of all the foreground pixels. The second command finds the minimum. Thus, x is the top row of the object. The third command isolates this top row, and the final command finds the leftmost column in it.

Given the indices x and y of the current pixel and the value dir, how do we implement Step 2? We give a simple example, shown in Figure 12.4. Suppose that in this particular example the current value of dir is 0, so that

dir+3 (mod 4)=3 .

The dotted arrows indicate the direction of traversing (starting from the pixel in direction 3 from P_k) until we reach a new foreground pixel. This pixel is then P_{k+1}.

We start by noting the row and column increments to the 4-neighbors of a pixel:

$$-1 \quad 0$$

$$0 \quad -1 \qquad 0 \quad 0 \qquad 0 \quad 1$$

$$1 \quad 0$$

Since we are looking at 4-connected boundaries, these are the only neighbors we need. We can put these into a matrix, with the first row corresponding to the increments in direction 0:

```
>> n=[0 1;-1 0;0 -1;1 0]
```

This means that the indices in `n(j,:)` correspond to the increments in indices in direction $j - 1$. Thus, given a direction `dir`, we can enter

```
>> newdir=mod(dir+3,4);
>> for i=0:3,j=mod(newdir+i,4)+1;im(x+n(j,1),y+n(j,2)),end
```

and this will traverse the neighborhood of our image `im` at position (x, y), starting from the correct direction. Notice that we set the following:

```
>> j=mod(newdir+i,4)+1;
```

The extra `+1` takes account of the fact that the modulus function returns values $0, 1, 2, 3$, but the rows of n are $1, 2, 3, 4$. As the neighborhood is traversed, all the values will be placed into a small vector `tt`, so that

```
>> tt(i+1)=image(x+n(j,1),y+n(j,2));
```

We can then easily find the first nonzero value with:

```
>> d=min(find(tt==1));
```

Now we can update `dir`, and the position of the current pixel:

```
>> dir=mod(newdir+d-1,4);
>> x=x+n(dir+1,1);y=y+n(dir+1,2);
```

```
function out=chaincode4(image)

n=[0 1;-1 0;0 -1;1 0];

flag=1;
cc=[];
[x y]=find(image==1);
x=min(x);
imx=image(x,:);
y=min(find(imx==1));
first=[x y];
dir=3;

while flag==1,
   tt=zeros(1,4);
   newdir=mod(dir+3,4);
   for i=0:3,
      j=mod(newdir+i,4)+1;
      tt(i+1)=image(x+n(j,1),y+n(j,2));
   end
   d=min(find(tt==1));
   dir=mod(newdir+d-1,4);
   cc=[cc,dir];
   x=x+n(dir+1,1);y=y+n(dir+1,2);
   if x==first(1) & y==first(2)
      flag=0;
   end;
end;

out=cc;
```

FIGURE 12.5 *A MATLAB function for obtaining the chain code of a 4-connected object.*

As we do this, we will place the most recent value of `dir` into a vector that will be our final chain code.

The function shown in Figure 12.5 is the complete code for the above algorithm with one change: we stop when we reach the original pixel.

We can test this with the shape in Figure 12.2 (we surround our image with 0s first):

```
>> test=[0 0 0 0 0 0 0;...
         0 0 1 1 1 0 0;...
         0 0 1 1 1 1 0;...
         0 0 1 1 1 1 0;...
         0 1 1 1 1 1 0;...
         0 1 1 1 1 1 0;...
         0 1 1 1 1 0 0;...
         0 0 0 0 0 0 0];
```

(continued)

```
>> chaincode4(test)

  ans =

    Columns 1 through 12

      3  3  3  2  3  3  0  0  0  1  0  1

    Columns 13 through 18

      1  1  2  1  2  2
```

and comparing this with the code given earlier, the function has indeed returned the correct chain code.

We can easily modify the program to perform chain codes for 8-connected boundaries. The above algorithm must be slightly changed; again, see Sonka et al. [35].

Step 1. Start by finding the pixel in the object that has the leftmost value in the topmost row; call this pixel P_0. Define a variable `dir` (for direction), and set it equal to 7 (since P_0 is the top-left pixel in the object, the direction to the next pixel must be 7).

Step 2. Traverse the 3×3 neighborhood of the current pixel in a counter-clockwise direction, beginning the search at the pixel in direction

$$\text{dir} + 7 \pmod 8 \quad \text{if dir is even}$$
$$\text{dir} + 6 \pmod 8 \quad \text{if dir is odd.}$$

This simply sets the current direction to the first direction counterclockwise from `dir`:

dir	0	1	2	3	4	5	6	7
dir + 7 (mod 8)	7	0	1	2	3	4	5	6
dir + 6 (mod 8)	6	7	0	1	2	3	4	5

The first foreground pixel will be the new boundary element. Update `dir`.

Step 3. Stop when the current boundary element P_n is equal to the second element P_1 and the previous boundary pixel P_{n-1} is equal to the first boundary element P_0.

Note that the choosing of the starting direction in Step 2 can be implemented by

```
>> newdir=mod(dir+7-mod(dir,2),8);
```

which produces dir+7 if dir is even and dir+6 if dir is odd. As well, we must take into account all possible directions from a pixel. The index increments are:

$$
\begin{array}{ccc}
-1 \quad -1 & -1 \quad 0 & -1 \quad 1 \\
0 \quad -1 & 0 \quad 0 & 0 \quad 1 \\
1 \quad -1 & 1 \quad 0 & 1 \quad 1
\end{array}
$$

These will all be placed in the array n,

```
>> n=[0 1;-1 1;-1 0;-1 -1;0 -1;1 -1;1 0;1 1];
```

where as before, direction 0 corresponds to row 1 of n.

The program is given in Figure 12.6.

This can be tested on out test image test:

```
>> chaincode8(test)

ans =

  Columns 1 through 12

     6    6    5    6    6    0    0    0    1    2    2    2

  Columns 13 through 15

     3    4    4
```

The answer is indeed the code we obtained earlier by following the arrows around the object.

12.2.1 Normalization of Chain Codes

There are two problems with the definition of the chain code as given in previous sections:

1. The chain code is dependent on the starting pixel.
2. The chain code is dependent on the orientation of the object.

Here we will look at the first problem. The idea is to normalize the chain code as follows: imagine the code to be written around the edge of a circle. We choose as our starting place the position for which the code, when read, will be the lowest possible integer. The result is the **normalized chain code** for our object.

```
function out=chaincode8(image)

n=[0 1;-1 1;-1 0;-1 -1;0 -1;1 -1;1 0;1 1];

flag=1;
cc=[];
[x y]=find(image==1);
x=min(x);
imx=image(x,:);
y=min(find(imx==1));
first=[x y];
dir=7;

while flag==1,
  tt=zeros(1,8);
  newdir=mod(dir+7-mod(dir,2),8);
  for i=0:7,
    j=mod(newdir+i,8)+1;
    tt(i+1)=image(x+n(j,1),y+n(j,2));
  end
  d=min(find(tt==1));
  dir=mod(newdir+d-1,8);
  cc=[cc,dir];
  x=x+n(dir+1,1);y=y+n(dir+1,2);
  if x==first(1) & y==first(2)
    flag=0;
  end;
end;

out=cc;
```

FIGURE 12.6 *A MATLAB function for obtaining the chain code of an 8-connected object.*

For example, suppose we have an object consisting of a 3 × 3 square:

```
>> a=zeros(5,5);a(2:4,2:4)=1

     0     0     0     0     0
     0     1     1     1     0
     0     1     1     1     0
     0     1     1     1     0
     0     0     0     0     0

>> c=chaincode4(a)

c =

     3     3     0     0     1     1     2     2
```

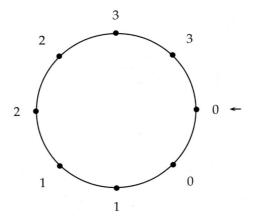

FIGURE 12.7 *A chain code written cyclically.*

Now let's put these codes around a circle as shown in Figure 12.7. The arrow indicates where we should start reading the code to obtain the lowest integer; in this case it is

```
0  0  1  1  2  2  3  3
```

But we can do this easily in MATLAB. We create a cyclic matrix: the top row is the chain code, and every row consists of a possible starting place around our circle. This can be done by advancing from one row to the next, each time moving the last element to the beginning. For our chain code above we can do the following:

```
>> m=c;
>> for i=2:8,m=[m;[m(i-1,8),m(i-1,1:7)]];end
>> m

m =

     3     3     0     0     1     1     2     2
     2     3     3     0     0     1     1     2
     2     2     3     3     0     0     1     1
     1     2     2     3     3     0     0     1
     1     1     2     2     3     3     0     0
     0     1     1     2     2     3     3     0
     0     0     1     1     2     2     3     3
     3     0     0     1     1     2     2     3
```

To find the row that contains the least integer we use the handy `sortrows` function, which sorts the rows lexicographically, first on the first element, then on the second element, and so on.

```
>> ms=sortrows(m)

ms =

     0     0     1     1     2     2     3     3
     0     1     1     2     2     3     3     0
     1     1     2     2     3     3     0     0
     1     2     2     3     3     0     0     1
     2     2     3     3     0     0     1     1
     2     3     3     0     0     1     1     2
     3     0     0     1     1     2     2     3
     3     3     0     0     1     1     2     2
```

Now the normalized chain code is just the first row:

```
>> ms(1,:)

ans =

     0     0     1     1     2     2     3     3
```

Let's try this with a slightly larger example, our `test` object from Figure 12.2:

```
>> c=chaincode4(test);
>> lc=length(c);
>> m=c;
>> for i=2:lc,m=[m;[m(i-1,lc),m(i-1,1:lc-1)]];end
>> ms=sortrows(m);
>> ms(1,:)

ans =

  Columns 1 through 11

     0    0    0    1    0    1    1    1    2    1    2

  Columns 12 through 18

     2    3    3    3    2    3    3
```

```
function out=normalize(c)
%
% NORMALIZE returns the vector which is the least integer of all cyclic
% shifts of V.
%
m=c;
lc=length(c);
for i=2:lc,m=[m;[m(i-1,lc),m(i-1,1:lc-1)]];end
ms=sortrows(m);
out=ms(1,:);
```

FIGURE 12.8 *A* MATLAB *function for normalizing a chain code.*

The only difference between this list of commands and the previous one is that we replace the numbers 8 and 7 with lc and lc-1. These commands can easily be put into a function, as shown in Figure 12.8.

12.2.2 Shape Numbers

We now consider the problem of defining a chain code that is independent of the orientation of the object. For example, let's create a simple L shape:

```
>> L=zeros(7,6);L(2:6,2:3)=1;L(5:6,4:5)=1

L =

        0     0     0     0     0     0
        0     1     1     0     0     0
        0     1     1     0     0     0
        0     1     1     0     0     0
        0     1     1     1     1     0
        0     1     1     1     1     0
        0     0     0     0     0     0
```

Then we can take its chain code,

```
>> c=chaincode4(L)

c =

  Columns 1 through 11

        3     3     3     3     0     0     0     1     2     2     1

  Columns 12 through 14

        1     1     2
```

and normalize it:

```
>> normalize(c)

   Columns 1 through 11

     0    0    0    1    2    2    1    1    1    2    3

   Columns 12 through 14

     3    3    3
```

Suppose we rotate the shape so that it has a different orientation (we use the rot90 function, which rotates a matrix by 90°):

```
>> L2=rot90(L)

L2 =

     0      0      0      0      0      0      0
     0      0      0      0      1      1      0
     0      0      0      0      1      1      0
     0      1      1      1      1      1      0
     0      1      1      1      1      1      0
     0      0      0      0      0      0      0
```

Now we can find the normalized chain code for this new orientation.

```
>> c2=chaincode4(L2)

c2 =

   Columns 1 through 11

     3    3    2    2    2    3    0    0    0    0    1

   Columns 12 through 14

     1    1    2
>> normalize(c2)

ans =

   Columns 1 through 11

     0    0    0    0    1    1    1    2    3    3    2

   Columns 12 through 14

     2    2    3
```

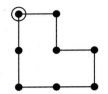

FIGURE 12.9 *A simple L shape.*

FIGURE 12.10 *The shape from Figure 12.9 rotated.*

Even when normalized, the chain codes are different.

To overcome this, we take differences of the chain code. For each two consecutive elements c_i and c_{i+1} their difference is defined as

$$c_{i+1} - c_i \quad (\text{mod } 4).$$

(If we were dealing with 8-connected boundaries, then we would take differences mod 8.) For an example, take the simple L shape shown in Figure 12.9. The chain code can be read easily starting from the point shown; it is

3 3 0 0 1 2 1 2.

To apply differences, repeat the first chain code number at the end, and then take differences along the entire length of the code:

3	3	0	0	1	2	1	2	3
	0	−3	0	1	1	−1	1	1
	0	1	0	1	1	3	1	1

The first row is just the chain code, with the first element repeated at the end, the second row contains the differences, and the third row these differences mod 4. The normalized version of these differences (which here is just the last row itself), is the **shape number** for this L shape.

Suppose this shape is rotated 90° to obtain the shape shown in Figure 12.10. The chain code for this shape is

3   2   3   0   0   1   1   2.

Even when normalized, the result is not the same as the chain code for this shape in its original orientation. But if the differences are obtained,

3		2		3		0		0		1		1		2		3
	-1		1		-3		0		1		0		1		1	
	3		1		1		0		1		0		1		1	

then the normalized third row is

0   1   0   1   1   3   1   1,

which is exactly the same code obtained above.

This can be done easily in MATLAB. Given our chain code c, we create a cyclically shifted code by moving the first element to the end:

```
>> c=chaincode4(a)

c =

     3     3     0     0     1     1     2     2

>> c1=[c(2:8)  c(1)]

c1 =

     3     0     0     1     1     2     2     3
```

Now we just subtract the two, mod 4:

```
>> mod(c1-c,4)

ans =

     0     1     0     1     0     1     0     1
```

The normalized version of this code is the shape number of our object. Let's try this with our L shape and its rotation.

```
>> c=chaincode4(L);
>> lc=length(c);
>> c1=[c(2:lc)  c(1)];
>> mod(c1-c,4)
```

(continued)

```
ans =

  Columns 1 through 11

     0    0    0    1    0    0    1    1    0    3    0

  Columns 12 through 14

     0    1    1
```

This is already normalized. Now for L2:

```
>> c=chaincode4(L2);
>> lc=length(c);
>> c1=[c(2:lc) c(1)];
>> mod(c1-c,4)

ans =

  Columns 1 through 11

     0    3    0    0    1    1    0    0    0    1    0

  Columns 12 through 14

     0    1    1
```

This needs to be normalized:

```
>> normalize(ans)

  Columns 1 through 11

     0    0    0    1    0    0    1    1    0    3    0

  Columns 12 through 14

     0    1    1
```

This is exactly the result we obtained for L.

12.3 Fourier Descriptors

The idea is this: suppose we walk around an object, but instead of writing down the directions, we write down the boundary coordinates. The final list of (x, y) coordinates can be turned into a list of complex numbers $z = x + yi$. The Fourier transform of this list of numbers is a **Fourier descriptor** of the object.

The beauty of a Fourier descriptor is that often only a few terms at the beginning of the transform are enough to distinguish objects or to classify them.

We can easily modify our function chaincode4.m to boundary4.m by replacing the lines

```
cc=[cc,dir];
x=x+n(dir+1,1);y=y+n(dir+1,2);
```

with

```
x=x+n(dir+1,1);y=y+n(dir+1,2);
cc=[cc;x y];
```

Thus, the variable cc contains a list of the boundary pixels. Suppose we have created our function, for example:

```
>> a=zeros(5,5);a(2:4,2:4)=1

a =

     0     0     0     0     0
     0     1     1     1     0
     0     1     1     1     0
     0     1     1     1     0
     0     0     0     0     0

>> b=boundary4(a)

b =

     3     2
     4     2
     4     3
     4     4
     3     4
     2     4
     2     3
     2     2
```

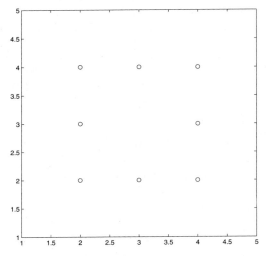

FIGURE 12.11 *Boundary pixels.*

Turning these into complex numbers is easy:

```
>> c=complex(b(:,1),b(:,2))

c =

   3.0000 + 2.0000i
   4.0000 + 2.0000i
   4.0000 + 3.0000i
   4.0000 + 4.0000i
   3.0000 + 4.0000i
   2.0000 + 4.0000i
   2.0000 + 3.0000i
   2.0000 + 2.0000i
```

These can be plotted:

```
>> plot(c,'o'),axis([1,5,1,5]),axis equal
```

The result is shown in Figure 12.11. Supposing we take the Fourier transform, and from it extract only a few terms:

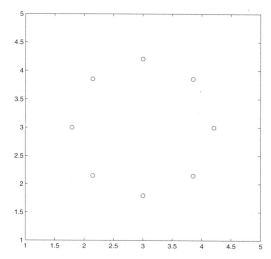

FIGURE 12.12 *The use of Fourier descriptors for approximating a boundary.*

```
>> f=fft(c)

f =

   24.0000 +24.0000i
        0 -  9.6569i
        0
        0
        0
        0 +  1.6569i
        0
        0

>> f1=zeros(size(f));
>> f1(1:2)=f(1:2);
>> plot(ifft(f1),'o'),axis([1.0,5.0,1.0,5.0]),axis square
```

The result is shown in Figure 12.12. We note several points:

1. The Fourier transform of c contains only three nonzero terms.

2. Only two terms of the transform are enough to begin to get some idea of the shape, size, and symmetry of the object.

3. Even though the shape itself has been greatly changed—a square has become a circle—many shape descriptors are still little changed (such as size and symmetry).

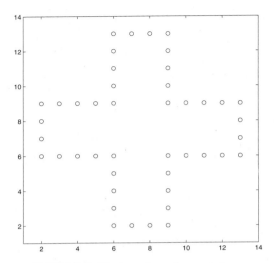

FIGURE 12.13 *The boundary of a cross shape.*

To give a slightly more substantial example, we shall create a cross shape, and experiment with it.

```
>> a=zeros(14,14);a(6:9,2:13)=1;a(2:13,6:9)=1;
>> b=boundary4(a);
>> c=complex(b(:,1),b(:,2));
>> plot(c,'o'),axis([1,14,1,14]),axis square
```

This is shown in Figure 12.13. Now we can obtain the Fourier transform and experiment with extracting different elements from it.

```
>> f=fft(c);
>> f1=zeros(size(f));
>> f1(1:2)=f(1:2);
>> plot(ifft(f1),'o'),axis([1,14,1,14]),axis square
```

This is shown in Figure 12.14(a). Taking eight terms

```
>> f1(1:8)=f(1:8);
>> plot(ifft(f1),'o'),axis([1,14,1,14]),axis square
```

is shown in Figure 12.14(b). The results after using 24 and 36 elements from the transform are shown in Figures 12.14(c) and (d).

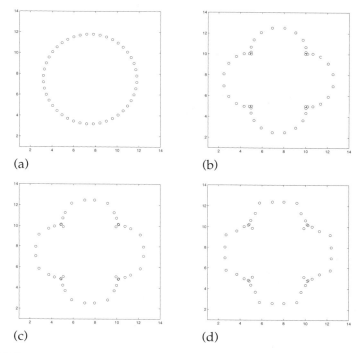

FIGURE 12.14 *Results after extracting different numbers of elements from the Fourier transform of the boundary. (a) After using 2 terms from the transform. (b) After using 8 terms from the transform. (c) After using 24 terms from the transform. (d) After using 36 terms from the transform.*

We will not, of course, obtain the exact boundary until we take all the terms of the transform, but even 8 terms from 44 give a rough idea of the shape and size.

EXERCISES

1. Find the chain codes, normalized chain codes, and shape numbers for each of the following 4-connected shapes:

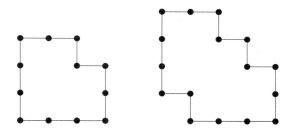

2. Now repeat Question 1 for all possible reflections and rotations of those shapes.

3. Repeat Questions 1 and 2 for the 8-connected shapes:

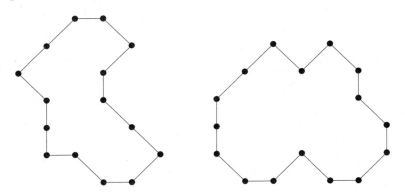

4. Check your answers to the previous questions with MATLAB.

5. Generate the shapes with the following 4-connected chain codes:

   a. 3 3 3 0 0 0 0 1 1 2 2 1 2 2
   b. 3 3 3 0 3 0 0 1 0 1 1 2 2 1 2 2

6. Generate the shapes with the following 8-connected chain codes:

   a. 5 6 7 6 0 0 1 2 2 4 3 4
   b. 5 6 7 7 1 7 1 2 2 3 5 3 4

7. Obtain the normalized chain codes and shape numbers of all the shapes in the previous questions. Check your answers with MATLAB.

8. Use MATLAB to generate a T shape, and obtain its Fourier descriptors. How many terms are required to identify the:

   a. Symmetry of the object?
   b. Size of the object?
   c. Shape of the object?

9. Repeat Question 8, but use an X shape.

10. Compare the results of Questions 8 and 9 with the results of the cross shape discussed in Section 12.3.

    In the three objects, how many terms are required to distinguish the following:

    a. Symmetries.
    b. Sizes.
    c. Shapes.

11. How does the size of an object affect its Fourier descriptors? Experiment with a 6 × 4 rectangle, and then with a 12 × 8 rectangle. Generalize your findings.

CHAPTER THIRTEEN

COLOR PROCESSING

For human beings, color provides one of the most important descriptors of the world around us. The human visual system is particularly attuned to two things: edges and color. We have mentioned that the human visual system is not particularly good at recognizing subtle changes in gray values. In this section we will investigate color briefly and discuss some methods of processing color images.

13.1 What Is Color?

Color study consists of

1. the physical properties of light that give rise to color,
2. the nature of the human eye and the ways in which it detects color, and
3. the nature of the human vision center in the brain and the ways in which messages from the eye are perceived as color.

13.1.1 Physical Aspects of Color

As we have seen in Chapter 1, visible light is part of the electromagnetic spectrum. The values for the wavelengths of blue, green, and red were set in 1931 by the CIE (Commission Internationale d'Eclairage), an organization responsible for color standards.

13.1.2 Perceptual Aspects of Color

The human visual system tends to perceive color as being made up of varying amounts of red, green, and blue. That is, human vision is particularly sensitive to these colors. This is a function of the cone cells in the retina of

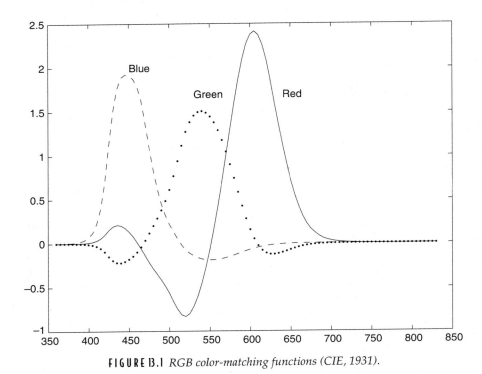

FIGURE 13.1 *RGB color-matching functions (CIE, 1931).*

the eye. These values are called the **primary colors.** If we add together any two primary colors we obtain the **secondary colors:**

$$\text{magenta (purple)} = \text{red} + \text{blue,}$$

$$\text{cyan} = \text{green} + \text{blue,}$$

$$\text{yellow} = \text{red} + \text{green.}$$

The amounts of red, green, and blue that make up a given color can be determined by a color matching experiment. In such an experiment, people are asked to match a given color (a **color source**) with different amounts of the additive primaries red, green, and blue. Such an experiment was performed in 1931 by the CIE, and the results are shown in Figure 13.1. Note that for some wavelengths, various of the red, green, or blue values are negative. This is a physical impossibility, but it can be interpreted by adding the primary beam to the color source to maintain a color match.

To remove negative values from color information, the CIE introduced the XYZ color model. The values of X, Y, and Z can be obtained from the corresponding R, G, and B values by a linear transformation:

$$\begin{bmatrix} X \\ Y \\ Z \end{bmatrix} = \begin{bmatrix} 0.431 & 0.342 & 0.178 \\ 0.222 & 0.707 & 0.071 \\ 0.020 & 0.130 & 0.939 \end{bmatrix} \begin{bmatrix} R \\ G \\ B \end{bmatrix}.$$

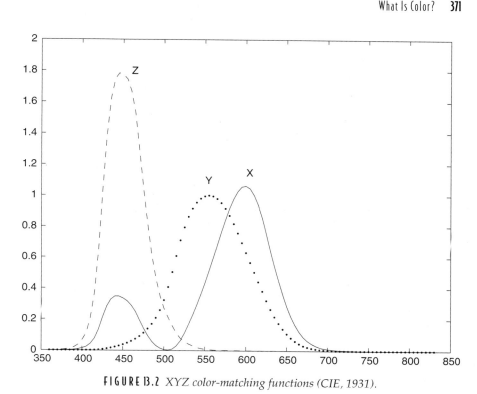

FIGURE 13.2 *XYZ color-matching functions (CIE, 1931).*

The inverse transformation is easily obtained by inverting the matrix:

$$
\begin{bmatrix} R \\ G \\ B \end{bmatrix} = \begin{bmatrix} 3.063 & -1.393 & -0.476 \\ -0.969 & 1.876 & 0.042 \\ 0.068 & -0.229 & 1.069 \end{bmatrix} \begin{bmatrix} X \\ Y \\ Z \end{bmatrix}.
$$

The XYZ color matching functions corresponding to the R, G, B curves of Figure 13.1 are shown in Figure 13.2. The matrices given are not fixed; other matrices can be defined according to the definition of the color white. Different definitions of white will lead to different transformation matrices.

The CIE required that the Y component corresponded with **luminance,** or perceived brightness of the color. That is why the row corresponding to Y in the first matrix (that is, the second row) sums to 1, and also why the Y curve in Figure 13.2 is symmetric about the middle of the visible spectrum.

In general, the values of X, Y, and Z needed to form any particular color are called the **tristimulus values.** Values corresponding to particular colors can be obtained from published tables. To discuss color independent of brightness, the tristimulus values can be normalized by dividing by $X + Y + Z$:

$$x = \frac{X}{X + Y + Z}$$

$$y = \frac{Y}{X + Y + Z}$$

$$z = \frac{Z}{X + Y + Z}$$

and so $x + y + z = 1$. Thus a color can be specified by x and y alone, called the **chromaticity coordinates.** Given x, y, and Y, we can obtain the tristimulus values X and Z by working through the above equations backward:

$$X = \frac{x}{y}Y$$

$$Z = \frac{1 - x - y}{y}Y.$$

We can plot a chromaticity diagram, using the `ciexyz31.txt`[1] file of XYZ values:

```
>> wxyz=load('ciexyz31.txt');
>> xyz=wxyz(:,2:4)';
>> xy=xyz'./(sum(xyz)'*[1 1 1]);
>> x=xy(:,1)';
>> y=xy(:,2)';
>> figure,plot([x x(1)],[y y(1)]),xlabel('x'),ylabel('y'),axis square
```

Here the matrix `xyz` consists of the second, third, and fourth columns of the data, and `plot` is a function that draws a polygon with vertices taken from the x and y vectors. The extra `x(1)` and `y(1)` ensures that the polygon joins up. The result is shown in Figure 13.3. The values of x and y, which lie within the horseshoe shape in Figure 13.3, represent values that correspond to physically realizable colors. A good account of the XYZ model and associated color theory can be found in Foley et al. [6].

---

[1] This file can be obtained from the Colour & Vision Research Laboratories at `http://www.cvrl.org`.

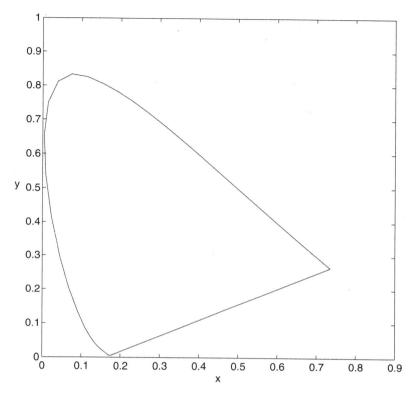

FIGURE 13.3 *A chromaticity diagram.*

13.2 Color Models

A **color model** is a method for specifying colors in some standard way. It generally consists of a three-dimensional coordinate system and a subspace of that system in which each color is represented by a single point. We will investigate three systems.

13.2.1 RGB

In this model, each color is represented as three values R, G, and B, indicating the amounts of red, green, and blue that make up the color. This model is used for displays on computer screens; a monitor has three independent electron "guns" for the red, green, and blue component of each color. We discussed this model in Chapter 2.

Note also from Figure 13.1 that some colors require negative values of R, G, or B. These colors are not realizable on a computer monitor or TV set on which only positive values are possible. The colors corresponding to positive values form the **RGB gamut.** In general, a color gamut consists of all the

```
function res=gamut()

global cg;
x2r=[3.063 -1.393 -0.476;-0.969 1.876 0.042;0.068 -0.229 1.069];
cg=zeros(100,100,3);
for i=1:100,
  for j=1:100,
    cg(i,j,:)=x2r*[j/100 i/100 1-i/100-j/100]';
    if min(cg(i,j,:))<0,
      cg(i,j,:)=[1 1 1];
    end;
  end;
end;
res=cg;
```

FIGURE 13.4 *Computing the RGB gamut.*

colors realizable with a particular color model. We can plot the RGB gamut on a chromaticity diagram, using the xy coordinates obtained above. To define the gamut, we will create a $100 \times 100 \times 3$ array and to each point (i, j) in the array, associate an XYZ triple defined by $(i/100, j/100, 1-i/100-j/100)$. We can then compute the corresponding RGB triple, and if any of the RGB values are negative, we can make the output value white. This is easily done with the simple function shown in Figure 13.4.

We can then display the gamut inside the chromaticity figure by:

```
>> imshow(cG),line([x' x(1)],[y' y(1)]),axis square,axis xy,axis on
```

The result is shown in Figure 13.5.

13.2.2 Hue, Saturation, and Value

Hue, saturation, and value is abbreviated HSV. These terms have the following meanings:

Hue: The "true color" attribute (red, green, blue, orange, yellow, and so on).

Saturation: The amount by which the color has been diluted with white. The more white in the color, the lower the saturation. Thus, a deep red has high saturation, and a light red (a pinkish color) has low saturation.

Value: The degree of brightness. A well-lit color has high intensity; a dark color has low intensity.

This is a more intuitive method of describing colors, and because the intensity is independent of the color information, this is a very useful model for image processing. We can visualize this model as a cone, as shown in Figure 13.6.

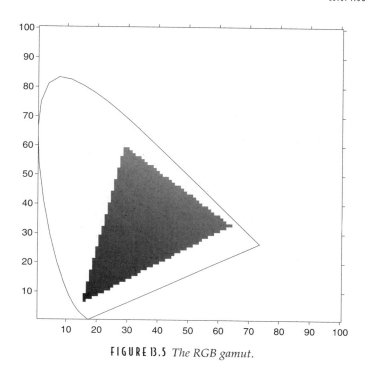

FIGURE 13.5 *The RGB gamut.*

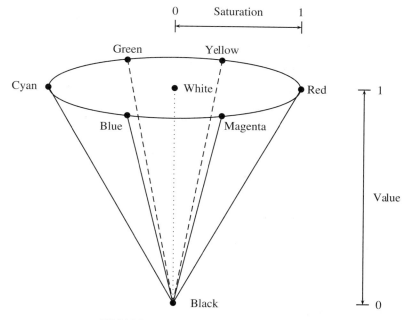

FIGURE 13.6 *The color space HSV as a cone.*

Any point on the surface represents a purely saturated color. The saturation is thus given as the relative distance to the surface from the central axis of the structure. Hue is defined to be the angle measurement from a predetermined axis, say red.

13.2.3 Conversion between RGB and HSV

Suppose a color is specified by its RGB values. If all the three values are equal, then the color will be a grayscale; that is, an intensity of white. Such a color, containing just white, will thus have a saturation of zero. Conversely, if the RGB values are very different, we would expect the resulting color to have a high saturation. In particular, if one or two of the RGB values are zero, the saturation will be one, the highest possible value.

Hue is defined as the fraction around the circle starting from red, which thus has a hue of zero. Reading around the circle in Figure 13.6 produces the following hues:

Color	Hue
Red	0
Yellow	0.1667
Green	0.3333
Cyan	0.5
Blue	0.6667
Magenta	0.8333

Suppose we are given three R, G, B values, which we suppose to be between 0 and 1. If they are between 0 and 255, we first divide each value by 255. We then define:

$$V = \max\{R, G, B\}$$

$$\delta = V - \min\{R, G, B\}$$

$$S = \frac{\delta}{V}$$

To obtain a value for hue, we consider several cases:

1. If $R = V$ then $H = \dfrac{1}{6}\dfrac{G - B}{\delta}$,

2. If $G = V$ then $H = \dfrac{1}{6}\left(2 + \dfrac{B - R}{\delta}\right)$,

3. If $B = V$ then $H = \dfrac{1}{6}\left(4 + \dfrac{R - G}{\delta}\right)$.

If H ends up with a negative value, we add 1. In the particular case $(R, G, B) = (0, 0, 0)$, for which both $V = \delta = 0$, we define $(H, S, V) = (0, 0, 0)$.

For example, suppose $(R, G, B) = (0.2, 0.4, 0.6)$ We have

$$V = \max\{0.2, 0.4, 0.6\} = 0.6$$

$$\delta = V - \min\{0.2, 0.4, 0.6\} = 0.6 - 0.2 = 0.4$$

$$S = \frac{0.4}{0.6} = 0.6667$$

Since $B = G$, we have

$$H = \frac{1}{6}\left(4 + \frac{0.2 - 0.4}{0.4}\right) = 0.5833.$$

Conversion in this direction is implemented by the `rgb2hsv` function. This is, of course, designed to be used on $m \times n \times 3$ arrays, but let's just experiment with our previous example:

```
>> rgb2hsv([0.2 0.4 0.6])

ans =

    0.5833    0.6667    0.6000
```

These are indeed the HSV values we have just calculated.
    To convert to RGB, we start by defining

$$H' = \lfloor 6H \rfloor$$
$$F = 6H - H'$$
$$P = V(1 - S)$$
$$Q = V(1 - SF)$$
$$T = V(1 - S(1 - F)).$$

Since H' is a integer between 0 and 5, we have six cases to consider:

H'	R	G	B
0	V	T	P
1	Q	V	P
2	P	V	T
3	P	Q	V
4	T	P	V
5	V	P	Q

Let's take the HSV values we computed above. We have

$$H' = \lfloor 6(0.5833) \rfloor = 3$$
$$F = 6(0.5833) - 3 = 0.5$$
$$P = 0.6(1 - 0.6667) = 0.2$$
$$Q = 0.6(1 - (0.6667)(0.5)) = 0.4$$
$$T = 0.6(1 - 0.6667(1 - 0.5)) = 0.4.$$

Since $H' = 3$, we have

$$(R, G, B) = (P, Q, V) = (0.2, 0.4, 0.6).$$

Conversion from HSV to RGB is implemented by the `hsv2rgb` function.

13.2.4 YIQ

This color space is used for TV and video in the United States and other countries where (the National Television Standards Commission) NTSC sets the video standard (Australia uses PAL (Phrase Alternating Line)). In this scheme Y is the luminance (this corresponds roughly with intensity), and I and Q carry the color information. The conversion between RGB is straightforward:

$$\begin{bmatrix} Y \\ I \\ Q \end{bmatrix} = \begin{bmatrix} 0.299 & 0.587 & 0.114 \\ 0.596 & -0.274 & -0.322 \\ 0.211 & -0.523 & 0.312 \end{bmatrix} \begin{bmatrix} R \\ G \\ B \end{bmatrix}$$

and

$$\begin{bmatrix} R \\ G \\ B \end{bmatrix} = \begin{bmatrix} 1.000 & 0.956 & 0.621 \\ 1.000 & -0.272 & -0.647 \\ 1.000 & -1.106 & 1.703 \end{bmatrix} \begin{bmatrix} Y \\ I \\ Q \end{bmatrix}$$

The two conversion matrices are, of course, inverses of one another. Note the difference between Y and V:

$$Y = 0.299R + 0.587G + 0.114B$$
$$V = \max\{R, G, B\}.$$

This reflects the fact that the human visual system assigns more intensity to the green component of an image than to the red and blue components. We note here that other transformations [7] RGB to HSV (and vice versa) have

$$V = 0.333R + 0.333G + 0.333B$$

where the intensity is a simple average of the primary values. Note also that the Y of YIQ is different from the Y of XYZ, with the similarity that both represent luminance.

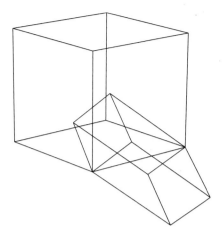

FIGURE 13.7 *The RGB cube and its YIQ transformation.*

Since YIQ is a linear transformation of RGB, we can picture YIQ to be a parallelepiped (a rectangular box that has been skewed in each direction) for which the Y axis lies along the central $(0,0,0)$ to $(1,1,1)$ line of RGB. Figure 13.7 shows this.

That the conversions are linear, and hence easy to do, makes this a good choice for color image processing. Conversion between RGB and YIQ are implemented with the MATLAB functions `rgb2ntsc` and `ntsc2rgb`.

13.3 Color Images in MATLAB

Since a color image requires three separate items of information for each pixel, a (true) color image of size $m \times n$ is represented in MATLAB by an array of size $m \times n \times 3$: a three-dimensional array. We can think of such an array as a single entity consisting of three separate matrices aligned vertically. Figure 13.8 shows a diagram illustrating this idea. Suppose we read in an RGB image:

```
>> x=imread('lily.tif');
>> size(x)

ans =

    186    230      3
```

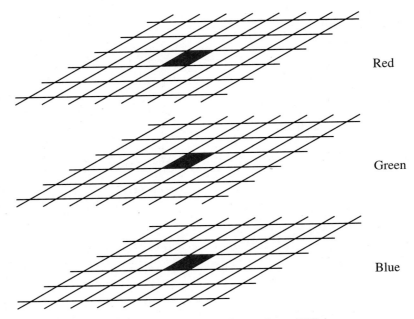

FIGURE 13.8 *A three-dimensional array for an RGB image.*

We can isolate each color component by the colon operator:

x(:,:,1)	is the first, or red component.
x(:,:,2)	is the second, or green component.
x(:,:,3)	is the third, or blue component.

The color components can all be viewed with imshow:

```
>> figure,imshow(x(:,:,1))
>> figure,imshow(x(:,:,1))
>> figure,imshow(x(:,:,2))
```

These are all shown in Figure 13.9. Notice how the colors with particular hues show up with high intensities in their respective components. For the rose in the top right of each photo and the flower in the bottom left of each photo both of which are predominantly red, the red component shows a very high intensity for these two flowers. The green and blue components show much lower intensities. Similarly, the green leaves—at the top left and bottom right in the photos—show up with higher intensity in the green component than the other two.

| Red component | Green component | Blue component |

FIGURE 13.9 *The components of an RGB color image.*

| Hue | Saturation | Value |

FIGURE 13.10 *The HSV components.*

We can convert to YIQ or HSV and view the components again:

```
>> xh=rgb2hsv(x);
>> imshow(xh(:,:,1))
>> figure,imshow(xh(:,:,2))
>> figure,imshow(xh(:,:,3))
```

These are shown in Figure 13.10. We can do precisely the same thing for the YIQ colorspace:

```
>> xn=rgb2ntsc(x);
>> imshow(xn(:,:,1))
>> figure,imshow(xn(:,:,2))
>> figure,imshow(xn(:,:,3))
```

These are shown in Figure 13.11. Notice that the Y component of YIQ gives a better grayscale version of the image than the value of HSV. The top-right rose, in particular, is quite washed out in Figure 13.10 (Value), but shows better contrast in Figure 13.11 (Y).

We will see below how to put three matrices, obtained by operations on the separate components, back into a single three-dimensional array for display.

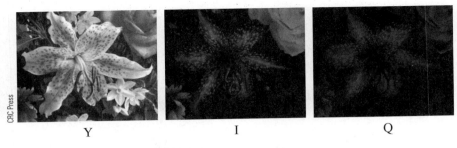

Y   I   Q

FIGURE 13.11 *The YIQ components.*

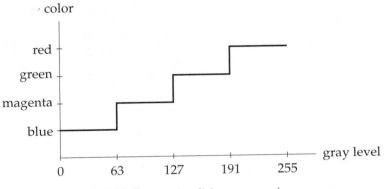

FIGURE 13.12 *Intensity slicing as a mapping.*

13.4 Pseudocoloring

Pseudocoloring means assigning colors to a grayscale image in order to make certain aspects of the image more amenable for visual interpretation—for example, for medical images. There are different methods of pseudocoloring.

13.4.1 Intensity Slicing

In this method, we break up the image into various gray level ranges. We simply assign a different color to each range. For example:

gray level:	0–63	64–127	128–191	192–255
color:	blue	magenta	green	red

We can consider this as a mapping, as shown in Figure 13.12.

13.4.2 Gray to Color Transformations

We have three functions, $f_R(x)$, $f_G(x)$, $f_B(x)$, that assign red, green, and blue values to each gray level x. These values (with appropriate scaling, if necessary) are then used for display. Using an appropriate set of functions can enhance a grayscale image with impressive results.

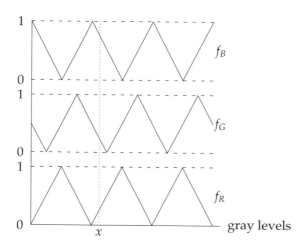

The gray level x in the diagram is mapped onto red, green, and blue values of 0.375, 0.125, and 0.75, respectively.

In MATLAB, a simple way to view an image with added color is to use imshow with an extra colormap parameter. For example, consider the image blocks.tif. We can add a color map with the colormap function; there are several existing color maps to choose from. An example of adding a colormap to an image is:

```
>> b=imread('blocks.tif');
>> imshow(b,colormap(jet(256)))
```

However, a bad choice of color map can ruin an image. An example of this, is applying the vga color map to the blocks image. As this colormap has only 16 rows, we need to reduce the number of grayscales in the image to 16. This is done with the grayslice function:

```
>> b16=grayslice(b,16);
>> figure,imshow(b16,colormap(vga))
```

If you view the output of these commands, you will see that the result, although undeniably colorful, is not really an improvement on the original image. The available color maps are listed in the help file for `graph3d`:

```
hsv         - Hue-saturation-value color map.
hot         - Black-red-yellow-white color map.
gray        - Linear grayscale color map.
bone        - Grayscale with tinge of blue color map.
copper      - Linear copper-tone color map.
pink        - Pastel shades of pink color map.
white       - All white color map.
flag        - Alternating red, white, blue, and black color map.
lines       - Color map with the line colors.
colorcube   - Enhanced color-cube color map.
vga         - Windows color map for 16 colors.
jet         - Variant of HSV.
prism       - Prism color map.
cool        - Shades of cyan and magenta color map.
autumn      - Shades of red and yellow color map.
spring      - Shades of magenta and yellow color map.
winter      - Shades of blue and green color map.
summer      - Shades of green and yellow color map.
```

There are help files for each of these color maps;

```
>> help hsv
```

The command above will provide some information on the `hsv` color map.

We can easily create our own color map. It must be created using a matrix with three columns, with each row consisting of RGB values between 0.0 and 1.0. Suppose we wish to create a blue, magenta, green, and red color map as shown in Figure 13.12. Using the RGB values:

Color	Red	Green	Blue
Blue	0	0	1
Magenta	1	0	1
Green	0	1	0
Red	1	0	0

we can create our color map with:

```
>> mycolormap=[0 0 1;1 0 1;0 1 0;1 0 0];
```

Before we apply it to the blocks image, we need to scale the image down so that there are only the four grayscales 0, 1, 2, and 3:

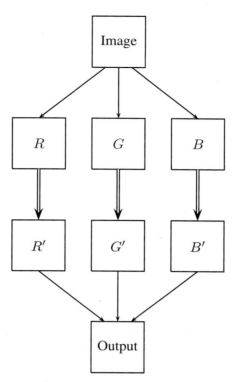

FIGURE 13.13 *RGB processing.*

```
>> b4=grayslice(b,4);
>> imshow(b4,mycolormap)
```

13.5 Processing of Color Images

There are two methods we can use:

1. We can process each RGB matrix separately.
2. We can transform the color space so that the intensity is separated from the color information, and process the intensity component only.

Schemas for these are given in Figures 13.13 and 13.14.
   We will consider a number of different image processing tasks and apply either of the above schema to color images.

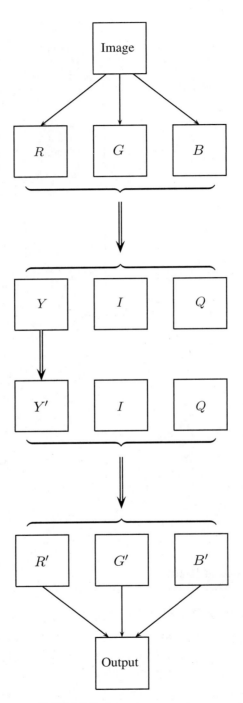

FIGURE 13.14 *Intensity processing.*

13.5.1 Contrast Enhancement

Contrast enhancement is best done by processing the intensity component. Suppose we start with the image cat.tif, which is an indexed color image, and convert it to a truecolor (RGB) image.

```
>> [x,map]=imread('cat.tif');
>> c=ind2rgb(x,map);
```

Now we have to convert from RGB to YIQ, to be able to isolate the intensity component:

```
>> cn=rgb2ntsc(c);
```

Now we apply histogram equalization to the intensity component and convert back to RGB for display:

```
>> cn(:,:,1)=histeq(cn(:,:,1));
>> c2=ntsc2rgb(cn);
>> imshow(c2)
```

If you view the result, you can see that the contrast has been enhanced. Whether this is an improvement is debatable, but it has had its contrast enhanced.

But suppose we try to apply histogram equalization to each of the RGB components:

```
>> cr=histeq(c(:,:,1));
>> cg=histeq(c(:,:,2));
>> cb=histeq(c(:,:,3));
```

Now we have to put them all back into a single three-dimensional array for use with imshow. The cat function is what we want to use:

```
>> c3=cat(3,cr,cg,cb);
>> imshow(c3)
```

The first variable for cat is the dimension along which we want our arrays to be joined. The result of these operations is not acceptable. If you view the image you will see some strange colors have been introduced; the cat's fur has developed a sort of purplish tint, and the grass color is somewhat washed out.

Low pass filtering　　　　　　　　　　High pass filtering

FIGURE 13.15 *Spatial filtering of a color image (shown in grayscale).*

13.5.2 Spatial Filtering

The schema we use depends on the filter. For a low-pass filter, say a blurring filter, we can apply the filter to each RGB component:

```
>> a15=fspecial('average',15);
>> cr=filter2(a15,c(:,:,1));
>> cg=filter2(a15,c(:,:,2));
>> cb=filter2(a15,c(:,:,3));
>> blur=cat(3,cr,cg,cb);
>> imshow(blur)
```

A grayscale version of the result is shown in Figure 13.15. We could also obtain a similar effect by applying the filter to the intensity component only. But for a high-pass filter, for example an unsharp masking filter, we are better off working with the intensity component only:

```
>> cn=rgb2ntsc(c);
>> a=fspecial('unsharp');
>> cn(:,:,1)=filter2(a,cn(:,:,1));
>> cu=ntsc2rgb(cn);
>> imshow(cu)
```

A grayscale version of the result is shown in Figure 13.15. In general, we will obtain reasonable results using the intensity component only. Although we can sometimes apply a filter to each of the RGB components, as we did for the blurring example above, we cannot be guaranteed a good result. The problem is that any filter will change the values of the pixels, and this may introduce unwanted colors.

13.5.3 Noise Reduction

As in Chapter 8, we will use the image twins.tif, but now in full color.

```
>> tw=imread('twins.tif');
```

We will add noise and look at the noisy image and its RGB components:

```
>> tn=imnoise(tw,'salt & pepper');
>> figure,imshow(tn(:,:,1))
>> figure,imshow(tn(:,:,2))
>> figure,imshow(tn(:,:,3))
```

These are all shown in Figure 13.16. It appears that we should apply median filtering to each of the RGB components. This is easily done:

```
>> trm=medfilt2(tn(:,:,1));
>> tgm=medfilt2(tn(:,:,2));
>> tbm=medfilt2(tn(:,:,3));
>> tm=cat(3,trm,tgm,tbm);
>> imshow(tm)
```

A grayscale version of the result is shown in Figure 13.17(a). In this instance we cannot apply the median filter to the intensity component only, because the conversion from RGB to YIQ spreads the noise across all the YIQ components. If we remove the noise from Y only,

```
>> tnn=rgb2ntsc(tn);
>> tnn(:,:,1)=medfilt2(tnn(:,:,1));
>> tm2=ntsc2rgb(tnn);
>> imshow(tm2)
```

then the noise has been slightly diminished, as shown in grayscale in Figure 13.17(b), but it is still there. If the noise applies to only one of the RGB components, then it would be appropriate to apply a denoising technique to this component only.

Also note that the method of noise removal must depend on the generation of noise. In the example above we tacitly assumed that the noise was generated after the image had been acquired and stored as RGB components. But because noise can arise anywhere in the image-acquisition process, it is quite reasonable to assume that noise might affect only the brightness of the image. In such a case denoising the Y component of YIQ will produce the best results.

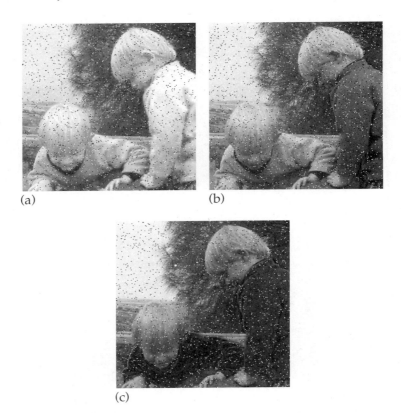

FIGURE 13.16 *Components of a noisy color image. (a) The red component. (b) The green component. (c) The blue component.*

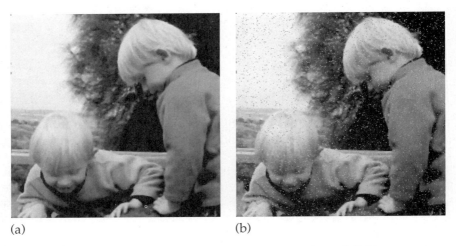

FIGURE 13.17 *Attempts at de-noising a color image. (a) De-noising each RGB component. (b) De-noising Y only.*

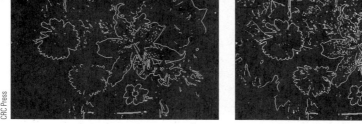

fe1: Edges after `rgb2gray`   fe2: Edges of each RGB component

FIGURE 13.18 *The edges of a color image.*

13.5.4 Edge Detection

An edge image will be a binary image containing the edges of the input. We can go about obtaining an edge image in two ways:

1. We may take the intensity component only and apply the `edge` function to it.
2. we may apply the `edge` function to each of the RGB components and join the results.

To implement the first method, we start with the `rgb2gray` function:

```
>> fg=rgb2gray(f);
>> fe1=edge(fg);
>> imshow(fe1)
```

Recall that `edge` with no parameters implements Sobel edge detection. The result is shown in Figure 13.18. For the second method, we can join the results with the logical "or":

```
>> f1=edge(f(:,:,1));
>> f2=edge(f(:,:,2));
>> f3=edge(f(:,:,3));
>> fe2=f1 | f2 | f3;
>> figure,imshow(fe2)
```

This is also shown in Figure 13.18. The edge image `fe2` is a much more complete edge image. Notice that the rose now has most of its edges, where in image `fe1` only a few were shown. Also note that there are the edges of some leaves in the bottom left of `fe2` that are completely missing from `fe1`. The success of these methods will also depend on the parameters of the edge function chosen, for example, the threshold value used. In the examples shown, the edge function has been used with its default threshold.

EXERCISES

1. Work through all the examples in this chapter and note the output of each sequence of operations.

2. By hand, determine the saturation and intensity components of the following image, where the RGB values are as given:

(0,1,1)	(1,2,3)	(7,7,7)	(5,1,2)	(1,1,7)
(2,1,2)	(1,7,7)	(2,0,2)	(3,3,2)	(5,5,0)
(4,4,4)	(4,6,7)	(4,5,6)	(1,5,7)	(3,6,7)
(3,0,3)	(5,2,2)	(1,1,1)	(6,6,0)	(2,2,2)
(1,2,1)	(0,4,4)	(3,1,6)	(3,3,3)	(2,4,6)

3. Suppose the intensity component of an HSV image was thresholded to just two values. How would this affect the appearance of the image?

4. By hand, perform the conversions between RGB and HSV or YIQ for the values:

R	G	B	H	S	V
0.5	0.5	0			
0	0.7	0.7			
0.5	0	0.5			
			0.33	0.5	1
			0.67	0.7	0.7
			0	0.2	0.8

R	G	B	Y	I	Q
0.3	0.3	0.7			
0.7	0.9	0			
0.8	0.8	0.7			
			1	0.3	0.3
			0.5	0.5	0.5
			0	1	1

You may need to normalize the RGB values.

5. Check your answers to the conversions in Question 3 by using the MATLAB functions rgb2hsv, hsv2rgb, rgb2ntsc, and ntsc2rgb.

6. Threshold the intensity component of a color image, say flowers.tif, and see if the result agrees with your guess from Question 2 above.

7. The image spine.tif is an indexed color image; however the colors are all very close to shades of gray. Experiment with using imshow on the index matrix of this image with varying color maps of length 64.

Which color map seems to give the best results? Which color map seems to give the worst results?

8. View the image autumn.tif. Experiment with histogram equalization on
   a. The intensity component of HSV.
   b. the intensity component of YIQ.

   Which seems to produce the best result?

9. Create and view a random patchwork quilt with:

```
>> r=uint8(floor(256*rand(16,16,3)));
>> r=imresize(r,16);
>> imshow(r),pixval on
```

What RGB values produce
a. A light brown color?
b. A dark brown color?

Convert these brown values to HSV, and plot the hues on a circle.

10. Using the flowers image, see if you can obtain an edge image from the intensity component alone that is as close as possible to the image fe2 in Figure 13.18. What parameters to the edge function did you use? How close to fe2 could you get?

11. Add Gaussian noise to an RGB color image x with

```
>> xn=imnoise(x,'gaussian');
```

View your image, and attempt to remove the noise with
a. Average filtering on each RGB component.
b. Wiener filtering on each RGB component.

12. Take the twins image and add salt and pepper noise to the intensity component. This can be done with

```
>> ty=rgb2ntsc(tw);
>> tn=imnoise(ty(:,:,1).'salt & pepper');
>> ty(:,:,1)=tn;
```

Now convert back to RGB for display.

a. Compare the appearance of this noise with the salt and pepper noise applied to each RGB component as shown in Figure 13.16. Is there any observable difference?

b. De-noise the image by applying a median filter to the intensity component.

c. Now apply the median filter to each of the RGB components.

d. Which gives the best results?

e. Experiment with larger amounts of noise.

f. Experiment with Gaussian noise.

CHAPTER FOURTEEN

IMAGE CODING AND COMPRESSION

14.1 Lossless and Lossy Compression

We have seen that image files can be very large. It is thus important for both reasons of storage and file transfer to make these file sizes smaller, if possible. In Section 1.9 we touched briefly on the topic of compression; in this section we investigate some standard compression methods. It will be necessary to distinguish between two different classes of compression methods: **lossless compression,** where all the information is retained, and **lossy compression,** where some information is lost.

Lossless compression is preferred for images of legal, scientific, or political significance, where loss of data, even that of apparent insignificance, could have considerable consequences. Unfortunately, this style tends not to lead to high compression ratios. However, lossless compression is used as part of many standard image formats.

14.2 Huffman Coding

The idea of Huffman coding is simple. Rather than using a fixed-length code (8 bits) to represent the gray values in an image, we use a variable-length code, with smaller-length codes corresponding to more, probable gray values.

An example will make this clear. Suppose we have a 2-bit grayscale image with only four gray levels: 0, 1, 2, and 3, with the probabilities 0.2, 0.4, 0.3, and 0.1, respectively. That is, 20% of pixels in the image have gray value 50; 40% have gray value 100, and so on. The table below shows fixed-length and variable-length codes for this image:

Gray value	Probability	Fixed code	Variable code
0	0.2	00	000
1	0.4	01	1
2	0.3	10	01
3	0.1	11	001

Now consider how this image has been compressed. Each gray value has its own unique identifying code. The average number of bits per pixel can be calculated easily as the expected value (in a probabilistic sense):

$$(0.2 \times 3) + (0.4 \times 1) + (0.3 \times 2) + (0.1 \times 3) = 1.9.$$

Notice that the longest code words are associated with the lowest probabilities. This average is indeed smaller than 2.

This can be made more precise by the notion of **entropy,** which is a measure of the amount of information. Specifically, the entropy H of an image is the theoretical minimum number of bits per pixel required to encode the image with no loss of information. It is defined by

$$H = - \sum_{i=0}^{L-1} p_i \log_2(p_i),$$

where the index i is taken over all grayscales of the image, and p_i is the probability of gray level i occurring in the image. Very good accounts of the basics of information theory and entropy are given by Roman [29] and Welsh [39]. In the example given above,

$$H = -(0.2 \log_2(0.2) + 0.4 \log_2(0.4) + 0.3 \log_2(0.3) + 0.1 \log_2(0.1)) = 1.8464.$$

This means that no matter what coding scheme is used, it will never use less than 1.8464 bits per pixel. On this basis, the Huffman coding scheme given above, giving an average number of bits per pixel much closer to this theoretical minimum than 2, provides a very good result.

To obtain the Huffman code for a given image we proceed as follows:

1. Determine the probabilities of each gray value in the image.
2. Form a binary tree by adding probabilities two at a time, always taking the two lowest available values.
3. Now assign 0 and 1 arbitrarily to each branch of the tree from its apex.
4. Read the codes from the top down.

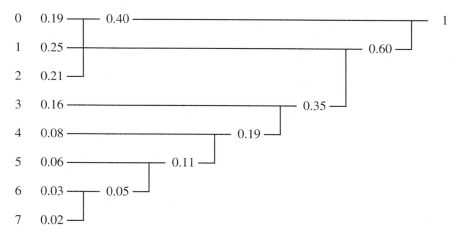

FIGURE 14.1 *Forming the Huffman code tree.*

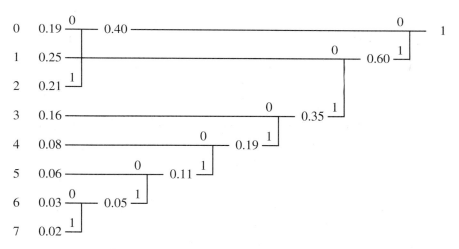

FIGURE 14.2 *Assigning 0s and 1s to the branches.*

To see how this works, consider the example of a 3-bit grayscale image (so the gray values are 0–7) with the following probabilities:

gray value	0	1	2	3	4	5	6	7
probability	0.19	0.25	0.21	0.16	0.08	0.06	0.03	0.02

For these probabilities, the entropy can be calculated to be 2.6508. We can now combine probabilities two at a time as shown in Figure 14.1.

Note that if we have a choice of probabilities, we choose arbitrarily. The second stage consists of arbitrarily assigning 0s and 1s to each branch of the tree just obtained. This stage is shown in Figure 14.2.

To obtain the codes for each gray value, start at the 1 on the top right and work back toward the gray value in question, listing the numbers passed on the way. This produces:

Gray value	Huffman code
0	00
1	10
2	01
3	110
4	1110
5	11110
6	111110
7	111111

As above, we can evaluate the average number of bits per pixel as an expected value:

$$(0.19 \times 2) + (0.25 \times 2) + (0.21 \times 2) + (0.16 \times 3)$$
$$+ (0.08 \times 4) + (0.06 \times 5) + (0.03 \times 6) + (0.02 \times 6) = 2.7,$$

which is a significant improvement over 3 bits per pixel and very close to the theoretical minimum of 2.6508 given by the entropy.

Huffman codes are uniquely decodable, in that a string can be decoded in only one way. For example, consider the string

$$1 \quad 1 \quad 0 \quad 1 \quad 1 \quad 1 \quad 0 \quad 0 \quad 0 \quad 0 \quad 0 \quad 1 \quad 0 \quad 0 \quad 1 \quad 1 \quad 1 \quad 1 \quad 1 \quad 0$$

to be decoded with the Huffman code generated above. There is no code word 1 or 11, so we may take the first 3 bits, 110, as being the code for gray value 3. Notice also that no other code word begins with this string. For the next few bits, 1110 is a code word; no other begins with this string, and no other smaller string is a code word. Thus we can decode this string as gray level 4. Continuing in this way we obtain:

as the decoding for this string.

For more information about Huffman coding and its limitations and generalizations, see Gonzalez and Woods [7] and Rabbani and Jones [27].

14.3 Run-length Encoding

Run-length encoding (RLE) is based on a simple idea: to encode strings of 0s and 1s by the number of repetitions in each string. RLE has become a standard in facsimile transmission. For a binary image, there are many different implementations of RLE. One method is to encode each line separately, starting with the number of 0s. So the following binary image,

```
0 1 1 0 0 0
0 0 1 1 1 0
1 1 1 0 0 1
0 1 1 1 1 0
0 0 0 1 1 1
1 0 0 0 1 1
```

would be encoded as

(123)(231)(0321)(141)(33)(0132)

Another method [35] is to encode each row as a list of pairs of numbers, the first number in each pair giving the starting position of a run of 1s and the second number its length. Thus, the above binary image would have the encoding

(22)(33)(1361)(24)(43)(1152)

Grayscale images can be encoded by breaking them up into their bit planes, which were discussed in Chapter 3.

To give a simple example, consider the following 4-bit image and its binary representation:

```
10   7   8   9      1010   0111   1000   1001
11   8   7   6      1011   1000   0111   0110
 9   7   5   4  ⟶   1001   0111   0101   0100
10  11   2   1      1010   1011   0010   0001
```

We may break it into bit planes as shown:

```
0  1  0  1     1  1  0  0     0  1  0  0     1  0  1  1
1  0  1  0     1  0  1  1     0  0  1  1     1  1  0  0
1  1  1  0     0  1  0  0     0  1  1  1     1  0  0  0
0  1  0  1     1  1  1  0     0  0  0  0     1  1  0  0
   0th plane      1st plane      2nd plane      3rd plane
```

Each plane can then be encoded separately using our chosen implementation of RLE.

However, there is a problem with bit planes, and that is that small changes of gray value may cause significant changes in bits. For example, the change from value 7 to 8 causes the change of all 4 bits, since we are changing the binary strings 0111 to 1000. The problem is, of course, exacerbated for 8-bit images. For RLE to be effective, we hope that long runs of very similar gray values would result in very good compression rates for the code. But this may not be the case. A 4-bit image consisting of randomly distributed 7s and 8s would thus result in uncorrelated bit planes and little effective compression.

To overcome this difficulty, we may encode the gray values with their binary **Gray codes.** A Gray code is an ordering of all binary strings of a given length so that there is only one bit change between one string and the next. Thus, a 4-bit Gray code is

15	1	0	0	0
14	1	0	0	1
13	1	0	1	1
12	1	0	1	0
11	1	1	1	0
10	1	1	1	1
9	1	1	1	0
8	1	1	0	0
7	0	1	0	0
6	0	1	0	1
5	0	1	1	1
4	0	1	1	0
3	0	0	1	0
2	0	0	1	1
1	0	0	0	1
0	0	0	0	0

See Rabbani and Jones [29] for discussion and detail. To see the advantages, consider the following 4-bit image with its binary and Gray code encodings:

8	8	7	8	1000	1000	0111	1000	1100	1100	0100	1100
8	7	8	7	1000	0111	1000	0111	1100	0100	1100	0100
7	7	8	7	0111	0111	1000	0111	0100	0100	1100	0100
7	8	7	7	0111	1000	0111	0111	0100	1100	0100	0100

where the first binary array is the standard binary encoding, and the second array is the Gray codes. The binary bit planes are

0	0	1	0	0	0	1	0	0	0	1	0	1	1	0	1
0	1	0	1	0	1	0	1	0	1	0	1	1	0	1	0
1	1	0	1	1	1	0	1	1	1	0	1	0	0	1	0
1	0	1	1	1	0	1	1	1	0	1	1	0	1	0	0
0th plane				1st plane				2nd plane				3rd plane			

and the bit planes corresponding to the Gray codes are

0	0	0	0		0	0	0	0		1	1	1	1		1	1	0	1
0	0	0	0		0	0	0	0		1	1	1	1		1	0	1	0
0	0	0	0		0	0	0	0		1	1	1	1		0	0	1	0
0	0	0	0		0	0	0	0		1	1	1	1		0	1	0	0

0th plane · 1st plane · 2nd plane · 3rd plane

Notice that the Gray code planes are highly correlated except for one bit plane, whereas all the binary bit planes are uncorrelated.

14.3.1 Run-length Encoding in MATLAB

We can experiment with RLE by writing a simple function to implement it. To make it easy, we will stick with single binary images. Our output will be a single vector, giving the number of 0s and 1s, alternating through our image row by row. We start by putting our image into a single row. For a binary image im, this can be done with the two commands

```
L=prod(size(im));
im=reshape(im',1,L);
```

To find the number of beginning 0s, we obtain the position of the first 1, thus:

```
min(find(im==1))
```

We append one less than this result to our output vector. It may well be that there are no further 1s, in which case we have reached the end of the file, and we stop by appending the current length of our image to the output vector. We now change to look for the place of the next 0; we can use the min(find) command again, but we first reduce our image by the number of 0s we have already found.

The following table shows how we can implement RLE:

Image	Looking for	Place	RLE output
			[ ]
[0 0 1 1 1 0 0 0 1]	1	3	[2]
[1 1 1 0 0 0 1]	0	4	[2 3]
[0 0 0 1]	1	4	[2 3 3]
[1]	0	Not found	[2 3 3 1]

```
function out=rle(image)
%
%   RLE(IMAGE) produces a vector containing the run-length encoding of
%   IMAGE, which should be a binary image.   The image is set out as a long
%   row, and the conde contains the number of zeros,   followed by the number
%   of ones, alternating.
%
%   Example:
%
%     rle([1 1 1 0 0;0 0 1 1 1;1 1 0 0 0])
%
%     ans =
%
%        0    3    4    5    3
%
L=prod(size(image));
im=reshape(image',1,L);
x=1;
out=[];
while L ~= 0,
  temp=min(find(im == x));
  if isempty(temp),
    out=[out L];
    break
  end;
  out=[out temp-1];
  x=1-x;
  im=im(temp:L);
  L=L-temp+1;
end;
```

FIGURE 14.3 *A MATLAB function for obtaining the run-length code of a binary image.*

Here is one more example:

Image	Looking for	Place	RLE output
			[ ]
[1 1 1 0 0 0 0 1 1]	1	1	[0]
[1 1 1 0 0 0 0 1 1]	0	4	[0 3]
[0 0 0 0 1 1]	1	4	[0 3 4]
[1 1]	0	Not found	[0 3 4 2]

Notice that in this second example, since the length of our initial run of 0s was found to be zero, we do not reduce the length of our image in the next step.

Figure 14.3 shows the implementation of this algorithm in MATLAB.

Now we can test this on a few images.

```
>> c=imread('circles.tif');
>> cr=rle(c);
>> whos c cr
  Name       Size          Bytes   Class
   c         256x256       65536   uint8 array (logical)
   cr        1x693          5544   double array
```

We can reduce the size of the output by storing it using the data type `uint16` (unsigned 16-bit integers).

```
>> cr=uint16(cr);
>> whos cr
   Name         Size                 Bytes   Class

   cr           1x693                 1386   uint16 array
```

Even if the original circles image was stored as 1 bit per pixel or eight pixels per byte, we would have a total of

$$\frac{65,536}{8} = 8,192 \text{ bytes,}$$

still more than the run-length code. In this example, RLE provides a reasonable amount of compression.

```
>> t=imread('text.tif');
>> tr=rle(t);
>> whos t tr
   Name         Size                 Bytes   Class

   t            256x256              65536   uint8 array (logical)
   tr           1x2923               23384   double array
```

Again, better compression can be obtained by changing the data type.

```
>> tr=uint16(tr);
>> whos tr
   Name         Size                 Bytes   Class

   tr           1x2923                5846   uint16 array
```

Although this compression is not as good as that for the previous image, it is still better than the minimum of 8,192 bytes for the original image.

14.4 The JPEG Algorithm

Lossy compression trades some acceptable data loss for greater rates of compression. Of the many compression methods available, the algorithm developed by the Joint Photographic Experts Group (JPEG) has become one of the most popular. It uses **transform coding,** where the coding is done not on the pixel values themselves, but on a transform.

The heart of this algorithm is the **discrete cosine transform** (DCT), with a definition similar to the Fourier transform. Although it can be applied to an array of any size, in the JPEG algorithm it is applied only to 8×8 blocks. If $f(j, k)$ is one such block, then the forward (two-dimensional) DCT is defined as:

$$F(u, v) = \frac{C(u)C(v)}{4} \sum_{j=0}^{7} \sum_{k=0}^{7} f(j, k) \cos \left(\frac{(2j + 1)u\pi}{16} \right) \cos \left(\frac{(2k + 1)v\pi}{16} \right)$$

and the corresponding inverse DCT as

$$f(i, j) = \sum_{u=0}^{7} \sum_{v=0}^{7} f(u, v)C(u)c(v) \cos \left(\frac{(2j + 1)u\pi}{16} \right) \cos \left(\frac{(2k + 1)v\pi}{16} \right),$$

where $C(w)$ is defined as

$$C(w) = \begin{cases} \frac{1}{\sqrt{2}} & \text{if } w = 0 \\ 0 & \text{otherwise.} \end{cases}$$

The DCT has a number of properties that make it particularly suitable for compression:

1. It is real-valued, so there is no need to manipulate complex numbers.
2. It has a high information-packing ability because it packs large amounts of information into a small number of coefficients.
3. It can be implemented very efficiently in hardware.
4. Like the FFT, there is a "fast" version of the transform that maximizes efficiency.
5. The basis values are independent of the data [7].

Like the two-dimensional FFT, the two-dimensional DCT (given above) is separable and thus can be calculated by a sequence of one-dimensional DCTs. First, we apply the one-dimensional DCT to the rows, then to the columns of the result.

To see an example of the information-packing capabilities, we consider the simple linear sequence given by:

```
>> a=[10:15:115]

a =

    10    25    40    55    70    85    100    115
```

We will apply both the FFT and DCT to this sequence, remove half the result, and invert the remainder. First apply the FFT:

```
>> fa=fft(a);
>> fa(5:8)=0;
>> round(abs(ifft(fa)))


ans =


    49    41    56    57    71    70    85    90
```

Now apply the DCT (using the dct and idct functions):

```
>> da=dct(a);
>> da(5:8)=0;
>> round(idct(da))


ans =


    11    23    41    56    69    84   102   114
```

Notice how much closer the DCT result is to the original, despite of the loss of information from the transform. This example is illustrated in Figure 14.4.

The JPEG baseline compression scheme is applied as follows:

1. The image is divided into 8×8 blocks, with each block transformed and compressed separately.

2. For a given block, the values are shifted by subtracting 128 from each value.

3. The DCT is applied to this shifted block.

4. The DCT values are normalized by dividing by a normalization matrix Q. It is this normalization that provides the compression by making most of the elements of the block zero.

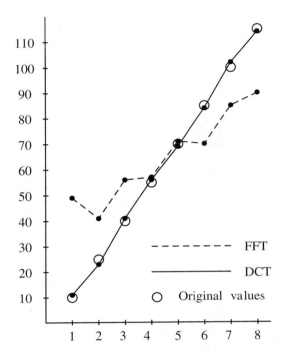

FIGURE 14.4 *Comparison of the FFT and the DCT.*

5. This matrix is formed into a vector by reading off all nonzero values from the top left in a zigzag fashion:

6. The first coefficients of each vector, which will be the largest elements in each vector and which are known as the DC coefficients, are encoded by listing the difference between each value and the values from the previous block. This helps keep all values (except for the first) small.

7. These values are then compressed using RLE.

8. All other values (known as the **AC coefficients**) are compressed using a Huffman coding.

The amount of lossy compression can be changed by scaling the normalization matrix Q in step 4 above.

To decompress, the steps above are applied in reverse; the Huffman encoding and RLE can be decoded with no loss of information. Having done that, then the following occurs:

1. The vector is read back into an 8×8 matrix.

2. The matrix is multiplied by the normalization matrix.

3. The inverse DCT is applied to the result.

4. The result is shifted back by 128 to obtain the original image block.

The normalization matrix that has been used by the JPEG group is

$$\begin{bmatrix} 16 & 11 & 10 & 16 & 24 & 40 & 51 & 61 \\ 12 & 12 & 14 & 19 & 26 & 58 & 60 & 55 \\ 14 & 13 & 16 & 24 & 40 & 57 & 69 & 56 \\ 14 & 17 & 22 & 29 & 51 & 87 & 80 & 62 \\ 18 & 22 & 37 & 56 & 68 & 109 & 103 & 77 \\ 24 & 35 & 55 & 64 & 81 & 104 & 113 & 92 \\ 49 & 64 & 78 & 87 & 103 & 121 & 120 & 101 \\ 72 & 92 & 95 & 98 & 112 & 100 & 103 & 99 \end{bmatrix}$$

We can experiment with the DCT and quantization using standard MATLAB functions. The two-dimensional DCT and inverse DCT are implemented with the functions dct2 and idct2, respectively.

To see all this in action, we take an 8×8 block from an image.

```
>> c=imread('caribou.tif');
>> x=151;y=90;
>> block=c(x:x+7,y:y+7)

block =

      87      95      92      73      59      57      57      55
      74      71      68      59      54      54      51      57
      64      58      57      55      58      65      66      65
      57      63      68      66      74      89      98     104
      95     109     117     114     119     134     145     140
     128     139     146     139     140     148     151     143
     137     135     125     118     137     156     154     132
     122     119     113     110     128     144     140     142
```

Now we subtract 128 from each value of the block:

```
>> b=double(block)-128

b =

    -41   -33   -36   -55   -69   -71   -71   -73
    -54   -57   -60   -69   -74   -74   -77   -71
    -64   -70   -71   -73   -70   -63   -62   -63
    -71   -65   -60   -62   -54   -39   -30   -24
    -33   -19   -11   -14    -9     6    17    12
      0    11    18    11    12    20    23    15
      9     7    -3   -10     9    28    26     4
     -6    -9   -15   -18     0    16    12    14
```

and apply the DCT:

```
>> bd=dct2(b)

bd =

 -225.3750  -30.7580   17.3864    5.6543  -22.3750   -1.8591    3.7575    1.7196
 -241.5333   52.0722    0.8745  -21.2434    8.1434    1.8639    0.9420   -1.3369
   -2.5427   50.9316    5.0847    9.1573    1.5820   -3.8454    1.5706   -0.6043
  102.5557   23.3927  -11.5151  -12.7655  -10.6629    2.8179   -3.6743    1.2462
   -2.3750  -20.7081    3.5090  -10.3182   -1.3750   -2.4723    0.3054   -0.7308
  -12.7510    1.5740    2.7664    8.1034   -5.2779    1.0922   -1.6694    1.0561
    6.6005    7.8668   -4.9294   -7.0092    2.1860    0.8872    0.6653   -0.1783
   10.6630    0.4486   -0.1019    7.9728   -4.0241    2.4364   -2.3823    0.6011
```

We now need to enter our normalization matrix and divide it by:

```
>> q = [16 11 10 16 24 40 51 61;...
12 12 14 19 26 58 60 55;...
14 13 16 24 40 57 69 56;...
14 17 22 29 51 87 80 62;...
18 22 37 56 68 109 103 77;...
24 35 55 64 81 104 113 92;...
49 64 78 87 103 121 120   101;...
72 92 95 98 112 100 103 99];
>> bq=round(bd./q)

bq =

   -14    -3     2     0    -1     0     0     0
   -20     4     0    -1     0     0     0     0
     0     4     0     0     0     0     0     0
     7     1    -1     0     0     0     0     0
     0    -1     0     0     0     0     0     0
    -1     0     0     0     0     0     0     0
     0     0     0     0     0     0     0     0
     0     0     0     0     0     0     0     0
```

At this stage we have turned our block into one containing mostly 0s. If we were to output a vector from this block, it would be

```
-14 -3 -20 0 4 2 0 0 4 7 0 1 0 -1 -1 0 0 0 -1 0 -1 EOB
```

where EOB signifies the end of the block. By this stage we have reduced an 8 × 8 block to a vector of length 21, containing only small values.

To uncompress, we take the vector and reorder its elements into the matrix bq above. Multiplying by the normalization matrix produces:

```
>> bq2=bq.*q

bq2 =

    -224    -33     20      0    -24      0      0      0
    -240     48      0    -19      0      0      0      0
       0     52      0      0      0      0      0      0
      98     17    -22      0      0      0      0      0
       0    -22      0      0      0      0      0      0
     -24      0      0      0      0      0      0      0
       0      0      0      0      0      0      0      0
       0      0      0      0      0      0      0      0
```

Now we apply the inverse DCT.

```
>> bd2=idct2(bq2)

bd2 =

   -48.1431  -39.4257  -39.8246  -53.5852  -65.6253  -68.5089  -70.4960  -74.9017
   -52.5762  -46.8345  -50.6187  -65.1825  -74.3228  -71.8983  -68.6282  -69.8981
   -70.6699  -66.1335  -69.6750  -80.0362  -81.2435  -69.9392  -59.8115  -57.6095
   -68.4457  -61.8134  -60.1283  -62.2478  -54.7898  -37.7751  -26.0007  -24.2342
   -29.6526  -21.6215  -16.7263  -14.7648   -5.2632    9.2177   14.8476   11.3981
     1.6297    7.3329    9.2805    8.8036   15.4106   24.9217   24.0240   15.7152
     3.0533    4.5797    1.2799   -2.1680    4.6076   15.8252   16.2949    8.4867
    -2.8366   -4.0640  -10.3394  -14.0550   -3.8001   13.2610   19.3977   14.9470
```

Finally we add 128 to each value and round off:

```
>> b2=round(bd2+128)

b2 =

    80    89    88    74    62    59    58    53
    75    81    77    63    54    56    59    58
    57    62    58    48    47    58    68    70
    60    66    68    66    73    90   102   104
    98   106   111   113   123   137   143   139
   130   135   137   137   143   153   152   144
   131   133   129   126   133   144   144   136
   125   124   118   114   124   141   147   143
```

It can be seen that these values are very close to the values in the original block. The differences between original and reconstructed values are:

```
>> double(block)-double(b2)

ans =

     7     6     4    -1    -3    -2    -1     2
    -1   -10    -9    -4     0    -2    -8    -1
     7    -4    -1     7    11     7    -2    -5
    -3    -3     0     0     1    -1    -4     0
    -3     3     6     1    -4    -3     2     1
    -2     4     9     2    -3    -5    -1    -1
     6     2    -4    -8     4    12    10    -4
    -3    -5    -5    -4     4     3    -7    -1
```

The algorithm works best on regions of low frequency; in such cases the original block can be reconstructed with only very small errors.

We can experiment with JPEG compression by using the blkproc function, which applies a function to each block in the image, the size of the blocks being given as parameters to blkproc. We will design two functions: jpg_in, which applies JPEG compression to each 8 × 8 block, and jpg_out, which reverses the compression. For each function we will include a further parameter, n, which will be used to scale the normalization matrix. These functions are shown in Figure 14.5. Now we can apply them to the matrix of the caribou image.

```
function out=jpg_in(x,n)
q=[16 11 10 16 24 40 51 61;...
   12 12 14 19 26 58 60 55;...
   14 13 16 24 40 57 69 56;...
   14 17 22 29 51 87 80 62;...
   18 22 37 56 68 109 103 77;...
   24 35 55 64 81 104 113 92;...
   49 64 78 87 103 121 120 101;...
   72 92 95 98 112 100 103 99];
bd=dct2(double(x)-128);
out=round(bd./(q*n));
```

```
function out=jpg_out(x,n)
q=[16 11 10 16 24 40 51 61;...
   12 12 14 19 26 58 50 55;...
   14 13 16 24 40 57 69 56;...
   14 17 22 29 51 87 80 62;...
   18 22 37 56 68 109 103 77;...
   24 35 55 64 81 104 113 92;...
   49 64 78 87 103 121 120 101;...
   72 92 95 98 112 100 103 99];
out=round(idct2(x.*q*n)+128);
```

FIGURE 14.5 MATLAB *functions for experimenting with JPEG compression.*

```
>> cj1=blkproc(c,[8,8],'jpg_in',1);
>> length(find(cj1==0))

ans =

      51940
```

We have applied the compression scheme to each 8×8 block of the image, up to the point of dividing by the quantization matrix and rounding off. The point of the second command is to show how much information has been lost at this stage. The original image contained 65,536 different items of information (the pixel values), each between 0 and 128. But now we have only $65,536 - 51,940 = 13,596$ items of information, and their maxima and minima are:

```
>> max(cj1(:)),min(cj1(:))

ans =

      60


ans =

     -45
```

Thus, the information is not only far less in number, but also in range. Now we can go backward:

```
>> c1=jpg_out(cj1,2);
>> c1=uint8(c1);
```

(a)   (b)

FIGURE 14.6 *An image before and after JPEG compression and decompression.*

The original image and result c2 are shown in Figure 14.6. There is no apparent difference between the images—they look identical. However, they are not identical

```
>> max(double(c(:))-double(c1(:)))

ans =

    31

>> min(double(c(:))-double(c1(:)))

ans =

   -26
```

We can see the difference (scaled for viewing)

```
>> imshow(mat2gray(double(c)-double(c1)))
```

in Figure 14.7. We can experiment with different levels of quantization. Suppose we take our extra parameter n to be 2. This has the effect of doubling each value in the normalization matrix, thus should set more of the DCT values to 0:

FIGURE 14.7 *The difference between an image and its JPEG decompression.*

(a)   (b)

FIGURE 14.8 *JPEG compression with a scale factor of 2.*

```
>> cj2=blkproc(c,[8,8],'jpg_in',2);
>> length(find(cj2==0))

ans =

       56729
```

This means that only 8,807 values are nonzero. We can also find that the maximum and minimum values of `cj` are 30 and −22. We can now decompress and display the result and the difference with the same commands as above. The results are shown in Figure 14.8. Now we will try a scale of 5:

(a)   (b)

FIGURE 14.9 *JPEG compression with a scale factor of 5.*

```
>> cj5=blkproc(c,[8,8],'jpg_in',5);
>> length(find(c5==0))

ans =

       61512
```

The result and difference image are shown in Figure 14.9. At this stage we may be losing some fine detail, but the image is still remarkably good. We also note that as the scale factor increases, the range of values after the quantization decreases. For the matrix cj above, the maximum and minimum are 12 and −9.

Finally we shall try a scale factor of 10:

```
>> cj10=blkproc(c,[8,8],'jpg_in',10);
>> length(find(cj10==0))

ans =

       63684
```

The maximum and minimum are 6 and −4, and we have only 1,852 items of information. The results are shown in Figure 14.10. This image certainly shows considerable degradation; however, the animal is still quite clear.

Capt. Budd Christman/NOAA Corps.

(a)   (b)

FIGURE 14.10 *JPEG compression with a scale factor of 10.*

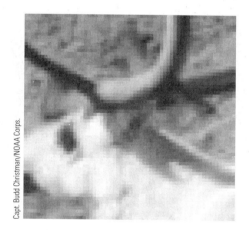

Capt. Budd Christman/NOAA Corps.

FIGURE 14.11 *An image close-up.*

We can see the results of JPEG compression and decompression by looking at a close-up of the image. We will investigate that portion of the animal around the top of the head,

```
>> imshow(imresize(c(68-31:68+32,56-31:56+32),4))
```

which is shown in Figure 14.11. The same areas, with the scales of 1 and 2, are shown in Figure 14.12. The close-ups, with the scales of 5 and 10, are shown in Figure 14.13. Notice that blockiness becomes more apparent as the scale factor increases. This blockiness is due to the working of the algorithm, because each 8×8 block is processed independently of the others.

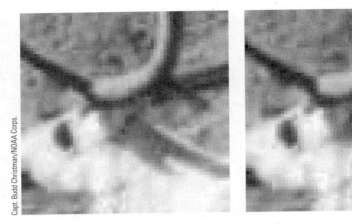

FIGURE 14.12 *Close-ups after the scale factors of 1 and 2.*

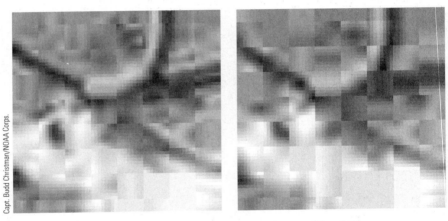

FIGURE 14.13 *Close-ups after the scale factors of 5 and 10.*

This process tends to produce discontinuities in the output and is one of disadvantages of the JPEG algorithm for high levels of compression.

In Chapter 15 we will see that some of these disadvantages can be overcome by using wavelets for compression.

We have seen how changing the compression rate may affect the output. The JPEG algorithm, however, is particularly designed for storage. For example, suppose we take the original block from the caribou image, but divide it by double the quantization matrix. After reordering, the output vector will be

```
7  -1  -10  0  2  1  0  0  2  4  0  1  0  -1  EOB.
```

This vector is further encoded using Huffman coding. To do this, each element of the vector (except for the first), that is, each AC value, is defined to be in a particular category depending on its absolute value. In general, the value 0 is given category 0, and category k contains all elements x whose absolute value satisfies

$$2^k \le |x| \le 2^{k+1} - 1.$$

The categories are also used for the differences of the first (DC) value. The first few categories are:

Range	DC category	AC category
0	0	Not applicable
$-1, 1$	1	1
$-3, -2, 2, 3$	2	2
$-7, \ldots, -4, 4, \ldots, 7$	3	3
$-15, \ldots, -8, 8, \ldots, 15$	4	4

To encode the vector, the category is used with all nonzero terms, along with the number of preceding 0s. For example, for the vector above see the following:

Values:	7	-1	10	0	2	1	0	0	2	4	0	1	0	-1
Category:	1		4		2	1			2	3		1		1
Preceding zeros:	0		0		1	0			2	0		1		1

For each nonzero AC value, a binary vector is produced containing the Huffman code for its particular category and run of preceding 0s. This is followed by a sign bit (0 for negative, 1 for positive) and, for category k, a run of $k - 1$ bits indicating the position within that category. The Huffman code table is provided as part of the JPEG baseline standard. For the first few categories and runs they are as follows:

Run	Category	Code
0	0	1010
0	1	00
0	2	01
0	3	100
0	4	1011
1	1	1100
1	2	111001
1	3	1111001
1	4	111110110
2	1	11011
2	2	11111000
2	3	1111110111

A full table is given by Gonzalez and Woods [7]. For the nonzero AC values in the vector above, the output binary strings will be created from:

Run	Category	Code	Sign	Position
0	1	00	0	0
0	4	1011	1	011
1	2	111001	1	0
0	1	00	1	1
2	2	11111000	1	0
0	3	100	1	00
1	1	1100	1	0
1	1	1100	0	0

The output string of bits for this block will consist of the code for the difference of the DC coefficient, followed by

0000/10111011/11100110/0011/1111100010/100100/110010/110000,

where the lines show just the individual strings. Assuming 8 bits for the first code, the entire block has been encoded with only 60 bits,

$$60/64 \approx 0.94 \text{ bits per pixel,}$$

a compression rate of over 8.5.

For a detailed account of the JPEG algorithm, see Pennebaker [24].

EXERCISES

1. a. If you have knowledge of data structures, implement your own Huffman coding functions. You will need to implement a tree structure in MATLAB — one way of doing this is with a nested cell array. (Look up the help for cell.) Otherwise, download a Huffman code example from the MATLAB central file exchange.

   b. Using your function, test it on the examples given in Section 14.2.

2. Construct a Huffman code for each of the probability tables given:

gray scale		0	1	2	3	4	5	6	7
probability	(a)	.07	.11	.08	.04	.5	.05	.06	.09
	(b)	.13	.12	.13	.13	.12	.12	.12	.13
	(c)	.09	.13	.15	.1	.14	.12	.11	.16

In each case determine the average bits per pixel given by your code.

3. From your results of Question 1, what do you think are the conditions of the probability distribution that gives rise to a high compression rate using Huffman coding?

4. Encode each of the following binary images using RLE:

a

1	0	0	1	1	1
0	1	0	1	1	1
1	0	0	1	1	1
0	1	1	1	0	1
1	0	1	0	1	1
0	1	1	1	1	0

b

1	0	1	0	0	0
0	0	1	1	0	1
1	1	0	0	0	0
0	0	0	0	1	1
1	1	1	1	0	0
1	1	1	0	0	0

5. Using RLE, encode each of the following 4-bit images:

a

1	1	3	3	1	1
1	7	10	10	7	1
6	13	15	15	13	6
6	13	15	15	13	6
1	7	10	10	7	1
1	1	3	3	1	1

b

0	0	0	6	12	12	1	9
1	1	1	6	12	11	9	13
2	2	2	6	11	9	13	13
8	10	15	15	7	5	5	5
14	8	10	15	7	4	4	4
14	14	5	10	7	3	3	3

6. Check your answers to Questions 3 and 4 with MATLAB. You can isolate the bit planes by using the technique discussed in Section 3.4.

7. Encode the preceding images using the 4-bit Gray code, and apply RLE to the bit planes of the result. Compare the results obtained using Gray codes and standard binary codes.

8. Write a MATLAB function for restoring a binary image from a run-length code. Test it on the images and codes from the previous questions.

9. The following are the RLEs for a 4 × 4 four-bit image from most- to least-important bit planes:

```
3   1   2   2   1   4   1   2
1   2   1   2   1   2   1   2   1   3
2   1   2   1   2   2   1   5
0   3   1   3   2   3   1   2   1
```

Construct the image.

10. a. Given the following 4-bit image, transform it to a 3-bit image by removing the least most significant bit plane. Construct a Huffman code on the result and determine the average number of bits per pixel used by the code.

```
0   4   4   4   4   4   6   7
0   4   5   5   5   4   6   7
1   4   5   5   5   4   6   7
1   4   5   5   5   4   6   7
1   4   4   4   4   4   6   7
2   2   8   8   8  10  10  11
2   2   9   9   9  12  13  13
3   3   9   9   9  15  14  14
```

b. Now apply Huffman coding to the original image and determine the average number of bits per pixel used by the code.

c. Which of the two codes gives the best rate of compression?

11. Apply JPEG compression to an 8 × 8 block consisting of

a. All the same value.

b. The left half one value, and the right half another.

c. Random values uniformly distributed in the 0–255 range.

Compare the length of the code vector in each case and the results of decompression.

12. Open the image `engineer.tif`. Using the JPEG compression commands described above, attempt to compress this image using greater and greater compression rates. What is the largest quantization scale factor for which the image is still recognizable? How many 0s are in the DCT block matrix?

13. Apply the given JPEG Huffman codes to the vector

−14 −3 −7 0 4 2 0 0 4 3 0 1 0 −1 −1 0 0 0 −1 0 −1 EOB

and determine the compression rate.

CHAPTER FIFTEEN

WAVELETS

15.1 Waves and Wavelets

We have seen in Chapters 7 and 14 that the discrete Fourier transform (DFT) and its cousin, the discrete cosine transform (DCT), are of enormous use in image processing and image compression. But, as we saw with the Fourier transform, this power does not come without cost. In particular, because the Fourier transform is based on the idea of an image being decomposed into periodic sine or cosine functions, we must assume some sort of periodicity in the image to make the theory fit the practice. This periodicity was obtained by assuming that the image "bent" to meet itself at the top and bottom and at the left and right sides. If so, however, this means that we have introduced unnecessary discontinuities in the image, and these may affect the transform and our use of it.

The idea of wavelets is to keep the wave concept, but drop the periodicity. We may consider a **wavelet** to be a little part of a wave, a wave that is only nonzero in small region. Figure 15.1 illustrates the idea. Figure 15.1(a) is just the graph of

$$y = \sin(x)$$

for $-10 \leq x \leq 10$, and Figure 15.1(b) is the graph of

$$y = \sin(x)e^{-x^2}$$

over the same interval.

Suppose we are given a wavelet. What can we do with it? Well, if

$$f = w(x)$$

is the function that defines our wavelet, we can

- dilate it by applying a scaling factor to x: $f(2x)$ would "squash" the wavelet, and $f(x/2)$ would expand it;

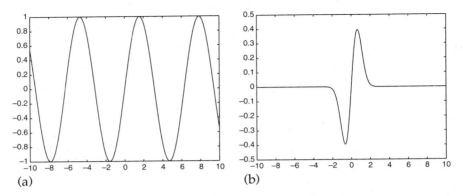

FIGURE 15.1 *Comparing a wave and a wavelet. (a) A wave. (b) A wavelet.*

- translate it by adding or subtracting an appropriate value from x: $f(x-2)$ would shift the wavelet 2 to the right; $f(x+3)$ would shift the wavelet 3 to the left; and
- change its height by simply multiplying the function by a constant.

Of course we can do any or all at once:

$$6f(x/2 - 3), \quad \frac{1}{3}f(16x + 17), \quad f(x/128 - 33.5), \quad \dots$$

Let

$$w(x) = \sin{(x)}e^{-x^2}$$

be the function shown in Figure 15.1(b). Figure 15.2 shows some dilations and shifts of this wavelet.

Given our knowledge of the working of the Fourier transform, it should come as no surprise that given a suitable starting wavelet $w(x)$, we can express any function $f(x)$ as a sum of wavelets of the form

$$aw(bx + c).$$

Moving into two dimensions, we can apply wavelets to images in the same way we applied sine and cosines with the Fourier transform.

Using wavelets has provided a new class of very powerful image-processing algorithms: wavelets can be used for noise reduction, edge detection, and compression. The use of wavelets has superseded the use of the DCTs for image compression in the JPEG2000 image compression algorithm.

A possible problem with wavelets is that the theory, which has been very well researched, can be approached from many different directions.

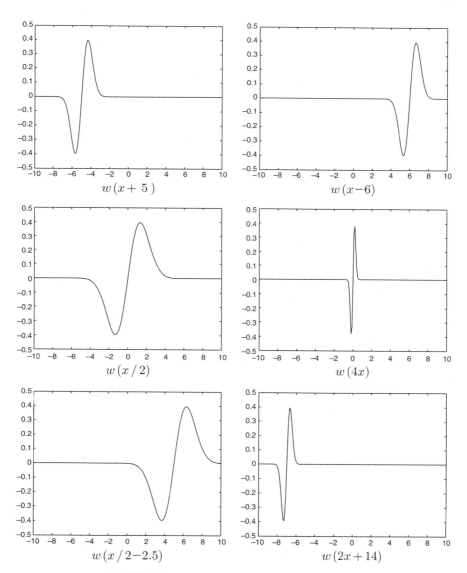

FIGURE 15.2 *Shifts and dilations of the wavelet $w(x)$.*

There is thus no "natural" method of presenting wavelets: it depends on your background and on the use to which the wavelets will be put. Also, much of the writing on wavelets tends to dive into the theory very quickly. In this chapter, however, we will look at the very simplest examples of the use of wavelets and their application to images.

15.1.1 A Simple Wavelet Transform

To obtain a feeling for how a wavelet transform works and behaves, we will look at a very simple example. All wavelet transforms work by taking weighted averages of input values and providing any other necessary information to be able to recover the original input.

For our example, we will perform just two operations: averaging of two values and differencing. For example, suppose we are given two numbers, 14 and 22. We can easily create their average,

$$\frac{14 + 22}{2} = 18.$$

To recover the original two values from their average, we need a second value, the difference, obtained by subtracting the average from the first value:

$$14 - 18 = -4.$$

From the average and the difference we can obtain the original two numbers by adding and subtracting the difference and the average:

$$18 + (-4) = 14$$
$$18 - (-4) = 22.$$

In general, if a and b are our two numbers, we create an average s and a difference d by

$$s = \frac{a + b}{2}$$
$$d = a - s.$$

We can then recover the two original numbers with

$$a = s + d$$

and

$$b = s - d.$$

Let's take a simple vector v of eight elements and create two new vectors v_1 and v_2 of four elements each. Vector v_1 will consist of the averages of each of the pairs of elements from v, and vector v_2 will consist of the differences of the first four elements of v with the elements of v_1. We start with

$$v = [71, \quad 67, \quad 24, \quad 26, \quad 36, \quad 32, \quad 14, \quad 18].$$

Then,

$$v_1 = \left[\frac{71 + 67}{2}, \quad \frac{24 + 26}{2}, \quad \frac{36 + 32}{2}, \quad \frac{14 + 18}{2} \right]$$
$$= [69, \quad 25, \quad 34, \quad 16]$$

and

$$v_2 = [71 - 69, \quad 24 - 25, \quad 36 - 34, \quad 14 - 16]$$
$$= [2, \quad -1, \quad 2, \quad -2].$$

The concatenation of v_1 and v_2 is the **Discrete wavelet transform at 1 scale** of the original vector:

$$d_1 = [69, \quad 25, \quad 34, \quad 16, \quad 2, \quad -1, \quad 2, \quad -2].$$

We can continue by performing this same averaging and differencing for the first four elements of the result; this will involve the concatenation of two vectors of two elements each:

$$v_1 = \left[\frac{69 + 25}{2}, \quad \frac{34 + 16}{2} \right]$$
$$= [47, \quad 25]$$
$$v_2 = [69 - 47, \quad 34 - 25]$$
$$= [22, \quad 9]$$

Replacing the first four elements of d_1 above with this new v_1 and v_2 produces

$$d_2 = [47, \quad 25, \quad 22, \quad 9, \quad 2, \quad -1, \quad 2, \quad -2],$$

which is the **Discrete wavelet transform at 2 scales** of the original vector. We can go one more step, replacing the first two elements of d_2 with their average and difference:

$$d_3 = [36, \quad 11, \quad 22, \quad 9, \quad 2, \quad -1, \quad 2, \quad -2],$$

and this is the **Discrete wavelet transform at 3 scales** of the original vector.

To recover the original vector, we simply add and subtract, first using only the first two elements, then the first four, and finally all of them:

$$[36 + 11, \quad 36 - 11, \quad 22, \quad 9, \quad 2, \quad -1, \quad 2, \quad -2]$$
$$= [47, \quad 25, \quad 22, \quad 9, \quad 2, \quad -1, \quad 2, \quad -2]$$
$$[47 + 22, \quad 47 - 22, \quad 25 + 9, \quad 25 - 9, \quad 2, \quad -1, \quad 2, \quad -2]$$
$$= [69, \quad 25, \quad 34, \quad 16, \quad 2, \quad -1, \quad 2, \quad -2]$$
$$[69 + 2, \quad 69 - 2, \quad 25 + (-1), \quad 25 - (-1), \quad 34 + 2, \quad 34 - 2,$$
$$16 + (-2), \quad 16 - (-2)]$$
$$= [71, \quad 67, \quad 24, \quad 26, \quad 36, \quad 32, \quad 14, \quad 18].$$

At each stage, the averaging vector produces a lower-resolution version of the original vector. Wavelet transforms produce a mix of lower resolutions of the input and the extra information required for inversion.

We notice that the differences may be small if the input values are close together. This concept leads to an idea for compression: we apply a threshold by setting to zero all values in the transform that are less than a predetermined value. Suppose we take a threshold of zero, so that after thresholding d_3 becomes:

$$d_3' = [36, \quad 11, \quad 22, \quad 9, \quad 2, \quad 0, \quad 2, \quad 0].$$

If we now use this as the starting place for our adding and subtracting, we end up with

$$v' = [71, \quad 67, \quad 25, \quad 25, \quad 36, \quad 32, \quad 16, \quad 16].$$

Notice how close this is to the original vector, despite the loss of some information from the transform.

15.2 A Simple Wavelet: The Haar Wavelet

The Haar wavelet has been around for a long time and has been used with images as the **Haar transform.** Only recently has the Haar transform been viewed as a simple wavelet transform. In fact, the Haar wavelet is the simplest possible wavelet, and for that reason it is a good starting place.

The Haar wavelet is defined by the function

$$\psi(x) = \begin{cases} 1 & \text{if } 0 < x < 1/2 \\ -1 & \text{if } 1/2 \le x < 1 \\ 0 & \text{otherwise} \end{cases}$$

and is shown in Figure 15.3. As with our wavelet function $w(x)$, we can compress and expand this wavelet horizontally or vertically and shift it.

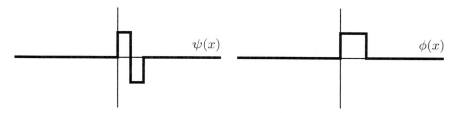

FIGURE 15.3 *The Haar wavelet and pulse function.*

15.2.1 Applying the Haar Wavelet

Given the Haar wavelet, what do we do with it? That is, how do we use the Haar wavelet in a wavelet transform? We haven't yet defined what a wavelet transform is or what it might look like. Without going into too many details, a wavelet transform can be defined in much the same way as the DFT or the DCT: it is a sum of function values multiplied by wavelet values. In comparison, for the DFT we multiplied function values by complex exponentials, and in the DCT we multiplied our function values by cosines.

The discrete wavelet transform (DWT) can be written [7] as:

$$W_\phi(j_0, k) = \frac{1}{\sqrt{M}} \sum_x f(x) \phi_{j_0,k} x \tag{15.1}$$

$$W_\psi(j, k) = \frac{1}{\sqrt{M}} \sum_x f(x) \psi_{j,k}(x), \tag{15.2}$$

where the subscripts on $\phi(x)$ and $\psi(x)$ represent different dilations and shifts of the basic functions. Then we can recover $f(x)$ with

$$f(x) = \frac{1}{\sqrt{M}} \sum_k W_\phi(j_0, k) \phi_{j_0,k} x + \frac{1}{\sqrt{M}} \sum_{j=j_0}^{\infty} W_\psi(j, k) \psi_{j,k}(x).$$

(See Gonzalez and Woods [7].) But what these expressions really show is that the DWT has the same basic appearance as the DFT and DCT: in each case we form a sum of input values multiplied by the values from a particular class of functions. The form of the equations above indicates that the discrete wavelet transform can be written as a matrix multiplication, as we saw for the DFT. We will show below how this is done.

Notice that the Haar wavelet can be written in terms of the simpler pulse function:

$$\phi(x) = \begin{cases} 1 & \text{if } 0 \leq x < 1 \\ 0 & \text{otherwise,} \end{cases}$$

using the relation

$$\psi(x) = \phi(2x) - \phi(2x - 1). \tag{15.3}$$

We can see that this is true by noting that $\phi(2x)$ is equal to 1 for $0 \leq x \leq 1/2$ and that $\phi(2x - 1)$ is equal to 1 for $1/2 \leq x < 1$.

The pulse function also satisfies the equation

$$\phi\left(\frac{x}{2}\right) = \phi(x) - \phi(x - 1). \tag{15.4}$$

In the theory of wavelets, the "starting wavelet," in this case our function $\psi(x)$, is called the **mother wavelet,** and the corresponding function $\phi(x)$ is called the **scaling function** (and sometimes called a **father wavelet**).

We can also write our scaling expression seen in Equation 15.4 as

$$\phi(x) = \phi(2x) + \phi(2x - 1). \tag{15.5}$$

Equations (15.4) and (15.5) are important because they tell us how the wavelets are rescaled at different resolutions. Equation (15.5) is a very important equation: it is called the **dilation equation,** because it relates the scaling function to dilated versions of itself. Generalizations of this equation, as we will see below, have led to wavelets other than the Haar wavelet. Equation (15.3) is the **wavelet equation** for the Haar wavelet. Note that the dilation and wavelet equations have the same right-hand side, except for a change of sign. These can be generalized to produce

$$\phi(x) = \cdots + h_{-2}\phi(2x + 2) + h_{-1}\phi(2x + 1) + h_0\phi(2x)$$
$$+ h_1\phi(2x - 1) + h_2\phi(2x - 2) + h_3\phi(2x - 3) + \cdots \tag{15.6}$$
$$\psi(x) = \cdots - h_{-2}\phi(2x - 3) + h_{-1}\phi(2x - 2) - h_0\phi(2x - 1)$$
$$+ h_1\phi(2x) - h_2\phi(2x + 1) + h_3\phi(2x + 2) - \cdots, \tag{15.7}$$

where the values h_i are called the **filter coefficients** or the **taps** of the wavelet. A wavelet is completely specified by its taps.

We thus have for the Haar wavelet

$$\phi(x) = h_0\phi(2x) + h_1\phi(2x - 1) \tag{15.8}$$
$$\psi(x) = h_1\phi(2x) - h_0\phi(2x - 1), \tag{15.9}$$

where $h_0 = h_1 = 1$. It is actually these h_i values that we use in a calculation of the DWT. We can put them into a DWT matrix:

$$H_{2^n} = \begin{bmatrix} 1 & 1 & 0 & 0 & 0 & 0 & \cdots & 0 & 0 & 0 & 0 \\ 0 & 0 & 1 & 1 & 0 & 0 & \cdots & 0 & 0 & 0 & 0 \\ 0 & 0 & 0 & 0 & 1 & 1 & \cdots & 0 & 0 & 0 & 0 \\ \vdots & \vdots & \vdots & \vdots & \vdots & \vdots & & \vdots & \vdots & \vdots & \vdots \\ 0 & 0 & 0 & 0 & 0 & 0 & \cdots & 1 & 1 & 0 & 0 \\ 0 & 0 & 0 & 0 & 0 & 0 & \cdots & 0 & 0 & 1 & 1 \\ 1 & -1 & 0 & 0 & 0 & 0 & \cdots & 0 & 0 & 0 & 0 \\ 0 & 0 & 1 & -1 & 0 & 0 & \cdots & 0 & 0 & 0 & 0 \\ 0 & 0 & 0 & 0 & 1 & -1 & \cdots & 0 & 0 & 0 & 0 \\ \vdots & \vdots & \vdots & \vdots & \vdots & \vdots & & \vdots & \vdots & \vdots & \vdots \\ 0 & 0 & 0 & 0 & 0 & 0 & \cdots & 1 & -1 & 0 & 0 \\ 0 & 0 & 0 & 0 & 0 & 0 & \cdots & 0 & 0 & 1 & -1 \end{bmatrix}$$

If v is the vector we investigated earlier, then $vH_8 = d_1$. We can obtain d_2 and d_3 by multiplying the first values of the vector by the appropriate sized H matrix.

Let's try this in MATLAB:

```
>> h8=[1 1 0 0 0 0 0 0;0 0 1 1 0 0 0 0;...
       0 0 0 0 1 1 0 0;0 0 0 0 0 0 1 1;...
       1 -1 0 0 0 0 0 0;0 0 1 -1 0 0 0 0;...
       0 0 0 0 1 -1 0 0;0 0 0 0 0 0 1 -1];
>> h4=[1 1 0 0;0 0 1 1;1 -1 0 0;0 0 1 -1];
>> h2=[1 1;1 -1];
>> v=[71 67 24 26 36 32 14 18];
>> d1=v*h8'/2

d1 =

      69     25     34     16      2     -1      2     -2

>> d2=d1;d2(1:4)=d1(1:4)*h4'/2

d2 =

      47     25     22      9      2     -1      2     -2

>> d3=d2;d3(1:2)=d2(1:2)*h2'/2

d3 =

      36     11     22      9      2     -1      2     -2
```

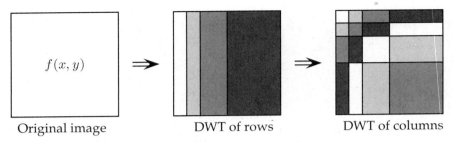

Original image   DWT of rows   DWT of columns

FIGURE 15.4 *The standard decomposition of the two-dimensional DWT.*

The extra divisions by 2 are done because the Haar matrix, as we have given it, simply adds two numbers instead of taking their average; it is done similarly for the difference.

We have suppressed some numeric detail for simplicity in our previous discussion. To be precise, the values of h_0 and h_1 for the Haar wavelet are

$$h_0 = h_1 = \frac{1}{\sqrt{2}},$$

and the matrix H_{2^n} given above should have the factor $\frac{1}{\sqrt{2}}$ in front of it.

Any wavelet transform can be computed by matrix multiplications. But as we have seen in our discussion of the DFT, this can be very inefficient. Happily, many wavelet transforms can be quickly computed by a fast algorithm that is similar in style to the average/difference method we saw earlier. These methods are called **lifting methods** [19].

If we go back to our averaging and differencing example, we can see that the averaging part of the transform corresponds to low-pass filtering, in that we are coarsening or blurring our input. Similarly, the differencing part of the transform corresponds to a high-pass filter of the sort we examined in our discussion of edges in Chapter 9. Thus, a wavelet transform contains within it both high- and low-pass filtering of our input, and we can consider a wavelet transform entirely in terms of filters. This approach will be discussed in Section 15.4.

15.2.2 Two-Dimensional Wavelets

The two-dimensional wavelet transform is separable, which means we can apply a one-dimensional wavelet transform to an image in the same way as for the DFT: we apply a one-dimensional DWT to all the columns and then one-dimensional DWTs to all the rows of the result. This is called the **standard decomposition,** and it is illustrated in Figure 15.4.

We can also apply a wavelet transform differently. Suppose we apply a wavelet transform (say, using the Haar wavelet) to an image by columns, then by rows, but using our transform at one scale only. This technique will produce a result in four quarters: the top left will be a half-sized version of

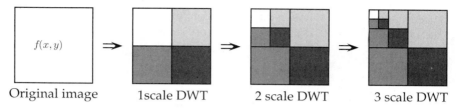

FIGURE 15.5 *The nonstandard decomposition of the two-dimensional DWT.*

the image and the other quarters high-pass filtered images. These quarters will contain horizontal, vertical, and diagonal edges of the image. We then apply a one-scale DWT to the top-left quarter, creating smaller images, and so on. This is called the **nonstandard decomposition,** and it is illustrated in Figure 15.5.

15.3 Wavelets in MATLAB

Although there is a wavelets toolbox produced by the Mathworks,[1] we will not assume that you have access to it. However, there are a number of publicly available wavelet toolboxes available, which, if not as full featured, contain enough functionality for our purposes.

We will use the UviWave toolbox, developed at the University of Vigo in Spain. Its home page is http://www.tsc.uvigo.es/~wavelets/uvi_wave.html, but it can also be found at other places on the Web. Assuming that you have downloaded and installed the toolbox, let's try it, using the same vector as above:

```
>> >> [h,g,rh,rg]=daub(2)
h =
    0.7071    0.7071
g =
   -0.7071    0.7071
rh =
    0.7071    0.7071
rg =
    0.7071   -0.7071
```

Here h and g are the low-pass and high-pass filter coefficients for the forward transform; rh and rg are the low-pass and high-pass filter coefficients for the inverse transform. The daub function produces the filter coefficients for

---

[1] See http://www.mathworks.com/products/wavelet/ for more information.

a class of wavelets called **Daubechies wavelets**, of which the Haar wavelet is the simplest. Now we can apply the DWT to our vector:

```
>> w=wt(v,h,g,3)

w =

   101.8234   31.1127   44.0000   18.0000    2.8284   -1.4142    2.8284   -2.8284
```

This is, in fact, the same as our vector d_3 from above, except for scaling factors. If we divide the first two elements by $(\sqrt{2})^3$, the next two by $(\sqrt{2})^2$, and the last four by $\sqrt{2}$,

```
>> w./sqrt(2).^[3 3 2 2 1 1 1 1]

ans =

    36.0000   11.0000   22.0000    9.0000    2.0000   -1.0000    2.0000   -2.0000
```

we have d_3 from above. We can reconstruct the original vector now:

```
>> iwt(w,rh,rg,3)

ans =

    71.0000   67.0000   24.0000   26.0000   36.0000   32.0000   14.0000   18.0000
```

We could construct our original d_3 by adjusting h and g to remove the scaling values:

```
>> h=[1 1]/2,g=[-1 1]/2

h =

     0.5000     0.5000


g =

    -0.5000     0.5000

>> wt(v,h,g,3)

ans =

    36    11    22     9     2    -1     2    -2
```

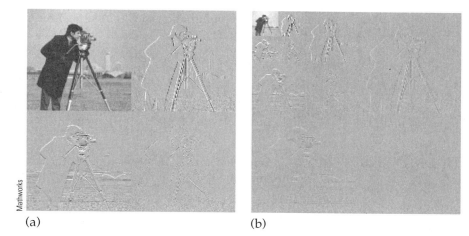

(a)   (b)

FIGURE 15.6 *Different scales of DWT applied to an image. (a) One scale. (b) Three scales.*

Let's try an image. We will apply the Haar wavelet to an image of size 256 × 256, at one and three scales. For display, it will be necessary to scale parts of the image for viewing.

```
>> c=imread('cameraman.tif');
>> [h,g,rh,rg]=daub(2);
>> cw1=wt2d(double(c),h,g,1);
>> m1=2.4*ones(2,2);m1(1,1)=1;m1=imresize(m1,128,'nearest');
>> imshow(mat2gray(cw1).*m1)
>> cw3=wt2d(double(c),h,g,3);
>> m3=2.4*ones(8,8);m3(1,1)=1;m3=imresize(m3,32,'nearest');
>> figure,imshow(mat2gray(cw3).*m3)
```

The result is shown in Figure 15.6. In each case the scaling matrix m1 or m3 simply has 1s over the image in the upper left and 2.4s everywhere else.

We notice that this wavelet transform uses the nonstandard decomposition. To see what a standard decomposition looks like, we use the wt function, which, when applied to a matrix, produces the DWTs of all the rows. Thus, we perform a wt operation, followed by a transposition (to bring the columns into row positions), then another wt, and finally another transposition.

```
>> cw2=wt(wt(double(c),h,g,2)',h,g,2)';
>> m2=2.4*ones(4,4);m2(1,1)=1;m2=imresize(m2,64,'nearest');
>> cw3=wt(wt(double(c),h,g,3)',h,g,3)';
>> imshow(mat2gray(cw2).*m2)
>> figure,imshow(mat2gray(cw3).*m3)
```

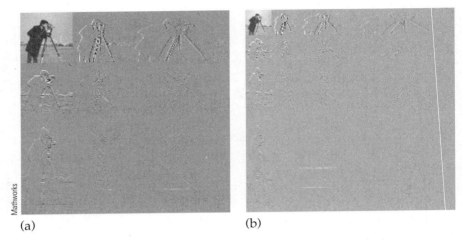

FIGURE 15.7 *Different scales of DWT applied to an image, using the standard decomposition. (a) Two scales. (b) Three scales.*

This is shown in Figure 15.7. Although it is not easy to see, you can just notice that in the standard decomposition, the filtered images in the transform are squashed, rather than all retaining their shape as in the nonstandard decomposition.

15.4 The Daubechies Wavelets

We have seen that the dilation and wavelet equations for the Haar wavelet are particular examples of the general Equations (15.6) and (15.7). However, it is not at all obvious that there are any other solutions. One of the many contributions of Ingrid Daubechies to the theory of wavelets was to define an entire class of wavelets that may be considered as solutions to these equations.

The Daubechies 4 wavelet has a scaling function $\phi(x)$ and wavelet function $\psi(x)$, which satisfy the equations

$$\phi(x) = h_0\phi(2x) + h_1\phi(2x - 1) + h_2\phi(2x - 2) + h_1\phi(2x - 2) \tag{15.10}$$

$$\psi(x) = h_0\phi(2x - 1) - h_1\phi(2x) + h_2\phi(2x + 1) - h_3\phi(2x + 2), \tag{15.11}$$

where the values of the filter coefficients are

$$h_0 = \frac{1 + \sqrt{3}}{4\sqrt{2}} \approx 0.48296$$

$$h_1 = \frac{3 + \sqrt{3}}{4\sqrt{2}} \approx 0.83652$$

$$h_2 = \frac{3 - \sqrt{3}}{4\sqrt{2}} \approx 0.22414$$

$$h_3 = \frac{1 - \sqrt{3}}{4\sqrt{2}} \approx -0.12941.$$

These can be obtained with the `daub` function of `UviWave`:

```
>> [h,g,rh,rg]=daub(4)
h =
    -0.1294      0.2241      0.8365      0.4830
g =
    -0.4830      0.8365     -0.2241     -0.1294
rh =
     0.4830      0.8365      0.2241     -0.1294
rg =
    -0.1294     -0.2241      0.8365     -0.4830
```

The four vectors contain the same values, but in different orders and with different signs. As for the Haar wavelet, we can apply the Daubechies 4 wavelet by a matrix multiplication; the matrix for a one-scale DWT on a vector of length 8 is

$$\begin{bmatrix} h_0 & h_1 & h_2 & h_3 & 0 & 0 & 0 & 0 \\ 0 & 0 & h_0 & h_1 & h_2 & h_3 & 0 & 0 \\ 0 & 0 & 0 & 0 & h_0 & h_1 & h_2 & h_3 \\ h_2 & h_3 & 0 & 0 & 0 & 0 & h_0 & h_1 \\ h_3 & -h_2 & h_1 & -h_0 & 0 & 0 & 0 & 0 \\ 0 & 0 & h_3 & -h_2 & h_1 & -h_0 & 0 & 0 \\ 0 & 0 & 0 & 0 & h_3 & -h_2 & h_1 & -h_0 \\ h_1 & -h_0 & 0 & 0 & 0 & 0 & h_3 & -h_2 \end{bmatrix}.$$

Notice that the filter coefficients overlap between rows, which is not the case for the Haar matrix H_{2^n}. This means that the use of the Daubechies 4 wavelet will have smoother results than using the Haar wavelet. The form of the matrix above is similar to circular convolution with the one-dimensional filters

$$\begin{bmatrix} h_0 & h_1 & h_2 & h_3 \end{bmatrix}$$

and

$$\begin{bmatrix} h_3 & -h_2 & h_1 & -h_0 \end{bmatrix}.$$

The discrete wavelet transform can indeed be approached in terms of filtering; the two filters above are then known as the low-pass and high-pass

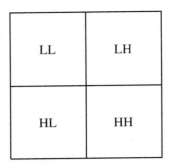

FIGURE 15.8 *The one-scale wavelet transform in terms of filters.*

filters, respectively. Steps for performing a one-scale wavelet transform are given by Umbaugh [37]:

Step 1. Convolve the image rows with the low-pass filter.

Step 2. Convolve the columns of the result of Step 1 with the low-pass filter and rescale this to half its size by subsampling.

Step 3. Convolve the result of Step 1 with the high-pass filter and again subsample to obtain an image of half the size.

Step 4. Convolve the original image rows with the high-pass filter.

Step 5. Convolve the columns of the result of Step 4 with the low-pass filter and rescale this to half its size by subsampling.

Step 6. Convolve the result of Step 4 with the high-pass filter and again subsample to obtain an image of half the size.

At the end of these steps there are four images, each half the size of the original. They are

1. the low-pass/low-pass image (LL), the result of Step 2,
2. the low-pass/high-pass image (LH), the result of Step 3,
3. the high-pass/low-pass image (HL), the result of Step 5, and
4. the high-pass/high-pass image (HH), the result of Step 6.

These images can then be placed into a single image grid as shown in Figure 15.8.

The filter coefficients of a wavelet are such that the transform may be inverted precisely to recover the original image. Using filters, this is done by taking each subimage, zero interleaving to produce an image of double the size and convolving with the inverse low-pass and high-pass filters. Finally, the results of all the filterings are added. For the Daubechies 4 wavelet, the inverse low-pass and high-pass filters are

$$\begin{bmatrix} h_2 & h_1 & h_0 & h_3 \end{bmatrix}$$

and

$$\begin{bmatrix} h_3 & -h_0 & h_1 & -h_2 \end{bmatrix},$$

respectively.

A further approach to the DWT may be considered as a general-ization to filtering. It is called **lifting** and is discussed by Jensen and la Cour-Harbo [19]. Lifting starts with a sequence $s_j[n], n = 0 \ldots 2^j - 1$ and produces two sequences $s_{j-1}[n], n = 0 \ldots 2^{j-1} - 1$ and $d_{j-1}[n], n = 0 \ldots 2^{j-1} - 1$, each half the length of the original. The lifting scheme for the Haar wavelet may be described as

$$d_{j-1}[n] = s_j[2n + 1] - s_j[2n]$$
$$s_{j-1}[n] = s_j[2n] + d_{j-1}[n]/2.$$

A lifting scheme for the Daubechies 4 wavelet is

$$s_{j-1}^{(1)}[n] = s_j[2n] + \sqrt{3}s_j][2n + 1]$$

$$d_{j-1}^{(1)}[n] = s_j[2n + 1] - \frac{1}{4}\sqrt{3}s_{j-1}^{(1)}[n] - \frac{1}{4}\left(\sqrt{3} - 2\right)s_{j-1}^{(1)}[n - 1]$$

$$s_{j-1}^{(2)} = s_{j-1}^{(1)}[n] - d_{j-1}^{(1)}[n + 1]$$

$$s_{j-1}[n] = \frac{\sqrt{3} - 1}{\sqrt{2}}s_{j-1}^{(2)}[n]$$

$$d_{j-1}[n] = \frac{\sqrt{3} + 1}{\sqrt{2}}d_{j-1}^{(1)}[n].$$

Both the Haar and Daubechies 4 schemes can be reversed; see Jensen and la Cour-Harbo [17] for details. A single lifting, as shown above, produces a one-scale wavelet transform. To produce transforms of higher scales, lifting can be applied to s_{j-1} to produce s_{j-2} and d_{j-2}, then to s_{j-2}, and so on. In each lifting scheme, the sequence s_{j-1} may be considered as the subsampled low-pass version of s_j, and the sequence d_{j-1} may be considered as the sub-sampled high-pass version of s_j. Thus, a single lifting scheme provides, in effect, both the low-pass and high-pass filter results. Applying a lifting to an image, first to all the rows, and then to all the columns of the result, will produce a one-scale wavelet transform.

We might hope that since the scaling and wavelet functions $\phi(x)$ and $\psi(x)$ have such simple forms for the Haar wavelet, as we saw in Figure 15.3, the same would be true for the Daubechies 4 wavelet. We can plot a wavelet by inverting a basis vector: a vector consisting of all 0s except for a single 1.

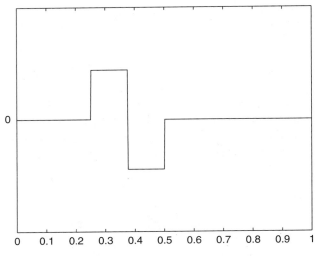

FIGURE 15.9 *A plot of the Haar wavelet.*

Following Jensen and la Cour-Harbo [17], we will choose a vector whose sixth element is 1. We will experiment first with the Haar wavelet:

```
>> [h,g,rh,rg]=daub(2);
>> t=zeros(1,512);t(6)=1;
>> td=iwt(t,rh,rg,9);
>> plot([1:512]/512,td)
```

The result is shown in Figure 15.9. Other basis vectors produce similar results, but with the wavelet scaled or translated. The vector we have chosen seems to produce the best plot. For the Daubechies 4 wavelet, we repeat the above four commands, but begin with:

```
>> [h,g,rh,rg]=daub(4);
```

The result is shown in Figure 15.10. This is a very spiky and unusual graph! It is, in fact, a fractal, and unlike the Haar wavelet, the function cannot be described in simple terms.

15.5 Image Compression Using Wavelets

Wavelets provide some of the most powerful tools known for image compression. As we stated earlier, they have replaced the use of the DCT in the JPEG2000 algorithm. In this section we will investigate what information we can remove from the DWT of an image and still retain most of the original information.

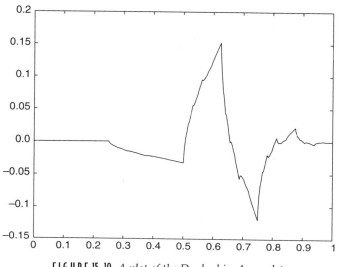

FIGURE 15.10 *A plot of the Daubechies 4 wavelet.*

15.5.1 Thresholding and Quantization

The idea is to take the DWT of an image and, for a given value d, set all values x in the DWT for which $|x| \leq d$ to 0. This is at the basis of the JPEG2000 compression [37]. We will try this using the Daubechies 4 wavelets and $d = 10$.

```
>> c=imread('caribou.tif');
>> imshow(c);
>> cw=wt2d(double(c),h,g,8);
>> length(find(abs(cw)<=10))

ans =

        47427
>> cw(find(abs(cw)<=10))=0;
>> cw=round(cw);
>> ci=iwt2d(cw,rh,rg,8);
>> imshow(mat2gray(ci))
```

We are thus removing nearly three-quarters of the information from the DWT. We further simplify the result by quantizing; in this case we use the round function to turn fractions into integers. Figure 15.11(a) shows the original caribou image, and Figure 15.11(b) shows the result of the above commands. The result is indistinguishable from the original image. We can use different wavelets by using either daub(2) or daub(6) to

(a)   (b)

FIGURE 15.11 *An example of wavelet compression. (a) Original image. (b) Result after thresholding and inversion.*

(a)   (b)

FIGURE 15.12 *Use of different wavelets. (a) Using the Haar wavelet. (b) Using the Daubechies 6 wavelet.*

obtain the Haar filter coefficients or the filter coefficients of the Daubechies 6 wavelet. The results of thresholding (again with $d = 10$) are shown in Figure 15.12(a and b). We could clearly obtain higher compression rates by removing more information; this can be obtained by increasing the threshold value d. We will try with $d = 30$ and $d = 50$.

(a)   (b)

FIGURE 15.13 *Examples of wavelet compression. (a) Using d = 30. (b) Using d = 50.*

```
>> cw=wt2d(double(c),h,g,8);
>> length(find(abs(cw)<=30))

ans =

      61182

>> cw(find(abs(cw)<=30))=0;
>> cw=round(cw);
>> ci=iwt2d(cw,rh,rg,8);
>> imshow(mat2gray(ci))
>> cw=wt2d(double(c),h,g,8);
>> length(find(abs(cw)<=50))

ans =

      63430

>> cw(find(abs(cw)<=50))=0;
>> cw=round(cw);
>> ci=iwt2d(cw,rh,rg,8);
>> figure,imshow(mat2gray(ci))
```

Figure 15.13(a) shows the result with $d = 30$, and Figure 15.13(b) shows the result with $d = 50$. Notice that with a threshold value of 50, we are discarding 63,430 items of information, leaving only 2,106 nonzero values. However, the result is extremely good when compared with the results of JPEG compression as shown in Figure 14.10 in Chapter 14.

Capt. Budd Christman/NOAA Corps.

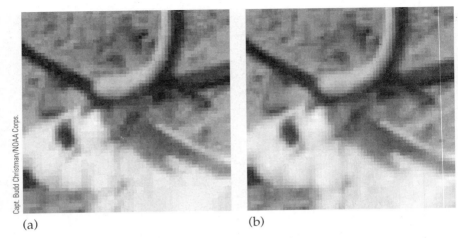

Capt. Budd Christman/NOAA Corps.

(a)   (b)

FIGURE 15.14 *Close-ups of wavelet compression using* $d = 10$. *(a) Using the Haar wavelet.*
(b) Using the Deubechies 6 wavelet.

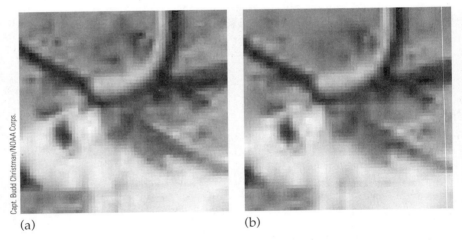

Capt. Budd Christman/NOAA Corps.

(a)   (b)

FIGURE 15.15 *Close-ups of wavelet compression using the Daubechies 6 wavelet. (a) Using*
$d = 30$. *(b) Using* $d = 50$.

As in Chapter 14, we will investigate the appearance of the image with
a close-up. Figure 15.14(a) shows the close-up using the Haar wavelet and
$d = 10$; Figure 15.14(b) shows the result using the Daubechies 6 wavelets and
$d = 10$. Figure 15.15(a) shows the close-up using the Daubechies 6 wavelet
and $d = 30$; Figure 15.15(a) shows the result using the same wavelet and
$d = 50$. Even though we can see that we are losing some fine detail, the
result is far superior to the result obtained by using the JPEG compression
algorithm.

Capt. Budd Christman/NOAA Corps.

FIGURE 15.16 *An image after DWT extraction and inversion.*

15.5.2 Extraction

Here we cut off a portion of the DWT, setting all values to 0, and inverting the rest. This is not a standard method of compression, but it does gives reasonably good results. It also has the advantage of being easier to compute than thresholding and quantization. For example, suppose we keep just the upper-left 100×100 elements of the transform:

```
>> [h,g,rh,rg]=daub(4);
>> cw=wt2d(double(c),h,g,8);
>> temp=zeros(size(c));
>> temp(1:100,1:100)=cw(1:100,1:100);
>> ci=iwt2d(temp,rh,rg,8);
>> imshow(mat2gray(ci))
```

The result is shown in Figure 15.16. Notice that whereas we took only 10,000 elements of the 65,536 elements of the transform—less than a one-sixth—the output is remarkably good. Figure 15.17(a) shows the results after extracting the top left 50×50 elements of the DWT and Figure 15.17(b) shows the result after extracting the top left 20×20. The left-hand figure is quite blurry, but because we have used only 2,500 of the possible 65,536 elements of the transform, this is to be expected. On the right, with only 400 elements used, the figure is basically unrecognizable. Even so, we can still distinguish size, shapes, and grayscales.

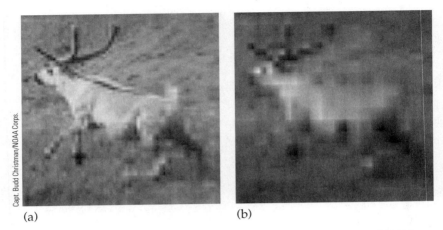

Capt. Budd Christman/NOAA Corps.

(a)   (b)

FIGURE 15.17 *Compression by DWT extraction. (a) Taking* 50×50 *elements. (b) Taking* 20×20 *elements.*

15.6 High-Pass Filtering Using Wavelets

If we look at a wavelet transform, then apart from the rescaled image in the top left, the rest is high-frequency information. We would expect then, that if we were to eliminate the top-left corner by setting all the transform values to 0, the result after inversion would be a high-pass-filtered version of the original image.

We will perform a two-scale decomposition (with Daubechies 4 wavelet) on the Caribou image, and remove the image from the top left.

```
>> cw=wt2d(double(c),h,g,2);
>> cw(1:64,1:64)=0;
>> ci=iwt2d(cw,rh,rg,2);
>> imshow(mat2gray(ci))
```

The result of this extraction and inversion is shown in Figure 15.18(a). We can do the same thing using a three-scale decomposition, which will mean that the corner image will be half the size.

```
>> cw=wt2d(double(c),h,g,3);
>> cw(1:32,1:32)=0;
>> ci=iwt2d(cw,rh,rg,3);
>> imshow(mat2gray(ci))
```

The result is shown in Figure 15.18(b). These images can be thresholded to produce edge images.

We can be more specific in the part of the transform we eliminate or keep and extract the horizontal or vertical edges only.

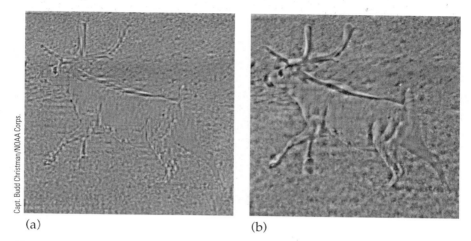

Capt. Budd Christman/NOAA Corps.

(a)   (b)

FIGURE 15.18 *High-pass filtering with wavelets. (a) Using a two-scale decomposition. (b) Using a three-scale decomposition.*

15.7 Denoising Using Wavelets

Since noise can be considered as a high-frequency component, some form of low-pass filtering should remove it. As we did for compression, we can remove such components by thresholding. To compare with the results obtained in Chapter 8, we will use a gray version of the twins image, converted to type double.

```
>> tw=imread('twins.tif');
>> t=im2double(rgb2gray(tw));
>> tg=imnoise(t,'gaussian');
```

Now we can attempt some noise removal. We will assume that all the filter coefficients are those of the Daubechies 4 wavelet.

```
>> imshow(tg);
>> tw=wt2d(tg,h,g,4);
>> length(find(abs(tw)<0.1))

ans =

        42384

>> tw(find(abs(tw)<0.15))=0;
>> ti=iwt2d(tw,rh,rg,4);
>> figure,imshow(mat2gray(ti))
```

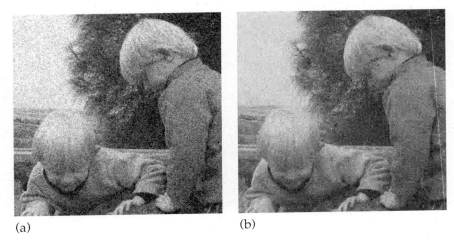

(a)   (b)

FIGURE 15.19 *Denoising using wavelets. (a) Original noise image. (b) Result of wavelet filtering.*

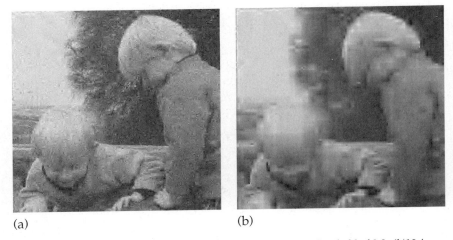

(a)   (b)

FIGURE 15.20 *Denoising using different thresholds. (a)Using a threshold of 0.2. (b)Using a threshold of 0.5.*

The noisy image is shown in Figure 15.19(a) and the result of the wavelet filtering commands is shown in Figure 15.19(b). At this level of thresholding, not much of the noise has been removed, although there has been some slight reduction. Figure 15.20(a) shows the result using a threshold of 0.2, and Figure 15.20(b) shows the result using a threshold of 0.5. The results compare very favorably to those we investigated in Chapter 8; however, we can see that too high a threshold results in unacceptable blurring of the image.

EXERCISES

1. For each of the sequences apply, by hand, the simple wavelet transform discussed in Section 15.1 at one, two, and three scales.

   a. 20 38 6 25 30 29 21 32
   b. 30 11 0 38 0 15 22 32
   c. 7 38 19 11 24 14 32 14

2. Check your answers with MATLAB using the filter coefficients

   ```
   >> h=[1 1]/2,g=[-1 1]/2
   ```

3. Work backward from the transforms and obtain the original sequence.

4. Determine the filter coefficients rh and rg to perform the calculations in Question 3.

5. Repeat the calculations above in MATLAB using the Haar wavelet transform, obtaining the filter coefficients with the command

   ```
   >> [h,g,rh,rg]=daub(2)
   ```

6. Obtain a 256×256 grayscale image. Obtain the DWT at one, two, and three scales using daub(2), daub(4), and daub(6). Are there any observable differences in the outputs of the transform for the different wavelets?

7. Write a MATLAB function showdwt, which will scale the result of a two-dimensional wavelet transform for easier viewing.

8. Obtain the following grayscale image:

   ```
   >> f=imread('flowers.tif');
   >> fg=rgb2gray(f);
   >> f=im2uint8(f(30:285,60:315));
   ```

   Perform the forward DWT at eight scales using the Daubechies 4 wavelet. For each of the following values of d, make all elements of the transform whose absolute values are less than d equal to zero. Determine the number of zeros in the result. Quantize the result by using the floor or round functions. Invert the result and display.

   a. 10
   b. 25
   c. 50
   d. 60

   At what values of d do you notice degradation in the result?

9. Repeat Question 8 for some very large values of d: 100, 200, 300, . . .
What is the size of d that renders the image completely
unrecognizable? How many 0s are in the transform?

10. Repeat Questions 8 and 9 with an image of a face. If you don't have
one, you can obtain some faces with:

```
>> load gatlin.mat
>> g=im2uint8(ind2gray(X(31:286,41:296),map));
```

11. Choose any of your 256 × 256 grayscale images. Add Gaussian noise
with mean 0 and with standard variations 0.01, 0.02, 0.05, and 0.1. For
each noisy image, attempt to denoise it with wavelets. How reasonable
a result can you obtain for the noise with the higher standard
deviations?

CHAPTER SIXTEEN

SPECIAL EFFECTS

We have seen a great many different methods of changing the appearance of an image, and usually our need for the particular change was motivated by a problem: we may have needed to remove something from an image (noise, for example), to improve the appearance of the image, to calculate some aspect of the image (size, position, number of components, etc.).

However, there is another totally different aspect of image processing—that of adding some sort of special effect to an image. We may want to make this change for effect alone, or simply for fun. There are a great many different effects possible, and in this chapter we will look at a few of them. Here we are encroaching on the area of computer graphics. However, our algorithms involve the changing of either the value or the position of pixels, and we can achieve many effects with very simple means.

16.1 Polar Coordinates

Many effects have a radial nature; their appearance radiates outward from the center of the image. To achieve these effects, we need to transform our image from Cartesian coordinates to polar coordinates and back again.

THE ORIGIN Suppose we have an image of size rows × cols. If the dimensions are odd, we can choose as our origin the very center pixel. If the dimensions are even, we choose as origin a pixel at the top left of the bottom-right quadrant. So, in a 7×9 image, our origin would be at pixel $(4, 5)$, and in a 6×8 image, our origin would be at position $(4, 4)$. We can express the origin formally by

$$x_0 = \lceil (r + 1)/2 \rceil$$
$$y_0 = \lceil (c + 1)/2 \rceil,$$

where r and c are the numbers of rows and columns, respectively, and $\lceil x \rceil$ is the **ceiling function,** which returns the smallest integer not less than x. Of course, if one dimension is odd and the other even, the origin will be at the center of the odd dimension and in the first place of the second half of the even dimension.

Thus, we can find coordinates of the origin by:

```
>> ox=ceil((rows+1)/2)
>> oy=ceil((cols+1)/2)
```

POLAR COORDINATES   To find the polar coordinates, we apply the usual formulas

$$r = \sqrt{x^2 + y^2}$$
$$\theta = \tan^{-1}(y/x),$$

which can be implemented for an array by using the the meshgrid function, where the indices are offset by the values of the origin:

```
>> [y,x]=meshgrid([1:cols]-oy,[1:rows]-ox);
>> r=sqrt(x.^2+y.^2);
>> theta=atan2(y,x);
```

We can easily go back, using the fact that the (x, y) coordinates corresponding to the polar coordinates (r, θ) are

$$x = r \cos \theta$$
$$y = r \sin \theta.$$

Thus we have

```
>> x2=round(r.*cos(theta))+ox
>> y2=round(r.*sin(theta))+oy
```

and these arrays will contain the same indices as the original arrays.

EXAMPLE   We have seen in Chapter 3 that an image can be pixelated, that is, be shown in large blocks of low resolution, by using the imresize function. We can achieve the same effect, however, by using the mod function. In general, $\text{mod}(x, n)$ is the remainder when x is divided by n. For example see the following:

```
>> x=1:12

x =

     1    2    3    4    5    6    7    8    9   10   11   12

>> mod(x,4)

ans =

     1    2    3    0    1    2    3    0    1    2    3    0
```

If x is divisible by 4, then there is no remainder, and the mod function returns 0. If we subtract the mod values from the original, we obtain repetition, which in an image would produce a pixelated effect:

```
>> x-mod(x,4)

ans =

     0    0    0    4    4    4    4    8    8    8    8   12
```

Thus, a subtraction of moduli from the radius and argument values should produce a radial pixelated effect.

We can try it with the flowers image, which for simplicity we will turn into a grayscale image.

```
>> f=imread('flowers.tif');
>> fg=rgb2gray(f);
>> [rows cols]=size(fg)

rows =

    362


cols =

    500

>> ox=ceil((rows+1)/2)

ox =
```

(continued)

```
    182

>> oy=ceil((cols+1)/2)

oy =

    251

>> [y,x]=meshgrid([1:cols]-oy,[1:rows]-ox);
>> r=sqrt(x.^2+y.^2);
>> theta=atan2(y,x);
```

This is just the standard setup. Now we perform the pixelation:

```
>> r2=r-mod(r,5);
>> theta2=theta-mod(theta,0.087);
```

Since the angles are given as radians, we use a small value in the modulus; here, $0.087 = 5\pi/180$.

Now we transfer back into Cartesian coordinates:

```
>> x2=r2.*cos(theta2);
>> y2=r2.*sin(theta2);
```

To obtain an image for display, we must adjust the indices x2 and y2 by adding ox and oy to them, rounding them off, and making sure that the row indices are between 1 and rows and that the column indices are between 1 and cols:

```
>> xx=round(x2)+ox;
>> yy=round(y2)+oy;
>> xx(find(xx>rows))=rows;
>> xx(find(xx<1))=1;
>> yy(find(yy>cols))=cols;
>> yy(find(yy<1))=1;
```

Now we can use these new indices xx and yy to obtain an image from the original flower image matrix fg. To do this, we could use a double loop,

```
>> for i=1:rows,...
     for j=1:cols,...
        f2(i,j)=fg(xx(i,j),yy(i,j));...
     end;...
   end;
```

The original `fg`   The pixelated `f2`

FIGURE 16.1 *Radial pixelation.*

or more simply the `sub2ind` function, which does exactly the same thing:

```
>> f2=fg(sub2ind([rows,cols],xx,yy));
```

Now we can display the original and the result.

```
>> imshow(fg),figure,imshow(f2)
```

The results are shown in Figure 16.1.

16.2 Ripple Effects

We will investigate two different ripple effects: bathroom-glass ripples, which give the effect of an image seen through wavy glass, such as is found in bathrooms, and pond ripples, which approximate a reflection in the surface of a pond.

We have seen that subtracting moduli produces a pixelated effect. A bathroom-glass effect can be obtained by adding moduli:

```
>> x=1:12;
>> x+mod(x,4)

ans =

   2    4    6    4    6    8   10    8   10   12   14   12
```

Notice that though the values increase from left to right, they do in small runs that seem to overlap. The appearance will be of a ripple across the image. We will experiment first using Cartesian coordinates:

```
>> [y,x]=meshgrid(1:cols,1:rows);
>> y2=y+mod(y,32);
>> y2(find(y2<1))=1;
>> y2(find(y2>cols))=cols;
```

Here we have just added moduli across the columns, then adjusted the result to ensure that the values stay with the column range. Now we can use sub2ind to create a new image:

```
>> ripple1=fg(sub2ind([rows cols],x,y2));
>> imshow(ripple1)
```

We can, of course, do the same thing down the rows,

```
>> x2=x+mod(x,32);
>> x2(find(x2<1))=1;
>> x2(find(x2>rows))=rows;
>> ripple2=fg(sub2ind([rows cols],x2,y));
>> imshow(ripple2)
```

or even both at once.

```
>> ripple3=fg(sub2ind([rows cols],x2,y2));
>> imshow(ripple3)
```

To obtain a radial ripple, corresponding to ripples on a pond, we create our polar coordinate matrices r and theta as above, and then do the following:

```
>> r2=r+mod(r,10);
>> x2=r2.*cos(theta);
>> y2=r2.*sin(theta);
```

Now we create the indices xx and yy as in the pixelation example above.

```
>> ripple4=fg(sub2ind([rows,cols],xx,yy));
>> imshow(ripple4)
```

All results are shown in Figure 16.2.

ripple1   ripple2

ripple3   Radial ripple: `ripple4`

FIGURE 16.2 *Bathroom-glass rippling on an image.*

To obtain the pond ripple effect, we move the pixels around by using a sine wave. For Cartesian effects we use:

```
>> [y,x]=meshgrid(1:cols,1:rows);
>> y2=round(y+3*sin(x/2));
>> x2=round(x+3*sin(y/2));
```

As above, we ensure that the values of x2 and y2 fit within the row and column bounds.

```
>> ripple5=fg(sub2ind([rows cols],x,y2));
>> ripple6=fg(sub2ind([rows cols],x2,y));
>> ripple7=fg(sub2ind([rows cols],x2,y2));
```

For a radial sine wave ripple, we adjust r first.

```
>> r2=r+sin(r/2)*3;
```

FIGURE 16.3 *Pond rippling on an image.*

After that, we create x2 and y2 as above, and turn them back into indices xx and yy with the appropriate bounds.

```
>> ripple8=fg(sub2ind([rows cols],xx,yy));
```

These new ripples are shown in Figure 16.3. The effects can be varied by changing the parameters to the sine functions in the commands above.

16.3 General Distortion Effects

The rippling effects in the previous section are examples of more general effects called **distortion effects.** Here it is not so much the value of the pixels that are changed as their position. All distortion effects work in much the same way, which we shall describe in a sequence of steps. Suppose we have an effect that involves Cartesian coordinates only.

1. Start with an image matrix $p(i, j)$ of size $m \times n$.
2. Produce two new indexing arrays (the same size as the matrix): $x(i, j)$ and $y(i, j)$.
3. Create a new image $q(i, j)$ by

$$q(i, j) = p(x(i, j), y(i, j)).$$

We have seen above that the arrays $x(i, j)$ and $y(i, j)$ may be created by a procedure that produces values that may be fractional or be outside the bounds of the image matrix. Thus, we will need to ensure that the indexing arrays contain integers only and that for all i and j, $1 \leq x(i, j) \leq m$ and $1 \leq y(i, j) \leq n$.

If we have an effect that requires polar coordinates, we add a few steps to the procedure above:

1. Start with an image matrix $p(i, j)$ of size $m \times n$.
2. Create the arrays $r(i, j)$ and $\theta(i, j)$ containing the polar coordinates of each position (i, j).
3. Produce new arrays $s(i, j)$ and $\phi(i, j)$ by adjusting the values of r and θ.
4. Write these new arrays out to Cartesian indexing arrays (the same size as the matrix):

$$x(i, j) = s(i, j) \cos (\phi(i, j)) + o_x$$
$$y(i, j) = s(i, j) \sin (\phi(i, j)) + o_y$$

where (o_x, o_y) are the coordinates of the polar origin.
5. Create a new image $q(i, j)$ by

$$q(i, j) = p(x(i, j), y(i, j)).$$

As above, we must ensure that the indexing arrays contain only integers and have the appropriate bounds.

We have seen above how to implement various distortion effects in MATLAB, so just by changing the functions used to distort the indexing arrays or the polar coordinates we can achieve many different effects.

FISHEYE   The fish-eye lens effect can be obtained very easily with polar coordinates. Here are the relevant commands:

```
>> R=max(r(:));
>> r=r.^2/R;
```

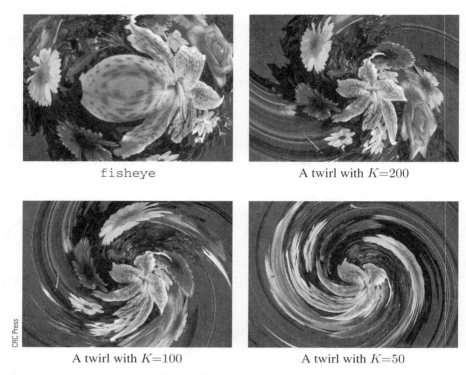

FIGURE 16.4 *Fisheye and twirls.*

To put these into context, we will list the entire sequence of commands for use with the flower matrix `fg`:

```
>> [rows,cols]=size(fg);
>> ox=ceil((rows+1)/2);
>> oy=ceil((cols+1)/2);
>> [y,x]=meshgrid([1:cols]-oy,[1:rows]-ox);
>> r=sqrt(x.^2+y.^2);
>> theta=atan2(y,x);
>> R=max(r(:));                % Here is where we implement the fisheye effect
>> s=r.^2/R;
>> x2=round(s.*cos(theta))+ox; % Now we write out to the indexing arrays...
>> y2=round(s.*sin(theta))+oy;
>> x2(find(x2<1))=1;           % ...and ensure that their bounds are correct
>> x2(find(x2>rows))=rows;
>> y2(find(y2<1))=1;
>> y2(find(y2>cols))=cols;
>> fisheye=fg(sub2ind([rows cols],x2,y2)); % Create the new image...
>> imshow(fisheye)                         % ...and view it
```

The result is shown in Figure 16.4.

TWIRL   A twirl or swirl effect, as of the top of a cup of coffee being swirled with a spoon, is also very easily done. Again, it is a polar effect. A twirl effect can be obtained by

$$s(i, j) = \theta(i, j) + r(i, j)/K,$$

where K can be changed to adjust the amount of twirl. A small value provides more twirl, a large value less. So given the arrays r and theta, and a value K, the relevant commands are:

```
>> phi=theta+(r/K);
>> x2=round(r.*cos(phi))+ox;
>> y2=round(r.*sin(phi))+oy;
```

Figure 16.4 shows the results of twirls with different values of K.

JITTER   The jitter effect is more easily implemented than described. It is like a radial bathroom-glass effect, but instead of manipulating the r matrix to obtain a ripple effect, we manipulate the theta matrix.

```
>> phi=theta+mod(theta,0.1396)-0.0698;
```

Here, $0.1396 = 8\pi/180$, and $0.0698 = 4\pi/180$. The result is shown in Figure 16.5.

CIRCULAR SLICE   This is another effect obtained by manipulating the angle. It's implementation is similar to that of the jitter effect:

```
>> phi=theta+mod(r,6)*pi/180
```

We include the extra $\frac{\pi}{180}$ factor to convert to radians. The result, which has a rippling appearance, is shown in Figure 16.5.

SQUARE SLICE   The square slice is a Cartesian effect. It works by cutting the image into small squares and perturbing them a little. It uses the sign function, which is defined as:

$$\text{sign}(x) = \begin{cases} 1 & \text{if } x > 0, \\ 0 & \text{if } x = 0, \\ -1 & \text{if } x < 0. \end{cases}$$

We start with

```
>> [y,x]=meshgrid(1:cols,1:rows);
```

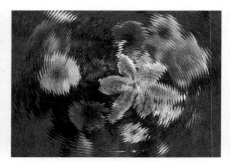

Jitter   Circular slice

FIGURE 16.5 *Jitter and circular slice.*

and then implement the slice distortion with:

```
>> K=8;
>> Q=10;
>> x2=round(x+K*sign(cos(y/Q)));
>> y2=round(y+K*sign(cos(x/Q)));
```

The values K and Q influence the size of the squares and the amount of perturbation. A large value of K produces a very perturbed image; a large value of Q produces large squares. After rounding, fixing the bounds, and writing to a new image, results are shown in Figure 16.6.

FUZZY EFFECT   This effect is obtained by replacing each pixel with a randomly selected pixel from its neighborhood. To do this, we simply add random values to the index matrices x and y. If we are choosing values from a 7×7 neighborhood, then we randomize the indices with integer values chosen from $-3, -2, -1, 0, 1, 2, 3$. We can achieve this with:

```
>> x2=x+floor(7*rand(rows,cols)-3);
>> y2=y+floor(7*rand(rows,cols)-3);
```

For a $(2N + 1) \times (2N + 1)$ neighborhood, our randomization commands would be

```
>> x2=x+floor((2*N+1)*rand(rows,cols)-N);
```

and the process would be done similarly for y2. Results are shown in Figure 16.7. For a large value of N, the result begins to take on a frosted-glass effect.

CRC Press

FIGURE I6.6 *The square-slice effect.*

CRC Press

FIGURE I6.7 *The fuzzy effect using different neighborhoods.*

I6.4 Pixel Effects

In a sense, all image effects are pixel effects, since we are always dealing with pixels. However, in the previous sections, we didn't change the values of the grayscales explicitly; we merely copied them to different positions in the output arrays. Many effects, however, take the pixel values and apply some sort of processing routines to them.

```
function out=mode(mat)
%
% Finds a most commonly occuring value in a matrix
%
h=hist(mat(:),0:255);
temp=find(h==max(h(:)))-1;
n=floor(rand*length(temp))+1;
out=temp(n);
```

FIGURE 16.8 *A simple program for computing the mode.*

5×5   9×9

FIGURE 16.9 *The oil painting effect with different filter sizes.*

OIL PAINTING This effect is very popular and is included in most image manipulation and photo-handling software. In concept it is very simple. It works by means of a nonlinear filter; the output of the filter is the most common pixel value in the filter mask.

The most commonly occurring value in a neighborhood is called the statistical **mode.** To implement this we need to write a small function. We use the `hist` function to create a list of the frequencies of each value in our neighborhood and find the values that occur most often. We then pick a random one. Figure 16.8 shows our function. Now we apply it, to the flowers image, for instance.

```
>> fo=nlfilter(double(fg),[5,5],'mode');
>> imshow(uint8(fg))
```

The result is shown in Figure 16.9. We can obtain a more "painterly" effect by choosing a larger block size in `nlfilter`. The use of `nlfilter` can be very slow; if you have access to the MATLAB compiler, you will achieve faster results by writing a program called, say `oilify.m`, and compiling it. Such a function is given in Figure 16.10. Given the slowness of `nlfilter`, it would be much faster to use this function.

```
function out=oilify(im,s)
%
% Produces an "oilpaint" effect by taking the pixel value most commonly
% occurring in a (2s+1)x(2s+1) neighbourhood of each pixel.
%
[rows,cols]=size(im);
out=zeros(rows,cols);
la=(2*s+1)^2;
for i=s+1:rows-s,
  for j=s+1:cols-s,
    a=double(im(i-s:i+s,j-s:j+s))+1;
    h=zeros(1,256);
    for k=1:la,
      h(a(k))=h(a(k))+1;
    end;
    [p,q]=sort(h);
    out(i,j)=q(256)-1;
  end
end
if isa(im,'uint8'),
  out=uint8(out);
end;
```

FIGURE 16.10 *A MATLAB function for creating oil paintings.*

SOLARIZATION   Solarization is a photographic effect that is obtained by applying diffuse light to a developing photograph and then continuing with the development. The result, which seems somehow magical, is that the image can be partly positive and partly negative.[1] This effect has been used by many photographers, but can be a fairly hit or miss affair in the photographic darkroom. However, it is very easy to create solarization effects digitally.

We have seen examples of solarization functions in Chapter 4; now we explore how they can be applied.

A simple solarization effect can be obtained by taking the complement of all pixels in an image $p(i, j)$ whose grayscales are less than 128:

$$\text{sol}(i, j) = \begin{cases} p(i, j) & \text{if } p(i, j) > 128, \\ 255 - p(i, j) & \text{if } p(i, j) \leq 128. \end{cases}$$

This is very straightforward:

```
>> fgd=double(fg);
>> u=double(fg>128);
>> sol=u.*fgd+(1-u).*(255-fgd);
>> imshow(uint8(sol)),figure,imshow(mat2gray(sol))
```

---

[1] A good account of solarization can be found at http://www.cchem.berkeley.edu/wljeme/ SOUTLINE.html.

CRC Press

FIGURE 16.11 *The solarization effect.*

CRC Press

```
sol1                                    sol2
```

FIGURE 16.12 *More solarization effects.*

We display the result twice; the second time the image is shown with better contrast. These images are shown in Figure 16.11. We can make more interesting solarization effects by varying the complementation according to the value of the row or column. All we need to do is to change the matrix u above:

```
>> u1=double(fg > 255*x/(2*rows));
>> sol1=u1.*fgd+(1-u1).*(255-fgd);
>> u2=double(fg > 255*y/(2*cols));
>> sol2=u2.*fgd+(1-u2).*(255-fgd);
>> imshow(uint8(sol1)),figure,imshow(uint8(sol2))
```

The results are shown in Figure 16.12.

16.5 Color Images

Most of the effects discussed look far more dramatic when applied to color images. For all the distortion effects, application to a color image means applying the effect to each of the RGB components separately. Recall that distortion effects don't change the values of the pixels so much as their

```
function out=twirl(img,K)

% TWIRL(IMG,K) creates a twirl effect on an image IMG, where K provides the
% amount of twirl.  The larger the value of K, the smaller the amount of twirl.
%
% IMG can be an image of type UINT8 or DOUBLE, and greyscale or RGB.
%
%  Example:
%
%     f=imread('flowers.tif');
%     f2=twirl(f,100);
%     imshow(f2)

sf=size(size(img));
if sf(2)==2,
  out=makeTwirl(img,K);
elseif sf(2)==3,
  out=cat(3,makeTwirl(img(:,:,1),K),...
      makeTwirl(img(:,:,2),K),...
      makeTwirl(img(:,:,3),K));
end;

function res=makeTwirl(im,K)
[rows,cols]=size(im);
ox=ceil((rows+1)/2);
oy=ceil((cols+1)/2);
[y,x]=meshgrid([1:cols]-oy,[1:rows]-ox);
r=sqrt(x.^2+y.^2);
theta=atan2(y,x);
phi=theta+(r/K);
x2=round(r.*cos(phi))+ox;
y2=round(r.*sin(phi))+oy;
%
% Now fix the bounds on  x2 and y2 so that
% 1 <= x2 <= rows and 1 <= y2 <= cols.
%
x2(find(x2>rows))=rows;
x2(find(x2<1))=1;
y2(find(y2>cols))=cols;
y2(find(y2<1))=1;
%
% Use x2 and y2 to write out to the new image.
%
res=zeros(size(im));
res=im(sub2ind([rows,cols],x2,y2));
if isa(im,'uint8'),
  res=uint8(res);
end;
```

FIGURE 16.13 *A MATLAB function for performing general twirls.*

position. Thus, in order to maintain the colors, we need to shift all the RGB components.

This is most easily done with a MATLAB function. Figure 16.13 shows, as an example, how to turn the twirl process into a function that can handle both grayscale and color images.

Oil painting is again done by applying the effect to each of the color components separately.

EXERCISES

1. Experiment with changing the parameters for the effects described in this chapter. For example, see if you can use the pond ripple effect to obtain pictures like this:

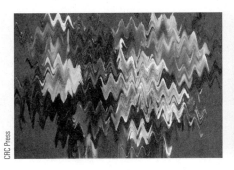

2. Write some MATLAB functions to implement all the effects given. Include some parameters to change the output.

3. Extend your functions so that they can be applied to color images.

4. In Holzmann's book [15], many other effects are described. For example, the following pictures show the result of a random tile effect, where the image is broken up into squares that are then shifted by a random amount.

See if you can write a function to implement this effect and then extend your function to work with color images.

5. See if you can use the mode command (discussed in the oil painting effect) in conjunction with the `colfilt` command (discussed in chapter 5), to provide a faster oil painting routine than was possible with `nlfilter`.

Basic Use of Matlab

A.1 Introduction

Matlab is a data analysis and visualization tool that has been designed with powerful support for matrices and matrix operations. As well, Matlab has excellent graphics capabilities, and its own powerful programming language. One of the reasons that Matlab has become such an important tool is through the use of sets of Matlab programs designed to support a particular task. These sets of programs are called **toolboxes,** and the particular toolbox of interest to us is the Image-Processing Toolbox.

Rather than give a description of all of Matlab's capabilities, we will restrict ourselves to just those aspects concerned with handling of images. We will introduce functions, commands, and techniques as required. A Matlab **function** is a keyword that accepts various parameters and produces some sort of output: for example a matrix, a string, a graph, or figure. Examples of such functions are sin, imread, and imclose. There are many functions in Matlab, and as we shall see, it is very easy (and sometimes necessary) to write our own. A **command** is a particular use of a function. Examples of commands might be:

```
>> sin(pi/3)
>> c=imread('cameraman.tif');
>> a=imclose(b);
```

As we will see, we can combine functions and commands or put multiple commands on a single input line.

Matlab's standard data type is the matrix—all data are considered to be matrices of some sort. Images, of course, are matrices whose elements are the gray values (or possibly the RGB values) of its pixels. Single values are considered by Matlab to be 1×1 matrices, while a string is merely a $1 \times n$ matrix of characters, n being the string's length.

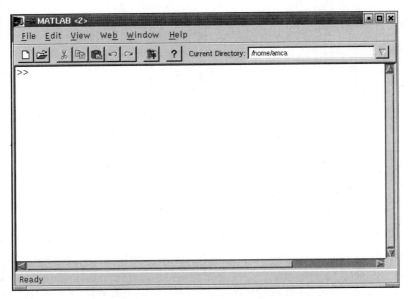

FIGURE A.1 *The MATLAB command window ready for action.*

In this appendix we will look at the more generic MATLAB commands and discuss images in the chapters.

When you start up MATLAB, you have a blank window called the Command Window in which you enter commands. This is shown in Figure A.1. Given the vast number of MATLAB's functions and the different parameters they can take, a command line-style interface is, in fact, much more efficient than a complex sequence of pull-down menus.

The prompt consists of two right arrows:

```
>>
```

A.2 Basic Use of MATLAB

If you have never used MATLAB, we will experiment with some simple calculations. We first note that MATLAB is *command line driven*; all commands are entered by typing them after the prompt symbol. Let's start off with a mathematical classic:

```
>> 2+2
```

What this means is that you type in

```
2+2
```

at the prompt, and then press your Enter key. This sends the command to the MATLAB kernel. What you should now see is:

```
ans =

      4
```

MATLAB, of course, can be used as a calculator; it understands the standard arithmetic operations of addition (as we have just seen), subtraction, multiplication, division, and exponentiation. Try these:

```
>> 3*4

>> 7-3

>> 11/7

>> 2^5
```

The results should not surprise you. Note that for the output of 11/7 the result was given only to a few decimal places. In fact MATLAB does all its calculations internally to double precision. However, the default display format is to use only eight decimal places. We can change this by using the format function. For example:

```
>> format long
>> 11/7

ans =

    1.57142857142857
```

Entering the command format by itself returns to the default format.

Matlab has all the elementary mathematical functions built in:

```
>> sqrt(2)

ans =

    1.4142

>> sin(pi/8)

ans =

    0.3827

>> log(10)

ans =

    2.3026

>> log10(2)

ans =

    0.3010
```

The trigonometric functions all take radian arguments, and `pi` is a built-in constant. The functions `log` and `log10` are the natural logarithm and logarithms to base 10.

A.3 Variables and the Workspace

When using any sort of computer system, we need to store things with appropriate names. In the context of Matlab, we use **variables** to store values. Here are some examples:

```
>> a=5^(7/2)

a =

  279.5085

>> b=sin(pi/9)-cos(pi/9)

b =

   -0.5977
```

Note that although a and b are displayed using the short format, MATLAB in fact stores their full values. We can see this with:

```
>> format long;a,format
a =
      2.795084971874737e+02
```

We can now use these new variables in further calculations:

```
>> log(a^2)/log(5)

ans =

     7
>> atan(1/b)

ans =

   -1.0321
```

A.3.1 The Workspace

If you are using a windowed version of MATLAB, you may find a Workspace item in the View menu. This lists all your currently defined variables, their numeric data types, and their sizes in bytes. To open the workspace window, use the View menu, and choose Workspace. The same information can be obtained using the whos function:

```
>> whos
   Name        Size              Bytes   Class
    a           1x1                   8   double array
    ans         1x1                   8   double array
    b           1x1                   8   double array
  Grand total is 3 elements using 24 bytes
```

Note also that ans is variable. It is automatically created by MATLAB to store the result of the last calculation. A listing of the variable names only is obtained using who:

```
>> who

Your variables are:

a      ans   b
```

The numeric date type `double` is MATLAB's standard for numbers; such numbers are stored as double-precision 8-byte values.

Other data types will be discussed below.

A.4 Dealing with Matrices

MATLAB has an enormous number of commands for generating and manipulating matrices. Since a grayscale image is a matrix, we can use some of these commands to investigate aspects of the image.

We can enter a small matrix by listing its elements row by row, using spaces or commas as delimiters for the elements in each row and semicolons to separate the rows. Thus the matrix

$$a = \begin{bmatrix} 4 & -2 & -4 & 7 \\ 1 & 5 & -3 & 2 \\ 6 & -8 & -5 & -6 \\ -7 & 3 & 0 & 1 \end{bmatrix}$$

can be entered as

```
>> a=[4 -2 -4 7;1 5 -3 2;6 -8 -5 -6;-7 3 0 1]
```

A.4.1 Matrix Elements

Matrix elements can be obtained by using the standard row, column-indexing scheme. For our image matrix a above, the command

```
>> a(2,3)

ans =

    -3
```

returns the element of the matrix in row 2 and column 3.

MATLAB also allows matrix elements to be obtained using a single number; this number being the position where the matrix is written out as a single column. Thus, in a 4×4 matrix as above, the order of elements is

$$\begin{bmatrix} 1 & 5 & 9 & 13 \\ 2 & 6 & 10 & 14 \\ 3 & 7 & 11 & 15 \\ 4 & 8 & 12 & 16 \end{bmatrix}.$$

So the element a(2,3) can also be obtained as a(10):

```
>> a(10)

ans =

    -3
```

In general, for a matrix M with r rows and c columns, element $m(i, j)$ corresponds to $m(i + r(j - 1))$. Using the single indexing allows us to extract multiple values from a matrix:

```
>> a([1 6 11 16])

ans =

    4    5    -5    1
```

To obtain a row of values, or a block of values, we use MATLAB's colon operator (:). This generates a vector of values; the command

```
>> a:b,
```

where a and b are integers, lists all integers from a to b. The more general version of this command,

```
i:b,
```

lists all values from a by increment i up to b. For example

```
>> 2:3:16
```

generates the following list:

```
ans =

    2  5  8  11  14
```

Applied to our matrix a, this command, for example

```
>> a(2,1:3)

ans =

     6      -8     -5
```

lists all values in row 2 that are between columns 1 and 3, inclusive. Similarly,

```
>> a(2:4,3)

ans =

    -3
    -5
     0
```

lists all the values in column 3 that are between rows 2 to 4, inclusive. And we can choose a block of values such as

```
>> a(2:3,3:4)

ans =

    -3      2
    -5     -6
```

which lists the 2-by-2 block of values that lie between rows 2 to 3 and columns 3 to 4.

The colon operator by itself lists all the elements along that particular row or column. So, for example, all of row 3 can be obtained with:

```
>> a(3,:)

ans =

     6      -8     -5     -6
```

and all of column 2 with

```
>> a(:,2)

ans =

    -2
     5
    -8
     3
```

Finally, the colon on its own lists all the matrix elements as a single column:

```
a(:)
```

shows all the 16 elements of a.

A.4.2 Matrix Operations

All the standard operations are supported. We can add, subtract, multiply and invert matrices, and take matrix powers. For example, with the matrix a from above, and a new matrix b defined by

```
>> b=[2 4 -7 -4;5 6 3 -2;1 -8 -5 -3;0 -6 7 -1]
```

we can have, for example:

```
>> 2*a-3*b

ans =

     2   -16    13    26
   -13    -8   -15    10
     9     8     5    -3
   -14    24   -21     1
```

As an example of matrix power see the following:

```
>> a^3*b^4

ans =

      103788     2039686     1466688      618345
      964142     2619886     2780222      345543
    -2058056    -2327582      721254     1444095
     1561358     3909734    -3643012    -1482253
```

Inversion is performed using the `inv` function:

```
>> inv(a)

ans =

   -0.0125     0.0552    -0.0231    -0.1619
   -0.0651     0.1456    -0.0352    -0.0466
   -0.0406    -0.1060    -0.1039    -0.1274
    0.1082    -0.0505    -0.0562     0.0064
```

A transpose is obtained by using the apostrophe:

```
>> a'

ans =

     4     1     6    -7
    -2     5    -8     3
    -4    -3    -5     0
     7     2    -6     1
```

As well as these standard arithmetic operations, MATLAB supports some geometric operations on matrices; `flipud` and `fliplr` flip a matrix up and down and left and right, respectively, and `rot90` rotates a matrix by 90°:

```
>> flipud(a)
ans =
     -7      3      0      1
      6     -8     -5     -6
      1      5     -3      2
      4     -2     -4      7
>> fliplr(a)
ans =
      7     -4     -2      4
      2     -3      5      1
     -6     -5     -8      6
      1      0      3     -7
>> rot90(a)
ans =
      7      2     -6      1
     -4     -3     -5      0
     -2      5     -8      3
      4      1      6     -7
```

The reshape function produces a matrix with elements taken column by column from the given matrix.

```
>> c=[1 2 3 4 5;6 7 8 9 10;11 12 13 14 15;16 17 18 19 20]

c =

     1     2     3     4     5
     6     7     8     9    10
    11    12    13    14    15
    16    17    18    19    20

>> reshape(c,2,10)

ans =

     1    11     2    12     3    13     4    14     5    15
     6    16     7    17     8    18     9    19    10    20

>> reshape(c,5,4)

ans =

     1     7    13    19
     6    12    18     5
    11    17     4    10
    16     3     9    15
     2     8    14    20
```

Reshape produces an error if the product of the two values is not equal to the number of elements of the matrix. Note that we could have produced the original matrix above with

```
>> c=reshape([1:20],5,4])'
```

All these commands work equally well on vectors. In fact, MATLAB makes no distinction between matrices and vectors, a vector merely being a matrix with number of rows or columns equal to 1.

THE DOT OPERATORS   A very distinctive class of operators in MATLAB are those that use dots; these operate in an element-wise fashion. For example, the command

```
a*b
```

performs the usual matrix multiplication of a and b. But the corresponding dot operator,

```
a.*b,
```

produces the matrix whose elements are the products of the corresponding elements of a and b. That is, if

```
c=a.*b
```

then $c(i, j) = a(i, j) \times b(i, j)$:

```
>> a.*b

ans =

       8      -8     28     -28
       5      30     -9      -4
       6      64     25      18
       0     -18      0      -1
```

We have dot division and dot powers. The command a.^2 produces a matrix with element being a square of the corresponding elements of a:

```
>> a.^2

ans =

    16     4    16    49
     1    25     9     4
    36    64    25    36
    49     9     0     1
```

Similarly we can produce a matrix of reciprocals by writing 1./a:

```
>> 1./a

ans =

    0.2500   -0.5000   -0.2500    0.1429
    1.0000    0.2000   -0.3333    0.5000
    0.1667   -0.1250   -0.2000   -0.1667
   -0.1429    0.3333       Inf    1.0000
```

The value Inf is MATLAB's version of infinity. It is returned for the operation $1/0$.

OPERATORS ON MATRICES   Many functions in MATLAB, when applied to a matrix, work by applying the function to each element in turn. Such functions are the trigonometric and exponential functions and logarithms. Using functions in this way means that in MATLAB many iterations and repetitions can be done with **vectorization** rather than by using loops. We will explore this next.

A.4.3 Constructing Matrices

We have seen that we can construct matrices by listing all their elements. However, this can be tedious if the matrix is large or if it can be generated by a function of its indices.

Two special matrices are the matrix consisting of all zeros and the matrix consisting of all ones. These are generated by the zeros and ones functions respectively. Each function can be used in several different ways:

zeros(n)   If n is a number, it will produce a zeros matrix of size $n \times n$.

zeros(m,n)   If m and n are numbers, they will produce a zeros matrix of size $m \times n$.

zeros(m,n,p, . . .)   Where m, n, p, and so on are numbers, they will produce an $m \times n \times p \times \cdots$ multidimensional array of zeros.

zeros(a)   Where a is a matrix, it will produce a matrix of zeros of the same size as a.

Matrices of random numbers can be produced using the rand and randn functions. They differ in that the numbers produced by rand are taken from a uniform distribution on the interval $[0, 1]$, and those produced by randn are take from a normal distribution with mean zero and standard deviation one. For creating matrices, the syntax of each is the same as the first three options of zeros above. The rand and randn functions on their own produce single numbers taken from the appropriate distribution.

We can construct random integer matrices by multiplying the results of rand or randn by an integer and then using the floor function to take the integer part of the result:

```
>> floor(10*rand(3))

ans =

     8     4     6
     8     8     8
     5     8     6

>> floor(100*randn(3,5))

ans =

  -134   -70  -160   -40    71
    71    85  -145    68   129
   162   125    57    81    66
```

The floor function will be automatically applied to every element in the matrix.

Suppose we wish to create a matrix, every element of which is a function of one of its indices: for example, the 10×10 matrix A, for which $A_{ij} = i+j-1$. In most programming languages, such a task would be performed using nested loops. We can use nested loops in Matlab, but it is easier here to use dot operators. We can first construct two matrices: one containing all the row indices and one containing all the column indices:

```
>> rows=(1:10)'*ones(1,10)

rows =

    1    1    1    1    1    1    1    1    1    1
    2    2    2    2    2    2    2    2    2    2
    3    3    3    3    3    3    3    3    3    3
    4    4    4    4    4    4    4    4    4    4
    5    5    5    5    5    5    5    5    5    5
    6    6    6    6    6    6    6    6    6    6
    7    7    7    7    7    7    7    7    7    7
    8    8    8    8    8    8    8    8    8    8
    9    9    9    9    9    9    9    9    9    9
   10   10   10   10   10   10   10   10   10   10

>> cols=ones(10,1)*(1:10)

cols =

    1    2    3    4    5    6    7    8    9   10
    1    2    3    4    5    6    7    8    9   10
    1    2    3    4    5    6    7    8    9   10
    1    2    3    4    5    6    7    8    9   10
    1    2    3    4    5    6    7    8    9   10
    1    2    3    4    5    6    7    8    9   10
    1    2    3    4    5    6    7    8    9   10
    1    2    3    4    5    6    7    8    9   10
    1    2    3    4    5    6    7    8    9   10
    1    2    3    4    5    6    7    8    9   10
```

Now we can construct our matrix using `rows` and `cols`:

```
>> A=rows+cols-1

A =

    1    2    3    4    5    6    7    8    9   10
    2    3    4    5    6    7    8    9   10   11
    3    4    5    6    7    8    9   10   11   12
    4    5    6    7    8    9   10   11   12   13
    5    6    7    8    9   10   11   12   13   14
    6    7    8    9   10   11   12   13   14   15
    7    8    9   10   11   12   13   14   15   16
    8    9   10   11   12   13   14   15   16   17
    9   10   11   12   13   14   15   16   17   18
   10   11   12   13   14   15   16   17   18   19
```

The construction of rows and cols can be done automatically with the meshgrid function:

```
[cols,rows]=meshgrid(1:10,1:10)
```

will produce the two index matrices above.

The size of our matrix a can be obtained by using the size function:

```
>> size(a)

ans =

     4     4
```

which returns the number of rows and columns of a.

A.4.4 Vectorization

Vectorization, in MATLAB, refers to an operation carried out over an entire matrix or vector. We have seen examples of this already in our construction of the 10×10 matrix A above and in our use of the dot operators. In most programming languages, applying an operation to elements of a list or array will require the use of a loop or a sequence of nested loops. Vectorization in MATLAB allows us to dispense with loops in almost all instances and is a very efficient replacement for them.

For example, suppose we wish to calculate the sine values of all the integer radians 1 to 1 million. We can do this with a for loop,

```
>> for i=1:10^6,sin(i);end
```

and we can measure the time of the operation with MATLAB's tic, toc timer: tic starts a stop watch timer and toc stops it and prints out the elapsed time in seconds. Thus, on my computer:

```
>> tic,for i=1:10^6,sin(i);end,toc

elapsed_time =

   27.4969
```

We can perform the same calculation with

```
>> i=1:10^6;sin(i);
```

and print out the elapsed time with:

```
>> tic,i=1:10^6;sin(i);toc

elapsed_time =

   1.3522
```

Note that the second command applies the sine function to all the elements of the vector 1:10^6, whereas with the for loop, sine is only applied to each element of the loop in turn.

As another example, we can easily generate the first 10 square numbers with:

```
>> [1:10].^2

ans =

  1 4 9 16 25 36 49 64 81 100
```

Here, [1:10] generates a vector consisting of the numbers 1 to 10, and the dot operator .^2 squares each element in turn.

Vectorization can also be used with logical operators. We can obtain all positive elements of the matrix a above with:

```
>> a>0

ans =

    1    0    0    1
    1    1    0    1
    1    0    0    0
    0    1    0    1
```

The result consists of 1s only in the places where the elements are positive.

MATLAB is designed to perform vectorized commands very quickly, and whenever possible such a command should be used instead of a for loop.

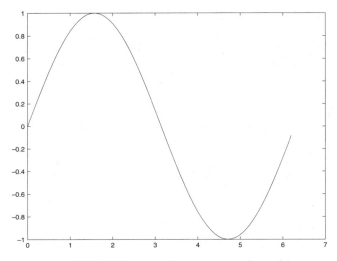

FIGURE A.2 *A simple plot in* Matlab.

A.5 Plots

Matlab has outstanding graphics capabilities. But we shall just look at some simple plots. The idea is straightforward: we create two vectors x and y of the same size, then the command

```
plot(x,y)
```

will plot y against x. If y has been created from x by using a vectorized function $f(x)$, the plot will show the graph of $y = f(x)$. Here's a simple example:

```
>> x=[0:0.1:2*pi];
>> plot(x,sin(x))
```

The result is shown in Figure A.2. The plot function can be used to produce many different plots. We can, for example, plot two functions simultaneously with different colors or plot symbols. For example

```
>> plot(x,sin(x),'.',x,cos(x),'o')
```

produces the graph shown in Figure A.3.

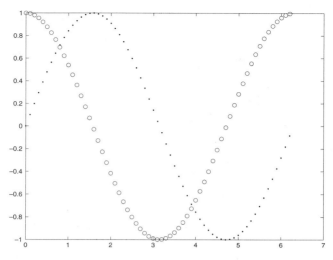

FIGURE A.3 *A different plot in* MATLAB.

A.6 Help in MATLAB

MATLAB comes with a vast amount of online help and information. There is so much, in fact, that it's quite easy to use MATLAB without a manual. To obtain information on a particular command, you can use `help`. For example:

```
>> help for

FOR    Repeat statements a specific number of times.
    The general form of a FOR statement is:

        FOR variable = expr, statement, ..., statement END

    The columns of the expression are stored one at a time in
    the variable and then the following statements, up to the
    END, are executed. The expression is often of the form X:Y,
    in which case its columns are simply scalars. Some examples
    (assume N has already been assigned a value).

        FOR I = 1:N,
            FOR J = 1:N,
                A(I,J) = 1/(I+J-1);
            END
        END
```

(continued)

```
FOR S = 1.0: -0.1: 0.0, END steps S with increments of -0.1
FOR E = EYE(N), ... END  sets E to the unit N-vectors.

Long loops are more memory efficient when the colon
expression appears in the FOR statement since
the index vector is never created.

The BREAK statement can be used to terminate
the loop prematurely.

See also IF, WHILE, SWITCH, BREAK, END.
```

If there is too much information, it may scroll past you too fast to see. In this case you can turn on the MATLAB pager with the command

```
>> more on
```

For more help on `help`, try:

```
>> help help
```

Better-formatted help can be obtained with the `doc` function, which opens up a help browser that interprets HTML-formatted help files. The result of the command

```
>> doc help
```

is the window shown in Figure A.4.

You can find more about the `doc` function with either of these commands:

```
>> doc doc
>> help doc
```

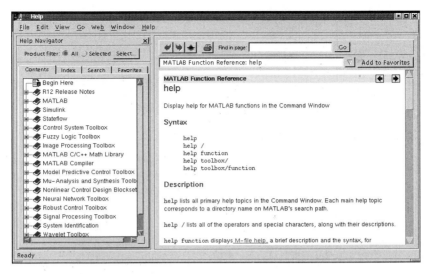

FIGURE A.4 *The* MATLAB *help browser.*

If you want to find help on a particular topic, but don't know the function to use, the `lookfor` function is extremely helpful. The command

    lookfor topic

lists all commands for which the first line of the help text contains the string `topic`. For example, suppose we want to find out if MATLAB supports the exponential function

    e^x.

we would do this in the following way:

```
>> lookfor exponential
EXP      Exponential.
EXPINT Exponential integral function.
EXPM     Matrix exponential.
EXPM1  Matrix exponential via Pade approximation.
EXPM2  Matrix exponential via Taylor series.
EXPM3  Matrix exponential via eigenvalues and eigenvectors.
BLKEXP Defines a function that returns the exponential of the input.
```

We now know that the function is implemented using `exp`. We could have used

```
>> lookfor exp
```

and this would have returned many more functions.

Note that MATLAB convention is to use uppercase names for functions in help texts, even though the function itself is called in lowercase.

A.7 Programming in MATLAB

MATLAB has a very rich programming language. Only a small set of functions is actually built in to MATLAB, others are written in MATLAB's own programming language. We consider two distinct programs: script files and functions.

A.7.1 Script Files

A script file is simply a list of commands to be executed. It may be that we will execute the same sequence of commands many times, in which case it is more efficient to write a file containing those commands. If the file is called `script.m` and placed somewhere on the path, then simply entering `script` at the prompt will execute all the commands in it. Of course, you can use any name you like for your script file! However, it is conventional to end MATLAB files with the extension `.m`.

A.7.2 Functions

As we have seen, a function is a MATLAB command that takes an input (one or several variables) and returns one or several values. Let's look at a simple example: writing a function that returns the number of positive values of a matrix. This function will take a matrix as input and return a single number as output. We have seen that

```
>> a>0
```

produces a matrix with 1s in the positions of positive elements. Thus, the sum of all elements in this new matrix is the number we require. We can obtain the sum of matrix elements using the `sum` function. If applied to a vector, `sum` produces the sum of all its elements. If applied to a matrix, however, `sum` produces a vector whose elements are the sums of the matrix columns:

```
>> sum(a)

ans =

     4      -2      -12       4

>> sum(a>0)

ans =

     3       2        0        3
```

We have two options here. We can use `sum` twice

```
>> sum(sum(a>0))

ans =

     8
```

or we could convert the matrix to a vector by using the colon operator before finding the positive elements:

```
>> sum(a(:)>0)

ans =

     8
```

Our function must have a name; let's call it `countpos`. A function file starts with the word `function`. The first line defines how the function is called. After that come some lines of help text, and finally the code. Our `countpos` function is shown in Figure A.5.

If this file is saved as `countpos.m` somewhere on the path, we can use `countpos` exactly as we use any other MATLAB function or function,

```
>> countpos(a)

>> help countpos

>> doc countpos
```

```
function num=countpos(a)

% COUNTPOS finds the number of positive elements in a matrix.   The matrix can
% be of any data type.
%
% Usage:
%
%    n=countpos(a)

num=sum(a(:)>0);
```

FIGURE A.5 *A simple MATLAB function.*

and the command

```
>> lookfor count
```

will include a reference to countpos.

Finally, if we want to explore functions in more detail, we can use type, which lists the entire program corresponding to that function or command. So we can enter

```
>> type countpos.m
```

to see a listing of our new function.

EXERCISES

1. Perform the following calculations in MATLAB:

$$132 + 45, \quad 235 \times 645, \quad 12.45/17.56. \quad \sin(\pi/6), \quad e^{0.5}, \quad \sqrt{2}$$

2. Now enter format long and repeat the above calculations.

3. Read the help file for format and experiment with some of the other settings.

4. Enter the following variables: $a = 123456$, $b = 3^{1/4}$, $c = \cos(\pi/8)$. Now calculate

$$(a + b)/c, \quad 2a - 3b, \quad c^2 - \sqrt{a - b}, \quad a/(3b + 4c), \quad \exp(a^{1/4} - b^{10})$$

5. Find the MATLAB functions for the inverse trigonometric functions $\sin^{-1}$, $\cos^{-1}$, and $\tan^{-1}$. Then calculate

$$\sin^{-1}(0.5), \quad \cos^{-1}(\sqrt{3}/2), \quad \tan^{-1}(2)$$

Convert your answers from radians to degrees.

6. Using vectorization and the colon operator, use a single command each to generate

   a. the first 15 cubes,
   b. the values $\sin(n\pi/16)$ for n from 1 to 16,
   c. the values $\sqrt{n}$ for n from 10 to 20.

7. Enter the following matrices:

$$A = \begin{bmatrix} 1 & 2 & 3 \\ 2 & 3 & 4 \\ 3 & 4 & 5 \end{bmatrix}, \quad B = \begin{bmatrix} -1 & 2 & -1 \\ -3 & -4 & 5 \\ 2 & 3 & -4 \end{bmatrix}, \quad C = \begin{bmatrix} 0 & -2 & 1 \\ -3 & 5 & 2 \\ 1 & 1 & -7 \end{bmatrix}$$

Now calculate:

$$2A - 3B, \quad A^T, \quad AB - BA, \quad BC^{-1}, \quad (AB)^T, \quad B^T A^T, \quad A^2 + B^3$$

8. Use the det function to find the determinant of each of the matrices in Question 7. What happens if you try to find the inverse of matrix A?

9. Write a little function issquare, which will determine whether a given integer is a square number. Thus:

```
>> issquare(9)

ans =

     1

>> issquare(9.000)

ans =

     1

>> issquare(9.001)

ans =

     0

>> issquare([1:10])

ans =

     1    0    0    1    0    0    0    0    1    0
```

10. Enter the command

```
>> imshow(issquare(reshape([1:65536],256,256)))
```

What are you seeing here?

11. Plot the function *tan(x)* with the following commands:

```
>> x=[0:0.1:10];
>> plot(x,tan(x))
>> figure,plot(x,tan(x)),axis([0,10,-10,10])
```

What does the `axis` function do? Read the help file to find out. Experiment with changing the last two numbers in `axis` for the command above.

The Fast Fourier Transform

We have discussed the Fourier transform and its uses in Chapter 7. However, as we know, the Fourier transform gains much of its usefulness by the existence of a fast algorithm to compute it. We look briefly at one version of the fast Fourier transform (FFT) here. More details can be found in Gonzalez and Woods [7] and in Walker [38].

To begin, we shall look at the very simple discrete wavelet transform (DFT) for a two-element vector, where for convenience we will omit the scaling factor:

$$\begin{bmatrix} X_0 \\ X_1 \end{bmatrix} = \begin{bmatrix} 1 & 1 \\ 1 & -1 \end{bmatrix} \begin{bmatrix} x_0 \\ x_1 \end{bmatrix}$$

$$= \begin{bmatrix} x_0 + x_1 \\ x_0 - x_1 \end{bmatrix}.$$

We can express this combination with a butterfly diagram as shown in Figure B.1. We will see how this butterfly diagram can be extended to vectors of greater length. In general, a butterfly diagram will consist of nodes joined as shown in Figure B.1, with scaling factors as shown in Figure B.2.

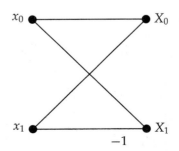

FIGURE B.1 *A butterfly diagram.*

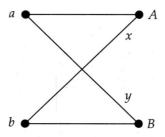

FIGURE B.2 *A general butterfly.*

In this figure, we have

$$A = a + xb,$$
$$B = a + yb.$$

By convention, if a scaling factor is not specified, it is assumed to be 1.

We can extend this to the DFT for a four-element vector, starting with its matrix definition.

$$
\begin{bmatrix} X_0 \\ X_1 \\ X_2 \\ X_3 \end{bmatrix} =
\begin{bmatrix} 1 & 1 & 1 & 1 \\ 1 & -i & -1 & i \\ 1 & -1 & 1 & -1 \\ 1 & i & -1 & -i \end{bmatrix}
\begin{bmatrix} x_0 \\ x_1 \\ x_2 \\ x_3 \end{bmatrix}
$$

$$
= \begin{bmatrix} x_0 + x_1 + x_2 + x_3 \\ x_0 - ix_1 - x_2 + ix_3 \\ x_0 - x_1 + x_2 - x_3 \\ x_0 + ix_1 - x_2 - ix_3 \end{bmatrix}
$$

$$
= \begin{bmatrix} (x_0 + x_2) + (x_1 + x_3) \\ (x_0 - x_2) - i(x_1 - x_3) \\ (x_0 + x_2) - (x_1 + x_3) \\ (x_0 - x_2) + i(x_1 - x_3) \end{bmatrix}
$$

$$
= \begin{bmatrix} x_0' + x_1' \\ x_2' - ix_3' \\ x_0' - x_1' \\ x_2' + ix_3' \end{bmatrix}
$$

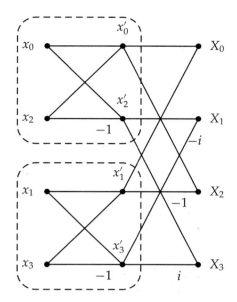

FIGURE B.3 *A butterfly diagram for a four-element FFT.*

This means we can obtain a four-element DFT by a two-stage process; first we create intermediate values x_i':

$$x_0' = x_0 + x_2$$
$$x_1' = x_1 + x_3$$
$$x_2' = x_0 - x_2$$
$$x_3' = x_1 - x_3$$

and use these new values to calculate the final values:

$$X_0 = x_0' + x_1'$$
$$X_1 = x_2' - ix_3'$$
$$X_2 = x_0' - x_1'$$
$$X_3 = x_2' + ix_3'$$

The butterfly diagram for this is shown in Figure B.3. Note that it consists of two simple butterfly diagrams on the left, joined together with more butterflies on the right.

Note that the order of the original element x_i has been changed; we will discuss this more on the next page.

To apply the same idea to an eight-element vector, we consider the general term of the transform:

$$X_k = \omega^0 x_0 + \omega^k x_1 + \omega^{2k} x_2 + \omega^{3k} x_3 + \cdots + \omega^{7k} x_7 \qquad \text{where } \omega = e^{-2\pi i/8}$$

$$= \underbrace{\omega^0 x_0 + \omega^{2k} x_2 + \omega^{4k} x_4 + \omega^{6k} x_6}_{\text{even values}} + \underbrace{\omega^k x_1 + \omega^{3k} x_3 + \omega^{5k} x_5 + \omega^{7k} x_7}_{\text{odd values}}$$

$$= \omega^0 x_0 + \omega^{2k} x_2 + \omega^{4k} x_4 + \omega^{6k} x_6 + \omega^k (x_1 + \omega^{2k} x_3 + \omega^{4k} x_5 + \omega^{6k} x_7).$$

Now, let $z = \omega^2 = e^{-2\pi i/4}$. Then,

$$X_k = (z^0 x_0 + z^k x_2 + z^{2k} x_4 + z^{3k} x_6) + \omega^k (z^0 x_1 + z^k x_3 + z^{2k} x_5 + z^{3k} x_7). \quad \text{(B.1)}$$

If we examine at the brackets in this expression, we note that the first bracket is the kth term of the DFT of (x_0, x_2, x_4, x_6), and the second bracket is the kth term of the DFT of (x_1, x_3, x_5, x_7). Thus, we can write

$$X_k = \text{DFT}(x_0, x_2, x_4, x_6)_k + \omega^k \text{DFT}(x_1, x_3, x_5, x_7)_k.$$

To make the argument easier to follow, let us write

$$(Y_0, Y_1, Y_2, Y_3) = \text{DFT}(x_0, x_2, x_4, x_6)$$
$$(Y'_0, Y'_1, Y'_2, Y'_3) = \text{DFT}(x_1, x_3, x_5, x_7).$$

Thus we have

$$X_k = Y_k + \omega^k Y'_k.$$

There is a slight problem here: the DFT of a four element vector has only four terms, so that k here only will take values 0–3, and we need values 0–7. However, if we look back at Equation (B.1), we can see that if k takes values 4–7, the powers of z just cycle round again, since $z^4 = 1$. Thus, for these values of k we have

$$X_k = Y_{k-4} + \omega^k Y'_{k-4}.$$

This means that the indices for X_k can take all values between 0 and 7, but the indices of Y_k and Y'_k only take on values 0–3.

We can check this in MATLAB. Recall that to obtain a correct result, the $\texttt{fft}$ function must be applied to a *column* vector.

Let us first create an eight-element vector, and obtain its Fourier transform:

```
>> x=2:9

x =

    2    3    4    5    6    7    8    9

>> fx=fft(x')

fx =

   44.0000
   -4.0000 + 9.6569i
   -4.0000 + 4.0000i
   -4.0000 + 1.6569i
   -4.0000
   -4.0000 - 1.6569i
   -4.0000 - 4.0000i
   -4.0000 - 9.6569i
```

Now we will split up the vector into even and odd parts and put their Fourier transforms together using the formula above:

```
>> even=[2 4 6 8];odd=[3 5 7 9];
>> feven=fft(even');
>> fodd=fft(odd');
>> X=zeros(8,1);
>> omega=exp(-2*pi*sqrt(-1)/8);
>> for i=0:3,X(i+1)=feven(i+1)+omega^i*fodd(i+1);end
>> for i=4:7,X(i+1)=feven(i-3)+omega^i*fodd(i-3);end
>> X

X =

   44.0000
   -4.0000 + 9.6569i
   -4.0000 + 4.0000i
   -4.0000 + 1.6569i
   -4.0000
   -4.0000 - 1.6569i
   -4.0000 - 4.0000i
   -4.0000 - 9.6569i
```

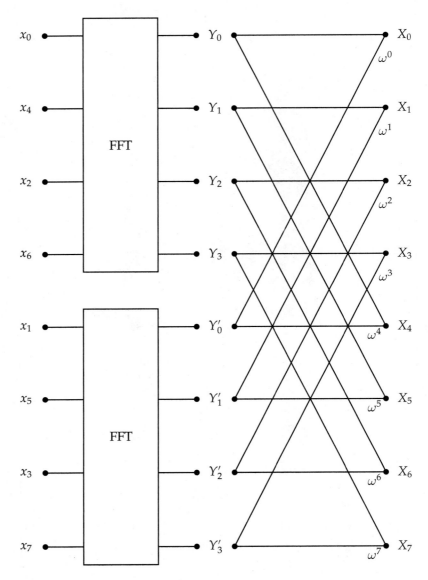

FIGURE B.4 *A butterfly diagram for an eight-element FFT.*

This result agrees with the Fourier transform obtained from above. Note that in the for loops we used indices $i + 1$ and $i - 3$. We did this because the theory starts indices at 0, but MATLAB starts indices at 1.

As with the four-element transform, we can express the eight-element transform by using a butterfly diagram. Such a diagram, treating the

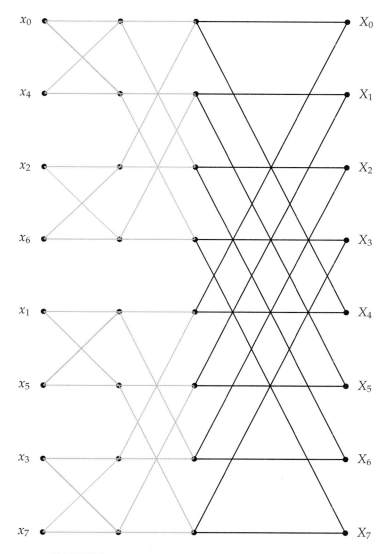

FIGURE B.5 *A complete butterfly diagram for an eight-element FFT.*

four-element FFT as a black box, is shown in Figure B.4. Note that as in Figure B.3 the order of the original elements is changed.

If we now replace the black box FFTs from Figure B.4 with the four-element butterfly diagram of Figure B.3, we obtain a complete butterfly diagram for eight elements, which is given in Figure B.5. To show the structure of the diagram, we have left out the multiplication factors, which are simply inherited from their respective diagrams.

We have noted that the input values in our butterfly diagrams are not given in their correct order. The ordering we require can be obtained by **binary bit reversal.** Suppose we list the input elements x_i in order, but replace the indices with their binary expansions:

$$
\begin{array}{cccccccc}
x_0 & x_1 & x_2 & x_3 & x_4 & x_5 & x_6 & x_7 \\
= \quad x_{000} & x_{001} & x_{010} & x_{011} & x_{100} & x_{101} & x_{110} & x_{111}
\end{array}
$$

Now we replace each index with the reversal of its bits and go back to decimal:

$$
\begin{array}{cccccccc}
x_{000} & x_{100} & x_{010} & x_{110} & x_{001} & x_{101} & x_{011} & x_{111} \\
= \quad x_0 & x_4 & x_2 & x_6 & x_1 & x_5 & x_3 & x_7
\end{array}
$$

Now we have the new order for input into the FFT.

The particular form of the FFT we have developed here is known as the decimation in time, 2-radix FFT. We can describe its general workings as follows:

1. Reorder the initial 2^n vector elements by binary bit reversal.
2. Butterfly the elements two at a time, using scaling factors 1 and -1.
3. Butterfly the resulting elements four at a time, using the scaling factors $1, \omega, \omega^2$ and ω^3, with $\omega = \exp(2i\pi/4)$.
4. Butterfly the resulting elements eight at a time, using the scaling factors $1, \omega, \omega^2, \ldots, \omega^7$, with $\omega = \exp(2i\pi/8)$.
5. Continue until we butterfly all elements together using scaling factors ω^k, with $\omega = \exp(2i\pi/2^n)$.

In practice, an FFT program will use a divide and conquer strategy: the initial vector is broken up into smaller vectors, the algorithm is applied recursively to these smaller vectors, and the results are "butterflied" together.

There are many other forms of the FFT, but they all work by the same basic principle of dividing the vector into shorter lengths. Clearly, we will obtain the greatest speed for vectors whose lengths are a power of 2 (such as the examples above), but we can also apply similar schemes to other lengths.

BIBLIOGRAPHY

1. Gregory A. Baxes. *Digital Image Processing: Principles and Applications*. John Wiley and Sons, 1994.
2. Wayne C. Brown and Barry J. Shepherd. *Graphics File Formats: Reference and Guide*. Manning Publications, 1995.
3. John F. Canny. A computational approach to edge detection. *IEEE Transactions on Pattern Analysis and Machine Intelligence*, 8(6):679–698, 1986.
4. Kenneth R. Castleman. *Digital Image Processing*. Prentice Hall, 1996.
5. Ashley R. Clark and Colin N. Eberhardt. *Microscopy Techniques for Materials Science*. CRC Press, 2002.
6. James D. Foley, Andries van Dam, Steven K. Feiner, John F. Hughes, and Richard L. Phillips. *Introduction to Computer Graphics*. Addison-Wesley, 1994.
7. Rafael Gonzalez and Richard E. Woods. *Digital Image Processing*. Addison-Wesley, second edition, 2002.
8. Richard W. Hall, T. Y. Kong and Azriel Rosenfeld, Shrinking Binary Images, in T. Y. Kong and Azriel Rosenfeld, eds, *Topological Algorithms for Digital Image Processing*, pp. 31–98, Elsevier North-Holland, 1996.
9. Richard W. Hall, Parallel Connectivity-Preserving Thinning Algorithms, in T. Y. Kong and Azriel Rosenfeld, eds, *Topological Algorithms for Digital Image Processing*, pp. 145–180, Elsevier North-Holland, 1996.
10. Duane Hanselman and Bruce R. Littlefield. *Mastering Matlab 6*. Prentice Hall, 2000.
11. Robert M. Haralick and Linda G. Shapiro. *Computer and Robot Vision*. Addison-Wesley, 1993.
12. Stephen Hawley. Ordered dithering. In Andrew S. Glassner, editor, *Graphics Gems*, pages 176–178. Academic Press, 1990.
13. M. D. Heath, S. Sarkar, T. Sanocki, and K. W. Bowyer. A robust visual method for assessing the relative performance of edge-detection algorithms. *IEEE Transactions on Pattern Analysis and Machine Intelligence*, 19(2):1338–1359, 1997.
14. Robert V. Hogg and Allen T. Craig. *Introduction to Mathematical Statistics*. Prentice-Hall, fifth edition, 1994.
15. Gerard J. Holzmann. *Beyond Photography: The Digital Darkroom*. Prentice Hall, 1988.
16. Adobe Systems Incorporated. *PostScript(R) Language Reference*. Addison-Wesley Publishing Co., third edition, 1999.
17. Anil K. Jain. *Fundamentals of Digital Image Processing*. Prentice Hall, 1989.
18. Glyn James and David Burley. *Advanced Modern Engineering Mathematics*. Addison-Wesley, second edition, 1999.

19. Arne Jensen and Anders la Cour-Harbo. *Ripples in Mathematics: The Discrete Wavelet Transform*. Springer-Verlag, 2001.

20. David C. Kay and John R. Levine. *Graphics File Formats*. Windcrest/McGraw-Hill, 1995.

21. V. F. Leavers. *Shape Detection in Computer Vision Using the Hough Transform*. Springer-Verlag, 1992.

22. Jae S. Lim. *Two-Dimensional Signal and Image Processing*. Prentice Hall, 1990.

23. William B. Pennebaker and Joan L. Mitchell. *JPEG Still Image Data Compression Standard*. Van Nostrand Reinhold, 1993.

24. James R. Parker. *Algorithms for Image Processing and Computer Vision*. John Wiley and Sons, 1997.

25. Maria Petrou and Panagiota Bosdogianni. *Image Processing: The Fundamentals*. John Wiley and Sons, 1999.

26. William K. Pratt. *Digital Image Processing*. John Wiley and Sons, second edition, 1991.

27. Majid Rabbani and Paul W. Jones. *Digital Image Compression Techniques*. SPIE Optical Engineering Press, 1991.

28. Greg Roelofs. *PNG: The Definitive Guide*. O'Reilly and Associates, 1999.

29. Steven Roman. *Introduction to Coding and Information Theory*. Springer-Verlag, 1997.

30. Azriel Rosenfeld and Avinash C. Kak. *Digital Picture Processing*. Academic Press, second edition, 1982.

31. John C. Russ. *The Image Processing Handbook*. CRC Press, second edition, 1995.

32. Dale A. Schumacher. A comparison of digital halftoning techniques. In James Arvo, editor, *Graphics Gems II*, pages 57–71. Academic Press, 1991.

33. Jean Paul Serra. *Image Analysis and Mathematical Morphology*. Academic Press, 1982.

34. Melvin P. Siedband. Medical imaging systems. In John G. Webster, editor, *Medical Instrumentation: Application and Design*, pages 518–576. John Wiley and Sons, 1998.

35. Milan Sonka, Vaclav Hlavac, and Roger Boyle. *Image Processing, Analysis and Machine Vision*. PWS Publishing, second edition, 1999.

36. David S. Taubman and Michael W. Marcellin. *Jpeg2000: Image Compression Fundamentals, Standards, and Practice*. Kluwer Academic Publishers, 2001.

37. Scott E. Umbaugh. *Computer Vision and Image Processing: A Practical Approach Using CVIPTools*. Prentice Hall, 1998.

38. James S. Walker. *Fast Fourier Transforms*. CRC Press, second edition, 1996.

39. Dominic Welsh. *Codes and Cryptography*. Oxford University Press, 1989.

40. CIE. (1932). *Commission Internationale de 1' Éclairage Proceedings, 1931*. Cambridge: Cambridge University Press.

41. Guild, J. (1931). The colorimetric properties of the spectrum. *Philosophical Transactions of the Royal Society of London, A230*, 149–187.

42. Wright, W. D. (1928–29). A re-determination of the trichromatic coefficients of the spectral colours. *Transactions of the Optical Society, 30*, 141–164.

Chapter 3: pp. 44, 45, 47, Capt. Budd Christman, NOAA Corps; p. 49, Mathworks. **Chapter 4:** p. 71, Mathworks, pp. 75, 77, CRC Press; p. 80, Mathworks. **Chapter 5:** pp. 96, 99, 101, 104, 111, Mathworks. **Chapter 6:** pp. 125, 129, 132, 136, Mathworks; p.m. 137–38, The National Gallery, London, England. **Chapter 7:** pp. 169, 170, 171, 172, 176, 177, 178, 179, Mathworks. **Chapter 8:** p. 210, 211, Mathworks. **Chapter 9:** pp. 218, 219 (top) CRC Press; p. 219 (bottom), 220, Mathworks; p. 222, CRC Press; p. 223, Mathworks; p. 226 (top left and bottom right), Mathworks; p. 226 (top right and bottom left), CRC Press; pp. 227, 228, 233, 234, 235, 237, 240, 244, CRC Press; pp. 255, 256, Mathworks. **Chapter 10:** p. 265, CRC Press; 268, Mathworks; pp. 271, 272, 276, 280, CRC Press; pp. 294, 296, Capt. Budd Christman/NOAA Corps. **Chapter 11:** p. 300, Mathworks; pp. 310, 321, CRC Press; p. 334 (top left), CRC Press; p. 342, CRC Press. **Chapter 13:** pp. 381, 382, 391, CRC Press. **Chapter 14:** pp. 412, 413, 414, 415, 416, Capt. Budd Christman/NOAA Corps. **Chapter 15:** pp. 433, 434, Mathworks; pp. 440, 441, 442, 443, 444, 445, Capt. Budd Christman/NOAA Corps. **Chapter 16:** pp. 453, 455, 456, 458, 460, 461, 462, 464, 466, CRC Press.